URBAN POVERTY AND THE UNDERCLASS

Studies in Urban and Social Change

Published by Blackwell in association with the *International Journal of Urban and Regional Research*. Series editors: Chris Pickvance, Margit Mayer and John Walton

Published

Forthcoming

URBAN POVERTY AND THE UNDERCLASS
A READER

Edited by Enzo Mingione

The right of Enzo Mingione to be identified as editor of this work has been asserted in
accordance with the Copyright, Designs and Patents Act 1988.

First published 1996

First published in USA
2 4 6 8 10 9 7 5 3 1

Blackwell Publishers Ltd
108 Cowley Road
Oxford OX4 1JF
UK

Blackwell Publishers Inc
238 Main Street
Cambridge, Massachusetts 02142
USA

British Library Cataloguing in Publication Data
A CIP catalogue record for this book is available from the British Library.

Library of Congress Cataloging-in-Publication Data
Urban poverty and the underclass: a reader / edited by Enzo Mingione.
    p.   cm. -- (Studies in urban and social change)
  Includes bibliographical references and index.
  ISBN 0–631–20036–3. -- ISBN 0–631–20037–1
  1. Urban poor. 2. Urban poor--Europe. 3. Socially handicapped. 4. Socially
handicapped--Europe. 5. Homelessness. I. Mingione, Enzo. II. Series.
HV4028.U73   1996
362.5′09173′2--dc20   96–365
                                                                              CIP

Typeset in 10.5 on 12 pt Baskerville by Photoprint, Torquay, Devon
Printed and bound in Great Britain by Hartnolls Limited, Bodmin, Cornwall

This book is printed on acid-free paper

Contents

Figures

Maps

Tables

Preface

The story of this book begins in Los Angeles three days before the Rodney King riots in 1992, when many of its authors took part in a round-table conference on urban poverty at UCLA. In the US the debate on the urban underclass was then at its peak, and in Europe the question of social exclusion was emerging. Here the focus was particularly on the neighbourhoods in crisis and the decaying peripheries with their segregated minorities and immigrants, but also on poorly educated long-term unemployed young people and families in serious economic difficulty. As so often happens, after having discussed and analysed worsening ghettoization and racial tensions, the participants in the conference were taken by surprise by the violence of the riots. It confirmed the correctness of the analyses but was in fact unforeseeable. Anyone who studies poverty knows that even the most intolerable forms of hardship and discrimination are not synonymous with conflict and rioting. This gives rise to a first interpretative signpost, also applicable to this volume: the big cities of the industrialized countries are to a growing extent factories of heightened social privation, often concentrated among discriminated social groups segregated in decaying areas, the effects of which cannot be predicted either in the short run or, even less so, in the long run.

The contributions to the UCLA round table, supplemented by a few other articles, were published in a special issue of the *International Journal of Urban and Regional Research* in 1993. However, we held the debate to be of such importance as to merit a practically new and updated publication. Apart from Herbert Gans and Loïc Wacquant, the contributors to the special issue – Fainstein, Marcuse, Mingione, Morlicchio, Morris and Silver – have all written entirely new chapters for this book.

At its hub lies a problem that is crucial for the understanding of contemporary societies: the existence of a growing area of great social privation, even in the opulent societies, and its increasing concentration and radicalization in the big cities, in certain decaying neighbourhoods and to the detriment of disadvantaged groups such as minorities and immigrants. The numbers and percentages involved or the rising trend are in themselves not so important as the fact that an important qualitative transformation is firmly believed to be taking place. For example, with regard to Italy, Nicola Negri and Chiara Saraceno (*Le politiche contro la povertà in Italia*, Bologna, Il Mulino, 1996) have analysed the most recent data elaborated by the Government Commission on Poverty for the years 1993 and 1994. They note that there was only a slight increase in those under the poverty line but big variations in the economic condition of different typologies of poor people. In particular, their concentration in the regions of the South has increased and within the poverty in this part of the country there has been a rise in the proportion of large families in difficulty.

Processes of impoverishment are also tending to change in contexts in which there is increasing instability of working careers and of family and community support networks and where state welfare intervention is in a condition of financial, political and ideological crisis. Robert Castel (1995) has defined these phenomena in terms of *Les Métamorphoses de la question sociale*, the change from a regime based on stable salaried employment to a much more heterogeneous and precarious regime. It is no longer mainly a question of potentially transitory phenomena reflecting a continuum of economic stratification from those with more to those with less resources. More and more frequently they lead to a, possibly irreversible, horizontal divide between the inserted and the excluded. This divide is huge precisely in the case of urban poverty, above all when characterized by institutional obtuseness such as that towards ghetto dwellers and the homeless.

Considerable theoretical and methodological difficulties arise in addressing the question of urban poverty from a comparative multinational perspective. To start with, the various studies carried out are little acquainted with one another. Not only has the debate on the underclass in the US not been linked up with the work on social exclusion in Europe, but also both of these research paths have failed to take into account the classic studies of poverty and even the more recent debate on the analytical concepts and tools for tackling the question. The ample literature on the underclass and ghetto poor in American cities makes no reference, for example, to the recent debate between Peter Townsend and Amartya Sen on relative deprivation, the use of poverty lines and the linkage between existing indicators and concepts that are difficult to make operational. On the whole, the problem of the underclass has been viewed as specific to the US with no counterpart in the other industrialized countries. The analytical indicators used in the debate – the population with an income below the US poverty line, the recipients of state welfare benefits, unwed teenage mothers and so on – have not been rooted in the theoretical and conceptual tradition of the studies of poverty from Rowntree on.

The same thing occurred in Europe when social exclusion became the centre of attention in place of poverty. Still now, the term gives the impression more of an intuitive short cut than a concept and a narrative generated by a thoroughly critical reflection. The analytical definition of the concept of social exclusion is emerging a posteriori. Hence it is only now that the main guidelines to the question are coming into focus. These are its connection with the original conceptualization of poverty in industrial societies – the threshold of shame that according to Adam Smith rules out the possibility of being integrated into the community of belonging; the importance of the temporal nature of processes and of the institutional aspects that make clear the confines of the concept beyond the generic binary mechanism of outside and inside applying to any form of social organization; and a strong link between what is understood as the epicentre of social exclusion in Europe and the phenomena characterizing the problem of the underclass or the ghetto poor, namely, institutional discrimination and territorial segregation. Most recently, Robert Castel has proposed to clarify the analytical confines of the concept of social exclusion by referring to the institutional processes (official discrimination) of spatial segregation and the confining of certain groups of the population to particularly disadvantaged conditions. This avoids confusing exclusion with the myriad forms of social marginalization revolving around 'the deterioration of working conditions or the weakening of support based on sociality'.

The first part of this book deals specifically with the comparative theoretical and analytical framework for the question of urban poverty in industrialized societies as a form of social exclusion. In the first chapter, I have attempted to put together the basic elements of the theoretical narrative on urban poverties and to supply the key factors for a comparative analysis of phenomena that occur in different cultural contexts and are studied from diverse methodological perspectives, in some cases stressing individual downdrift and in others the socio-institutional conditions of exclusion.

In the second chapter, Giuseppe Micheli introduces the question of individual drift and, consequently, of those concatenations of conditions and events leading to social exclusion. This is a crucial point in the path followed in this volume since it allows us to verify the compatibility between the two different frames of reference from which students of urban poverties nowadays operate: that of individual drift and that of chronic social contexts. This theme is taken up again in my concluding chapter.

Saskia Sassen then discusses the factors of economic–occupational transformation that have brought about a big increase in the risk of exclusion, particularly concentrated in large cities (beginning with the global cities) in some decaying neighbourhoods and to the detriment of certain social groups. It is the new service employment regimes that inhibit the traditional opportunities and hopes of social mobility which characterized the systems of social integration typical of the Fordist and welfarist societies.

Antonio Tosi looks at the problem of the homeless in relation to the discussion of current social exclusion. This is an important exercise within the comparative narrative because it dispels a serious ambiguity. The homeless are seen as, at the same time, victims of the severest marginalization syndrome and a result solely of the housing problem. The interpretational framework set up by Tosi serves to introduce the accurate treatment of the problem in the second part of the book: that undertaken by Marcuse apropos advanced homelessness in the big American cities.

In the final chapter of the first part, Hilary Silver reconstructs the cultural and political diversity that lies behind the various narratives and emphases in different national contexts with reference to the US, the UK and France. This is an indispensable exercise for rendering comparable narratives which, despite tackling similar problems, adopt different points of view, stereotypes and idiosyncratic positions due to their formulation within diverse national histories and socio-political cultures.

The second part of the book is dedicated to the underclass debate, with particular attention being paid to the big American cities, but not only. All the authors belong to a current that is highly critical of the use of the term 'underclass', mistakenly overloaded with stereotyped deviant behaviours. The term is now more and more frequently dropped in favour of 'ghetto poor'.

Herbert Gans and Norman Fainstein demonstrate that the dispute over the underclass is in no way a simple matter of terminology. The conflation into a single term of economic disadvantage, institutional isolation, lack of employment opportunities, ethnic origins, cultural characteristics, forms of deviant behaviour and spatial concentration misses the point that these factors act as a sequence of causes within an ongoing process. Consequently political bias leads to attention being focused automatically on the presumed behaviour and cultural deviance exhibited by the victims.

Lydia Morris pays special attention to the malign circuits that are established between employment system and social exclusion. The persistence and spread of bad jobs together with the fact that these are systematically done by disadvantaged social groups, women, immigrants and poorly educated members of ethnic minorities, generate a syndrome in which a high potential of exclusion is reproduced institutionally.

The hyper-ghettoization and advanced homelessness in the big American cities are at the centre of Peter Marcuse's contribution. Prominence is given particularly to the profound historical changes that have brought the ghetto and the homeless, as well as racial divisions, into the contemporary syndrome of social exclusion.

Logan, Alba and McNulty also address the problem of ethnic minorities in New York and Los Angeles. They examine the gap between the opportunities offered to some groups by ethnic enclaves and entrepreneurship and the great disadvantages weighing down large sections of other minorities. In New York these are above all blacks and Puerto Ricans, while in Los Angeles the protagonists of social exclusion are chiefly recent immigrants from Mexico and other countries in Central America.

In the final chapter of the second part, Loïc Wacquant's comparative analysis of the ghetto in south Chicago and the decaying quarter of La Corneuve on the outskirts of Paris focuses directly on the question of the differences between Europe and the US in the processes of institutional and spatially segregated marginalization. Here emerge the issues relating to welfare as a bulwark against the more heightened and violent forms of social exclusion. The American ghetto is far more closed, penalizing and violent than the decaying French periphery. Among other differences, Wacquant points to the role played by an interventionist state welfare apparatus in contrast with the institutional abdication that characterizes life in the American hyper-ghetto.

This last theme is the predominant one in the third and final part of the book. Here the attempt is made to understand in the light of empirical data on poverty in European cities to what extent economic and social transformations and the redefinition of welfare systems are triggering processes of territorial concentration and segregation and helping to turn urban poverty into forms of social exclusion like those found in the big American cities.

Nick Buck analyses UK data on the spatial and social concentration of families with no stable links with the world of work. His conclusion is that despite a tendential increase in territorial concentration and consequent activation of malign circuits of exclusion, the alarm surrounding the formation of an urban underclass in the UK has little justification as things now stand. Here too, as in the preceding chapter and those following, it is observed that though differing from one another and all more or less in crisis, European welfare systems have maintained their capacity to check the uncontrolled spread of heightened forms of institutional discrimination, of which the ghetto poor and the advanced homelessness in American cities are the most evident examples.

The other three chapters in the last part present a comparison between two pairs of cities in Italy and Germany, one prosperous and the other beset by problems. Milan and Stuttgart, the prosperous cities, have certainly been affected by processes of socio-economic transformation that increase the risk of being involved in impoverishment drift, but these phenomena have not gelled into accentuated forms of spatial segregation and institutional discrimination. These cases also show the crisis of welfare intervention and the formation of a nucleus of irreversible marginalization, though there is clearly no sign of an urban underclass in gestation. The situation is different in Berlin and, above all, Naples. In the latter in particular, the intertwining of a failed industrial development, de-industrialization and a serious and persistent jobs crisis is reflected in the areas of highly concentrated social privation both in some inner city neighbourhoods and in the decaying periphery. A markedly low standard of living, lack of opportunities and discrimination in the access to services give rise to vast areas of hardship even if here we do not find the ethnic division characterizing the American ghetto and, to some degree, the poor quarters inhabited by minorities and immigrants in northern European cities. The case of Naples delineates a different borderline in the debate on urban social exclusion in big cities. The reasons for this are both the high concentrations of poor subjects in neighbourhoods that are not marked by ethnic divisions and the fact that the institutional apparatus is at the same time actively present, as in the European model, and discriminatory, as in the American model, above all as regards local welfare, education and health services. It would be interesting to extend Wacquant's comparative analysis to a poor

Neapolitan neighbourhood, where the mix between institutional support, ethnic–cultural divisions, opportunities and resources for economic mobility is different, as is the role played by deviant behaviour and violence, mostly monopolized by the criminal organization known as the Camorra.

Finally, in the Conclusion I have tried to gather together the various threads of the contributions in order to take stock. It is not my intention to bring the debate to a close but rather to indicate the paths that need to be followed to intensify the comparative analysis in relation to a complicated theme that is at the same time vulnerable to political conditioning.

It is now up to the reader to judge whether the essays collected together in this volume make a sufficiently cohesive and incisive contribution to the construction of a comparative narrative on urban poverties in industrially advanced countries; a narrative that takes into account the fact that it is precisely these forms of poverty, accompanied by territorial segregation and/or institutional discrimination, that best exemplify the emerging question of social exclusion. Today, the narrative on social exclusion – but the terms used are not so important since the Wilsonian approach to the underclass debate and also the hyper-ghetto and advanced homelessness lie fully within the scope of the question – constitutes a crucial node in the interpretation of contemporary societies because it represents a clear qualitative advance on the 'modern' interpretation of poverty as the lower layer in a cohesive system of economic stratification that is kept open to entry and exiting by strong processes of mobility. Thus, the hypothesis of a regime and social order different from that in which we lived up to the 1960s is put forward. Urban poverties may be considered as the front line of this new regime, but much work still needs to be done to bring to light the details of the very complex pattern that is emerging.

This Preface and chapters 1, 2, 13 and 16 were translated by Paul Goodrick, lecturer in English at Milan State University, chapter 4 was translated by James Davis and chapter 14 by Jehanne-Marie Marchesi.

A particular word of thanks goes to David Benassi, who not only assisted me in my contacts with the other contributors but also helped considerably with some difficult editorial work, in particular desk revision and ensuring text uniformity, as well as drawing up the index and the bibliography.

Enzo Mingione

Part I

What is
Urban Poverty?

1

Urban Poverty in the Advanced Industrial World: Concepts, Analysis and Debates

Enzo Mingione, University of Padova

URBAN POVERTY: CONCEPTS AND MEASURES

There is little doubt that poverty is still a serious problem in the advanced industrial world. Despite affluence there are households and individuals that face great difficulties and are unable to get by. For the very reason that they are poor, instead of receiving help from their affluent communities, they are viewed with suspicion and fear, marginalized and excluded. Besides this fact, two questions for research make up the core of this volume: are there forms of severe urban poverty that are now on the increase? Are they more and more concentrated in large cities and in some areas (inner city ghettos or decaying peripheries)? These forms of poverty lie at the heart of the debates on social exclusion and the underclass and are discussed as such instead of the subjects who in general find themselves in economic difficulties in the affluent societies. Forms of poverty are assumed to be persistent and to have no permanent solutions under the present conditions of economic development and welfare provision. Consequently, they constitute serious fissures in the social systems of welfare capitalism (see Tosi and Marcuse herein). In order to prepare the ground for discussion of these forms of urban poverty, it is essential that we first assess the concept of poverty in general and the forms of measurement that are used in research and policy making.

Generally, our visions of poverty focus on people who persistently face economic difficulties and therefore cannot satisfy their basic needs. This rough and ready definition already raises various problems. The poor are such not because the amount of resources at their disposal is low but because they are insufficient[1] for socially acceptable conditions of life in a particular historical community. Poverty is a reflection not of the resources that people have but rather of the ones they are effectively able to use in order to satisfy basic needs (Sen 1985, 1992). Basic needs vary greatly at different moments of the life-course and under different social and community conditions,[2] and they depend ultimately on the chain of events in individual life histories. It is known, for example, that the elderly have a low amount of needs when physically autonomous and well integrated in family, friendship and neighbourhood networks, and, conversely, they have a high number of requirements when chronically ill, non-autonomous and socially isolated. Then there is the serious controversy over whether resources should be considered insufficient when they do not provide for anything beyond pure survival or, rather, when they do not permit integration into the community in which the poor live and non-exclusion from the same minimum opportunities and rights of the non-poor; hence the still open debate on the concepts of absolute and relative poverty. Last but not least, anyone who is in difficulty for a sufficiently long period of time, so that his/her standard of life is seriously affected, is considered to be poor, as against people with only temporary problems.

From these preliminary considerations there immediately emerges an important point. Our conceptual vision of poverty is inconsistent with macro forms of measurement that can be used for comparative analysis. The identification of the poor on a large scale takes place in two different ways that are highly problematic with respect to our vision of poverty. The first method of identification, and the most widely used for international comparison, is to take as being poor the households or individuals living below the poverty lines – conventional yardsticks of spendable income or expenditure, fixed officially by governments either in relation to the average per capita income of the population or in relation to a fixed national minimum considered indispensable for survival.[3] The second method, less used in international comparisons and macro analysis due to the obvious difficulty of comparing highly diversified conditions of welfare provision, is to consider as poor those individuals assisted by specific welfare programmes.

Both the absolute version of the poverty line, which is nearly everywhere used as an operative instrument for establishing admission to welfare programmes, and the relative version, which, on the other hand, is the preferred instrument for comparative studies and official statistics, are at the same time useful but inaccurate. They measure what it is possible to measure, that is, the level of monetary income or expenditure at a certain moment of time. As such they do not tell us anything about duration in time, sufficiency of resources in terms of satisfying basic needs, the variety of resources (including social and informal kinds) and their effective utilization, the variability of social and demographic backgrounds, and other aspects that are considered necessary in order to identify and understand poverty. It is worth mentioning some of the distortions that are particularly important for the problems dealt with in this volume.

As the poverty lines measure the population living below a standard calculated solely on the basis of the possession or use of monetary resources, they systematically overestimate the poor by including individuals and groups who can count on hidden resources and/or who have needs well below the average or who live in particularly inexpensive areas. The two most frequently mentioned cases are the rural population and the healthy and not socially isolated elderly, especially when they are homeowners. Conversely, the poverty lines dramatically underestimate some factors that are typical of urban poverty: the much higher than average cost of living, the lack of opportunities for self-provisioning and self-help, the negative impact of greater social instability and isolation. As will be seen in many of the essays included here, this point further highlights the dramatic picture in the US in particular, for which we have significant data on the concentration of the population below the federal poverty line in urban ghettos. This concentration is even greater and the conditions of life of the poor are much worse than we would expect from the macro data. As this volume shows, although for Europe we do not have locally disaggregated macro data, it is reasonable to assume that here also processes of concentration, ghettoization and deterioration of the life conditions of the urban poor are under way.

Identification of the poor with welfare clients who are in economic difficulty has some grave limitations. As already stated, it is extremely problematic for comparative purposes. Welfare programmes are diversified and variously selective even at the local level, not to mention the international level. They are selective in two different ways. From an institutional perspective, they fix minimum requirements for admission to aid. These are usually variations of the survival minimum which have the same characteristics as the absolute line of poverty. In addition, however, not all those entitled to aid apply for it. What we have here is a selection process that involves not only a question of information and efficiency but also cultural bias, discrimination and stigmatization, which discourage potential clients for reasons of self-confidence and pride. Paradoxically, the more efficient, generous, well organized and less discriminatory a programme is, the more poverty it discovers.[4] This, however, has very little to do with reality. In fact, the opposite is often true. In conditions where welfare programmes are inefficient, restrictive and discriminatory there is more poverty. This is evident if we compare the Scandinavian countries (more welfare clients and less poverty) to the US or Italy where, in the first case, the stigmatization of welfare dependents is strong and, in the second, welfare programmes are not particularly efficient and well organized. In both cases, we have relatively fewer welfare clients and more real poverty. The same obviously occurs with changes in welfare provisions: the more they become efficient, generous and non-discriminatory, the more welfare clients there are and the less poverty there is, and vice versa.[5]

The main advantage of the study of poverty through welfare clients is the fact that this may provide important longitudinal data. Welfare clients' panels[6] identify the long-term histories of the poor, the events and conditions that affect the impoverishment trajectories and those that favour the exit from poverty. This last observation gives me the opportunity to introduce the reasons for a main difference in the angle of approach to the study of urban poverty, a difference which also runs through this volume. While the majority of authors insist on the features of areas of chronic poverty, the conditions of life of large urban groups that survive in a general climate of deprivation from childhood to death, others (see in particular Micheli and Zajczyk herein) focus on the life trajectories of impoverishment. These different angles are equally important in that they are complementary within an attempt to understand the reality of urban poverty today. Where, as in the case of American cities, it is possible to document specifically the features of areas of concentrated chronic poverty, these very features are the object of discussion rather than the chain of events in the life histories of the poor. Where already constituted areas of chronic poverty exist, the histories of impoverishment usually repeat common features (early dropping out from school, discrimination in access to welfare services, teenage pregnancy or early marriage for females, joblessness and prison for males, etc.), which need to be checked against the specific different conditions of social groups and localities. Conversely, where such chronic areas do not exist or their features are not available through disaggregated institutional data, it is particularly useful to focus on individual life histories. I will discuss this point at greater length in the concluding chapter.

Throughout the long phase of industrial development in the nineteenth and twentieth centuries up to the end of the post-war expansion in the early 1970s, poverty involved mainly two phenomena: the rural population subjected to the growing pressure of market competition and to the progressive erosion of the margins of subsistence arrangements; and the life conditions of the mass of the more or less recently urbanized working class without craft skills, uprooted from traditional forms of sociality and at the mercy of a labour market that was highly dynamic but in which the excess of supply, fed by new waves of migration, over demand, limited by increases in labour productivity, tended to remain chronic. It is particularly this latter phenomenon that attracted the modern scientific and political attention towards poverty in industrialized countries. And it is not by chance that this attention developed above all in the English cities where early and radical industrialization and de-ruralization led to the concentration of vast masses of people uprooted from traditional forms of social support[7] and made them totally dependent on wages, the labour market and monetary consumption (the so-called cash nexus).

The first to study the phenomenon of poverty systematically[8] was Seebohm Rowntree in York (1901, 1941 and 1951 with Lavers). His definition was a very pragmatic one, lying at the root of the conceptualization of absolute poverty: the poor are those who are unable to achieve physical survival. He attempted to establish a fixed value-free criterion by which to measure poverty, one that ideally could be applied to all societies. This measure was based on a basket of goods held to be indispensable by studies on the minimum energy levels required for health and physical efficiency. By attaching a price to these goods a threshold was determined, which made it possible to classify those with fewer resources as poor.[9] The poverty condition was thus equated with the subsistence minimum, to be ascertained in turn. The pioneering investigations of Rowntree made it possible to identify urban poverty as a new phenomenon, qualitatively different from the traditional rural kind. In the new industrial cities, the combination of fully commodified standards of life, growing individualism and diversified opportunities for raising resources on a labour market, persistently characterized by a surplus of labour supply, meant that a sizeable part of the population was left in a condition of great difficulty.

In order to test the assumption of individual responsibility Rowntree had to find a level of income at which the individualistic hypothesis no longer held: that is, a minimum subsistence level which left no room for discretion in evaluation. The results of his studies pointed to structural variables such as insufficient income from work, unemployment, old age, death and illness of the breadwinner as the main causes of poverty. The structural nature of these causes was confirmed by the fact that in British cities the picture changed considerably following the implementation of the Beveridge Report (1942); in the third study (conducted in the late 1940s and published in 1951) only old age and illness still appeared as poverty-causing factors. The importance of intervention by the welfare state in response to the processes of pauperization arising out of the way the market functions was, therefore, increasingly evident.

Once again, it was in urban contexts, and under the very conditions created by the development of different forms of welfare capitalism, that the concepts of relative poverty and privation were put forward.[10] The absolute definition of poverty and the assumption that it can be used as a universal criterion have been increasingly criticized.[11] Different population groups have different needs and the choice of goods to be included in the basket is likewise arbitrary and standardizes modes of consumption without taking into account likes, habits, cultural traditions, the life cycle, age or family typologies. Moreover, in a climate of welfare capitalism increasing importance is given to access to or exclusion from essential life resources, like health and education services, means of transportation or minimum status symbols, which in turn regulate the distribution of crucial working opportunities and life chances. Post-war economic expansion and the growing extent of social intervention by the state altered the socio-economic conditions of social reproduction processes and the relative nature of the concept of poverty became the fundamental benchmark for most studies conducted since the 1970s in European countries.

It is above all Townsend who has theorized that it is ontologically impossible to define universal standards that do not take diversified social conditions into account. On the basis of the concept of relative poverty those considered to be poor are 'individuals, families and groups in the population . . . when they lack the resources to obtain the types of diet, participate in the activities and have the living conditions and amenities which are customary, or at least widely encouraged or approved, in the societies to which they belong' (Townsend, 1979: 31). The idea is that in complex modern societies poverty cannot be defined only by the material level of survival but has to be extended to the entire stratum of families and individuals that, though managing to survive, are actually excluded from most of the benefits typical of industrial societies in terms of education, health, culture and, more generally, social integration. The consequence is that they find themselves relegated into highly malign circuits of social marginalization. Townsend's goal has been to construct a synthesized index ('deprivation index') from complex indicators pertaining to two main categories: available resources and life-styles. As to the first, he starts from the presupposition that in no society does income alone, understood as cash earnings, allow a person's economic position to be adequately measured; he thus maintains that it is more useful and significant to consider all available resources. To construct the living standard indicator, he takes a set of 'primary', therefore necessary, 'goods/services' whose availability or access is held to be normal in the context in question. Living conditions play a fundamental role in Townsend's definition and to make it operational he uses two key concepts, relative privation and reference group, introduced by Runciman in the 1960s.[12]

Both Rowntree and Townsend have directly influenced the construction of useful yardsticks for the definition and implementation of social policies. On one side, all those methods based on an official 'vital minimum' for calculating the needy part of the population (for example, the Federal Poverty Standard in the US, Supplementary Benefit in the UK or *Sozialhife* in Germany) are certainly closer to Rowntree's approach. On the other, starting from the conceptualization of relative poverty and the way the poverty line is formulated,[13] the idea has emerged of establishing a conventional threshold of income/consumption capacity (variable from one society to another) below which subjects are considered to be poor. From this has been derived the International Standard Poverty Line.

WHAT IS NEW IN URBAN POVERTY?

It is clear from the previous section that while industrializing cities have been the main arena for the identification of modern forms of poverty, the concepts and measures, and obviously the social policies, relating to the phenomenon have been applied generally. With the exception of the UK, where de-ruralization happened early and radically, up to recent times economic poverty remained heavily concentrated in less developed rural areas everywhere in the industrialized world. A paradoxical consequence was that most of the features that have been emphasized in the debates on poverty, typical of urban areas, did not apply to the majority of the poor.[14] Today, although the progressive depopulation of the countryside combined with agricultural protectionism has not eradicated rural poverty entirely, it has helped to limit it considerably. It should be noted, in particular, that it was only in the 1950s and 1960s that both in the US and in many countries of continental Europe the less developed rural regions were abandoned *en masse*, producing also a shift out of traditional rural poverty offset by increasing urban poverty; but due to time lags, differences in quality and generational gaps this process went largely unnoticed.[15]

At the same time, welfare programmes were developed to try and deal with working-class poverty and integrate growing masses of proletarianized workers and their families into modern systems of citizenship. All of this occurred in conditions of rapid upward social mobility, driven by the growth of large manufacturing concerns as the mainstay of rising productivity and by the parallel diffusion of mass consumerism. In such a context it is no wonder that little was said about poverty. The crucial problem was to develop welfare pro-grammes that would employ at least a part of the resources created by growth to protect weaker individuals and families from exposure to the devastating effects from the way the labour market worked. In other words, the forms of poverty that arose within a context of de-ruralization and proletarianization were not thought to be necessarily in conflict with the development of modern citizenship systems. Also, the particularly virulent levels found in nineteenth-century English cities, the great crisis of the 1930s, the emphasis of the Chicago School on the 'unhealthy and contagious intimacy' (Park, 1925: 45) in great cities or the misery in the backward rural regions were largely ignored. Such poverty appeared to be the painful, but transitory, price to pay for industrial modernization. The very resources that the process of impoverishment itself helped to produce through a constant provision of low-cost labour seemed sufficient to guarantee social integration, at least from one generation to the next. Thus at present, in entering into new debates on forms of severe poverty, typical of advanced industrial cities, there is confusion as to what is really new and what is only a new version of an old story that was largely forgotten during the golden age of post-war expansion. In fact, elements of both continuity and discontinuity are contained in this story. In this regard, recent contributions to the general debate on poverty, characterized by a renewed attention to 'absolute poverty' (Milano, 1988; Sen, 1992), constitute an important clarification in approaching the essential theme of this book, that is, urban social exclusion and the chronic urban poor, whether homeless and vagrant or ghettoized or segregated in derelict peripheries or decaying inner cities.

Concentrating on relative deprivation has the merit of putting one's finger on the fact that in advanced welfare societies a particularly low standard of living, independently of the capacity to survive, may constitute the starting point for malign circuits of social exclusion. On the other hand, however, it obscures the fact that large groups of people are in very serious difficulties and, at the same time, neglected or stigmatized by welfare programmes. The specific features of the processes of social marginalization and the chain of events and conditions that lead to social exclusion[16] remain largely hidden by viewing poverty as synonymous with low income. Income level is not necessarily an index of poverty: what we have is a static description of the amount of income available to or spent by diverse family typologies relative to an average or to a conventional minimum in a given country. In addition, the measurement of poverty according to income levels lowers or raises the number of poor independently of the course of poverty in absolute terms. In Sen's view, the problem of poverty cannot be resolved by studying economic resources but rather the capability of using this income to attain the social objectives and life conditions held to be necessary in each case. The level and variety of resource functioning, and thus the system of goods and incomes required to achieve them, 'are different in different societies and depend on a standard of life considered acceptable in a given context' (Sen, 1993: 310).

On the other hand, the cumulative effects of the disadvantages must also be taken into account and so 'those that experience the greatest difficulty in obtaining an income are precisely the people that have the greatest difficulty in using such an income to improve their living standard' (Sen, 1993: 313). It is likely that this difficulty grows in relation to the type of person and the kind of area in which the individual subject is inserted. In other words, it is one thing to be inserted in a chronically depressed area and quite another in a socially more supportive area. In general, the fact that niches of poverty may persist even in conditions of affluence and after the impact of fiscal and welfare redistribution entails the need to qualify poverty as exclusion from access to a minimum of resources held to be vital. Such exclusion forms the basis for both a social definition of poverty and a definition of social policies in terms of citizenship.[17] Consequently, now much more than in the past, the social construction of 'poverty' is indissolubly linked to the modern system of citizenship and to the welfare mix. As we will see again in the next section, by welfare mix is meant that combination of opportunities and support which should ensure every citizen is able to satisfy survival needs and achieve life standards that lead to acceptance in the community of belonging and permit, as Adam Smith once said, a minimum of self-confidence.

Summing up what has been said so far, the debate on urban poverty today reflects two different narratives (and research methodologies) which are complementary in understanding reality but very difficult to link together.[18] The first narrative is a macro one and focuses on all the risk of impoverishment indicators, including the poverty lines but also the general interconnections with factors, events or social typologies like unemployment, single parenthood, old age, mental illness, membership of a disadvantaged group or segregated residence in a decaying neighbourhood or in a less developed region. In its various versions, this narrative does not focus on the 'poor', in the sense of people for whom the malign circuits of exclusion are activated with serious consequences in terms of the transformation of their capacity to adopt 'normal' life strategies (see Micheli herein), but rather on 'poverty', that is, a broad social area where the potential for malign circuits to become activated is high. Once it is accepted that through this narrative we are unable to identify the 'real poor', there is a considerable degree of consensus on the general features and the 'new' consequences of the phenomenon in terms of rupture of the citizenship bond and formation of chronic areas, either dispersed or concentrated, of social destitution. But it is only through the second narrative,[19] focusing on the life histories and social processes involving the behaviour of and chain of events affecting the individuals and households for which the malign circuits are effectively activated, that we can develop our understanding of the poor and establish an effective connection between, on one side, factors and conditions and, on the other, behaviour. The two narratives cannot be connected either logically (the first operates with potential and quantitative correlations while the second deals with effective phenomena and qualitative processes) or technically (the quantitative data produced by the first cannot be corroborated with precision in the second, as what matters here is the typology of processes rather than numbers that cannot be representative). This has the effect of leaving the debate open.

In general, the new forms of severe urban poverty are viewed as critical problems in respect of citizenship systems that are being remoulded in line with changing social conditions. By excluding a growing number of individuals from full citizenship, the diffusion of poverty constitutes a serious threat to social cohesion. The problem is not the revolt of the poor, who are such also because they have no voice or political representation, but rather the weakening of the social bond as a whole in a situation where solidarity and certainties are fading away even for those who are not poor. The aim here, therefore, is not to describe poverty in diverse urban areas, but to discuss the impact of the phenomenon as a critical factor with regard to social cohesion in the process of transformation that is affecting the citizenship systems of the advanced industrial world.

Traditional forms of poverty have not ceased to exist and cannot be ignored. Many features of widespread typologies of poor individuals and households in contemporary cities are, in some ways and under different conditions, similar to those found in the past. This is particularly true in the case of large families supported by a single low-income worker (see Morlicchio herein), especially if insecurely employed, or in the case of socially isolated individuals. However, what is new and important is that the poor as such lie beyond the reach of relatively massive welfare intervention by the state.

The poor are ignored or untouched by welfare intervention or, in most cases, they are discriminated against and insufficiently protected by a powerful apparatus set up for the very purpose of achieving social integration and equal opportunities. This fact changes the nature of the problem considerably, not only when moving from the past to the present but also from the less developed (where material poverty is massive but rarely entails social exclusion) to the advanced industrial countries.

Furthermore, the post-Fordist transition has reopened the question in terms that are quite new because the processes of impoverishment are no longer controlled by the dynamics of change that were typical of the expansionary phase led by the large manufacturing concerns and mass consumerism; and it is also in this sense that there is today a growing tension between poverty and the system of citizenship. It is no longer possible to rely on decisive extensions of the stable employment base providing adequate incomes or on sufficiently high rates of economic growth to compensate for social exclusion always and to the extent necessary. Both employment and the family are becoming less stable and thus more problematic and selective in protecting individuals from falling into malign circuits of impoverishment. These transformations create new tensions on the welfare state intervention front, which is already seriously troubled by fiscal and financial difficulties.

The risks of falling into forms of chronic poverty are concentrated in cities for various reasons. Here it is particularly likely that economic poverty will become transformed into acute, progressive and unstoppable forms of social exclusion. Employment and demographic transformations are more radical and concur in continually bringing about new forms of vulnerability. The systems of kinship and community solidarity have been weakened by the instability, heterogeneity and anonymity of relations of sociality. The supply of public shelter is here more developed but also more overloaded by heterogeneous forms of demand that vary rapidly over time, and it is therefore more vulnerable to complexity and to financial collapse. It is also especially targeted to particular groups that are excluded from employment and consequently more likely to provoke objections from taxpayers. Moreover, the higher cost of living, the greater likehood of not finding suitable accommodation and the difficulty of adopting self-provisioning strategies make impoverishment sequences more frequent.

The debates on social exclusion and the underclass raise the question of the city mainly at a different logical level with respect to the question of the concentration of poverty in urban areas. It is not only a question of quantitative data on the presence of households with extremely low incomes but more one of the conditions of and prospects for the poor. It is argued that under present conditions the features characterizing the urban poor, concentrated in ghettos (Wilson, 1987 and 1993; Fainstein, Marcuse and Wacquant herein) or decaying peripheries (Morlicchio and Wacquant herein) or dispersed as homeless (Tosi and Marcuse herein), run a high risk of becoming chronic forms of social exclusion. These conditions derive, on one side, from decreasing opportunities and aid (from the state or from more fragile family and community structures) and, on the other, from the fact that the urban environment itself and social segregation constitute aggravating factors from the point of view of the life conditions of the poor, even apart from their numbers. Ethnographical studies and longitudinal researches on welfare clients tend to confirm this view, but it is difficult to find a definitive confirmation from empirical macro data for two reasons. The first is that it is too early to have confirmation of what we deduce to be a long-term process, but which began on a massive scale only a few years ago. Most of the data we use document what was happening in the 1970s and early 1980s while we assume (on the basis of local studies or of other macro indicators like the spread of long-term unemployment or of insufficiently paid unstable jobs or of single-parent households) that the phenomenon accelerated only thereafter. The second reason is that most of the institutional data are qualitatively inappropriate for confirming this hypothesis. For instance, the documentation available in the US on the progressive concentration of poverty in inner cities (from 32 per cent of the poor in 1970 to 42.4 per cent in 1990 – Danziger, Sandefur and Weinburg, 1994) does not tell us much about the conditions of and prospects for the poor in question. Hence, the current narratives on urban poverty as forms of social exclusion are based on plausible reasoning and on many different indicators, which, however, rarely match as they regard different population groups and different time-scales or only a section of the poor. The hypothesis of the city and of urban segregation as a factor producing chronic poverty leading towards malign circuits of exclusion is convincing but not fully documentable.

THE PROCESSES OF SOCIAL CHANGE AND ITS VARIOUS EFFECTS IN DIFFERENT COUNTRIES

The social transformations of the last few decades have led to the re-emergence of serious questions about impoverishment in practically all cities in the industrialized world. The new tensions result from the varying combined impact of post-Fordist economic accumulation based on the globalization and the increasingly important role of services (Sassen, 1991 and herein; Mingione, 1991a; Sayer and Walker, 1991; Esping-Andersen, 1994), the decline in stable employment in the big manufacturing factories and the increasing heterogeneity and instability of householding and demographic arrangements, which is eroding the crucial protective role of the nuclear family solidly embedded in local and kinship-based social conditions of solidarity. The intervention of differently structured welfare states, hampered by fiscal and financial difficulties and by increasing opposition to state expenditure from large politically organized groups of taxpayers, nowhere appears able to respond to the increasing pressure generated by post-Fordist problems, in particular the diffusion of chronic areas of poverty in large cities.[20]

There are two main points that need to be underlined: the decline of the family wage of the adult male breadwinner as the dominant form of the social division of labour in favour of a system centred on the multi-income household; and the substitution of the employment regime dominated by the large manufacturing concerns with the service employment regime (Sassen, 1991 and herein). The combination of these two transformations, on the one hand, and demographic and house-holding changes affecting the life-course, on the other, has helped to increase the risk of falling into poverty in different ways. In the advanced urban economies, since the early 1970s the volume of employment has increased, particularly due to the number of married women employed part- or full-time, but less than the volume of unemployment. The conditions of entry into first jobs for young males have deteriorated, deflating the myth of unlimited upward mobility. The balance between the loss of stable manufacturing jobs and the creation of precarious jobs in services is having a serious negative

Area	Fordist	Post-Fordist
ECONOMIC STRUCTURE	Predominance of manufacturing production in large concerns	Predominance of the financial cycle and of the service sector
ECONOMIC CYCLE VERSUS EMPLOYMENT	Crisis destroys jobs while growth creates new jobs	Growth does necessarily not creates new jobs. New investments in manufacturing may destroy jobs
EMPLOYMENT — Male	Full-time full-life as family income breadwinner	Diffusion of atypical and informal employment - no entry job at family income - employment instability - high youth unemployment - decreasing but persisting gender inequalities
EMPLOYMENT — Female	Partial or total exclusion from paid work, at least during intensive childcare phase	
WAGES	Family wage	Component and irregular wages
DIVISION OF UNPAID WORK	Completely and 'naturally' to women: part- or full-time housewives	Partial tension-ridden redistribution, but persistently and controversially in the hands of women - second shift versus involuntary housewife
DEMOGRAPHIC, FAMILY AND HOUSEHOLDING FEATURES	Standardized life-course based on: marriage at a 'proper' age	De-standardized unstable life-course: decline of marriage, at different later age
	stability of marriage	instability of marriage
	common - 2 or 3 - number of children	decline of birth rate - childbearing at different ages and fewer children
	central role of nuclear arrangements with dependent children	large part of life lived outside nuclear arrangements with dependent children
	average life-expectancy: a few years after pension	longer life-expectancy: 15-20 years beyond the pension age
CULTURAL FACTORS	Quantitative standard mass-consumerism; children-oriented individualism	Qualitative emphasis in consumption; 'hedonistic' individualism
WELFARE AND CITIZENSHIP	Centrality of the nation-state; Universalistic ideals and goals	Coexisting tendencies towards globalization and localism; Fragmentation, privatization and ad hoc programmes

Figure 1.1 The social transition hypothesis: features of change

impact (Standing, 1995), particularly in de-industrializing cities with radical forms of geographical and social concentration that penalize inner cities or some peripheries and less educated social groups. Under these conditions an increasing number of households, more and more heterogeneous relative to the two-parent nuclear family, are now without the protection of either a traditional breadwinner family-wage job or a multiple stable income arrangement.

In reality, the transformation processes are giving rise to different tensions because they interact with welfare systems that have grown up historically along diverse lines. In all cases, however, the transformation processes bring about difficulties, beginning with the three main areas that condition the forms of social integration and exclusion: the employment system; the system of householding and of primary solidarity; the welfare state and the regulatory authorities. In order to have a clearer idea of the impact of these transformation processes it is useful to adopt a view which overemphasizes (by dramatizing changes that in reality are slow, progressive and take place at different speeds and times and with diversified features in different places) the social transition from a Fordist to a post-Fordist regime (see figure 1.1).

In general, that is, excluding the question of particularly disadvantaged groups, such as minorities, immigrants and inhabitants of economically depressed regions, and concentrating on the risk of poverty within the life-course of common workers, two radical transformations within the last century can be pointed out. When at the beginning of this century Rowntree (1901: 169–72) studied the city of York, he noted that the risk of poverty was particularly concentrated in three periods of the life-course: childhood; early middle age (when a worker supports many dependants); old age. When he studied York in the late 1940s, only old age remained a substantial factor of impoverishment. Subsequently, the further development of welfare provisions and pension schemes attenuated the risk of poverty for the elderly. This transformation was due to the development of the family wage regime complemented by various forms of welfare and social insurance provisions, as shown in the left column (Fordist) of figure 1.1. Obviously, what is here called a 'Fordist regime' is an ideal construction, nowhere ever fully implemented and, in the different realities and at different times, characterized by serious inequalities and tensions.[21] However, the stability of employment and social insurance arrangements for the breadwinner providing a family income (if not for all, then what is more important, for an increasing number of adult males) and of the nuclear family set-ups, together with long-term economic growth at high rates and expanding state welfare expenditure, kept under control at least the general risk in the common worker's biography. The current changes as shown, again in a general ideal format, in the right-hand column of figure 1.1 (post-Fordist) are spreading the risk of impoverishment at various different time-points of individual biographies, particularly in connection with disadvantaged status and negative life events, like family crisis, job loss, long-term unemployment and mental illness. It is now more difficult to repeat on a general scale the Rowntree approach on the phases of the life-course because the risk is distributed in markedly different ways depending on the specific welfare systems. What can be said is that while childhood is once again a risk situation, particularly for children in a single-parent household and in large households supported by a single low-income worker, peaks of risk are appearing in the phases of biographies that, at the beginning of the century, were ones of relative abundance, that is, young adulthood and late middle age.

The current employment transformations that are having an influence on the risk of poverty are increases in unemployment and the fact that a large number of new jobs in the services sector are badly paid, insecure and unstable. In the last 20 years, there has been a sharp drop in employment in the manufacturing sector (particularly concentrated in some traditional industrial belts – inner cities or industrial peripheries – where the less skilled and educated part of the population is also concentrated), more or less counterbalanced by the increase in highly heterogeneous and relatively unstable forms of employment in services.[22] This transformation is radically altering the division of labour, based on stable occupations for adult male breadwinners earning a family wage, which had underpinned the ideology and life strategies of the Fordist era.

The labour market has begun to give rise to malign circuits that welfare systems have not managed to prevent or combat, above all because they are still largely structured according to the characteristics of the expansionary phase of employment in the big manufacturing plants. The unemployed and those in bad jobs are not necessarily poor, just as not all the poor are unemployed or in precarious occupations. Whether these two situations coincide depends on the individual's social and family profile, the protection given by welfare programmes, as well as the consequences that may derive from a failure for a certain time to be fully integrated into the employment system. The employment transformation contains the potential to augment the risk of poverty, which is then realized through the interplay of the other processes of change and the filter of complex systems of social insertion.

The socio-demographic changes in which we are interested most[23] are population ageing, the weakening of kinship networks (as a consequence of both increasing individualism and the falling birth-rate), the greater fragility of marriages, and the increase in migratory groups that are discriminated against and weakly inserted into networks of community solidarity. In all these cases, the primary support networks are less equipped to deal with difficult situations, and individuals are consequently more vulnerable to the risk of falling into poverty. But even here, the vulnerable socio-demographic typologies such as the dependent elderly, single-parent families, socially isolated individuals and households with limited resources overburdened by having to support many dependants or members in difficulties do not automatically imply a condition of poverty.

As for the welfare state, the (desired and unexpected) effects of the restructurings and privatizations deriving from both the fiscal crisis and the tendency to excessive growth of the demand for intervention and of state institutions must be taken into account. The link between the restructuring of state welfare programmes and poverty is more complex than appears at first sight. Obviously, there are also reductions in the number and quality of interventions and this has the almost automatic effect of removing shelter from social areas that are then more at risk. However, it is often the undesired effects that pave the way for uncontrollable tensions in the area of poverty.[24] Furthermore, the privatization of welfare services has, in general, made it possible to replace stably employed public sector workers with precarious workers employed by subcontracting agencies. In these cases, not only has the quality of the services declined but new individuals at risk of poverty have been created.

Besides the problems due to the financial collapse of the welfare state and those due to the overburdening demands for intervention and to unforeseen effects, there are new difficulties deriving from the decline in the national state's monopoly over regulatory action in favour of that by local and supranational bodies. Within this trans-formation, the application of state protection is not only weakened by the difficulty in co-ordinating programmes but, above all, by the increasingly problematic control over resources in a context of global mobility. In tandem, migratory mobility is also posing serious prob-lems in regard to the need to protect the life and work conditions of a highly differentiated, in terms of both original cultures and migratory plans, set of immigrants from the less developed world.

While it is not the case that all subjects under the weak or declining welfare umbrella are poor, it may be assumed that all the poor really *are* poor since comprehensive systems of welfare are not equipped to ensure that they are helped out of this condition. In the case of welfare programmes, too, we have a rough matrix for the potential impact on the features and spread of poverty. It has to be checked against the different welfare systems.

In order to understand how the various social environments filter the effects of the processes of change, made similar to a far-reaching extent by global interdependence, we have to approach the question from an intermediate level of theoretical abstraction. This entails assuming the existence of models and variants characterized by the crystallization over the medium-long period of several mixes of resources and social institutions that have become established in the historical development of capitalist industrial societies during the last two centuries.

The idea of the *Three Worlds of Welfare Capitalism* advanced by Esping-Andersen (1990) is a useful starting point.[25] The three areas on which he lays emphasis largely coincide with the spheres of social change mentioned above, that is: the family and voluntary support, the welfare state and the market as subsystems of responsibility in supplying welfare services.

The relative prominence of one subsystem compared to another characterizes the three models and may also characterize the variants inside each model. As can be seen in figure 1.2, the simple tripartition has been modified so as to identify important features in the processes that generate the risk of impoverishment, in particular the division between active and inactive state variants and that between cases where the persistent economic importance of family and kinship organization has been transformed into forms of innovative entrepreneurship and those where familism is heavily dependent on state assistance and the domination of the big company.

The characteristic feature of the 'conservative' model is the relatively greater importance of the family and voluntary organizations and a traditional state distrust of market forces, a full-blown resistance aimed at preventing whole-scale proletarianization that ends up fostering the adaptation of self-employment and family businesses as an alternative to maximized capitalist concentration. Variants of this kind are those where, in general, small family-based entrepreneurs have remained more dynamic, but also those where the model of the male 'breadwinner' wage worker has developed most fully and where the permanent presence in the labour market of married women has been relatively discouraged.

In this model, we can assume the existence of more pronounced 'statist' variants, as in the German and French cases, and variants with a more prominent familial component, as in the countries of

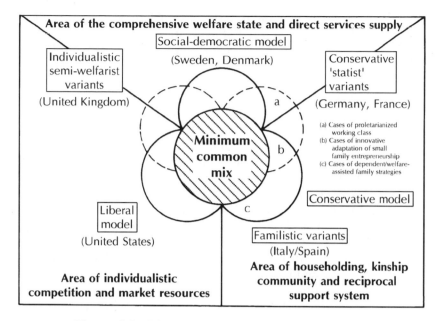

Figure 1.2   Models and variants of welfare systems

southern Europe (Mingione, 1995). Still in this same model, the division between regions where family entrepreneurship has developed a high capacity for adaptation and those where proletarianization has been more marked (the *Länder* in central-northern and eastern Germany) or where the entrepreneurial capacity of families has been stunted by late development (southern Italy) has played an important role in preventing or failing to prevent the creation and consolidation of substantial pockets of chronic poverty.

In all the 'conservative' cases, the production of poverty coagulates particularly at the intersection between, on one side, the sheltering capacity of the family, kin, community and voluntary organizations and, on the other, state policies of national insurance, income support and fiscal redistribution. The household and kinship system is over-loaded with responsibilities, and risks being dragged down into poverty whenever it has to support many individuals in need of special care, above all if state welfare is inefficient. The demographic transition is having a more radical effect in terms of the falling birthrate and delayed marrying age, but family structures are showing, at least for the time being, a great capacity for internal solidarity. In regions of entrepreneurial familism, those drifting into poverty are mainly individuals who have no family ties or have lost them. In regions of proletarianized or state-welfare-dependent familism, there is a trend towards family impoverishment syndromes, which are more serious in the big cities of southern Europe like Naples and Palermo where state intervention has always been less effective.

The 'liberal' model is characterized by a relatively greater expansion of the market, also as far as welfare services are concerned, and by more heightened forms of proletarianization, individualism and dependence on monetary income from waged employment. In this case, too, there are more 'statist' variants, like the UK, and more liberal-populist variants, like the US. In all these variants, poverty is more directly the product of labour market forces, where less competitive and skilled individuals are more vulnerable because they find less compensatory protection in both the family system and in state welfare services. Those malign circuits based on discrimination are particularly manifest where some social groups, such as minorities, recent immigrants and ex-workers, families trapped in de-industrialization zones, have less resources for acquiring usable entitlements on the labour market with the result that their weak position is handed down from one generation to the next. The rapid increase in precarious jobs in services has heightened the vulnerability of both discriminated social groups and regions hit by de-industrialization because the labour market continues to throw up syndromes of a social division of labour polarized between groups that cumulate many work and incomes chances and others excluded from the best working positions (Pahl, 1988; Morris, 1990, 1993 and herein; Buck herein). It is in these cases, in the capitals of de-industrialization, like Detroit or Liverpool, but also in the richer cities where world financial control is concentrated, like New York, Los Angeles or London (Sassen, 1991; Fainstein, Gordon and Harloe, 1992) that the spread of poverty is inexorably linked with the model of economic growth.

The Scandinavian 'welfarist' model is characterized by a greater development of the direct and universalistic creation of welfare services by the state. In countries with small populations and a relatively homogeneous identity, the process of proletarianization has been accompanied by costly systematic state intervention tending to cover all citizens, and not only workers, against the devastating effects of exposure to market forces. Here, the factors that pave the way for the risk of impoverishment are the fiscal tensions and vicious circles that can undermine the state's financial situation as a result of the growing number of individuals with a right to state protection, mostly the unemployed. The need to deal with structural changes in the employment system can give rise to difficulties that subsequently heighten the tensions in the system of state intervention. These tensions then bring about a fiscal crisis which short-circuits the state's capacity to protect subjects most at risk. Even if these cases are relatively more protected the fact remains that also in these variants the possible financial collapse of welfare policies will lead to the spread of impoverishment sequences, which state programmes with diminishing resources will be unable to reverse.

ISSUES AND TYPOLOGIES OF URBAN POVERTY IN A COMPARATIVE PERSPECTIVE

The final section of this chapter is devoted to introducing the general features of urban poverty in the five countries, the US, the UK, Germany, France and Italy, represented in this volume. Italy and Germany present serious problems of internal homogeneity. In the Italian case, poverty is particularly concentrated in the South and urban poverty is also extremely diversified in the two parts of the country; in the North it is more dispersed and individualized (Zajczyk, herein) while in the South it concerns predominantly large households segregated in decaying neighbourhoods in both inner cities and peripheries (Morlicchio, herein). In the German case, the unification of the country poses serious problems as the data used here refer only to the former Federal Republic and accurate documentation of the features of urban poverty in the eastern *Länder* is not yet available. The analysis of Berlin (Häussermann and Kazepov, herein) gives a first preliminary picture of urban poverty after unification.

The US and the UK both come under the liberal model of welfare capitalism, but the latter has a pronounced welfare framework dismantled only in part by the reforms of the Thatcher era. Germany (but in the East the Federal institutions were superimposed on a different system characterized by much higher rates of female employment and universalistic welfare provisions, even if at minimal levels – Leibfried et al., 1995) and France represent two rather different versions of the conservative statist variant. Italy represents the conservative familistic variant but extremely divided into an entrepreneurial version in the North and a state-dependent version in the South. Moreover, there are cultural differences between the five countries. These are discussed by Silver in chapter 5.

As expected, there are a few, controversial, indications to be culled from the comparative data available for all five countries on the population below the poverty line (taken to be 40 per cent of the average income) in the early 1980s (see table 1.1). Individuals with a

Table 1.1   Population under the poverty line taken as 40 per cent of the median income in the early 1980s

	1980		1985		1990
	n(000)	%	n(000)	%	%
Germany	2888	4.7	2590	4.2	
children	557	5.1(19.3)	549	5.9(21.2)	
elderly	616	6.4(21.3)	539	6.0(20.8)	
France	5757	10.7	4601	8.4	
children	1269	10.7(22.0)	1218	10.4(26.5)	
elderly	1364	18.9(23.7)	903	12.8(19.6)	
Italy	5167	9.2	5301	9.3	
children	1286	10.5(24.9)	1010	9.0(19.0)	
elderly	935	12.2(18.1)	930	12.8(17.5)	
United Kingdom	3678	6.5	5548	9.8	
children	1061	9.1(28.8)	1489	13.5(26.8)	
elderly	902	10.8(24.5)	1101	12.9(19.9)	
USA		13.0			13.5
children		17.9(38.0)			19.9(37.9)
elderly		15.7(13.2)			12.2(10.9)

Numbers in brackets are the proportions of children and elderly of all persons under the poverty line.
Source: Eurostat, 1990; for the USA, Danziger, Sandefur and Weinberg, 1994

particularly low income increased substantially in the UK and to a lesser extent in the US (but here starting from a much higher level) and in Italy. Conversely, their number decreased markedly in France and to a slight extent in the Federal Republic of Germany. The only trend which is both common and significant is the decline in the proportion of elderly among those in economic poverty, although it is only in the US in 1990 that this proportion is lower than that for the population as a whole.

Going beyond these data, which tell us little about the current features of the urban poor, we have to explore briefly the substantial issues and typologies which contribute to the understanding of the phenomenon in comparative terms. This will inevitably be somewhat controversial because, as already stated, the process of social exclusion is dynamic and cumulative and, consequently, the separation of issues and features creates distortions. Nevertheless, I will attempt to correct these by mentioning, whenever possible, the existing interconnections and any sequences of events and conditions.

Exclusion from Stable Employment

The relationship between exclusion from forms of good employment and poverty is not immediate.[26] In fact, it is influenced by various different factors, such as the duration of unemployment and of bad jobs, age, sex and inclusion in households with varying support capacities and the dimensions of social policies in favour of individuals in economic difficulties.

The literature has variously insisted on the fact that the transformations of the employment system have greatly contributed to increasing the risk of impoverishment, particularly in large metropolitan areas and to the disadvantage of certain social groups. In general, a strong statistical correlation has been noted between increases in levels of unemployment and the growth of the population living below the poverty line.[27] Thus, even in social contexts where the unemployed are directly protected by reasonable subsidies, higher levels of unemployment lead indirectly to increases in levels of poverty.

As already pointed out, unemployment levels have grown considerably from low 'frictional' levels in the early 1970s to much higher levels 30 years later (see table 1.2) (Standing, 1995). There are considerable differences in the levels between countries, though the lower levels in the US are in part due to the restrictive ways of measuring the phenomenon and in part explained by the wider diffusion of bad jobs. More important, however, is that in order to understand the connection between unemployment and poverty, we have to explore how far the unemployed enjoy dual protection: public subsidies and family, community or own resources. In addition, it is necessary to see what the indirect impact is of the increasing use of these support resources.

Table 1.2 Overall unemployment rate (1970–1990) and long-term unemployment rate (1975–1989) as a percentage of the total labour force

	Unemployment		Long-term unemployment	
	1970	*1990*	*1975*	*1989*
France	2.5	9.0	0.6	4.1
FRG	0.6	5.1	0.5	3.3
United Kingdom	2.2	6.9	0.5	2.5
Italy	5.3	9.9	2.0	8.3
USA	4.8	5.4	0.4	0.3

Source: OECD, 1991; Eurostat, 1988

Before taking into consideration how different 'models of unemployment' (who is unemployed, for how long, and how they are protected by different support sources) affect impoverishment paths in the different variants of urban industrialized society, another problem has to be mentioned (Gallie, 1994). A variably large group of people in poverty in large cities are out of work but not technically speaking unemployed as they are no longer looking for a regular job. Within the labour market structure of advanced industrial societies, a growing number of individuals stay permanently out of the official labour market because their professional credentials are not on a par with their expectations. The loops of severe impoverishment are often based on a progressive dequalification which leads to complete exclusion from the official labour market. Then there are the very poor, who take on temporary precarious jobs whenever available; but this does not solve their problems as a trend towards requalification is extremely unlikely. This direct connection between poverty and employment conditions should be considered as the parameter for any analysis that intends to go beyond the macro data on the numbers of poor in or out of work.

Among the cases considered here, only in Germany (and only in part) are the unemployed universally protected by state subsidies, that is, independently of the duration of unemployment and of previous work experience and insurance payments. In all the other variants, it is important to distinguish between what Therborn (1986) calls compensated (accompanied by sufficient subsidies) and punitive (low or no subsidies) forms of unemployment. Where subsidies are not universal, they usually protect for a varyingly limited time unemployed individuals with previous work experience.[28] Young people and women are largely excluded from subsidies, which are instead concentrated in favour of adult men who have lost their previous jobs. The former are supposed to be supported by other working members of the household, so that when they are socially isolated, live in low single-income households or, even worse, have to act as the breadwinner for a nuclear family (as in the case of single-parent households with dependent children) the risk of falling into impoverishment loops becomes very high.

If we exclude the universalistic countries, where the unemployed are all protected by subsidies, we have three variants depending on whether unemployment is particularly concentrated among young people (Italy), adult women (France) or adult men (the UK and the US). Regarding the risk of impoverishment, it is useful to mention the polarized distinction between the Italian (Pugliese, 1993; Mingione and Pugliese, forthcoming) and the British case (White, 1994; Morris, 1992; Buck, 1992 and herein).

In the Italian case, where long-term 'punitive' unemployment is particularly concentrated among southern youth (Reyneri, 1994), the risk of poverty affects especially low single-income households with poorly qualified dependent young adult children in large and medium-sized southern cities, first of all Naples (Morlicchio and Spanò, 1992; Morlicchio, herein). Even though we are unlikely to find a positive correlation between poverty and the unemployment status of the adult male head of a household, mass long-term youth unemployment erodes the resources of families with a single income where it is difficult for poorly educated children with low vocational qualifications to find a reasonable job. Here the connection between unemployment and poverty extends from the young adult children to the whole family structure.

In the British case, the extension of this connection between unemployment and poverty probably runs in the opposite direction: from the long-term unemployed father to his household. This is especially the case when he is no longer entitled to subsidies, far down a dequalification path and stuck in a low employment opportunity area in the rust belt cities. The social polarization and malign circuit of the 'work-poor household', suggested by Pahl (1989), take effect. Not only the unemployed subject but also his spouse and adult children are damaged by being confined in a low opportunity area and by the lack of information and social relations useful for finding good work opportunities and even informal work and self-provisioning (Morris, 1990, 1993 and herein).

These are only two of the many possible examples of how the diffusion of long-term urban unemployment can generate serious risk of impoverishment, through mass exclusion from work and progressive dequalification. It is necessary to make two observations concerning the indirect consequences of the relatively high levels of unemployment which are typical of advanced urban economies today. Even if a direct connection between unemployment and poverty is not always traceable, the difficulty in finding a good job is a crucial constituent factor in impoverishment loops which lead to social exclusion. This is due to the fact that the difficulty in finding a stable, sufficiently well-paid job, unfavourably concentrated among individuals and social groups with low educational and vocational qualifications condemned to living in city areas offering few opportunities, is part of a vicious circle of cumulative interlinked causation. The loss of self-confidence, physical and psychological illness, stigmatization of failure, alcohol or drug abuse, the difficulty in forming or maintaining a 'normal' family

cohabitation and a 'proper' housing arrangement are all interconnected elements which appear in the stages of the life history of the
socially excluded. A climate of high work instability and unemployment lies at the origins of these exclusion syndromes. In fact, it may be
true that many among the poor have problems finding a job because
they come from a first prison or drug addiction experience or from a
family breakup and a serious depression; but it is also true that the
impact of these events is minimal when and where the employment
climate is favourable.

The second consideration concerns the financial impact of high
levels of unemployment on the welfare systems, particularly but not
only when the unemployed are legally entitled to reasonable subsidies.
High levels of unemployment necessarily act as a constraint on public
expenditure, for different reasons. Not only do they compress income
and necessitate expanding some forms of expenditure to the detriment
of others, they also contribute to reorienting taxpayers against state
expenditure as in this particular case the lack of an immediate return
is so evident to public opinion. This is another dangerous malign
circuit which leads to the expansion of social exclusion: the higher the
number of poor the smaller the amount of state support they are likely
to receive.

The picture regarding the connection between employment conditions and urban poverty cannot be complete without some
considerations of the impact of the diffusion of insufficiently paid and
poorly tenured jobs in the services sector. This phenomenon is strictly
interlinked with higher levels of unemployment. Both trends are part
of a new employment regime (Sassen 1991 and herein: Lipietz, 1992).
Some of the poor are such because they remain out of work for a long
time as they cannot find or are unwilling to accept bad jobs; others,
conversely, are poor because they obtain only jobs which are
insufficiently paid, insecure and precarious. The number of the working
poor has increased dramatically in most of the large industrialized cities,
particularly in global cities (Sassen, 1991 and herein; Brown and Scase,
1991).

As I have already mentioned, unemployment and exclusive access
to bad jobs cannot be clearly distinguished as the main cause behind a
condition of poverty. A variable set of events accompany the circuit of
social exclusion. However, in many urban contexts, and particularly
in the US, a distinction can be made between poverty-affected social
groups due to 'unemployability' and others that are in this condition
because they are confined to bad jobs. The latter are more likely to be
women with family responsibilities or recent immigrant minorities
(Morris, herein).

The urban service employment regime is centred on a considerable increase of jobs in catering and hotels, office clerical work, leisure and entertainment, petty trade and commerce, maintenance and cleaning, security, etc. As Sassen explains in chapter 3, these jobs are characteristically labour intensive and require relatively few qualifications. Consequently, they are poorly paid and offer no career prospects. If they are done by a secondary worker the income generated may be sufficient to complement the household income, but in general it is insufficient on its own, also due to employment instability, to support a household. Thus, a family supported solely by the income deriving from one of these jobs finds itself in serious economic difficulties; this is also the case for large households supported by more than one of such working activities. The former is more likely to be a single-parent household where the only adult is a woman with low professional qualifications. The substantial increase in these households has led in most countries to the 'feminization of poverty' (Bane, 1988). The latter case is often found in immigrant communities, particularly Mexican and Central Americans in the large cities of the US but also ethnic minorities and recent immigrants in European cities.

The diffusion of these profiles of working poor has been more pronounced in the large financial centres like New York, Los Angeles and London, where the service employment regime has expanded completely unopposed (Sassen, 1991; Fainstein, Gordon and Harloe, 1992). The spread of the urban working poor has contributed to form a new large group of people, including an above average number of children, in serious economic difficulties and to concentrate the new poverty in the cities.[29] The realistic possibility that, particularly in the case of minorities and immigrants (and even more so if the latter are illegal), economic poverty may cumulate with serious discrimination in access to housing, health, education and other crucial services and the targeting of these groups for racist intolerance, constitutes another negative element in the picture of the malign circuit of social exclusion.

Demographic and Householding Factors

The protective capacity of family and community is weakening to a varying extent along two main lines: individuals may be socially isolated and hence more vulnerable for longer and longer periods during their life-course; and an increasing number of subjects are to be found in households and communities with highly insufficient resources. There is evidence from all five countries of both trends, though with cultural and socio-economic variations.

The only feature which is common to approximately the same extent in all advanced industrial societies is the lengthening of the duration of life. It is contributing to the ageing of the population and to the creation of a large group of single (predominantly females as their average life span is some years longer than that of males) or couple households characterized by low income (particularly in the case of women with an intermittent working life history on a low income) but also, and more importantly, by the need for specialized time-consuming care when physical autonomy is lost in old age. While the development of pension schemes and monetary assistance has kept economic poverty among the elderly under control, the second aspect is creating various difficulties in different welfare systems. The increasing need for care for the less autonomous elderly is met through different combinations of state, market and family resources. In the US, where the elderly are disproportionately non-Hispanic whites (which explains why they are a relatively small proportion of those below the poverty line – 11 per cent compared to approximately 20 per cent in the other countries), they are likely to be more isolated from family support and more dependent on market provision. This is probably creating an area of serious deprivation made up mainly of low-income elderly women prey to decreasing physical autonomy, socially isolated and with insufficient monetary resources to pay for expensive services outside Medicare. However, it is unlikely that this area of poverty will connect up with other forms of concentrated urban poverty.

In the UK also, the elderly in difficulty are likely to be relatively isolated from family support but more integrated into the local community compared to the high and long-distance mobility that is typical of their counterparts in the US. In the UK the problem is dealt with more by public programmes or mixed welfare provisions under the control of local authorities. There may be increasing geographical concentration of elderly deprivation, though the situation does not really resemble American ghetto poverty.

In the other three cases, the difficult problem of the elderly is still much more the responsibility of their families (particularly of adult women, daughters or daughters-in-law). The extent increases from the relatively low levels of France and Germany to the higher level of northern Italy and the peak of southern Italy. In all these cases, it is important to indicate two different situations of extreme difficulty: where a low-income elderly person with decreasing physical autonomy is isolated or has no nearby relatives; and where the problem of supporting an elderly relative aggravates the acute difficulties faced by an already weak family. Particularly this second case may contribute to the worsening of the conditions of life, above all in urban areas where disadvantaged groups are over-represented and public services poorly developed.

The declining rate, delaying and increasing instability (high divorce and separation rates) of marriage and the growing numbers of children born out of wedlock are differently distributed among the five countries and among the socially and locally disadvantaged groups in them. As a consequence, these factors have a diverse impact on the risks of social exclusion. There is a strong polarization between, on one side, the US, where in 1986 marriage and divorce rates were relatively high (respectively 9.7 per 1,000 women and 21.2 per 1,000 married women) as are the proportion of births out of wedlock (23.4) and the percentage of lone-parent families with children headed by a female (23), and, on the other, Italy, where all these indicators are much lower even if rising fast: the marriage rate stands at 5.2; divorce at less than 2; births out of wedlock at 5.6; lone mothers with children at 5 (Kamermann, 1995). The other countries lie in the middle with the UK closer to the US and Germany and France closer to Italy.

It could be said that there are two different modes of demographic and householding relations with a poverty risk. Both are increasingly vulnerable to impoverishment but in different ways. In the American mode, the risk is predominantly reflected in individualization (particularly in the case of young people and persons in between marriages) and in the increase in lone mothers. In the southern Italian mode, the risk is to a great extent transferred to families, particularly when they support children or the young adult long-term unemployed or a relatively large number of dependants. It is the southern Italian syndrome in particular that raises a controversial question. In the common way of perceiving marginalization processes, cumulation is normally insisted on as a crucial factor in impoverishment loops. It is argued that employment difficulties generate familial tensions and distortions and vice versa.[30] In the Italian case, these difficulties are absorbed by a traditional family structure which does not break down under the strain but extends the tensions to the other members.

In reality, this typology of 'familization' of poverty is not confined only to southern European cities and is not inconsistent with the current debates on social exclusion. The same syndrome is, for example, widespread among Latino migrants and minorities in the US (Moore and Pinderhughes, 1993) and among migrants and minorities in the other European countries. In all these cases, a two-parent nuclear household, which may be larger than average and also supported by other relatives, resists collapse under the pressures of joblessness or, more often, of extremely low worker incomes. However, these families also are in serious and persistent difficulties, because they cumulate disadvantages in other respects, in particular in terms of discrimination in the access to important services (like good education and health) or rights. Thus, in these cases too there is a local concentration of highly cumulative forms of chronic poverty even though the family and householding arrangements are different from those typical of the ghetto poor.

Disadvantaged Minorities and Immigrants

As can be seen in many of the chapters in this book, the debate on social exclusion and the underclass focuses in particular on disadvantaged minorities and immigrants, with the exception of Italy. In Naples areas of high concentration of disadvantages inhabited by the native population have developed, and in Milan both immigrants and the native population are protagonists of the drift into impoverishment, in different conditions but which rarely give rise to substantial and stable local concentrations. In this case, too, it is possible to speak of two polarized models: the US and northern Italy. In the first, very high concentrations of disadvantaged minorities in poor ghettos are recorded, which are increasingly internally homogeneous and where cumulative malign circuits of exclusion are evident (violence, low level of education, poor quality of services, absence of work opportunities, discrimination and so on). In the second, on the other hand, local concentration of those involved in exclusion drift is less probable and definitive, but above all it is not characterized by such a strong ethnic/racial 'closure' as can be found in the poor American ghettos. In chapter 11 Wacquant gives a very vivid idea of the differences, which would clearly be even greater in the case of Milan (see Zajczyk herein), where immigrants are far fewer in number and much less homogeneous than in La Courneuve on the outskirts of Paris.

Having made this initial clarification, which also derives from different cultural traditions (see Silver herein) as well as different realities, it is the case that several observations confirming, at least tendentially, the directions taken in the debate on social exclusion apply everywhere. They concern the fact that immigrants and disadvantaged minorities are more and more concentrated in large cities and, nearly always, in inner city or outer periphery ghettos (McFate, 1995). Though for different reasons, disadvantaged minorities and immigrants are doubly penalized in terms of access to job opportunities (Morris, 1994)[31] and access to welfare services such as health, information and education, which are also important instruments for social promotion.

It is these conditions that make it easier to structure the discourse on the chronic cumulation of disadvantages which triggers malign circuits and leads to social exclusion or the formation of an underclass. Conditions–behaviours–consequences concatenations differ and the degree of closure and discrimination against the poor community varies greatly (see Wacquant herein), but it is difficult to deny that these kinds of cumulative processes are under way in many big cities in the industrial world.

An important problem remains unsolved and it is dealt with in the concluding chapter. Arising above all out of the American debate on the underclass in the version put forward by Wilson (1987, 1993), socio-ethnic homogeneity and strong closed territorial segregation are seen to consititute essential factors in the discourse on urban poverty as a serious form of social exclusion. What needs to be asked, then, is whether the differences in terms of homogeneity or ghettoization or racial discrimination may alter the discourse to such a radical extent as to prevent the adoption of a common narrative encompassing all these phenomena. Certainly, the very different case of Milan where there is no substantial territorial segregation of the poor, let alone ethnic–racial homogeneity and closure, cannot be coherently tied into the narrative on the ghetto poor. Rather, there are other cases for which it will be necessary to reopen the debate in the conclusion. They are those in which forms of territorial segregation and the concentration and cumulation of disadvantages are recorded. In many of them, there is no predominant presence of disadvantaged ethnic minorities, as in Naples or the so-called white underclass in the US (Mincy, 1988) or the 'work-poor' families not belonging to minorities in the rust belt cities of the UK (Pahl, 1988; Buck, herein). In other cases, however, there is also a predominant presence of disadvantaged minorities, as in the Turkish quarters in German cities or the mostly North-African-inhabited districts of certain French cities or the parts of cities in the UK predominantly inhabited by West Indians or Asians, and also the neighbourhoods in the big American cities that are mainly inhabited by Chicanos and Central American immigrants. In every one of these cases, ghettoization is less traumatic than that suffered by the Afro-American and Puerto Rican ghetto poor; none the less malign circuits of serious marginalization are in progress that pass through exclusion from sufficiently stable and adequately paid work opportunities, heavy discrimination in access to minimum welfare services and visibly dilapidated habitations and life conditions. In conclusion, it is with reference to these cases that we will have to reopen the debate on the possibility that the various welfare and integration cultures or the differences in terms of familial and social strategies are of such a kind as to suggest diversified outcomes and interpretations.

NOTES

1   As underlined by Sen (1992: 111): 'In the income space, the relevant concept of poverty has to be *inadequacy* (for generating minimally acceptable capabilities) rather than *lowness* (independent from personal characteristics).'

2   It has been discovered that even the value for a minimum caloric diet for maintaining physical efficiency cannot be generalized. For example, both a majority of the elderly and large groups of people in developing countries maintain physical efficiency with diets below the minimum calculated standards (Sen 1981).

3   With the exception of the US, for analytical purposes the advanced industrial countries adopt the International Standard of Poverty Line (ISPL), that is, a conventional relative measure: households with an equivalent income (adjusted for household size and composition) below 50 per cent of average income. In the US, the Federal Poverty Standard (FPS), formulated by the Johnson administration in 1964 at the start of the 'War on Poverty', is a yardstick of absolute poverty; it is based on estimating the monetary cost of required food multiplied by three given that in the 1950s the average American family spent about one-third of its income on food products. Excluding inflation, the threshold value is more or less constant (in 1990 dollars around 13,300 for a family of four). In 1964 the American threshold was 50 per cent of the average income of a family of four; now it stands at 40 per cent. This means that today the number of poor in the US recorded by the FPS is lower than what would be indicated by the ISPL (Devine and Wright, 1993: 12–46).

4   Sen (1981, 1992), in particular, has developed this criticism using the example of the official Supplementary Benefit in the UK (the arguments he puts forward are, however, generally valid for any kind of social policy threshold). His objection rests essentially on the ontological impossibility of identifying the poor *tout court* as those who receive the minimum benefit. Any increase in the latter will also raise the number of poor people rather than reduce it.

5   The LIS (Luxembourg Income Studies) data (McFate et al., 1995; Mitchell, 1991) confirm the effectiveness of welfare provisions in lowering poverty rates. The comparison between poverty rates before tax and transfers and after tax and transfers leaves no room for doubt (see table 1.3).

6   Longitudinal panels and surveys supply data on the nature of poverty as a process, also identifying the most significant factors and events in impoverishment trajectories. The most interesting panel experiments are

Table 1.3   Percentage of all poor households lifted
out of poverty by tax and transfer programmes

	1979	*1986*
US	0.3	0.5
UK	33.0	46.1
West Germany	20.3	36.4
France	48.2	51.6

those of Bremen University (Longitudinal Social Assistance Sample –
LSA), Mannheim University (Socio-Economic Panel – SEP), the British
Household Panel Survey, and the Panel Study of Income Dynamics in
the US (Zajczyk, 1994: 56–62; Duncan et al., 1995: 91–2). The most
significant experience in Italy is the Veneto Social Survey (Micheli and
Laffi, 1995).

7   For several centuries enclosures had impeded communal land use,
thereby freeing labour power that was no longer able to reproduce itself
other than by offering itself on the urban labour market (Polanyi, 1944;
Marx, [1867] 1961; Novak, 1988). The accumulation of surplus
population in cities and the 'necessity' to force them into industrial
employment was at the origin of new policies towards poverty,
specifically the 'Poor Laws' of 1834 (see Polanyi, 1944).

8   At the same time also Charles Booth (1889) made a massive study of
poverty in London, but was less systematic and more moralistic than his
contemporary, Rowntree. Diffused urban poverty and pauperization in
industrially developing countries had already been clearly perceived as
an emerging serious phenomenon a few decades earlier by Tocqueville
(1835). The phenomenon was at the centre of Engels's analysis of *The
Conditions of the Working Class in England* (1969) and of parliamentary
reports (Blue Books) throughout the century. From the very beginning
there emerges an ideological opposition between a critical tradition,
emphasizing structural discrimination and social injustice against the
poor, and a cultural moralistic line, stressing the degraded moral
behaviour of the 'undeserving poor' (on this point see particularly
Morris, 1994).

9   Rowntree adopted a poverty line that reflected a restrictive criterion in
order to avoid any criticism of arbitrariness (and excessive generosity)
against his basket of goods and the results of his research, as well as the
ensuing social condemnation of the problem he identified. 'I purposely
adopted a standard which the most hard-boiled critic could not say was
extravagant' (Rowntree quoted in Briggs, 1961: 296).

10   In reality it resurfaced from early intuitions, among which one of
the most notable and quoted is the following consideration by Adam
Smith ([1776] 1812: 693): 'By necessaries I understand, not only the

commodities which are indispensably necessary for the support of life, but whatever the custom of the country renders it indecent for creditable people, even of the lowest order, to be without.'

11   This criticism appeared in the 1970s. Between the 1950s and 1970s the phenomenon of poverty seemed to have vanished from the agenda of social scientists. There are, of course, notable exceptions. Townsend has continued to study the problem (1952, 1970, 1979, 1985, 1990) and also in the US a large study group has been working on this theme (for example, Orshansky, 1965). See also Sen (1981).

12   In reality, the concept of 'relative privation' was introduced by Stouffer (1949). The term was next used by Merton ([1949] 1957), though it was Runciman who incorporated it into a systematic theory. The term 'reference group' was first coined by Herbert Hyman in 1942 ('The Psychology of Status' in *Archives of Psychology*) and the idea can be found even earlier in many social psychology texts.

13   It is preferable to see what Townsend himself says on how to determine the poverty line: 'households are ranked according to income and a criterion of deprivation applied. In descending the income scale, it is hypothesized that, at a particular point for different types of family, a significantly large number of families reduce more than proportionately their participation in the community's style of living. They drop out or are excluded. These income points can be identified as a poverty line' (Townsend, 1979: 249).

14   In this respect, it is particularly important to notice how the features of urban and rural poverty are largely different in terms of involvement in the labour market. Thus, it would be totally wrong to extend to the rural poor the features of marginal attachment to work that have been attributed to the 'idle' urban poor. It is from this very assumption of voluntary idleness that the behaviourist emphasis on the 'dangerous poor' in cities derives, which has been a constant feature of practically all social analysis undertaken during antiquity, the Middle Ages and more markedly on the eve of the industrial age with the build-up of urban overpopulation. Prejudice against the 'dangerous', deviant, undeserving and welfare-dependent poor (Dean and Taylor-Gooby, 1993; and Stern, 1993) has remained strong in the UK and, above all, the US. Moreover in the case of large American cities, the impact of the segregation of poverty and crime has been at the core of the analysis of the Chicago School in the period between the two world wars. For example, Park maintained that: 'In the great city the poor, the vicious, and the delinquent, crushed in an unhealthful and contagious intimacy, breed in and in, soul and body' (1925: 45).

15   In the US, for example, a large portion of the Afro-American ghetto poor of the 1980s are the children of families that moved in the immediate afterwar period from the less developed agricultural regions of the southern states to the frostbelt cities (Katz, 1986 and 1989). In the Italian case, a large portion of the population trapped in poverty today

are the children of those who migrated in the same period from the least developed southern agrarian regions to large cities, like Naples and Palermo, and have been stuck in precarious low-income building and trade jobs (Mingione, 1986).

16 Milano (1988) insists on some of these syndromes and processes – affecting particularly socially isolated, dequalified adult males cut out from welfare programmes – in his work, which may be considered the basis for the institution of the new programme of *Revenue Minimum d'Insertion* (RMI) in France.

17 Castel (1991: pp 147–8) stresses that the impoverishment process takes place following a fracture along two axes along which different areas of the social space run according to the level of *cohesion* they afford. The work relation axis (integration) defines 'a number of positions ranging from stable employment to the complete absence of work . . . On the relational insertion axis, it is equally possible to mark a range of positions between the inclusion in strong sociability networks and complete social isolation.'

18 What Bruckner (1995) attributes to the critical tradition may be extended to the great majority of poverty studies. 'In the critical tradition, a micro-level analysis provides a mirror image of the macro-level analysis; while this symmetry bears a certain attraction, we know that it is wrong.' This is the case because the data sets of the macro-level analysis (concerning people with incomes under the poverty line, or unemployed or single-parent households) are both static (Leibfried et al., 1995) and include different cases in respect of the data sets produced by the micro-level analysis (concerning people that are effectively in serious difficulties, that is, not potential poor but actually so).

19 This narrative often has a dynamic vocation oriented towards the life-course and the cumulation of negative events that produce marginalization loops (see herein Micheli; Leibfried et al., 1995). Also within this approach the micro–macro connection is impossible. As Micheli explains well, at the micro level, the transformation of the life strategies into malign circuits of deprivation is mediated by a great number of concomitant factors and psychological reactions.

20 This statement cannot be properly documented with data on the capacity of tax and welfare redistribution to lift people out of poverty (interpreted as low income). However, it is well known that the effectiveness of the US redistributive system is very low compared to European systems (McFate, Smeeding and Rainwater, 1995: 29 and ff; Burtless, 1994; Mitchell, 1991). The time trends in the early 1980s show that Sweden is among the few countries where this capacity was substantially decreasing, while it increased in France, the UK and West Germany. In the same period, however, poverty rates among non-elderly households increased substantially, particularly those headed by a 20–29 year old person. All these data refer to the low-income group and, consequently, they mean little with regard to the constitution of areas of urban social

exclusion. It is, in any case, interesting to note that the new tensions created by the post-Fordist transformations are so great, in terms of the increasing number of low-income households, that they cannot be contained even in the case of increasingly efficient tax and welfare redistribution.

21   As Morris discusses at length in chapter 8, the Fordist social regime was based on a very marked gender asymmetry to the disadvantage of women.

22   Job loss has mostly been in the manufacturing sector. In New York, from 1969 to 1989, 32 per cent of jobs in this sector were lost; in London, from 1971 to 1989, the figure is 47 per cent (Sassen, 1994a). This reduction corresponds to a shift (a typical phenomenon in big cities) of employment opportunities to the services sector, often resulting in underpaid and downgraded workers. In short, there is a profound gap between those employed in services who are protected and well paid and those employed precariously in services for very low pay, whose life-style consists of surviving on the fringes of society (Sassen, 1991 and herein; Esping-Andersen, 1993). In all the more industrialized countries, the service sector has been the most dynamic area of the labour market from the 1970s onward. However, service sector does not only mean 'advanced services' which involve skills and qualifications; above all, it means the rapid expansion of employment levels linked to low-level and unqualified services (Lipietz, 1992; Thernborn, 1986). For instance, in Milan two-thirds of new job starts have occurred in firms with less than 50 employees, while firms with less than 15 employees have provided 50 per cent of new jobs involving medium-to-low kinds of tasks in areas such as cleaning, catering and retail sales (Betelli, 1994).

23   By the term 'second demographic transition' (Lesthaeghe, 1991) is meant the sum of changes that have affected the Western family from the 1960s onward. These changes can be summed up in the following three points: (a) decline in fertility, together with a greater presence of women in the labour market, and the spread of more reliable contraceptive methods; (b) an increase in marital instability, therefore a greater number of separations and divorces; and (c) an increase in cohabitation between couples as an alternative to marriage (see Van de Kaa, 1980 and 1987; Shorter, 1975).

24   The classic example is the conditions for receiving monetary assistance for dependent children in the US (AFDC); by contributing to family instability, they eventually lead to impoverishment sequences (Wilson, 1993; McFate, 1991). A more recent example is the malign circuit produced by the rise in the number of unemployed subject to protection in the Scandinavian countries; it has led to cuts in other welfare programmes giving rise, in turn, to growing expenditure to cover the further rise in unemployment.

25   Esping-Andersen bases his typology on an evaluation of the degree of decommodification achieved by the welfare states of various countries. It

depends on the conditions for entitlements: in the liberal model reference is made to demonstrable abject need; in the conservative model to work performance; while in the social-democratic model we find the principle of the universal nature of citizens' rights. The author then proceeds to measure (for the methodology employed, see 1990: 77–8) the degree of decommodification, evaluating three areas of welfare: old-age pensions, sickness benefits and unemployment insurance. On the basis of the overall scores obtained, the author then constructs the clusters for his typology. Two main criticisms can be raised against Esping-Andersen's typology. The first is the arbitrary way in which cases are attributed to one cluster rather than another; the UK's decommodification score is 23.4, Australia's is 13.0, and Italy's 24.1, yet the UK belongs to the same cluster as Australia. The second criticism concerns the degree of heterogeneity in the conservative model, which other authors divide into separate models (Ferrera, 1993; Leibfried, 1992).

26   In their attempt to evaluate the impact of unemployment on poverty Gaffikin and Morrissey (1992) have compared the rate of unemployment, the extent of poverty, per capita GDP and per capita social expenditure, calculated as a percentage of GDP (source of information EEC 13/02/91, *Final Report of the Second European Poverty Programme*, EUROSTAT 1991 data relating to the year 1987). This comparison showed varying connections in the poverty–unemployment relation in member states. Denmark had the second lowest percentage of poor, the lowest rate of unemployment and the highest level of per capita GDP. Other countries, such as Germany, Spain, Ireland, Italy and Holland, showed a positive relation between the four variables and, therefore, a direct relation between unemployment and poverty (p. 37). Greece and Portugal had a high percentage of poor, a low level of GDP, but a low rate of unemployment. In the case of Belgium, a high rate of unemployment and a relatively low level of GDP were associated with the lowest extent of poverty and one of the highest levels of social spending. Thus, the data reveal cases with a high level of poverty and a low level of unemployment (Greece, Portugal) and cases with a high rate of unemployment and a low level of poverty (Belgium, Holland, France). The countries of the first group are generally those in which a sizeable part of the work-force is occupied in agriculture, which generates insufficient income. However, this is also the case in the US, where high levels of poverty are explained by the low level of per capita social spending and by the wide diffusion of insufficiently paid jobs. In the second group we find countries which offer a substantial income support to the unemployed (Atkinson and Micklewright, 1989).

27   As far as the countries of the European Union are concerned, the Second Report on Poverty concludes that poverty is generated principally by unemployment. A strict correlation between an increase in the extent of poverty and unemployment is immediately evident if one thinks that in the crucial period of industrial restructuring of the 1970s and 1980s

average unemployment increased three times, and at the same time the number of poor increased by 5 million (Donnison, 1991).

28   Some interesting considerations on the relation between unemployment and poverty may be made by looking at the distribution of unemployment benefits in the single states of the European Union. The ones which provide the highest benefits to their unemployed are those which have the lowest levels of poverty, while the ones providing the lowest benefits are those which show the highest levels of poverty (Commission of European Communities 13/02/91).

29   In the US urban poverty grew from the 1960s up to the mid-1980s, reaching levels unknown in Europe; even though the 1990 data show a relative improvement, particularly in New York, it is still at a record high level.

Table 1.4   Trends in poverty rates in New York City and Los Angeles County

	1969	1979	1982	1990
New York	14.9	20.0	24.0	19.2
Black	24.3	29.5	34.8	25.3
Hispanic	27.4	35.7	44.9	33.2
	1969	1979	1987	1990
Los Angeles	11.1	13.4	15.6	15.1
Black	24.2	23.2	24.5	21.2
Hispanic	16.6	19.2	25.2	22.9

Source: For New York, E. Tobier (1984) for 1969, 1979 and 1982; for Los Angeles, P. Ong et al. (1989) for 1969, 1979 and 1987

30   Apart from the obvious time sequences between joblessness and family crisis, there are other cases like the much discussed one pertaining to the Afro-American ghetto poor. As Devine and Wright (1993: 127–42) point out, it is precisely the different strategic picture, that is, one lacking the usual educational and occupational prospects and expectations, that fosters this family strategy transformation. Under the conditions in which teenagers live in the ghettos, not only does bringing a child into the world or not getting married not compromise any non-existent prospects, it also gives rise to some 'advantages' such as confirming one's femininity, marking the transition to adulthood, having a goal in life and so on. Obviously, marriage is out of the question because the male partner has no possibility of finding a job and maintaining the family. See also in this regard Sullivan, 1993; Testa et al., 1993; McLanahan and Garfinkel, 1993.

31   For instance, young ghetto Afro-Americans present very high long-term rates of unemployment, like young Neapolitans living in the poorest inner city and peripheral areas. Immigrants, in contrast, whether Latinos in American cities or immigrant minorities in European countries, are exposed to high risk of exclusion and marginalization, above all because they have bad jobs.

2

Downdrift: Provoking Agents and Symptom-Formation Factors in the Process of Impoverishment

Giuseppe A. Micheli,
Catholic University, Milan

DOWNDRIFT AS SYMPTOMATIC LIFE TRAJECTORIES

The exponential growth in the welfare-dependent population and the evidence of undiminished and newly diverging differences in the social, economic and even demographic life trajectories of the under-class (Michael and Tuma, 1985; Potter, 1991; Suchindran et al., 1985; McLanahan and Garfinkel, 1986) has led to a polarization of the debate in recent years. On one side there are those, like Murray (1984), who maintain that this state of affairs is due to cultural models that undermine the work ethic and family values; on the other, we have those, like Wilson (1987), who emphasize the decisive role of structural factors, such as unemployment or health and crime differentials, in producing demographic and social disorganization.

A not minor inconvenience with this resurfacing of polarized culture-of-poverty theories, hinging on the theme of the welfare dependency of single mothers and the hidden burden on mother-only families, is that the explanatory framework for poverty processes is reduced to two extreme ideal types: the individual who is totally in control of and responsible for his or her actions, and the individual who is totally other-directed and conditioned by his or her given situation. As Sullivan (1993) writes:

> Unfortunately the role of culture in these social changes remains . . . neglected . . . The neglect of culture leaves us in the dark as to how people deal collectively with economic disadvantage, prejudice and the dilemmas of procreating and raising families under such conditions. Lacking such an understanding, we are left with two sorts of explanatory framework, structural and individual, both of which beg crucial questions of how people in real communities devise collective response to their problems. Too extreme an emphasis on individual causation ignores growing evidence of the proliferation of low-wage jobs and increasing joblessness in inner city labor markets. Too much emphasis on structural causation ignores evidence that postponing childbearing leads to greater occupational success even within inner city populations. (1993: 66–7)

As is often the case, the pitfalls in the current debate appear in the same terms as in past debates. If we can interpret one of them correctly we may find some answers to the questions now being asked. Let us, then, go back half a century to when Faris and Dunham published a study on the ecology of *Mental Disorders in Urban Areas*. To explain the concentration of cases of schizophrenia in the inner city areas of Chicago and Providence, they assume that poverty and isolation are the determinant factors. But is it isolation, and with it the breakup of individual life trajectories, that causes social drift or poverty, and consequently social disorganization as an indivisible whole, that leads to isolation? Which one is the provoking agent? Their study expresses in a complete and paradoxical form the complexity and at the same time the ambiguity of the 'nature–nurture' dispute; at the time, it was put forward as a paradigm by the two opposed positions.

The muddle originated at the very start of research in this field. It was Burgess who, having urged Faris and Dunham to investigate epidemiological questions, shuffled the theoretical results around in his introduction to their book, published in 1939. In order to account for differentials in mental pathology, Faris and Dunham point to two factors that disorganize 'natural areas': social isolation and the transition between different cultures; as cultural factors they are always open to a twofold interpretation. What the two authors say on the opposition between marginalizing behaviour and social drift is, however, very clear:

> One interpretation frequently made of the concentration in the center of the city of insanity rates is that persons who are mentally abnormal fail

in their economic life and consequently drift down into the slum areas because they are not able to compete satisfactorily with others. Such a process is of course possible ... [However,] many of the cases of schizophrenia consist of persons who were born in and have always lived in deteriorated areas. These did not drift into the high-rate areas ... It is a question of whether this drift process, which undoubtedly contributes something to the apparent concentration of rates, is anything more than an insignificant factor in causing the concentration. (Faris and Dunham, 1939: 163)

In their search for alternative explanations to that of individual drift, Faris and Dunham look to contextual variables: from the social conditions in areas and isolation and social disorganization to minority status effect. Burgess, on the contrary, in the introduction interprets the collected data from a different angle; he espouses the hypothesis of territorial concentration as an effect of individual drift trajectories. Having picked up inheritance theories from a 1925 Myerson essay, he draws the following theoretical conclusion from the observations:

(a) a constitutional basis is an essential condition for a 'functional' as well as for an organic mental disorder ... It is possible though not certain that certain psychogenetic types may be more prodisposed to mental breakdown than others ... (b) the particular psychogenetic type of personality determines not the etiology but the symptoms of mental disorder ... (c) social conditions, while not primary in causation, may be underlying predisposing and precipitating factors. (Burgess, 1939: XV-XVI)

A misunderstanding between a book's authors and the writer of the introduction is undoubtedly an infrequent, odd but not insignificant event: it conceals a crucial aporia in their reasoning. They diverge on the role to be attributed to social interaction processes in the causal sequence of collective behaviour formation. However, they share the assumption that 'communication is essential for normal mental development and social isolation makes for mental breakdown' (pp. XV–XVI). Both positions share the image of social drift as a paralysing hold exerted by the network of interactions in which a person is inserted. But when we see which aspects of the network are emphasized, the picture is completely different: Faris and Dunham focus upon the crushing weight of the network (a cobweb in which a subject is trapped and has no freedom) while Burgess underlines the autonomy of individual choice in the trajectory that leads to the centre of the web.

Nevertheless, there are in this scientific dispute originating in the same book some, well-hidden, more refined analytical weapons than those wielded in the current debate on cultures of poverty. For instance, Faris and Dunham's analysis of the rates of psychiatric illness prevalent among black minorities ('rates for Negroes show a variation, being high in the central disorganized areas not populated primarily by members of their own race and low in the actual Negro areas' – Faris and Dunham, 1939: 169) constitutes one of the clearest pieces of empirical evidence for the role, anticipated by Durkheim, of minority group effects in collective behaviour formation.

Even more important, here, is the discovery that Burgess's second hypothesis ('the particular type of personality determines not the etiology but the symptoms of mental disorder') contains an extremely significant cognitive device, to which credit has been given only recently. This is the idea that a crisis behaviour can be read not as a unique and inevitable reaction to the succession of events (nor as the result of self-piloted 'rational choices', setting aside the context) but rather as a personalized symptomatic response to the interweaving of life events.

Poverty cannot be defined solely in terms of predetermined and totally passive behaviour or of totally self-determined perverse choices. It consists of entering into one life trajectory rather than another – that is, defined by some behaviours–symptoms and not by others – but which is characterized by irreversibility, with no return or exit, due to the interweaving of structural mechanisms and events and to the absence of a response by the context or the public sector.

From this perspective, it is no longer a matter of setting environmental influence against individual predisposition but of grasping the continuity running through three different states of 'poverty': a surmountable state of need (or 'critical normality'), one of acute, but contingent, crisis and hardship and one of extreme stable exclusion. These three states have often been studied as phenomena which do not intersect in any significant way. Yet they are linked together in that each life destiny is subject over time to the risk of passing from one to the other. It is true that in many cases during a life-course a subject drops into poverty in a drastically discontinuous way (mental disorder, physical handicap, denizenship). At other times, however, subjects slide or drift into extreme marginality gradually starting from situations of critical normality which have got out of control. It is therefore necessary to distinguish between impoverishment, understood as a process of both overall loss of strategic power and change in the strategic rationale underlying action, and poverty, understood as a final state of immobility totally devoid of strategic autonomy.

My aim here is to analyse the onset of household drift processes, seen as the entry of time trajectories for dealing with a crisis into a loop. Such a process does not necessarily show itself outside the household, as events and critical situations are often played down.

THE 'CULTURE MEDIUM' OF IMPOVERISHMENT

XX is 41 years old, married and has a good job. Suddenly he begins to suffer from insomnia, which makes it difficult for him to work. Nervous exhaustion is soon followed by the loss of his job. While being treated with drugs, he looks for another job but can only find temporary work. He separates from his wife. Poor medical care leads to drug poisoning. Helped by his sister, who gives up her own job, XX partially recovers but at a great monetary cost and without a stable solution for the future.

Three years from pensionable age, Mrs YY finds a job as a chambermaid to make up the missing contributions. One day, while cleaning a shower, she slips and breaks her ribs. Having lost her job, she spends three years in inactive convalescence while her artisan husband is not working very much. She never totally recovers and receives a monthly compensation payment at a 30 per cent disability rate. Still in much pain, she and her pensioner husband get by through spending less on food.

Since the birth of a child with brain disease three years ago, the life of ZZ and her husband has changed completely. The child's medical needs make it impossible for the mother to stay in work or only at considerable economic and organizational cost. Expenses mount and cuts have to be made in all their plans; it means not only giving up a career or buying the house but also those normal things in life like entertainment, holidays, friends and even doing things together: 'we are a bit trapped in here; a life of nothing but home and work. We don't even have friends any more.'

Married at a young age, WW now has five children between eight and twenty-one; one of them has a motor disability. Money is always short. The little girl's constant crying has badly affected the mother's nervous system. Depressed, WW stays in the house all day, which makes everything even more depressing. Her doctor advises her to spend a week in the mountains; but how? 'Once I was away from home ten days for an operation, and when I got back my husband looked as if he had been through an illness.' The couple asked the local

council for financial aid but did not receive it because the husband is
in work. 'Three daughters at boarding school with monthly fees to be
paid. How can you be relaxed?'

As these life stories drawn from a general social survey conducted in
the Veneto region in 1991 show, critical normality, hardship and
extreme poverty are much more interconnected than is generally
supposed. Yet they are usually investigated using distinct research
tools. Such specialization has certain limitations:

1 the cost of procedures prevents formulation of research projects combining
   several levels of measurement; although there will be an attempt to form
   an idea of the size and life scenarios of a population segment in a certain
   territory, no parameter will make it possible to link them with those of
   other segments;
2 even when multilevel measurements are carried out, the diverse methodologies used by researchers and their different receptiveness towards the
   dimensions of the reality prevent the results from being combined into a
   single picture.

To build a bridge between scenarios (quantitative, general) and
biographies (qualitative, particular) of poverty requires a well-defined
co-ordination of the measurement devices. The Veneto survey was
structured around a scheme that may be defined as 'two track and
three tier',[1] so as to cover a multiplicity of population segments
experiencing structural and existential tensions in incommensurable
ways. The most striking result of this survey is undoubtedly the fact
that poverty is intrinsically a process, which brings to mind through
spontaneous association the concept of 'chains of cause–effect
relations'. But is it possible to formulate an 'etiology' of poverty? A
situation of poverty as an end result cannot be put down to a single
'chain of cause–effect relations' for two closely connected reasons: (a)
different forms of poverty can be the outcome of identical trigger
conditions; and (b) the same final state may be the arrival point of
different causal chains, each sufficient but none in itself necessary. I
will dwell on this second reason and look more closely at the concept of
'necessary and sufficient cause'.

Mingione and Zajczyk (1992) say that if poverty is explained as a
cumulative process, then a bad job, unemployment and a low pension
are often necessary but insufficient elements in a concatenation of
events that leads to conditions of multiple deprivation. In 1974,
Mackie extended the idea of necessary and sufficient cause to complex
causation, introducing what he defines as 'INUS condition': insufficient but necessary part of a condition which is itself unnecessary but
sufficient. This idea has been translated into formal language by
Wunsch (1988). It is not, therefore, legitimate to look for 'causes' of

poverty; one should instead identify inus-conditions of single processes of drift.

If a single cause recurs in several 'sufficient minimal conditions', in several possible sequences that can all be followed by individual destinies and lead to an identical kind of poverty, the frequent occurrence of this cause in concomitance with a given state of crisis will be a reliable indicator of the latter's presence. For complex phenomena like poverties there is no single 'all-embracing cause'; nevertheless, for each poverty a league table of 'more probable than others' inus-causes, of 'more reliable than others' predictors, can be drawn up. Let us examine table 2.1 showing the predictive values, specific to the 'critical areas' studied in the Veneto social survey, of some indicators.[2]

It is not surprising that the probability of poor families containing a drug-addicted member is so high (almost nine times the average): they are a breeding ground for multifactor poverty. What is surprising, however, is that the probability of such an occurrence is significantly higher than average, though far less so, also among families in a condition of 'critical normality'. The presence of great nervous stress appears to be a further reliable predictor of a state of being at risk among families that make no use of public welfare services, even though its probability does not reach the levels recorded in self-proclaimed poor families.

Increasing failure to communicate within the family is also a strong signal of a 'terminal' state of poverty; among poor families it occurs seven times more frequently than the average. It is not, however, widespread in the other segments of the population lying between the standard normal and the poor family. On the contrary, the presence of a very elderly person, a disabled subject or several small children seems to intensify the network of intrafamily relations. Here is a case where an important resource for facing crises, the consolidation of communication and reciprocity between family members, may become in other crisis contexts a constraining or even aggravating factor.

These examples allow two conclusions to be drawn. First, while situations of serious poverty (here represented by poor families) show an all-round multifactorial condition, the critical situations 'on the borders', including those which make no use of public welfare services, in part reveal sets of predictors of difficulties that are specific to them.

The second conclusion concerns the significance to be attached to an 'etiology' of poverty. In my view, rather than search for unequivocal cause–effect relations it is useful to focus attention on the process itself that leads to an end state of serious poverty. What is to be

Table 2.1 Twenty predictors of specific criticalness

	Normal families	Critical normality	Very old in family	More than 3 children in family	Poorest	Handicap
	P(X) P(e)	 N.I.	5.5 N.I.	7.4 N.I.	2.2 N.I.	1.7 N.I.
Widowhoods	4.8	1.06	4.01	0.73	2.68	0.33
Separation/divorces	1.2	1.00	0.67	0.42	7.00	0.67
No adults with secondary education	71.9	1.02	1.07	1.05	1.34	1.10
One or more unemployed adults in family	6.7	0.74	0.60	1.69	9.82	2.36
Partner with unskilled job	36.7	0.91	1.57	1.01	2.11	0.61
Father with unskilled job	45.6	1.03	1.36	0.86	1.84	1.07
Original family with seven or more children	15.5	1.00	1.56	1.40	1.44	1.14
Mother's age at first child under twenty	12.2	1.16	1.00	1.07	1.61	1.03
Dwelling with no more than three rooms	20.2	0.99	0.87	0.86	2.71	0.95
Dwelling without areas of privacy	9.9	1.01	0.95	3.52	3.09	2.48
Laid off with benefits in the last five years	19.5	0.83	0.81	1.41	2.48	1.71
Monthly family budget in the red	8.6	2.08	1.62	2.02	6.57	1.83
Terminally ill subjects in dwelling	4.9	1.06	2.59	0.88	1.98	3.96
Drug addicts in dwelling	1.1	1.27	1.45	1.27	8.82	1.64
Nervous exhaustion subjects in dwelling	2.2	1.28	2.86	1.95	5.82	6.82
School dropouts in family	21.4	1.02	1.44	0.37	1.87	1.55
Perceived worsening of own status	11.4	1.07	1.54	1.14	2.59	1.38
Two or more welfare-dependent family members	4.7	1.17	3.04	0.30	7.02	4.85
No communication between cohabitant family members	7.0	1.06	0.69	0.41	3.68	0.50
No communication between non-cohabitant family members	17.7	0.92	0.99	1.06	1.73	1.29

understood by drift is the slipping from a state of even hard-won but reactive normality through one of critical and painful normality into a state of total submission to chronic suffering.

NON-LINEAR TRAJECTORIES

If the phenomenon of poverty is not a state of being but a downward-moving sequence through several stages, this condition of being a process entails adopting a transversal look at the different population segments. Buhr et al. (1989) underline the inability to grasp impoverishment processes of all those studies which use a discrete-time approach, with a single time observation point or, at most, two points that are merely compared in a static fashion. In particular, research projects of this kind are unable to distinguish between four types of 'welfare careers':

> the 'bridgers' (transitory recipients of welfare benefits with only temporary loss of social status), the 'marginalized' (recipients of welfare subjected to long-term processes of loss of status), the 'oscillators' (people swinging into and out of assistance, for whom loss of status is imminent but not (yet) permanent) and finally the 'escapers' (long-term recipients who eventually and unexpectedly manage to escape welfare dependence).

The results of cross-section analyses provide a classification of welfare users that is different from the above typology, but still static. For Buhr et al. this 'has a rather precarious implication: those who once became dependent on social assistance will remain so for most of the rest of their lives. Attempts by recipients – often visible only in a series of small steps – to overcome their status, can only insufficiently be accounted for in a cross-sectional analysis.'

In studying the life cycle of a psychologically sound family, McGoldrick and Carter (1991) place the dynamic connection between – what we would call – emotional and relational resources and consumption on a Cartesian plane. One axis is for the relational and functioning structures handed down from generation to generation (attitudes, taboos, expectations, emotionally important social and thematic perceptions with which persons grow up inside the family), which constitute something like the cards that are dealt to you: they are given. Here, they are referred to reductively as relational resources. On the other axis lies the anxiety produced by the stresses

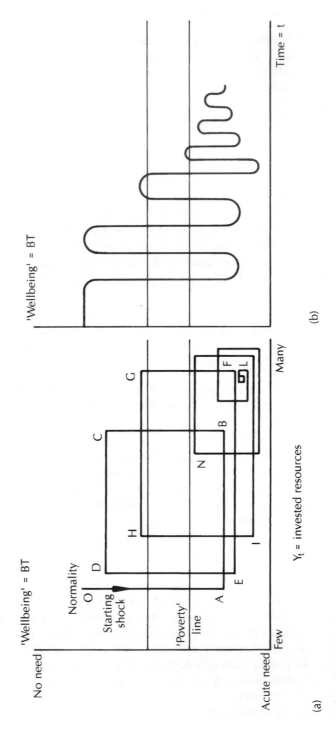

Figure 2.1 Chronicity as: (a) a non-linear trajectory on the wellbeing-invested resources plane, and (b) fluctuation over time of the state of need

on the family over time as it encounters the changes and transitions of the family life cycle. They are referred to here reductively as relational consumption.

Now, according to McGoldrick and Carter, a family will appear 'extremely disfunctional' – that is, it will enter into a psychological crisis that is so unbearable as to induce it to seek assistance – if considerable stress occurs. Translated into the terms of the question discussed here, a family becomes one 'in difficulty' when it experiences a life node characterized by acute need. But, they add, in a family where the other axis is already burdened by a heavy emotional load, even a light stress will produce a serious blockage in the system. Translated, this means that even a hardly perceptible aggravation in terms of family needs can produce a serious crisis (poverty) when the resources available to the household are either limited to begin with, due to environmental causes, or already depleted by previous crises.

McGoldrick and Carter's system comprising only relational axes can be extended so that it relates to the resources–consumption scheme used here to interpret family drift dynamics. On a plane where the family life trajectory co-ordinates are given by the degree of wellbeing (and inversely of need) and by the amount of invested resources (time, money and energy), a trajectory of drift into poverty is indicated by a loop, a spiral converging at a point on the plane lying below a threshold of satisfied wellbeing; this threshold can also be compared to a 'poverty line'.

Let us follow on the graph in figure 2.1(a) the course of a family life trajectory where a sudden shock occurs, an acute illness or deviant behaviour, the loss of a source of income or the irreversible loss (through departure or death) of a member. The drop in the household's 'wellbeing' (together with its increasing need) shifts the arrow indicating the life trajectory from point O to point A. In a crisis situation a family will tend to mobilize its resources; the increase in investment (point B) will bring about a concomitant return to the initial state of wellbeing (point C), permitting a gradual reduction in the use of resources until a return to 'normality' (D) is reached.

A temporary or reversible crisis is like a restitchable tear: the ABCD cycle closes without any apparent consequences. Supposing, however, that the first shock triggering the cycle is followed by a second: the repetition of the same crisis – the family head loses his/her job again – or the opening of a second front – a child has health problems. Once again, the family will tend to invest all the resources necessary to meet the new emergency. Nevertheless, the reiteration of a crisis or the opening of a second front generally involves a much bigger rupture in the family's material and symbolic organization. The effort required to

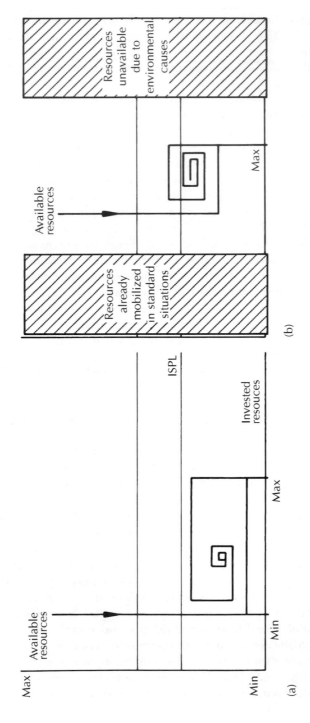

Figure 2.2 Modifications to trajectories due to: (a) intensification of initial shock, and (b) structural reduction in the usable investment surplus

overcome it will have to be greater and is difficult to summon up. In the second cycle (EFGH), the household uses up all its resources but is still only just able to scrape over a hypothetical threshold of reacquired family serenity. At this point the family's system of antibodies starts to weaken.

If a third shock, however small, occurs – perhaps provoked by the precarious balance of family roles left from the first two – the new organizational fluctuation (ILMN) will be unable to cross a crisis threshold despite utilizing all the resources still available. Any subsequent variations, induced by a chain of cause–effect relations between poverty factors, will lead the family to converge at a final state of immobility chronically below the poverty line, in which there are no extra resources to be invested and consequently all strategic action comes to a standstill.

Let us now follow the trajectory along the time axis, taking only the wellbeing–needs dimension into account. What we find is that the line oscillates above and below a threshold 'of poverty' (figure 2.1(b)) which the Bremen group uses to identify dynamically a particular type of poor: the oscillators or the marginalized. In figure 2.1 it is difficult to trace one factor, event or behaviour that is in itself a sufficient cause of family drift; many inus-causes could be traced in order to explain the triggering of the loop. As in all genuine vicious circles, the individual is not dragged into the abyss of poverty by a single catastrophe but slides down the slope bit by bit, 'guided gently by underlying influences' (Day, 1978).

It is, however, also possible to present situations in which one event, factor or behaviour turns out to be decidedly determinant. Figure 2.2 illustrates two models. In the first, 2.2(a) the shock dealt to the family in a state of 'normal' wellbeing is so violent that it prevents the reconstitution of acceptable conditions, whatever the investment of family resources: the unexpected onset of a degenerative or socially labelled illness can sometimes be a sufficient cause. But even non-catastrophic events or behaviour may in certain difficult situations be sufficient to cause drift. This occurs, 2.2(b), when the 'normal' state of the family rests on a routine level of investment that is already so high (for instance, presence of non-self-sufficient elderly or numerous offspring) as to prevent an adequate supplementary mobilization to meet the shock. In other words, it occurs when normality is based on a supportive network that is precarious (for example, without a reciprocity network ready to assist in emergencies, such as that found among poorly settled immigrants) to an extent which does not allow a valid response to the crisis factor. In this last case the area of resources on which the household cannot draw, marked out in figure 2.2(b), is that on the right and the constraints on the family's homeostatic reaction are predominantly environmental in nature.

TURNPIKES, TURN-OFFS AND ROUNDABOUTS

Faced with a single problem or a tangle of problems a household may not stop at an internal reorganization of tasks and duties. It may decide to externalize the costs of managing the crisis by seeking support in terms of assistance from specialist agencies or institutions. In order to understand the typology of external resources available to the family, let us imagine that the individual in difficulty is like a motorist on a motorway who, imperceptibly, is approaching a dead end of extreme poverty. Ahead of him lie three junctions, providing three turn-off strategies for changing direction and returning to the right route.

The first junction corresponds to the recourse to reciprocity procedures, ranging from exchanges based on solidarity with no expectation of an immediate return at one end to market exchanges at the other. If the first is impracticable, the second junction consists in the recourse to the welfare agencies. Not all the response strategies are equally accessible in every critical situation; while the recourse to the system of exchanges and reciprocity is preferred in situations that are undoubtedly critical but open to a favourable solution (looking after a child or an elderly dependant), where critical moments are difficult to overcome the choice of turning to the system of public (territorial and institutional) services prevails.

As a situation becomes more and more serious, it may be impossible for the motorist to take the second turn-off. That leaves the last junction: a strategy for making situations of serious difficulty bearable. There are many instances of family associationism aimed at satisfying a need expressed by a member: families with disabled members or children with Down's syndrome, communities for drug addicts or associations for alcoholics. Let us call these forms of association 'like-experience groups'. They constitute the recovery of a dimension of metanoia, in part abandoned by the philosophy of the welfare society. Their diffusion involves essentially life trajectories that are socially marked as deviant or different, but their philosophy of 'therapeutic' action now appears to extend well beyond such trajectories. Unlike a family choosing to close in on itself around a crisis point and shoulder the entire burden, the recourse to 'like-experience groups' is characterized by the acceptance of the idea of seeing one's own life condition mirrored in others.

Table 2.2 Strategies for dealing with a crisis according to social segment of population

Models for dealing with a crisis	Social groups that prefer models
Reciprocity networks	Couples with small children; single-parent families; tensions in family
Total institutions	Old couples
Private services market	Dual career couples; family with actually ill members
Public services market	Medium-sized cities; families with chronically sick members
Like-experience groups	Young/childless couples; single persons; big cities, high level of education

Source: Micheli (1992)

The array of strategies for dealing with a critical point in life is extensive and more articulated than the mere resort to the system of welfare agencies. Furthermore, the Veneto general social survey reveals that each solution is matched by socio-graphically well-defined population groups (table 2.2). In particular, it is the more dynamic segments of the population and those under transformation that opt for collectively formulated responses through exchanges of common experience. A shift in the image of welfare, too, is now under way, from the classical scheme of universal contribution to a mixed scheme in which a part of the system of guarantees remains universal and another part is hived off and underpinned by individualized contribution. This shift also turns out to be an option preferred, above all, by well-off families residing in big cities and with a high level of education. What we have, in short, is a world permeated by ideational change in which welfare is probably being revamped through the rise of a culture of the dynamics of like-experience groups alongside a 'culture of services'.

Let us return to our motorist in difficulty. The recourse to external resources (in the private market or in the reciprocity network), the delegating to the public sector and the entry into like-experience groups are the three main junctions open to an individual who wants to get off a path of drift. If he or she takes none of these, or does so but then returns onto the drift route, he or she will end up on an exitless roundabout, a closed circuit at the end of the motorway. In effect, all the cases that come under the typology in figure 2.2(a) and 2.2(b) are no longer normal 'organizational brain teasers' faced by families. They are no longer situations in which, even with the differences in strategy due to individual or family preferences, a solution can always be found for the problem encountered. What happens, for instance, if there is a seriously disabled or a drug-addicted child in the home? What happens if a family member is sent to prison or has a criminal record?

It is often emphasized that in situations of this kind the individual is trapped in a labyrinth of no answers, stripped of the capacity to manage his or her own affairs and reduced to a mere object of fate. Hence, a chronic condition appears to be a simple cultural product, at the end of trajectories of problems to which society's symbolic-normative system denies recognition: 'A chronic condition is a particular form of the relational system which an individual has with his environment. If you like, it is a gestalt' (Donati, 1991). Evidence of this production of a chronic condition as the absence of definitive responses is found by reconsidering the change in the psychiatric system in Italy at the end of the 1970s, when the mental hospitals were closed and the main focus of intervention was shifted to the local services. The reconstruction of an *ad hoc* psychiatric case-register (Baldwin, 1971) relating to an area in northern Italy comprising about 170,000 inhabitants (Carabelli and Micheli, 1986) makes it possible to follow the different destinies of two cohorts of psychiatric patients: those taken on in the four years preceding the reform and those in the following four years. The reform led to an increase in the medical help on offer; the most important novelties were the strengthening of the local out-patient service and the setting up from scratch of wards for short-term treatment in general hospitals.

Now, already in the pre-reform period 21 per cent of the new patients had more than one contact with a single agency and a further 13 per cent applied to several agencies (for in-patients and out-patients, private and public) over the four years. In the subsequent period, however, the 'recidivists' who applied to a single agency rose to 27 per cent and the commuters between several to 25 per cent. Also, the increased propensity to move from one agency to another was accompanied in the second four-year period by a sharp reduction in the average times of passing from one to the other. The result of the two combined processes was a thick web of commuting in a rapid time sequence. The apparent liberation of sick subjects, and of their choices, only produced a wild speeding up of their movements within a circuit of responses that remained partial and illusory. In the absence of a true lysis strategy for mental breakdowns (still not available today), the chronic condition due to institutionalization – cancelled by decree – resurfaced in the guise of a trans-institutional chronicity.

The concept of chronicity allows us to build a bridge between the microsociological concept of loop and irreversible crisis frameworks and the macrosociological frameworks brought together under the label of 'underclass'. McLanahan and Garfinkel (1993) help to clarify the close affinity between the two concepts:

> weak attachment to the labor force is a necessary but not sufficient condition for defining an underclass. Individuals who are temporarily out of work or ill or dependent on welfare are usually not viewed as part of the underclass, even though they may be living below the poverty line. Rather, it is the persistence of weak attachment that distinguishes underclass behavior and underclass neighborhoods from poverty areas and the poor in general.

If, says Booth, the poor person is the one who struggles to get the minimum indispensable means to live, the extremely poor person is the one who is no longer able to struggle. Although poverty is not a state but a process, extreme poverty most certainly is a state: the final one after a sequence of steps leading procedurally to drift.

In the approach adopted so far, chronicity is the terminal stage of individual life trajectories: it is the entry into a limit cycle (a loop) with no exit. But this limit cycle – and this must be underlined – is at the same time, and ambiguously, the end of a subjective and objective dual process. It is in fact by definition the outcome of a chain of self-developing autonomous choices, but at the same time also the result of a crushing of individual freedoms under the weight of an environment 'without answers'.

Verification of the dual nature of the process leading to poverty as a chronicity-producing condition lies in the doubling of the form that can be taken on by the final state in the gradual stripping away of identity. The first limit form is that of the purely other-directed individual who for conformity's sake adopts the 'modes of behaviour' typical of the agencies of social regulation to which he refers. It is the traditional syndrome of chronicity found in the elderly, long-term institutionalized patients and children in hospitals; it is the syndrome of resigned freezing of all action. Poverty is here like a motionless point of convergence (death point) along a path in a web.

In other cases, by contrast, the entry into loops involves the maintenance of an apparent autonomy in the debased form of permanent conflict with public interlocutors. Also in Italy, forms of marginality ('help-seeking yet help-rejecting') are increasing that are characterized by trans-institutional mobility, permanent roaming from one agency to the next, a chronic state of suffering together with urgent but unstructured demand, aggressive antagonism and low tolerance towards frustration.

In both the limit forms outlined it is easy to grasp the importance in the formation of poverty/chronicity of the role played by the circuit of services, by the interweaving of codified and selective responses and postponements and by the cumulation of social control and abandonment. It is much less easy to grasp the weight of strategic autonomy in a drift trajectory. In the irrational 'conflictual contractuality' of some and in the irrational 'syndrome of the purely acted' in others is there really nothing left of this autonomy?

SYMPTOMS AND RATIONALES

The notion that the individual acts with perfect rational choice in every circumstance is false. Linked to it is the even more pernicious idea that when the individual does not define his/her options on a rational choice basis, he/she is devoid of any strategic rationality whatsoever. It is worth repeating here some observations made elsewhere (Micheli, 1991 and 1993).

Although utilitarian reasoning does not solve many conundrums relating to the family economy it dominates the debate on family decisions, incorporating in the strategy of 'maximization of a well-ordered function' also many 'irrational' forms of behaviour, providing they are consistent with a set of opportunities. Thus, the search for an explanation of anomalous behaviour has for a long time mixed two different ways of dealing with the problem of 'non-rational' choices. On one side, there is the listing of the cost-benefit parameters for each behaviour and, on the other, the differentiation of rationales for evaluating not the result of an act but the act in itself, which does not always coincide with the strategy of maximization of the costs-benefits function. Following this second path, at least three other decision-making levels come to light that are clearly distinct from that of rational choice. The first is that of passive or inertial decisions, implicit in routine behaviour. Within a certain area of inertia, there is no movement from a position associated with a given utility towards another position, even if the latter implies a higher level of utility: the individual is only vaguely aware of why he/she is behaving in a certain way.

The second level is that of decisions taken on the basis of a convention in compliance with established collective norms. In this case too, the decisions are made outside of a procedure of maximization; they are based on an 'incomplete calculation'. This level is able to solve behaviour dilemmas like the so-called prisoner's dilemma since within certain limits behaviour according to convention can dominate or supplant other behaviour desirable on the basis of individual preferences.

The third level is that of decisions taken to bolster the meaning-giving system that is able to stabilize over time the symbolic content of the world of lived experiences, including the exchange values that underlie every rational choice decision-making strategy.

What we have here is not a single scheme for reading 'strategic rationality' but a typology of at least four distinct families of rational behaviour strategies. It involves not a compact monolithic rationale but a hierarchical decision-making structure that includes at least four decision-making levels: the inertial or drift level; that of utilitarian decisions; that of decisions made in compliance with a norm or to legitimize a belonging; and the level of bolstering any kind of identity.

Between the four strategic levels there is not only a precise difference in rational reasoning but also a hierarchization of intervention in the chosen situations. Different degrees of environmental pressure can make behaviour slide from minimal rationality to that in line with belonging and convention and to economic rationality, moving towards increasingly complete calculation. On the other hand, a sliding of the strategic level in the opposite direction, from economic calculation to the rationale of belonging, is sometimes able to solve dilemmas involving the apparent inconvenience of co-operative choices.

Both in the big decisions of life and in the small everyday ones there does not, therefore, exist, nor should one look for, a single paradigm of rationality, whether it be the utilitarian choice of Weberian paradigms, the inertia of the determinism of material structures, the rituality of microsociological paradigms of identity or the network of transactions, games and coalitions. Each of these mental schemes will find its correct application along diverse segments and at different vertices of the life trajectories, according to hierarchical sequential structures that are still totally open for investigation.

Many researchers into extreme poverties observe that in similar difficulties the behaviour of individuals or households is not rational, that is, it does not follow the rules of perfect neo-classical economic rationality. Negri (1991) says that the search for a point of equilibrium rationally adapted to constraints seems 'to be replaced by attitudes of escape and surrender that lead to situations of progressive uprooting, states of acceptance/resignation'. According to Laffi (1992) 'the poor do not do what we would like them to do.' The inability to use and manage money which marks the poor in the metropolitan area of Milan is no different from that of the unemployed in the classic Marienbad study. But the question, then, is 'what is the rationality that governs the existence of a person that does not have sufficient resources to live with dignity and why do the mental schemes that we hold appropriate fail?' (Laffi, 1992).

In answer to this question a first conjecture can be put forward starting from the proposed four-part typology of action strategies. There is in fact a fundamental difference between the four types of strategy identified. In two of them (inertial and convention-based choices) the individual adapts to an externally established order; in the other two decision-making modes it is instead the individual himself who becomes the maker of order, the formulator of rules (out of 'calculation' of interest or 'calculation' of identity). In G. H. Mead, the 'I' is the response of the organism to the attitude of others; the 'Me' is the organized set of attitudes of others which an individual assumes. The attitudes of others constitute the organized 'Me' and so an individual reacts to it as an 'I'. Using these concepts, we can say that two strategies depend on that socialized and objectified aspect which Mead calls 'Me'. Only two strategies, on the other hand, depend on the creative and innovatory component that he calls 'I'.

What we need, then, is an explanatory model of far greater complexity than those currently available, if we want to penetrate the objective and subjective mechanisms of drift. It must include a mapping of the strategies underlying different behaviours that, if not systematic, is at least more discerning; but above all it must be able to ferry the dispersed ranks of identifiable strategies over the swamp of mere listing to an overall etiological model for interpreting drift processes.

It seems to me that the keystone on which to organize such a model could be the category of symptom, which belongs to the tradition of social-psychological research. Walsh (1991) reminds us that the schools of communicational pragmatics and of the counter-paradox see normal families as extremely flexible, capable of using a vast repertory of behaviours to face problems. Pathological families, by contrast, display rigidities in functioning and a shortage of alternatives: the symptoms of psychological unease can thus be understood as communicative acts that appear 'when an individual is ensnared in a family structure and does not dispose of non-symptomatic means to change this situation'.

Already in 1978, in a fundamental study on the origins of female depression, Brown and Harris proposed to explain the onset of crisis points through the presence or absence of three types of factors: (a) the provoking agents that exert an influence at the moment the crisis begins; (b) the factors of vulnerability that influence whether the former have any effect or not; and (c) the symptom-formation factors that act on the severity of and form assumed by the crisis and, hence, also on the strategies chosen to face it. In this scheme, the symptom-formation factors are the new element that allow the explanatory models for certain choices of crisis subroutines to increase their heuristic capacity substantially. Different symptoms can arise from apparently identical situations, which is a considerable reversal of the principle that equal causes have equal results.

It is highly instructive to reread the stories of the life destinies of difficult families in the Veneto, distinguishing the intervening factors according to the role they played. On one side there are the crisis-triggering events (acute illness, mourning, separation, unemployment, isolation); on the other immunodepressive background factors, that is, factors which make the effect of events destructive (economic poverty, single family income, dropping out of school, precarious work or joblessness, no or an inadequate dwelling, precocity in key life transitions, non-integration into solidarity networks, lack of services in environment). Then there are also, and above all, those factors that direct the rationale of strategic action in the face of critical points and channel life destinies towards a reconstitution of equilibria rather than towards one or other possible outcomes of social drift. They are symptom-formation factors like subcultural belonging to social and cultural models (for example, insertion in or contiguousness with educated classes rather than deviant groups), generational and territorial models and family and subfamily models (for example, sibling birth order) extending to the Durkheimian effects of minority status. In the Brown and Harris model, they are the factors that act as reliable predictors of the symptom-selecting strategies adopted by the individual.

CONCLUSIONS

What mechanisms bring about the transformation of crisis trajectories, simple variants of normal life stories, into chronic states? A reading of the stories of difficult families in the Veneto as well as the reconstruction of the extreme poverty trajectories in the literature lead, in conclusion, to the formulation of four basic rules.

(1) The networks of public management of crisis subroutines (whether old age or psychiatric disorders, drug addiction or disablement, imprisonment or terminal illness) have difficulty in finding responses to the needs of the individual that are not fleeting and illusory. It is in the labyrinth of pseudo-responses that the gradual change of a crisis trajectory into a career of chronicity takes place.

(2)   The drift from critical normality into a chronic condition of poverty is, nevertheless, not only the inevitable outcome of the pressure from external agents; the victim also participates. In the course of the process he/she may change his/her own action strategy in order to reformulate a meaning-giving function. A frequently observed mechanism is that of the sliding from active strategies to adaptive strategies: the action strategy of normal or normal difficult families tends to privilege 'I' strategies, whereas that of 'poor' families (that is, having entered into a not reversible loop) gives much more space to 'Me' strategies.

(3)   Greater in-depth study is required to understand the decision-making mechanisms on the borders of poverty. Having identified which of the rationales the individual tends to privilege, the strategy that the individual in crisis will select, within the same rationale, is still in fact undefined. The alternative strategies can be many and quite different from one another. Let us consider the fourth-level strategies, existential reactions to a state of crisis aiming to reconstruct the individual's meaning-giving system. They can be multiple though all equally aimed at reconstituting the identity in crisis. Among them should also be included insertion in 'like-experience groups', which, as mentioned above, is the last turn-off for returning to the route of a meaningful life.

   However, when strategies of true 'metabolization of meaning' are beyond the individual's reach, other paths open up which are merely surrogates of them. They are of at least two types: (a) surrogate strategies of repressing or limiting exposure to external traumatic pressures (crisis conduct like flight, drug addiction and even self-destruction); (b) surrogate strategies of mimesis: inertial or gregarious adaption to other-directed 'modes of behaviour' (individual conformity or the chronic institutionalization of long-term patients, gregarious or crowd conduct) (Micheli, 1991).

(4)   Lastly, there is a final trace common to drift careers, which is inflected in the successive developments of generations. It is well known that a poorly educated couple is associated with an early entry into work for male offspring and with domestic chores for females. It seems natural for the children to interiorize the idea of schooling as a waiting period, to be shortened as much as possible in order to attain economic independence. Consistent with an action strategy centred on repression, subjects in drift undergo a true disarticulation of their perception and life project in time and in space. The individual's diminished resistance may then produce two parallel changes in the meaning-giving system that presides over the formation of 'symptoms': (a) the shortening of the distances that one is willing to go in order to deal with a crisis (syndrome of uprooting); (b) the shortening of the time that one is willing to wait to the same end ('hurry sickness': hence the precocity of life calendars).

These are perhaps the cornerstones of a great ideational change that is transforming the poverty-forming processes in our society. It is a change that is moving above individual destinies, which feeds on them and intervenes in them, contributing to the formation of 'context-bound' poverty.

NOTES

1   The first track is that of a general social survey standard. A random two-stage sample of the family population in the Veneto region was given a structured questionnaire, aimed at reconstructing the strategies for dealing with difficult situations in a 'normal' family. Two segments of population were in this way separated out and compared: a majority of 'normal' non-difficult families and a minority of 'normal' difficult families which, included in the random sample, declare the presence of substantial difficult points in the family. The second survey track is made up of a non-random sample of four types of difficult families that have already appeared in the welfare system: families with at least one member over 75, with at least three children under 14, with one disabled member and those in a state of poverty. These four family groups were given a structured questionnaire identical to that used for the random sample with the addition of some narrative windows in which the interview was continued in an unstructured form. In order to permit the greatest degree of comparability between different segments, the questionnaire used on the second track consisted of two blocks. One (narrative windows) aimed to supply raw data for a more sensitive qualitative reading of the survival processes 'at the margins' of poverty. The other (structured modules) aimed to build a bridge between the segments of 'normal' population (unknown to the world of welfare control and regulation agencies) and the population of 'users of services'.

2   Let $P(X)$ be the probability of observing in a universe of families one belonging to segment X (poor, with a disabled member or even simply difficult); it is estimated from the corresponding frequency in the general sample or on the basis of exogenous data. We wish to know the probability that we are dealing with a family of segment X if we observe a critical event E in it: the higher $P(X/E)$ relative to $P(X)$, the greater event E is a reliable diagnostic aid in pinpointing the particular difficult situation of segment X; that is, it is a good predictor of X. Since by definition $P(X/e) = P(e/X).P(X) > /P(e)$, the index number I. N. $(E/X) = P(X/e)/P(X) = P(e/X)/P(e)$ – determinable with the data available from a survey – expresses the capacity of the indicator E to predict specifically the existence of a segment X of chronicity.

3

Service Employment Regimes
and the New Inequality

Saskia Sassen, Columbia University, New York

Beyond the multiple causes that produce inequality and poverty through lack of employment, I argue that major changes in the organization of economic activity over the last 15 years have also emerged as a source of general economic insecurity and, particularly, of new forms of employment-centred poverty.

This is a broad subject; here I will confine myself to three processes: (a) the growing inequality in the profit-making capacities of different economic sectors and in the earnings capacities of different types of workers; (b) polarization tendencies embedded in the organization of service industries and the casualization of the employment relation; and (c) the production of urban marginality, particularly as a result of new structural processes of economic growth rather than those producing marginality through abandonment. These three dynamics are not necessarily mutually exclusive. I will examine how they operate in major cities. One of the working hypothesis in this chapter is that in global cities the impacts of economic globalization operate in part through these three dynamics. Such an analysis thus becomes a heuristic for capturing the ways in which economic globalization may or may not contribute to urban poverty in such cities.

Cities, particularly cities that are leading business centres, are a nexus where many of the new organizational tendencies come together. Many service activities have been decentralized through the new information technologies, and many other services dependent on vicinity to buyers follow distribution patterns of populations, firms and governments. But cities are key sites for the production of the most advanced services and of predominantly export-oriented services, and for service firms that operate in dense networks of firms. Cities are also key sites for the various labour markets these service firms need. They are the sites where the polarization tendencies embedded in the organization of service industries come to the fore and have distinctive impacts on urban economic and social configurations; these outcomes are sharpened in very large cities by the disproportionate concentrations of low-wage service jobs catering to commuters, tourists, as well as a mass of low-income residents. Many of these tendencies assume concrete forms in the urban landscape.

The first section focuses particularly on the major systemic tendencies in the organization of the economy and how they materialize in cities. The second section focuses on polarization tendencies in the service sector. And the third section briefly examines some of the impacts of these trends on urban space.

Throughout much of this chapter the empirical focus is on the US. To a considerable extent these trends towards greater inequality and insecurity are most advanced in the US because the government has never been as concerned with regulating economic and social conditions as is typical in western European countries. An important research question is how far the European countries will go towards deregulation of the economy and thereby stimulate some of these new trends.

INEQUALITY IN PROFIT-MAKING AND EARNINGS CAPACITIES

Inequality in the profit-making capacities of different sectors of the economy and in the earnings capacities of different types of workers has long been a feature of advanced economies. But what we see happening today takes place on an order of magnitude that distinguishes current developments from those of the post-war decades. The extent of inequality and the systems in which it is embedded and through which these outcomes are produced are engendering massive distortions in the operations of various markets, from investment to housing and labour.

Two of the major processes lying behind the possibility for the increased inequality in profit-making and earnings capacities are: (a) the ascendance and transformation of finance, particularly through securitization, globalization, and the development of new telecommunications and computer networks technologies; and (b) the growing service intensity in the organization of the economy generally which has vastly raised the demand for services by firms and households. In so far as there is a strong tendency towards polarization in the technical levels and prices of services as well as in the wages and salaries of workers in the service sector, the growth in the demand for services contributes to polarization and, via cumulative causation, to reproduce these inequalities. (For a fuller development of this argument see Sassen, 1994a: chapter 4.) Here I will particularly focus on these two major systemic tendencies in the economy and on how they materialize in cities.

The super-profit-making capacity of many of the leading service industries is embedded in a complex combination of new trends: technologies that make possible the hypermobility of capital at a global scale; market deregulation which maximizes the implementation of that hypermobility; financial inventions such as securization which liquify hitherto unliquid or relatively unliquid capital and allow it to circulate faster and hence make additional profits; the growing demand for services in all industries along with the increasing complexity and specialization of many of these inputs which has contributed to their valorization and often over-valorization, as illustrated in the unusually high salary increases beginning in the 1980s for top-level professionals. Globalization further adds to the complexity of these services, their strategic character, their glamour and therewith to their over-valorization.

The ascendance of finance and specialized services, particularly concentrated in large cities, creates a critical mass of firms with extremely high profit-making capabilities. These firms contribute to bid up the prices of commercial space, industrial services and other business needs, and thereby make survival for firms with moderate profit-making capabilities increasingly precarious. Among the latter, informalization of all or some of a firm's operations can emerge as one of the more extreme responses, further contributing to polarization in the urban economy. More generally, we see a segmentation between high-profit-making firms and relatively modest-profit-making firms.

The growth in the demand for service inputs, and especially bought service inputs, in all industries is perhaps the most fundamental condition making for change in advanced economies. It has had pronounced impacts on the earnings distribution, on industrial organization and on the patterns along which economic growth has spatialized. It has contributed to a massive growth in the demand for services by firms in all industries, from mining and manufacturing to finance and consumer services, and by households, both rich and poor.

The growing importance of services in economic organization can be seen in various types of data. All advanced economies have shown the most pronounced job growth in the so-called producer services (Castells and Aoyoma, 1994; Sassen 1994a: table 4.1). In the US, the sector with the largest share of new job growth from 1973 to 1987 was finance, insurance and real estate, which accounted for over 11 per cent of all new jobs; in the 1980s this sector accounted for 12 per cent and business services for almost 14 per cent of new jobs (though they are only 2 per cent of total jobs). At the other end of the spectrum, eating and drinking places, and retail each accounted for over 10 per cent of new jobs in the 1980s.[1] Another measure can be found in the value of bought service inputs in all industries. For this purpose I analysed the national accounts data over different periods beginning with 1960 for several industries in manufacturing and services. The results showed clearly that this value increased markedly over time (see Sassen and Orloff, forthcoming).

There are broader and more generalized tendencies towards a deeply embedded dualization in economic organization that are particularly evident in global cities. These general trends have to do with the enormous differentiation within each of the traditional categories, particularly manufacturing and services, depending on the intensity of the use of computers, information and control technologies in industry organization, and on whether an industry produces important inputs for other industries. Appelbaum and Albin (1990) have, in as far as this is possible given current data limitations, reclassified industries in terms of this variable across all major sectors of the economy.[2] Within the service sector, one grouping of industries can be characterized as 'knowledge and information intensive' (compare Appelbaum and Albin, 1990) and another subsector as labour intensive, and typically as having low productivity. The same can be found for manufacturing and other major sectors. Overall the employment, occupational, educational and earnings characteristics in each subsector tend to vary significantly.

Both the growing service intensity in the organization of the economy and the increased use of advanced technologies across all major sectors in the economy have a significant impact on the urban economy. Both entail a growing weight of specialized services in the economy. In so far as cities are preferred locations for the production of specialized services, cities re-emerge as significant production sites in advanced economies. This is a role they had lost to some extent when large-scale standardized mass manufacturing was dominant and necessarily left cities due to space requirements.

We see in cities the formation of a new urban economic core of financial and service activities that comes to replace the older typically more manufacturing oriented core of service and production activities. In the case of cities that are major international business centres, the scale, power and profit levels of this new core suggest that we are seeing the formation of a new urban economy. Even though these cities have long been centres for business and banking, since the early 1980s there have been dramatic changes in the structure of the business and financial sectors, as well as sharp increases in the overall magnitude of these sectors and their weight in the urban economy. This has had significant economic and social effects on cities in the US in the 1980s, a development also evident as of the mid-1980s in major European cities (see, for example, Kunzmann and Wegener, 1991; Frost and Spence, 1993; *Le Debat*, 1994; Sassen, 1994a: chapters 2, 3 and 5).[3]

This growth in services for firms is evident in cities at different levels of national urban systems. Some of these cities serve regional or subnational markets; others serve national markets and/or global markets. The specific difference that globalization makes in the context of a growing service intensity in the organization of the economy is to raise the scale and the complexity of transactions. This feeds the growth of top-level multinational headquarter functions and the growth of advanced corporate services. But even though globalization raises the scale and complexity of these operations, they are also evident at smaller geographic scales and lower orders of complexity, as in the case with firms that operate regionally. Thus while regionally oriented firms need not negotiate the complexities of international borders and the regulations of different countries, they are still faced with a regionally dispersed network of operations that requires centralized control and servicing, and with a growing need to buy insurance, legal, accounting, advertising and other such services. In this context, globalization becomes a question of larger scale and added complexity.

The implantation of global processes and markets in major cities has meant that the internationalized sector of the economy has expanded sharply and has imposed a new valorization dynamic – that is, a new set of criteria for valuing or pricing various economic activities and outcomes. This has had devastating effects on large sectors of the urban economy. It is not simply a quantitative transformation; we see here the elements for a new economic regime.

The ascendance of this specialized services-led economy, particularly the new finance and services complex, engenders what may be regarded as a new economic regime because although this sector may account for only a fraction of the economy of a city, it imposes itself on that larger economy. One of these pressures is towards polarization, as in the case with the possibility for superprofits in finance which in turn contributes to de-valorize manufacturing in so far as the latter cannot generate the superprofits typical in much financial activity.

High prices and profit levels in the internationalized sector and its ancillary activities, such as top-of-the-line restaurants and hotels, have made it increasingly difficult for other sectors to compete for space and investment. Many of these other sectors have experienced considerable downgrading and/or displacement, as, for example, neighbourhood shops tailored to local needs are replaced by up-market boutiques and restaurants catering to new high-income urban elites. Similarly in the valuation of labour inputs. One of the key outcomes of this transformation has been the significant growth of a high-income population particularly concentrated in cities and intimately linked to the ascendance of expertise and specialization in the organization of the economy. This ascendance of expertise in economic organization in turn has contributed to the valorization of specialized services and professional workers. And it has contributed to mark many of the 'other' types of economic activities and workers as unnecessary or irrelevant to an advanced economy. As I have sought to show at length elsewhere, many of these 'other' jobs are in fact an integral part of internationalized economic sectors, but not represented as such. This contributes to create a vast number of both low-income households and households earning very high incomes. The next two sections examine these issues in greater detail.

POLARIZATION TRENDS IN SERVICE EMPLOYMENT

The growth of services in terms of both jobs and firm inputs needs to be unbundled in order to capture the impact on questions of inequality and new forms of employment-centred poverty. Key issues are the types of jobs being created and the systemic tendencies organizing the service sector which are setting the terms of employment for today and tomorrow. Jobs and organization are, clearly, overlapping and mutually shaping factors. However, they do not overlap completely: the labour markets associated with a given set of technologies can, in principle, vary considerably and contain distinct mobility paths for workers. But today, sector organization, types of jobs, and labour market organization, are all strengthening the tendencies towards polarization.

Dualization in the Organization of Service Industries

Among the major systemic tendencies in the organization of the service sector contributing to polarization is the disproportionate grouping of service industries at either end of the technology spectrum. In the US, service industries that can be described as information- and knowledge-intensive have generated a significant share of all new jobs created over the last 15 years and have absorbed a disproportionate share of college graduates. Most of the other jobs created in the service sector fall at the other extreme. Appelbaum and Albin (1990) find that the first subsector generated over 9 million jobs from 1973 to 1987, while the second subsector added 11.2 million jobs. Each of these subsectors accounts for a considerable share of US jobs, with the first accounting for almost 30 per cent of all US jobs, and the second subsector for 39 per cent.[4]

These conditions of sharp growth at either end of the technology spectrum are continuing into the 1990s. Based on the data for 1992, the US Bureau of Labor Statistics projects a massive growth of low-wage service jobs, including service jobs catering to firms. Three service industries alone will account for about half of total US employment growth between 1992 and 2005: retail trade, health services and business services. Using the most detailed occupational classification (223 categories) the largest increases in terms of numbers of jobs are, in descending order: retail sales workers, registered nurses, cashiers, truck drivers, waiters and waitresses, nursing aides, janitors, food preparation workers, and systems analysts.[5] Most of these jobs do not require high levels of education and they are mostly not very highly paid. Nor does the BLS expect an increase in the median weekly wage of workers.

At the other extreme are jobs requiring a college degree. Their share was 23 per cent in 1992 and is projected to rise only by 1 per cent to 24 per cent by 2005. The knowledge- and information-intensive service subsector absorbed more than 5.7 million college-educated workers from 1973 to 1987. By 1987, over 40 per cent of workers with a college degree were employed in these service industries, compared to 17 per cent in the other service subsector. Indeed in the latter, 60 per cent of workers have never attended college. Furthermore, 20 per cent of workers with post-college education were in information- and knowledge-intensive service industries, compared to 6 per cent in the other services subsector.

Parallel segmentation is evident in terms of occupation. Managerial, executive and administrative occupations account for 17 per cent of all jobs in information- and knowledge-intensive service industries, which is double the percentage for other services. On the other hand, the latter subsector had, at 9.4 per cent, three times the share of supervisors as were found in the former. Information-, clerical- and computer-related-equipment operators were also most represented in information- and knowledge-intensive services, 8.5 per cent compared to 4.7 per cent in other services. Service and sales occupations are 40 per cent in other services, but only 16 per cent in information- and knowledge-intensive services. If we add up professionals, executives and kindred occupations we can see that they account for 34 per cent of workers in this subsector, compared to 14.6 per cent in other services.

The two broad occupational categories projected by the BLS to increase are professional specialty occupations and service occupations. The BLS data and projections show that the incomes in these two occupations in 1992 were 'on opposite ends of the earnings spectrum . . . earnings for service workers were about 40 per cent below the average for all occupational groups in 1992'. In combination with growth trends in industries and occupations this points to a maintenance and even increase in inequality in earnings, since most new jobs will be in low-paying service jobs and some of the professional specialty jobs may raise their levels of specialization and pay.

Appelbaum and Albin (1990) found that the differences they identified within the service sector are also evident in earnings. About 37 per cent (or 5.3 million jobs) of total new job growth in the US from 1979 to 1987 was in a group of service industries within the labour-intensive subsector where the median earnings of full-time year-round workers in 1986 was US $15,500. This is $7,000 less than the median of $22,555 of all full-time workers in this subsector (and almost $9,000 less than the median in durable goods manufacturing). Thus most new jobs in the labour-intensive subsector were in industries paying median wages and salaries under $15,500. Furthermore, these jobs were 37 per cent of new job growth in the 1980s, which is an increase over the 29 per cent share they had in the 1970s, signalling deterioration in the earnings of a growing share of workers in services. In contrast, public sector low-wage jobs, which are better paid and have more fringe benefits, saw a fall in their share of all new jobs, accounting for 26 per cent of jobs created in the 1970s and 22 per cent in the 1980s (or 3.2 million new jobs). The lowest paid hourly workers are part-time workers in the labour-intensive service industries, followed by full-time hourly workers in knowledge- and information-intensive service industries.[6] At the other end, the highest paid full-time hourly paid workers are in knowledge- and information-intensive manufacturing, followed by all other manufacturing.

A crucial and familiar form of segmentation is by sex. Seven out of every ten new jobs from 1973 to 1987 have been filled by women. Over 80 per cent of women hold jobs in service industries compared with about 55 per cent of men. The gendering of the employment transformation can be captured in the fact that women hold more jobs in knowledge- and information-intensive industries than men: about 34 per cent of jobs held by women are in these industries compared with about 25 per cent of jobs held by men. Differences by sex are also evident in terms of education. Thus, 38 per cent of women workers and 48 per cent of men in information- and knowledge-intensive services have a college degree, compared to respectively 15 per cent and 20 per cent in other services. Median earnings of women are higher in knowledge- and information-intensive services and manufacturing than in all other sectors; but they are always lower than the median for men in each sector.

The Casualization of the Employment Relation

In principle, the trends described above towards polarization in the job characteristics of the service sector could have left labour market organization unaffected. But they have not. We see a tendency towards a greater casualization of the employment relation. That is to say, it is not just a matter of an expansion of what are typically considered casual or unsheltered jobs, but a more fundamental transformation, one which also includes a growing array of high-paying professional jobs.

Two tendencies stand out. One is the weakening role of the firm in structuring the employment relation. More is left to the market. A second tendency in this restructuring of the labour market is what could be described as the shift of labour market functions to the household or community (see Sassen, 1995). Let me elaborate on each of these briefly.

Among the empirical referents for the weakening role of the firm in structuring the employment relation is the declining weight of internal labour markets. It corresponds to both the shrinking weight of vertically integrated firms and the restructuring of labour demand in many firms towards bipolarity – a demand for highly specialized and educated workers alongside a demand for basically unskilled workers whether for clerical, service, industrial service, or production jobs.

The shrinking demand for intermediate levels of skill and training has in turn reduced the need and advantages for firms of having internal labour markets with long promotion lines that function as training-on-the-job mechanisms. It has also reduced the need for firms to have full-time, year-round workers. And it has contributed to the rapid rise of employment agencies as intermediaries in the labour market; such agencies take over the demand and supply of a growing range of skills and occupations under highly flexible conditions.

These tendencies appear to be particularly evident in labour-intensive service industries, where the levels of skill required are often lower than in manufacturing. The higher growth of service as compared to manufacturing jobs thus carries additional consequences for the casualization of the employment relation.

Perhaps one of the most familiar and dramatic trends is the growth in part-time jobs. Over 60 per cent of all part-time workers in the US labour force are in labour-intensive services, which is also the sector that is expected to add the largest share of new jobs over the next decade.[7] Service workers are twice as likely to be in part-time jobs as average workers; involuntary part-time employment has grown significantly over the past decade (Carre, 1992).

The terms of employment have been changing rapidly over the last 15 years for a growing share of workers. In my reading, the overall tendency is towards a casualization of the employment relation that incorporates not only the types of jobs traditionally marked as 'casual' jobs, but also jobs at a high professional level which in many regards are not casual. It might be useful to differentiate a casualized employment relation from casual jobs in that the latter connotes such added dimensions as the powerlessness of the workers, a condition which might not hold for some of the highly specialized professional part-time or temporary workers. This is a subject that requires more research. (See Sassen 1994a: chapter 6)

The second tendency in the restructuring of labour markets I want to point out is the shift of labour market functions to the household or community. This is perhaps most evident in the case of immigrant communities. But it is also present in types of labour markets that are not necessarily embedded in immigrant communities or households.

There is a large body of evidence showing that once one or a few immigrant workers are hired in a given workplace, they will tend to bring in other members from their communities as job openings arise (Portes, 1995; Mahler, 1996). There is also evidence showing great willingness on the part of immigrant workers to help those they bring in with some training on the job, teaching the language, and just generally socializing them into the job and workplace. This amounts to a displacement of traditional labour market functions such as recruitment, screening and training from the labour market and the firm to the community or household. The labour market can then be reconceived as an activity space that contains a space dependency between employers and the community/household.[8]

Elsewhere (1995) I have examined how this space dependency between employers and low-wage workers contributes to the formation of distinctive localized labour markets and the extent to which the networks thus constituted also have the effect of restricting job opportunities for these workers. The formation of such localized labour markets and the enclosure of workers in these networks becomes particularly significant with the breakdown of internal labour markets in firms and the trend towards bipolarity in skill requirements generally in service industries. The overall effect is to further reduce the chances for upward mobility. While the case of immigrant workers makes this general dynamic clearer and more transparent, it actually encompasses a growing share of all low-wage workers.

In this restructuring of the labour market lie conditions for the growth of employment-centred insecurity and poverty and for urban marginality (see Sassen, 1994a: chapters 6 and 7). The casualization of the employment relation weakens and even eliminates the claims by workers on the firms where they work and hence can be seen as a weakening of the position of labour in the economy and corresponding institutional marginalization. Secondly, the displacement of labour market functions to the community or household raises the responsibility and the costs of participating in the labour force for workers, even if these costs are often not monetized.[9] These are all subjects that require new research given the transitions that we are living through.

TRENDS TOWARDS SPATIAL AND ORGANIZATIONAL POLARIZATION

These tendencies towards polarization assume distinct forms in the spatial organization of the urban economy and the structures for social reproduction that inscribe the urban landscape. Here I will touch only on a few aspects (see Sassen, 1994a: chapters 6 and 7; 1994b).

The rapid growth of industries with a strong concentration of high- and low-income jobs has assumed distinct forms in the consumption structure which in turn have a feedback effect on the organization of work and the types of jobs being created.[10] The expansion of the high-income work-force in conjunction with the emergence of new cultural forms have led to a process of high-income gentrification that rests, in the last analysis, on the availability of a vast supply of low-wage workers. As I have argued at greater length elsewhere, high-income gentrification is labour-intensive, in contrast to the typical US middle-class suburb that represents a capital-intensive process – tract housing, road and highway construction, dependence on private automobile or commuter trains, marked reliance on appliances and household equipment of all sorts, large shopping malls with self-service operations. High-income gentrification replaces much of this capital intensity with workers, directly and indirectly. Similarly, high-income residents in cities depend to a much larger extent on hired maintenance staff than the middle-class suburban home with its concentrated input of family labour and machinery.

Differences in the organization of work are evident both in the retail and in the production phase. High-income gentrification generates a demand for goods and services that are frequently not mass-produced or sold through mass outlets. Customized production, small runs, specialty items, fine food dishes are generally produced through labour-intensive methods and sold through small, full-service outlets. Subcontracting part of this production to low-cost operations, and also sweatshops or households, is common. The overall outcome for the job supply and the range of firms involved in this production and delivery is rather different from that characterizing the large department stores and supermarkets where standardized products and services are prevalent and hence acquisition from large, standardized factories located outside the city or the region are the norm. Proximity to stores is of far greater importance with customized producers. Further, unlike customized production and delivery, mass production and mass distribution outlets facilitate unionizing.

The expansion in the low-income population has also contributed to the proliferation of small operations that compete with large-scale standardized factories and large chain stores to meet the demand for low-price goods. In good part the consumption needs of the low-income population in large cities are met by manufacturing and retail establishments which are small, rely on family labour and often fall below minimum safety and health standards. Cheap, locally produced sweatshop garments, for example, can compete with low-cost Asian imports. A growing range of products and services, from low-cost furniture made in basements to 'gypsy cabs' and family daycare is available, often informally, to meet the demand from the growing low-income population.

There are numerous instances of how the increased inequality in earnings reshapes the consumption structure and how this in turn has feedback effects on the organization of work, both in the formal and in the informal economy: the creation of a special taxi line that only services the financial district and the increase of gypsy cabs in low-income neighbourhoods not serviced by regular cabs; the increase in highly customized woodwork in gentrified areas and low-cost rehabilitation in poor neighbourhoods; the increase of homeworkers and sweatshops making either very expensive designer items for boutiques or very cheap products.

Perhaps one of the clearest illustrations of the spatial impact of these trends towards polarization comes from a recent study on commercial bank branch closings and openings in the New York Metropolitan area presented to the New York State Legislature. It found a wave of bank branch closings which left several poor and minority communities without any banking services – this in the leading financial centre of the country. While an earlier wave of branch closings in the 1980s had been concentrated in low-income areas, the latest one affected the more modest segments of middle-income areas.[11] Five major New York City banks accounted for all except one of the closings of commercial branches in New York City neighbourhoods with more than 50 per cent minority populations.[12] However, branch services have increased in the suburbs and in high-income areas in New York City.[13] Banks have also been opening numerous 'personal financial centers' or 'private banking centers' in affluent areas of the City. In some of these branches customers must have $25,000 in their accounts to use the teller service. There is a strong trend towards offering less services to poor and middle-class neighbourhoods and an increasing array of specialized services to affluent consumers.

This illustrates a more general trend in the spatial organization of the urban economy – the even sharper trend today for leading sectors to be concentrated in the downtowns of cities, in suburban office complexes and in edge cities. There is hardly any economic growth in low-income communities. This unbalanced spatial distribution of growth has been much stronger over the last 15 years than in past historical periods when all large cities had a multitude of neighbourhood subeconomies, typically including commercial and manufacturing activities. Further, in so far as the ascendance of high-profit industries such as finance and specialized services has contributed to raise the price of commercial space and other business costs in the downtowns of large cities, small low-profit firms can hardly afford space in such central locations, even when there is an effective demand for their products or services.

Polarization among firms and households and in the spatial organization of the economy contribute, in my reading, towards the informalization of a growing array of economic activities. When firms with low or modest profit-making capacities experience an ongoing if not increasing demand for their goods and services from households and other firms in a context where a significant sector of the economy makes superprofits, they often cannot compete even though there is an effective demand for what they produce. Operating informally is one of the few ways in which such firms can survive: for example, using spaces not zoned for commercial or manufacturing uses, such as basements in residential areas, or space that is not up to code in terms of health, fire and other such standards. Similarly, new firms in low-profit industries entering a strong market for their goods and services may only be able to do so informally. Another option for firms with limited profit-making capabilities is to subcontract part of their work to informal operations.

One way of conceptualizing informalization in advanced urban economies today is to posit it as the systemic equivalent of what we call deregulation at the top of the economic system (see Sassen 1994b); this grounds it in major trends in advanced capitalism.[14] Both the deregulation of a growing number of leading information industries and the informalization of a growing number of sectors with low profit-making capacities can be conceptualized as adjustments under conditions where new economic developments and old regulations enter in growing tension.[15]

CONCLUSION

Developments in cities cannot be understood in isolation from fundamental changes in the larger organization of advanced economies. One way of conceiving of these transformations is as systemic transitions between different modes of social and economic organization. Thus we are seeing a transition from the relative obsoleteness of urban economies during the dominance of Fordism, to the revalorization of strategic components of urban space due to the increased service intensity in the organization of the economy. The ascendance of information industries and the growth of a global economy, both inextricably linked, have contributed to a new 'geography' of centrality and marginality. This new geography partly reproduces existing inequalities but also is the outcome of a dynamic specific to the current forms of economic growth. It assumes many forms and operates in many terrains, from the distribution of telecommunications facilities to the structure of the economy and of employment.

The new urban economy not only contributes to strengthen existing inequalities but sets in motion a whole series of new dynamics of inequality. The new growth sectors – specialized services and finance –

contain capabilities for profit making vastly superior to those of more traditional economic sectors. The latter are essential to the operation of the urban economy and the daily needs of residents, but their survival is threatened in a situation where finance and specialized services can earn superprofits.

We see sharp increases in socio-economic and spatial inequalities within major cities. This can be interpreted as merely a quantitative increase in the degree of inequality. But it can also be interpreted as social and economic restructuring and the emergence of new social forms and class alignments in large cities of highly developed countries: the growth of an informal economy; high-income commercial and residential gentrification; and the sharp rise of homelessness.

The observed changes in the occupational and earnings distribution are outcomes not only of industrial shifts but also of changes in the organization of firms and of labour markets. There has been a strengthening of differences within major sectors, notably within services. One set of service industries tends towards growing capital–labour ratios, growing productivity, intensive use of the most advanced technologies, and the other towards continued labour intensity and low wages. Median earnings and median educational levels are also increasingly diverging for each of these subsectors. These characteristics in each set of industries contribute to a type of cumulative causation within each set. The first group of industries experiences pressures towards even higher capital–labour ratios and productivity levels given high wages, while in the second group of industries, low wages are a deterrent towards greater use of capital-intensive technologies, and low productivity leads to even more demand for very low-wage workers. These conditions in turn contribute to reproduce the difference in profit-making capacities embedded in each of these subsectors.

The combination of economic, political and technical forces that has contributed to the decline of mass production as the central driving element in the economy has brought about a decline in a broader institutional framework that shaped the employment relation. The group of service industries that are the driving economic force in the 1980s and into the 1990s is characterized by greater earnings and occupational dispersion, weak unions, and mostly a growing share of unsheltered jobs in the lower-paying echelons along with a growing share of high-income jobs. The associated institutional framework shaping the employment relation is very different from the earlier one. This contributes to a reshaping of the sphere of social reproduction and consumption, which in turn has a feedback effect on economic organization and earnings. Whereas in the earlier period this feedback effect contributed to the reproduction and expansion of the middle class, currently it reproduces growing earnings disparity and labour market casualization. The overall result is a tendency toward increased economic polarization.

When we speak of polarization in the use of land, in the organization of labour markets, in the housing market and in the consumption structure, we do not necessarily mean that the middle class is disappearing. We are rather referring to a dynamic whereby growth contributes to inequality rather than expansion of the middle class, as was the case in the two decades after the Second World War in the United States and in many of the developed economies. Where the middle class represents a significant share of the population it is an important channel through which income and life-style coalesce into a dominant social form. In many of today's leading urban economies we see a segmenting of the middle class that has a sharper upward and downward slant than had been the case in other periods. The conditions that contributed to middle class expansion and politico-economic power – the centrality of mass production and mass consumption in economic growth and profit realization – have been displaced by new sources of growth. This is not simply a quantitative transformation; we see here the elements for a new economic regime.

NOTES

1 By 1987 business services provided 5.2 million jobs, or 5 per cent of total jobs, and had become a larger employer than construction and almost as large as transport and public utilities, and wholesale trade. Almost half of the new jobs in business services came from personnel supply services, and computer and data processing (see Bednarzik, 1990).

2 Appelbaum and Albin have proposed a taxonomy of firms and industries into broad sectors on the basis of 'information and knowledge intensity' – 'a multidimensional property of firms and industries, reflecting the nature of the output produced, the extent of computer rationalization of the production process, and the organizational adaptation to information and computation technologies' (1990: 32).

3 Manufacturing remains a crucial sector in all these economies, even when it may have ceased to be a dominant sector in major cities. Some have argued that the producer services sector could not exist without manufacturing (Cohen and Zysman, 1987; Markusen and Gwiasda, 1994). There is no consensus around this issue (see, for example, Noyelle and Dutka, 1988; Drennan, 1992). Drennan (1992) argues that a strong finance and producer services sector is possible in New York notwithstanding decline in its industrial base and that these sectors are so strongly integrated into the world markets that articulation with the

larger region becomes secondary. In a variant on both positions, I have long argued that manufacturing indeed feeds the growth of the producer services sector, but that it does so whether located in the area in question, somewhere else in the country, or overseas. Even though manufacturing – and mining and agriculture, for that matter – feeds growth in the demand for producer services, their actual location is of secondary importance in the case of global-level service firms. Second, the territorial dispersal of plants, especially if international, actually raises the demand for producer services in so far as it raises the complexity of management and financing. The growth of producer service firms headquartered in New York or London or Paris can be fed by manufacturing located anywhere in the world as long as it is part of a multinational corporate network. Third, a good part of the producer services sector is fed by financial and business transactions that either have nothing to do with manufacturing, as is the case in many of the global financial markets, or for which manufacturing is incidental, as in much merger and acquisition activity, which is centred on buying and selling firms rather than the buying of manufacturing firms as such.

4   Information- and knowledge-intensive manufacturing in the US accounts for only 3.2 per cent of US employment; the rest of manufacturing, for about 27 per cent. Note that women are far less represented in the 'rest of manufacturing' subsector than in the former; this is partly due to the feminization of the electronics assembly line.

5   Retail trade is expected to add the largest number of jobs, 4.5 million. Nearly half of these jobs will be for food service workers (cashiers and salespersons in eating and drinking places: these are not well-paid jobs, nor do they demand high levels of education). Next comes health services with an added 4.2 million jobs; within these the fastest-growing type of job is home care service, again mostly a low-paying job. Next are business services, with 3.1 million new jobs, which includes both low-wage and high-wage industries. One of the growth industries in business services is personnel supply services, such as temporary employment agencies; another growth sector is transportation, particularly trucking and warehousing.

6   Average hourly wages have been stagnant in the US since 1973, notwithstanding a rapid increase in the salaries of new professionals. And as has been documented in the 1990 census, income inequality increased over the previous 20 years.

7   Almost 30 per cent of all jobs in labour-intensive services are part time, compared to 17 per cent in information- and knowledge-intensive services. Part-time jobs are highly concentrated: restaurants and hotels, retail, and education account for 45 per cent of all part-time jobs, but only 25 per cent of all jobs in the economy. Nearly half of all workers in retail are part-time, compared with 10 per cent in administrative, managerial and supervisory occupations.

8   This space dependency is centred on the relation between workplace and

household, and between workplace and community. The exchange dynamic – a component of all markets – is therewith displaced from the centre of labour market operation where it is situated in the neo-classical model (see Sassen, 1995). When it comes to international labour migration, this reconceptualization views the act of migrating as a move from one particular local labour market (in the country of origin) to another particular local labour market (in the country of destination). This specific job search pattern has the effect of altering the geographic dimension often implied by job search models, especially among low-wage workers who have been found to have little geographic mobility. However, notwithstanding this wide-ranging area within which many immigrants search for jobs, they are actually largely moving within a very confined institutional setting, i.e. a *local* labor market, even when they travel long distances and improvise informal transportation systems. This is another way of conceptualizing the role of networks. These networks have spatial patterns, but they are not characterized by geographic proximity. Furthermore, while they may cover immense distances they do not necessarily offer great opportunities for mobility nor place immigrants in particularly competitive positions *vis-à-vis* natives in terms of upward job mobility. This is particularly so given the polarization tendencies evident in the distribution of jobs in services.

9   There is an interesting parallel here with one of the components of the service economy, that is, the shift of tasks traditionally performed by the firm onto the household: for example, furniture and even appliances sold unassembled to be put together by the buyer (Gershuny and Miles, 1983).

10 It is important here to keep in mind the distinction between what can be considered elements central to a theorization of informalization in advanced economies and the fact of possibly fairly generalized informal practices. The first seeks to identify what is distinct and can be used to specify the nature of the process in highly developed countries with extensive regulatory frameworks. Thus the finding that over half of all US households consume food produced informally (Institute for Social Research, 1987) does not by itself specify the informal economy. Generally the findings about US household use of informally produced and/or distributed services and goods describe a far more widespread condition than can be read as carrying theoretical meaning. For instance, over 27 per cent of US households bought informally produced home repairs, almost 21 per cent bought goods from informal sidewalk vendors, 15.5 per cent bought informal lawn and garden services, etc.

11 From 1985 to 1987, 55 full service commercial branches were closed, 34 in 1987 alone, which is the highest number for any one year in the last decade. The previous peak was in 1983 with 38 closings. From 1985 to 1987 was a period of extremely sharp growth in the financial industry in New York City. Thus this case makes it clear in yet another form that there is no trickle-down effect in financial growth.

12   During this period only two new full-service branches opened, one Chinese-owned in Chinatown and the other a small black-owned bank (Freedom National Bank), the only branch opened in New York City neighbourhoods with over 30 per cent black population. In all counties with black and Hispanic populations above the regional average, the number of residents per commercial bank branches increased. The Bronx, the borough with the highest percentage of black and Hispanic populations, had the most severe reduction in its commercial branch network, a 20 per cent loss from 1978 to 1987. Forty full-service commercial branches were closed over that period. In 1987 the Bronx had 30 per cent more residents per branch than it did in 1980. Brooklyn, the borough with the second highest proportion of blacks and Hispanics in 1987 had 14 per cent more residents per branch than it did in 1980 and has the highest ratio at almost 15,000 per branch (Port Authority of New York and New Jersey, Office of Economic and Policy Analysis, 1994).

13   This increase of 7 per cent cannot simply be explained as a function of population growth in the suburbs. In 1987 the outer boroughs had almost 12,000 residents per branch; the suburbs 3,000.

14   Linking informalization and growth takes the analysis beyond the notion that the emergence of informal sectors in cities like New York and Los Angeles is caused by the presence of immigrants and their propensities to replicate survival strategies typical of third world countries. Linking informalization and growth also takes the analysis beyond the notion that unemployment and recession generally may be the key factors promoting informalization in the current phase of highly industrialized economies. It points to characteristics of advanced capitalism that are not typically noted when informalization is thought of as imported via third world immigration.

15   'Regulatory fractures' is one concept I have used to capture this condition to indicate that there are situations not well designated as either violation or compliance. See also *Social Justice* (1993).

4

The Excluded and the Homeless: The Social Construction of the Fight Against Poverty in Europe

Antonio Tosi, Politecnico of Milan

In the political, professional and academic debate terms such as 'homeless', 'sans abri', 'senza casa', etc. offer us a set of concepts which can only be 'interchanged' at the cost of misunderstanding. The two main poles of current definitions make reference with equal relevance to two fundamental meanings of the word 'home': 'home' is a 'there' and a 'they' (Stone, 1994). Obviously the two conditions are not at all identical: many with no home have normal social relations and there are people with relational problems who live in houses. The question becomes further complicated if we consider that non-housing definitions may identify hardship in terms of poverty or in terms of (social) marginality/marginalization, and that they may define vulnerability in social terms or in terms of personal failings (disabilities).

Various expedients are used to handle the ambiguity of the terms (typological classification is the main one). Nevertheless, the problem – from an important point of view – remains unsolved. The two meanings given do not just identify different situations of hardship or categories of person, they also identify different social representations which correspond to different interpretations on an analytical level and different solutions to problems on a practical level. In constructing these representations the opposition of 'social' versus 'housing' is added to and correlates with other oppositions: a problem of (social) marginalization versus a problem of poverty; social problems as an illness or as deviance versus normality; the stress on personal data or disabilities versus the stress on structural factors, etc. There is a clear tendency in the debate to formulate explanations or proposals in terms of opposites and 'extremes' often at the risk of simplification and lack of credibility (Tosi and Cremaschi, 1989). An example of this is the attribution of the phenomenon to one type of factor only which would explain all (the increase in) homelessness, when the plurality of the types that constitute it is more than obvious and when generally even at an individual level it is rather the interaction or accumulation of different factors that creates the problem.

These simplifications, to be found also in the research literature, could not be explained if they were not backed by the interrelationships between the representations proposed and the social construction of the problem. The diffusion of images which appear 'noncredible' on the level of empirical verification can only be explained by the practical functions of the oppositions identified – to be appraised with reference to the political and public communication processes. I am thinking of the frequent underestimation of the components of marginalization in the processes that constitute homelessness or, from the opposite viewpoint, of the stubbornness with which many continue to deny the housing nature of the problem when the role of housing precariousness seems to be growing and in any case constitutes a distinctive feature of new homelessness. In effect, the 'natural' interrelationships between social theory and research on the one hand and social and political constructions on the other are in this case so closely woven as to represent an extreme case. In fact, it has frequently been claimed that the very subject of homelessness is determined by its political value, that it was in fact the need to deal with its socially alarming aspects (or to control its visibility) that 'invented' the field of homelessness.

In this chapter I assume that a constructivist point of view, that insists on the aspects in which the social/political construction interacts with the critical issues of the scientific debate, can clear up some of the fundamental points of the discussion on the homeless, and show the interest that this problem may have for the general debate on poverty and social policy. The basic idea is that the appropriate context for this operation is provided by the European debate on the ways of combating new poverty and by the application of the two categories that dominate the debate – 'social exclusion' and 'insertion' – to the problem of homelessness.

Certainly the comparisons that are suggested risk a certain dose of arbitrariness, above all because it is not possible here to cite the details and the contexts of the national experiences referred to. Nevertheless these limits do not constitute an obstacle to making the main point – the nature of the stakes being played for in the formulation of new social policies and their relationship with a new historical situation in which poverty and social policies are being determined.

The discussion revolves around the relationships exhibited by homelessness with three problems at the centre of the aforementioned European debate:

1 extreme poverty and social exclusion: what homelessness represents in the phenomenology of poverty and in the processes that produce it, and what – through homelessness – is given importance in the social construction of poverty;
2 the new insertion policies: what does experience of homelessness teach with respect to the 'ambiguity' of the notion of insertion – at the same time a reference for a strongly innovative effort to realize social efficacy by policies, and a possible reference for reducing them;
3 the territoriality of social exclusion and extreme poverty: why territorial dimensions assume such an important role in social constructions of poverty and what homelessness represents from this point of view. Homelessness involves specific territorial dimensions of extreme poverty: its dispersed character and the problems deriving from the presence of the poor in public places. An analysis of the social constructions, however, brings out its relations with the other, in some way opposed, dimension, that of the concentration of poverty, which in Europe is mainly represented in relation to the problems of urban ghettos and 'neighbourhoods in crisis'.

In Search of a Table of Concepts

It is perhaps useful to begin by breaking down the identifications and 'exchanges' that recur in public speech and to examine a series of possibilities of the type 'those of no abode are not the only ones without a house', or 'there are those without a house who are not of no abode'; 'it is possible to be excluded from housing without being socially excluded', etc. The operation involves putting a minimum of order in our concepts. This makes it possible to review the interpretations, to identify the operative and political implications and to explicitly define the relations between category systems and constructions. This can be done on the one hand by breaking down the concept of homelessness on the basis of the two dimensions already mentioned: homeless as 'of no abode' and homeless as 'excluded from housing'. The first term tries to hit on relational problems or elements of vulnerability or severe hardship which are suggested by the term 'homeless' in its more restricted or more conventional sense – those 'of no fixed abode', the roaming homeless (Nuy, 1993), etc. The second term on the other hand identifies the problem on the basis of the type of (non) accommodation adopted. Those with no accommodation (sleeping rough, etc.) are excluded, as are those that resort to temporary arrangements (temporary shelters, etc.) and also those whose housing is so inadequate that it cannot be considered as real housing (improper dwellings, etc.). Clearly the 'no abode' group represents just one of the categories populating the housing exclusion field. There are several others, some of which possess none of the relational problems and disabilities attributed to the homeless in the conventional sense: for example, many foreign immigrants. This distinction makes it possible to keep a check at least on some of the ambiguities implied by the terms 'homeless' and 'homelessness'. It can also be used to deal with the relationship between housing deprivation and poverty and to understand why homelessness is important in the construction of poverty.[1]

On the other hand, the concept of homelessness must be included in a larger table of concepts which – recognizing poverty as the context of the problem – also recognizes the new forms in which poverty manifests itself today and organizes the different conceptualizations. A variety of concepts is needed because the critical function of analysis is not to assign various situations to determined categories but to identify the processes that connect the different situations or that effect the 'passage' from one situation to another.

Two concepts are essential to this table, firstly there is 'extreme poverty' or 'great poverty'. This is effectively the fundamental point of reference, at least implicit, in the debate on homelessness – whatever means of identification is used, social, housing, etc. – and this concept is the best starting point from which to tie together the various themes that intertwine in the conceptual field of homelessness. Secondly there is the concept of 'social exclusion'. While this may be another way of defining extreme poverty, it introduces, however, a specific frame of reference which brings out historically new aspects of the problem of poverty.

'Extreme poverty' and 'great poverty' refer to a more accentuated degree of poverty, but also to something that may be different from poverty, or something that 'goes beyond poverty' (Council of Europe, 1993). Coming close to some connotations suggested by 'no abode', these terms refer to situations and experiences which do not form part of 'normal' poverty: disaffiliation, no home, etc. Moreover, with these terms the accent is placed on the cumulative character of the hardships and deprivations that constitute extreme poverty.

If the current debate on the homeless is considered, then the reference to extreme poverty also takes on important methodological significance. Homelessness is set in a network of factors which, according to current interpretations, constitute extreme poverty. What role do relational difficulties play in it? How does the lack or loss of a home come into the network of factors? What is the sequence of events? This contextual framework allows – on the basis of what happens in the studies on poverty – different combinations of factors to be made and encourages the combination of analysis at a structural level with individual level or biographical approaches, etc. As far as 'relational' dimensions are concerned, this means, for example, allowing notions of 'disaffiliation' which, as against psycho-social reductions or reductions in terms of disabilities, emphasize its social process character, its relationship with processes whereby work becomes more and more precarious and social ties more fragile, or with the absence of social protection – the 'objective' factors which lead to extreme poverty. As far as the housing dimension is concerned, the accent is placed on the connection between housing deprivation and poverty and the fact that housing exclusion may be suffered by various sectors of society and not just those of 'no abode'.

The reference to poverty poses two problems: (a) realizing that there is a difference between poverty and extreme poverty (and between their dynamics: the poor may decrease in number while the extreme poor increase – Avramov, 1994); and (b) locating the problem of extreme poverty in the wider question of poverty, of the employment crisis and of housing hardship. The stress on extreme poverty or on the homeless does in fact risk separating these from the wider questions, with serious practical consequences (Blasi, 1994).

It is clear then just how important – from both an analytical and political viewpoint – a bridging concept like 'risk' is. It makes it possible to connect extreme poverty (and homelessness) with vulnerability factors which involve wider sectors of society.

SOCIAL EXCLUSION

The most interesting uses of this concept put the accent on a process rather than a condition and thereby extend the analysis to the social/ systemic production of poverty and bring to the foreground the processes of disaffiliation which constitute the historically new aspect of the phenomenon. By connecting the process to a series of conditions, those which in another system of concepts would define the passage to post-Fordism, the debate on social exclusion considers the following to be fundamental:

- the new processes of disaffiliation resulting from an increase in social vulnerability which occurs when two vectors converge – the employment crisis and the various processes that make social ties more fragile. The latter have their roots in the transformation of family structures and models and in the decay of previous forms of sociality (Castel, 1991: 130–63).
- the constitution, in this way, of a 'supernumerary' population (1991), a population nobody knows what to do with, potentially chronic *laissés-pour-compte*, an unusable underclass (Lapeyronnie, 1990) etc.
- a modification of the systemic relations of inequality: 'the passage from a vertical society, a class society with people high-up and people low-down, to a horizontal society where the problem is not to be up or down but to be in or out' (Touraine, 1992b), and where the break between marginalized sectors and those that were able to 'modernize' is accentuated (Lapeyronnie, 1990).
- the importance of spatial/territorial mechanisms in the dynamics of exclusion (the partial correspondence between the cumulative character of disadvantages and their spatial concentration which gives rise to the problem of distressed urban areas', 'neighbourhood in crisis' etc.; the action of territorial processes and measures of control/segregation in exclusion) and the new processes that structure poverty in terms of territory (as emphasized for example in the US debate on the 'new outcast ghetto', Marcuse herein).

A fundamental feature of these conceptualizations is the accent on the 'risk' dimension that is implied in these processes, the idea that the area of vulnerability is – as much from the viewpoint of precarious employment as from that of the fragility of social ties – potentially more of a problem than the extent of current exclusion would suggest: the population at risk is much larger than that already excluded.

HOMELESSNESS, 1

The homeless provide a paradigmatic portrayal of the new processes of exclusion, particularly with regard to the aspects that are given importance in political debate. This can be seen for all the different meanings of the dimension 'home', and first of all for all the meanings strictly connected with housing. Here the conceptual distinction between homelessness in the sense of person of no (fixed) abode and homelessness as housing exclusion becomes important. The distinction makes it possible to understand why homelessness is important in the construction of social exclusion. The critical factor is the network of connections that have come into being between social exclusion and housing exclusion, a connection which has been defined in various ways: according to the role which, at a personal level, being without a home – however this may have occurred – plays in creating social exclusion as a global fact (Wodon, 1992); according to the growing importance that housing factors have or could have in social exclusion; according to the importance that a home has in terms of solutions, independently of individual case histories and whatever interpretation is made of the factors;[2] according to the tangibleness, in this field, of the size of the risk of exclusion – this tangibleness constitutes one of the most important elements in the representation of the 'structural' risk of social exclusion and its extent, that is, the fact that it 'could happen to anybody'.

But home is 'there' and 'they'. There is a meaning of the word 'home' that is quite marked in some of the terms that many languages employ for referring to the deepest aspects of the living experience: 'to dwell' as the relationship between social relations and places. In this sense, to have no home is an extreme expression of exclusion with strong symbolic overtones – having no niche, no 'shelter', no protection. The homeless are not necessarily the poorest, but those who do not have even a minimum of the social protection that derives from 'belonging' to a place.

In this sense too, the homeless communicate the risk of exclusion strongly. But they communicate it because they are highly visible. Visibility as a component (or cause?) of the problem is a feature that is emphasized by many in the debate on the homeless and is central in the construction of policies.

DUALISTIC HYPOTHESES

Naturally social exclusion is not an 'objective' fact, something that can be thought of as the inevitable result of the development mechanisms of society. It is a social process which brings policies and collective attitudes into play. In the first place – as is clear with unemployment – it is not an objective fact in the more obvious sense that 'excess' is the result of a model of development and management of society.[3]

The historical frame is that of the crisis of the 'unlimited collective responsibility' that has characterized the classic concepts of the welfare state. It is not, however, a question of discussing whether those models can be maintained. What constitutes the really new factor historically is the change of the scenario in which the heritage of the welfare state is put into question. The new processes of impoverishment and the crisis of the European welfare state contain in them the admissibility of an unprecedented 'dualism' in our societies, the hypothesis of a dual society and dualistic social policy models.

The 1960s represented a point of arrival for long term transformations. At the same time, it was a time for questioning the development model of modern societies as a whole or at least the 'progressist' portrayal of it that had been formed: the possibility of piloting growth to control its social repercussions, trust in the integrative capacities of increasing national wealth and in the property of a democratic society to ensure a minimum of social altruism . . . The possibility evoked with growing insistence that the current 'crisis' may lead to a dual society, is now being used to question this model. It is this which appears 'new' today . . . Dualism was not a possible scenario for the societies of the Ancien Régime, even if they were less egalitarian and had greater problems of under-employment and poverty. They had, however, strong traditional systems of regulation to control their areas of occupational instability and relational fragility . . . Later, the possibility of mass marginalization appeared with industrialization but seemed to have been avoided with the welfare state that gambled on the possibility of reconciling the differentiation of statuses with their complementarity, thanks to tempered use of social justice. The distance covered in this sense, beginning with pauperism at the beginning of the nineteenth century, was considerable. Thus while temptations towards dualism have always existed, as have the conditions of precariousness and vulnerability that could feed it, a society does not become dual unless it starts to set up a separation between its areas of integration and its areas of disintegration. Put in other terms, a society resigns itself to dualism when it accepts precariousness and vulnerability as a matter of fact – or when it pursues them in the name of productivity and efficiency of production on the one hand and of the promotion of unlimited individualism as a supreme ethical value on the other. (Castel, 1991: 166–7)

A CONFLICT OVER THE POOR

The retreat with respect to the model of 'unlimited collective responsibility' and universalistic citizenship yet again puts the treatment of the poor and of poverty and their relations with society into question. This questioning has the character of a conflict – which is part of the passage to post-Fordism and the corresponding falling apart of classic models of social policies. It is similar to the conflict that occurred when those models were founded. The old alternatives are being re-proposed, residual welfare models are opposed to comprehensive welfare models, and again discussion centres on the dissent over the recognized priorities for the poor in social policies and for the extreme poor within anti-poverty policies.

In this conflict over models a body of images are taken up that belong to the tradition of treatment of the poor. First of all, traditional identifications of the type, the poor as a danger (see Wihtol de Wenden, 1993), the (very) poor as an object of fear and disgust (Wagner, 1993), and so on are re-proposed. On an explanatory level, a well-known ideological structure is used again: the social/systemic production of the problem is denied; the accent is put on the individual character of the processes that constitute poverty and on the 'differentness' of the groups that are involved, etc. Finally a certain idea of 'social problems' is re-proposed – like foreign bodies to 'fight' excrescences of a system which as a whole functions well (Marcuse, 1988b) – which is the most consistent with the traditional regulatory welfare-assistance line of treatment of the poor (Tosi, 1994).

As is clear, it is a categorization system: fear, compassion, bother, refusal and indifference operate as functional categories consistent with specific constructions of the problem and therefore suggesting specific solutions. Fear and compassion result in proposals for control and social assistance measures. As a whole, this categorization system denotes a change of ideological and conceptual context of policies and collective representations. What is the game and what stakes are being played for here?

As the symbolic system constructed around the notions of danger and of differentness suggests, one of the possible meanings is the prevalence of a demand for the protection of society from the poor, which may replace policies aimed at integrating them. Certainly a distinction should be made between the various types of poverty. Negative representations have a logic and 'basis' which differ in part according to whether they relate to 'no abode', immigrants, drug addicts, etc. All these constructions do, however, although in different ways, question whether the poor actually 'belong' to the society in which they find themselves (Hopper and Baumohl, 1994; Autés, 1992) – with the possibility of denying that they belong in terms of rights. The very poor as objects of fear or compassion represent constructions that are opposed to the 'logic of rights'. The reduction is shown by the retreat on the content of rights, and even the movements in favour of the homeless can be pushed in this direction, as was noted for the US.

> Focusing on homelessness allows local élites to redefine the problem of the question of the 'rights' of the homeless in terms of the mere right to exist. The inevitable evolution of this discussion all too often leads to advocates finding themselves in the position of discussing, not the right to work or to the economic means for survival, but the right to sleep in a park or to beg in the metro. They find themselves fighting not for the creation of decent housing at affordable prices but for the siting in a particular district of emergency shelters in which and near which nobody (including the homeless) wants to live. (Blasi, 1994: 569)

CONTINUITY AND DISCONTINUITY

A powerful conceptual and technical apparatus is available for this reduction, the apparatus that grew up around the polarization of social policies and which – although with all the differences between national models – has characterized the tradition of the welfare state.[4]

> The subject of welfare corresponds to the institutionalization, beginning at the end of the nineteenth century, of two symmetrically opposite, although complementary approaches: defending society against the individual that threatens it and protecting the individual from the risks society forces him to run. There is no doubt that the same concern over improving the condition of the individual can be observed for both these viewpoints of welfare: concern that he integrates instead of doing harm or that he is protected instead of abandoned. These aims are pursued, however, by drawing a very distinct dividing line between two types of population and two methods of treatment. 'Welfare assistance' (and the defence of society which theoretically underlies the practice) considers its beneficiaries as (socially) marginal persons/groups to be subject to corrective protection as a condition for obtaining help or the suspension of a sanction. 'Welfare protection' considers its affiliates as normal persons and as having the right to that quasi-contract which is implied by providing social security, even automatically. (Donzelot, 1991: 18–19)

The first approach is close to and easily exchangeable with mere measures of control of a repressive type, even if the development of the welfare state, which also brought with it the development of its welfare assistance components, has progressively reduced the possibility of this exchange (Castel, 1991: 151).

As regards the historical polarization, the 'crisis' has two implications, opposite in effect, which together define the problematic character of social policies and the terms of the conflict surrounding the policies: (a) the distinction between the two types of measures is used again, in strict relation to reductions in social policies; (b) at the same time, because of the crisis of welfare models, the borderlines between the two types are narrowing.

The first possibility can be observed in the weight given to the different measures used to govern poverty and exclusion. On the one hand, in the new dualistic perspective, measures of control or repression are gaining ground over welfare measures. On the other hand, welfare assistance type measures may increase with respect to those based on a logic of rights and full welfare protection for various components of the excluded population.

The other possibility can be seen in the emergence of a new conception of welfare intervention which Donzelot has called 'welfare of the third type' (*social du troisième type*), which lies at the roots of the more innovative response to the new phenomena of poverty and exclusion.

'The crisis of the 1970s at one and the same time questioned each of its two constituent aspects and saw the disintegration of the dividing line that these drew between marginal and normal.' The classic clientele of the social services has been replaced by the growth of new forms of vulnerability – populations 'which could not be apprehended by the traditional procedures employed by the social services and which would not put up with guardianship caring methods, not considering themselves marginal either by vocation or constitution but in precarious conditions as a result of the crisis or because of society'. In a similar manner welfare protection has turned out to be ineffective when faced with growing unemployment, above all because of the difficulty in considering the condition as temporary. Thus

> certain methods of welfare assistance have entered into the class of 'welfare protection'. For example unemployment indemnities have increasingly taken on the form of training formulas which are in fact simply forms of psychological support camouflaged to a greater or lesser extent. On the other hand, welfare assistance progressively lost its optional, discretionary and guardianship type characteristics as income support measures of the 'minimum insertion wage' type were gradually introduced. (Donzelot, 1991: 19–20)

The narrowing of the borderline between the two approaches is manifested in what Donzelot calls 'transverse' social policies. The *Dévelopment social de quartier*, with its multidimensional characteristics, involvement of inhabitants and so on would represent a typical example of these. In these policies 'the two operations are unified into one single method, which we may call contractual involvement since it consists of meeting requests or demands by the offer of involvement; the principle of the contractual nature of the action is set against the automatic nature of a right' (Donzelot, 1991: 22).

Obviously, this is not a mere adaptation of policies to new demand, but an 'invention' which also reflects the new historical situation characterized by the crisis of the welfare state (but as an aspect of a more general transformation of the state – see Maclouf, 1992). The battle is being fought over the potentialities of this passage, over the capacity to develop this 'dislocation of the welfare question' positively. The emergence of a 'third type' of welfare indicates that we are not just in the presence of a retreat but also in a situation which is favourable for innovation. There is a considerable capacity to imagine positive new models of collective responsibility, including the technical aspects, to take the place of traditional welfare models. Battle on this front has commenced. It is therefore important to try to grasp, together with the potentialities, also the risks that the innovative formulas, formulas that are alternative to retreat and to strategies of control, may present. In this sense the broad debate on the significance of 'insertion' that has developed in France in relation to the RMI may be useful.[5]

INSERTION

The notion of 'insertion' (social or employment) is at the centre of new policies and is the notion which best expresses the innovative potential of projects for the fight against exclusion. In the debate on the homeless, the idea of (social) insertion has been ascribed to a 'liberal therapeutic' matrix (Wagner, 1993). Certainly its procedural model, the 'contract', comes from neo-liberal thought. It would, however, be reductive to identify as neo-liberal a cultural and political proposal that represents the major project for preventing the fall into dualism and for redesigning the basic notions of citizenship and the principles of social altruism and responsibility that belonged to the welfare state.

Given the semantic uncertainty surrounding the term 'insertion' (Maclouf, 1992: 122 and 128), it may be useful to try to understand the problem by citing some of the elements of the context and the historical situation which to some extent have already been mentioned: the need to deal with 'new profiles of the poor' (Castel and Laé, 1992), and – only partly correlated – the crisis of the welfare state and the transformations of the role of the state. A concise understanding, which usefully also cites the destructuring of the conditions which constituted the context of integration policies, has been proposed by Maclouf (1992: 133): 'the field of insertion is the set of voluntary initiatives, of public or private sector origin, that are designed to bring, in a flexible manner, those categories of persons defined as precarious into a more nebulous society. Whereas in the previous decades integration was the means by which well-defined groups participated in a clearly structured society.'

It is in this context that the innovative points of the new measures, as compared to traditional systems of welfare, should be assessed. They are: (a) the passage, in the portrayal of the beneficiaries of the policies, from the idea of 'recipient' to that of active individuals, 'considered as actors determining their own future', 'encouraged to involve themselves in the development of their insertion or training'

(Maclouf, 1992: 130); and (b) the change of 'sites' in the management of the poor; that is, the passage 'from a problem of managing categories of individuals with handicaps to a problem of territorial management of populations at risk' (Autés, 1992: 93 and 102).

The fundamental 'ambiguity' of the RMI is a perfect illustration of the different value that can be attributed to the notion of insertion.

> The RMI has two great merits: a rejection of sectorial treatment of disadvantaged populations and a refusal to abandon particularly unfortunate categories by playing the card of making insertion for all an imperative. However, if it is true that the populations it benefits are in fact heterogeneous, then the system is perpetually exposed to the risk of falling back into the re-categorization and dualistic functioning that it is intended to replace. (Castel and Laé, 1992: 18–19)

In effect, if 'for a large proportion of the beneficiaries returning to work is a distant prospect' – which is what represents a general structural obstacle to insertion – the different types of recipients will have different chances of returning to work. A classification system that is frequently used by operators goes like this: there are those that can get back into work with a little support, those who are 'away for a considerable time' and those for whom returning to work is unrealistic (Autés, 1992: 112). It is not therefore easy to treat the populations for whom these measures were devised homogeneously. Inserting people back into the world of work takes on a different meaning for different populations.

The distinction/opposition between 'social' insertion and 'work' insertion that marked the parliamentary debate on the setting up of RMI in France and which is commonly used by workers in the sector is crucial to the unveiling of this 'ambiguity'. It is not easy to tell what the relationships of continuity and discontinuity are between these forms and conceptions of insertion. With respect to a paradigm, social insertion is worth 'less' than insertion into work, there is 'a difference in value' (Castel and Laé, 1992). 'It is as if the conception of insertion were driven by the idea that the only true insertion is work and that at the worst, social insertion is a makeshift measure and at best the first stage of vocational insertion.' In this context, the distinction/opposition may contain 'the germs of a principle of division of the beneficiaries into categories' (Autés, 1992: 116 and 101). The opposition between work insertion and social insertion, however, could reveal 'divergent philosophies and the first signs of a break between income and work, and, at a deeper level, another type of definition of citizenship and social relationships in the making'. For this opening, which defines the great horizon of the new policies, it is necessary to 'maintain the tension of the two logics that support them: on the one hand the philosophy of insertion through work and on the other the philosophy of insertion through citizenship' – rather than oppose or order work insertion and social insertion (1992).

CONTRACT

The opposition comes from the meaning of the notion 'contract'. This notion too has a multiplicity of meanings – which again can be considered 'at one and the same time a source of perverse tendencies and rich in guarantees for the future' (Castel and Laé, 1992: 24). There is one idea of contract that comes directly from a conservative version of citizenship and this deserves illustration because it expresses all the risks and the possible reductive implications of the idea of insertion.

> Citizenship has been redefined by the right using the language of obligation and responsibility. In the first place, the obligation to work imposed on the poor with the intention of combating the 'culture of dependence'. In the second place, the 'new model' of citizen who, in the name of self-esteem and of responsibility, must pay for his 'share' of the local/social services. In the third place, the new model of citizen is also an active citizen. (IMI, 1992)

The ideological sense of this interpretation comes from the distance between the high model of relations between individual and society that is represented – founded on the ethic of work and of responsibility, etc. – and a reality of insertion, with the exposure to the risks of precariousness that it involves. The model may be inappropriate and/or difficult to implement and the reality of the effects quite different from those the model portrays.

The conservative and reductionist conception of citizenship may cause direct damage to the welfare content of insertion programmes. Behind these representations there could be 'tolerance of a high threshold of exclusion and marginalization' (Noel, 1991: 192). This would be indicated, as has been said of the RMI in France, by the improbability of the services requested in exchange or at least the different meanings these would have for the different types of recipients that were mentioned, 'the capacity to enter into a contract with an institution is a characteristic of social integration. To ask the recipients of RMI to commit themselves to a contract is in most cases to ask the impossible of them. It is demanding strategies from the excluded that even the upper layers of the population are incapable of, "construct a consistent life-course", "have a career plan" ' (Noel, 1991: 196).[6]

Behind this 'distance' lie images of a wage-earning and working society that are no longer realistic and the subordination of insertion to systemic-based hypotheses. This has led, for example, to the setting up of training as the main answer to unemployment. But this answer does not change the causes of weakness that have made these persons unemployed, nor the fact that if the demand for labour does not increase then training is of little use. On the other hand, as Noel points out (1991: 195), the answers are dominated by the logic of the demand for labour and concern over conflict in society, 'without trying to solve the problem faced by millions of individuals because they are unemployed, poor, excluded. Nobody has really asked what their potentials, their abilities and their aspirations are. No attempt has been made to value them.'

Given this distance and these contradictions, the offer of a contract may in reality mean precarious integration or even – in the dualist logic of differentiated protection – the sanctioning of exclusion itself.

Against this there is the great innovative potential of the notion of insertion and this lies in its 'median and transitory position'. To summarize the point in the words of Castel and Laé, these measures

> are a way of promoting belonging and the future . . . Institutionalizing not-belonging by means of a contract providing access to a right and a contract clearly stating the effort to be made on the part of society provides a positive context that implies a protocol for access to other rights, both in the near and distant future, the terms of which are not defined . . . But the RMI remains a particularistic right because it concerns those that populate this extreme zone of social space in which exclusion from the world of work and relational isolation combine their stigmatizing effects . . . Basically, the opposition between the good poor and the bad poor that we have known for centuries is reactivated by opposition between those whose chances of finding a job are almost intact and those for whom a possible vocation is simply mimed as if, as the probability of work decreases it is replaced by a pseudo legal contract of a permanent waiting list. (1992: 29–30)

The critical point then, concerns the nature of the work that is being spoken of and the social ties that the insertion projects should favour or reconstruct. To continue with Castel and Laé,

> Putting people on a permanent waiting list, but for what job? Our society does not seem mature enough for frank recognition of forms of activity that are not directly connected with productive work. The different value attributed to work insertion and social insertion

translates as this inability to legitimize 'occupations' that do not fit in to
a productive logic. This is where the ambiguity of an insertion contract
arises. (1992: 29–30)

Thus we also run into a cultural limit to the insertion project and at
the same time and once again we appreciate the future prospective
value of one of the two 'philosophies' of insertion, that which alludes to
a possible break between income and work and to new conceptions of
citizenship and social relationships. The debate on RMI has therefore
a general value. It raises questions which do not just concern work
insertion nor just those types of social figures to which RMI policies
are addressed. It does in fact concern the whole question of the
meaning of 'positive' policies aimed at the insertion of disadvantaged
groups.

HOMELESSNESS, 2

When all is said and done, the general key to dealing with the risks
implicit in the new measures is obvious, as Castel (1991: 168) observes
with regard to French legislation on RMI. It is a question of
positioning the insertion policies in a context of broader policies: 'a
twofold social policy – one, mainly preventive, would consist of
controlling areas of vulnerability by means of general measures, while
the other, mainly rehabilitative, would be aimed at reducing areas of
disaffiliation by means of concrete measures of insertion.'

This possibility is not just, however, faced with the difficulties of
implementation given the structural and ideological constraints that I
have mentioned. There is also the problem of designing the measures
according to the different needs of the figures that populate the area of
exclusion. As I have already mentioned, the dualism of the policies
may derive from selective application of the idea of insertion itself.
Selection could be radical; there could be categories of the poor to
whom the hypothesis is not applicable and who as such receive
treatment only in terms of welfare assistance, or in terms of control, as
is 'normal' for gypsies and new immigrants.

The arguments that developed in the debate on RMI are also
applicable to the homeless. What must be specifically added is that the
possible incongruence of 'insertion' and 'contract' formulas may be
greater for the homeless. In effect, putting the emphasis on their
vulnerability, insertion hypotheses tend to accentuate the 'liberal-

therapeutic' approach. This risks producing a double incongruence on the two poles that constitute homelessness. In fact the persons involved are often – as is increasingly frequent with the new figures of the homeless – persons who do not present disabilities nor traits of marginalization to justify the 'therapeutic' aims of insertion projects. On the other hand the disabilities may be such as to make the possibility of insertion doubtful, if it is interpreted according to current models. In fact, the homeless are more probable recipients of mere 'welfare assistance' and control measures.

Work insertion for the homeless is usually dealt with by means of the 'halfway measures' (Jencks, 1994) often employed to deal with vulnerable groups. They are motivated on one side by protectionist considerations, aimed at providing supplementary guarantees for the recipients, and on the other by considerations motivated by 'realism'. But what type of 'realism' is this? Up to what point is it consideration of the capacities and interests of the individuals in question and how much is it, on the other hand, a consideration of the compatibility of the proposals formulated with the 'political' or expenditure 'constraints'? And at what point does 'taking note' of the constraints become in the end a retreat consistent with dualism? Typically these measures may on the one hand be adaptation and strong protection – on the basis of the recognition of needs that are specific and the requirement for supplementary resources to deal with them – while on the other they may be a reduction to 'precarious insertion'. As for the recipients of RMI – but in a more accentuated manner – 'there is a risk of integrating the excluded in semi-protected, precarious and badly paid work. This would involve integration into precariousness which would mean passing from exclusion to the segregation of a dual society' (IMI, 1992).

Here it is more evident how important it is that there be a possibility of offering activity that is not determined in terms of productivity, without this becoming a 'motive' and mechanism for welfare-assisted precariousness. In the debate on insertion, the homeless introduce the subject on behalf – so to speak – of the persons concerned, and this is precisely what in conventional terms is called putting the accent on the 'subjective' vulnerability of the homeless (ideologically on their personal vulnerability). The possible incongruence of a certain idea of (re-)insertion becomes therefore more evident, together with how far-reaching, if the examples of insertion preached in the projects are to be taken seriously, the implications of these formulas may be, 'the employment of poorer "performing" individuals . . . involves a radical change in the development model' (Noel, 1991: 199).

THE HOMELESS, POVERTY AND TERRITORIAL PROCESSES

In order to take another step forward in this reconstruction of the meaning of the problem of the homeless, discussion of the effectiveness of policies must be left, to go back to the subject of the social construction of the problem and the relative policies. It is a question of understanding why the problem of homelessness is so important in the construction of policies and in the conflict over the poor. There are various possible answers to this question, which in various ways relate to the different aspects of social exclusion that are given importance in regard to the homeless: their paradigmatic expression of extreme poverty, their visibility, the strong communication of the risk of exclusion that this 'emergent' part of the problem involves. This explains, for instance, why the subject of homelessness is of strategic importance in the game of redefining social policies after the crisis of the classic welfare state models – the accent on the homeless or on extreme poverty could, for example, mean a reduction in policies, 'cutting out' that of the homeless from wider problems of poverty, housing hardship, etc. Or on the other hand it explains public concern over the subject due to the risk of a 'crisis of legitimization' that the presence of the homeless could feed – 'because it exposes misery in the midst of plenty, and represents alienation from the home in a home-based society'. This would explain the defensive nature of 'neutralization' of the strategies adopted: isolation, concealment, segregation (Marcuse, 1988b).

There is, however, a further reason to be found in the close relationship – almost an identification – between the treatment of the problem of the homeless and the management of its space–territorial aspects. The treatment of the homeless reveals the importance of the space–territory dimension in the construction of social exclusion and the related policies. This takes us back to the relationships between social exclusion and the space–territorial mechanisms that accompany the transition to the post-industrial city (Marcuse herein) – including the interactions of these with policies for the management of territoriality that express all the ambivalence of the new social policies. I will mention only the 'negative' processes: new forms of segregation (gentrification, the growth of 'abandoned' areas, etc.), the strengthening of barriers between areas, the multiplication of actions of territorial control (defence of the neighbourhood), etc. – processes that may find support at a political level both through urban policies that result in favouring segregative mechanisms and by policies of direct control of the territory, for example, expulsion from areas to be protected, etc.

While rationales of control/repression, as far as the homeless are concerned, have not reached the extent nor the harshness and cruelty in Europe as they have in countries like the USA, nevertheless processes and measures of territorial control are applied widely on different categories of the poor (immigrants, nomads) and affect the homeless to a certain extent.

The reference concerning territorial treatment is to the management of the risk implied by social exclusion. The risk may be seen as danger in terms of law and order or as a problem of prevention to stop a situation of risk precipitating into one of exclusion. There are two main spatial circumstances with which risk is associated, the presence of poor in urban public places and the residential concentration of the poor. In the negative representations of exclusion oriented towards control, it is the two things together – exclusion and place – that create the problem, 'supernumeraries' in the 'wrong' places, 'in places where they are neither welcome nor tolerated' (Hopper and Baumohl, 1994: 531).

This negative type of treatment is frequent with the homeless (at least those 'on the streets') – often applied to their presence in public places. Here they are in a category together with the other various types of the poor (immigrants, etc.) towards whom attitudes of rejection are multiplying. This is an expression of a general mechanism: the tendency towards 'restrictive citizenship' and to an abandonment of the universalistic vision of the welfare state is accompanied by the idea of a privileged community. The expulsion of 'outsiders' appears as an obvious implication. Now, in this perspective, community has a strong territorial meaning, as traditional notions of community, and expulsion takes on meanings that are 'naturally' territorial.

For the homeless, as for categories subject to strong rejection, 'negative' territorial measures combine explicitly dissuasive techniques (evictions, etc.) and control of visibility. Here territory is clearly a dimension through which rejection and closure are expressed, and it is clear that control of visibility is a decisive element – as a way of identifying the problem and as an aim of the policies. In the new ideological context, the elimination of the visibility may appear as a solution. Protection of society may become protection from visibility, which in this framework is synonymous with existence, hence all those policies that consist of moving and concealing the problem populations.

Territorial aspects of exclusion are not only employed by proposals and policies that are reductionist in character, but also by those that are positively innovative, where again we find the problem of 'insertion'. There is a specific type of concentration – the 'run-down district', the 'neighbourhood in crisis' – which is subjected to specific policies at the centre of the fight against exclusion in Europe.

Here the innovative components of the new policies are more evident. The local anti-poverty policies (*développement social des quartiers*, rehabilitation of distressed suburban areas, etc.) are targeted at degradation or segregation. As opposed to defensive, segregative policies, exclusion – at least in the best examples – is 'combated', the 'risk' is attacked. Again we meet the new virtuous circles hypothesized by the new policies. In the background there is the grand model of the 1980s European policies for fighting poverty: the local integrated project – holistic, inter-institutional, contractual, participative, etc. (Jacquier, 1991).

Naturally the ambivalence of this model should also be discussed and, as far as its concrete application is concerned, note should be taken of the different versions, looking into the discriminants between the different 'requalification' strategies (see Tosi, 1994). But at least on the level of representations, these local policies develop a genuine counter-model with respect to policies of control, and to the reduction of social policies and dualistic hypotheses. It is a counter-model that is capable of portraying, together with the RMI, the potentials and the possible future of the idea of insertion.

'Territorialize' means '*décloisonner*: removing the barriers created by categorial policies'. It also means new consideration of social ties and new hypotheses of citizenship:

> 'Territorialize' also means multiplying the places for speech, meeting places for social actors and the objects of negotiation. 'Territorialize' means politicizing local spaces in the sense of making them the object of an unceasing democratic debate. It means reviving democracy in the place where it is most necessary, where it makes an appeal to the mobilization of citizens in the fellowship of everyday life: democracy comes from below. (Autés, 1992: 119)

NOTES

1   The concept of housing exclusion is based on a number of assumptions, and has a number of implications (Tosi and Ranci, 1993). In the presence of a phenomenon which is subject to double identification – in terms of the

various social figures of poverty and social marginality, and in terms of the different types of (non) accommodation, – the field is decidedly defined with reference to the latter criterion. Identification of the social figures follows, starting from the accommodation situations. The social figures designated as homeless according to the most common, restrictive, meanings of the term are only specific figures among those in the field. In terms of accommodation, identification is wider with respect to what is suggested by the idea of homelessness in its narrow sense. The field includes, besides (a) persons with no accommodation, roofless, people sleeping rough etc., and (b) people who find shelter through temporary accommodation in institutions or in the private sector, also (c) people who are subject to (substantially) unacceptable housing conditions. Reference to exclusion thus implies the idea of a continuity between the excluded from housing and the badly housed – particularly evident in situations of unsuitable accommodation. At the same time, it is assumed that, however, the distinction between the two concepts should be maintained, even if it may be empirically difficult to distinguish between the two situations. A major theoretical reason for adopting an enlarged view and for assuming continuity between the two areas is the methodological necessity (Avramov, 1994) of shifting the focus from 'situation' to 'process', and from 'actual exclusion' to the 'risk of exclusion'. Given these relationships, assumptions about homelessness as the 'result' of poverty, or of social marginality, or of lack of affordable housing etc. are untenable. Instead, the heterogeneity is recognized of the problem of homelessness – the variety of figures and processes constituting it, and the impossibility of reducing the problem to any single explanation.

2 'Independently of why people are on the street, giving them a place which offers a minimum of privacy and of stability is usually the most important thing that we can do to improve their lives. Without stable housing nothing else can improve easily' (Jencks, 1994: 107).

3 'Unemployment is not an accident, but a decision a society makes to deal with a period of economic uncertainty and difficulty by excluding some of its members' (Noel, 1991: 199). 'Everywhere in Europe, the increased flexibility of the labour market, the privatization of public sector organizations and restructuring carried out in the name of competition has reduced consumption and increased inequalities. Nevertheless, this is the defeatist strategy that governments wish to employ', by also translating it into the field of social policies with proposals to eliminate the minimum wage, reduce social services, etc. (Halimi, 1994).

4 For analysis of the differences between national models in terms of political and cultural construction see Silver herein.

5 Set up in France in 1988, the RMI (*Revenue Minimum d'Insertion* – Minimum Insertion Wage) is a mechanism for ensuring a minimum wage to the most disadvantaged sectors of society. With financial assistance, it involves the stipulation of 'insertion contracts', that is, it provides support to make up the 'integration deficit', providing people in difficulty with a means that

enables them to avoid exclusion and to return to being normal members of society (see Castel and Laé, 1992).

6   'As far as I am concerned,' J. F. Noel added, 'I have a university education, 20 years of professional career, a totally chaotic life path and no plans for more than a year ahead. What about you?' (1991: 196).

5

Culture, Politics and National Discourses of the New Urban Poverty

Hilary Silver, Brown University, Providence

A decent provision for the poor is the true test of a civilization.

Dr Samuel Johnson

Renaming a social problem often designates a qualitative break with the past. Historically, new vocabularies distinguishing among the socially disadvantaged coincided with important social, economic and political transitions and with changes in provisions for the poor. For example, the ideas of 'poverty' and 'unemployment' were transformed by the 'moral imagination', redefining the central social problems associated with two great social transformations and addressed with new types of social policy (Himmelfarb, 1984; Patterson, 1981; Katz, 1993, 1989; Topalov, 1994). Today, the languages used in twentieth-century political struggles to institute and extend Western welfare states are again being superceded. Global economic restructuring appears associated with a 'new poverty' – at once persistent, urban and group based – in the advanced capitalist democracies of the West.[1]

Yet, it is still unclear what this new poverty shall be called. Different countries use different terminology. In France, new poverty discourse centres on the term 'exclusion', which 'has become in official language the social question *par excellence*' (Castel, 1995: 426). However, as the EC Commission (1992: 32) noted, national debates emphasize some aspects of 'exclusion' over others. If the term 'exclusion' is increasingly used in Britain and the US, its usages and meanings are different from those in France. Furthermore, there seems to be a consensus – both in France (Weimberg and Ruano-Borbalan, 1993; Nasse, 1992) and beyond (EC Commission, 1992: 10; Abou Sada et al., 1994) – that 'social exclusion' has many meanings, and so is difficult to define. In some respects, it is an 'essentially contested concept', an appraisive and complex notion open in meaning, explicable in terms of its parts, and inevitably involving endless disputes when it is used (Gallie, 1956). Selecting among the various meanings of 'exclusion' will necessarily entail the adoption of particular values and world-views (Silver, 1994).

Indeed, political and intellectual debates in all three national settings imbue new poverty rhetorics, often intentionally, with contested nuances. While 'exclusion' discourse dominates in France, the notion of an 'underclass' is prevalent in American discourse. Yet within the US, the 'underclass' takes on different connotations depending upon the political ideology of the person using the term. Although one finds references to 'the underclass' in Britain and France, few politicians use it. Rather, British and French intellectuals use the term somewhat differently than Americans. Why do poverty discourses tend to be nationally specific? This chapter offers three interrelated explanations: one historical, the second comparative and the third political.

NATIONAL PARADIGMS OF POVERTY DISCOURSE

Why do French politicians and intellectuals speak more about 'exclusion' while those in 'Anglo-Saxon' countries refer to the 'underclass'? One obvious possibility is that the 'new poverty' really is different in France than in the US and the UK. Considerable research has documented national differences in the extent and nature of poverty, inequality, long-term unemployment and other quantitative indicators of disadvantage. Comparing the three countries considered here, there appears to be some trade-off between unemployment and incomes, with the former worst in France and the latter worst in the US (for example, Freeman, 1994; OECD, 1993; Smeeding et al., 1990). Poverty and income inequality rose in all three countries but at different rates, partly reflecting differences in state redistributive efforts (Green, Coder and Ryscavage, 1991; O'Higgins, Schmaus and Stephenson, 1990; Castles and Mitchell, 1991). Wage inequality and wage differentials by skill also rose more in countries with more decentralized labour markets and wage-setting systems, especially the

US and UK (Freeman and Katz, 1994; Deakin and Wilkinson, 1991; OECD, 1993). Thus, it might be expected that the 'new poverty' will be discussed in different terms where it has different manifestations.

However, that real national differences partly correspond to different policy interventions suggests that politics plays a role in creating these empirical conditions. Thus, even if poverty itself influences discourse about it, the causality may also run the other way. To be sure, renaming the new poverty is unlikely to make it disappear, as governments in all three countries discovered after redefining social statistics during the last decade. But reducing the new poverty will still require political action to enact new social and economic policies. Poverty discourse is central to the symbolic politics that make such changes possible.

A second plausible explanation for national differences is conjunctural. During the 1980s when the new poverty was identified, the Socialists were in power in France while the Republicans controlled the White House and the Conservatives governed Great Britain. However, even discounting the spells of 'cohabitation' in France and Democratic congresses in the US, partisan dominance cannot explain why the opposition in these countries also adopted terms like 'exclusion' and the 'underclass'. For that, national patterns of symbolic politics must be examined.

Names for the new poor are best understood in the context of conflicting paradigms of national identity, political ideology and social science. A paradigm is 'a constellation of beliefs, values, techniques, and so on shared by the members of a given community' (Kuhn, 1970: 175). Paradigms 'specify not only what sorts of entities the universe does contain, but also, by implication, those that it does not' (p. 7). Because they are taken for granted, national 'paradigms' rule things in and out of political debate. They are ontologies that render reality comprehensible and mingle elements of what 'is' and 'ought' to be. Paradigms also provide criteria for choosing problems that are assumed to have solutions (p. 37). Accordingly, poverty discourses provide an implicit explanation of social reality, a theory of a social problem's causes. Depending upon the paradigm in which they are embedded, poverty discourses attribute responsibility for the problem and shape the policy agenda.

Paradigms help explain – that is, render meaningful – differences across countries in new poverty discourses. In particular, political cultures, those historically grounded symbols and meanings that order the life of the community or nation-state as a whole (Hunter, 1991), contain two types of paradigms useful in interpreting national poverty discourse. First, poverty discourse assumes a distinctive national cast partly because it invokes paradigms of citizenship and nationhood. It draws upon a particular cultural heritage and political history, however 'imagined' or 'invented' that tradition may be (Hobsbawm and Ranger, 1983; Anderson, 1991). Since poverty is a condition that potentially divides national societies, poverty discourse appeals to pre-existing socially constructed formulas of national unity. The 'excluded' and the 'underclass' can be understood in relation to the assumptions underlying what it means to be American, British or French. Second, new poverty discourse is nationally specific because 'old' poverty discourse was too. The terms under which the working class was politically incorporated and the rhetoric justifying earlier social policies vary cross-nationally and impart cultural continuity to contemporary discussions of poverty. 'Ways of understanding the new situation necessarily draw on traditional languages and tools of comprehension' (Katznelson, 1992: 296). However, the historical memory brought to bear on new terms is selective; symbolic interpretations of new social conditions may entail a 'rewriting' of history (Topalov, 1994). The variable meaning of terms for the new poverty thus offers a window on political cultures in general.

Political cultures cut across party ideology 'to express common (though contested) aspirations regarding the management of state and nation'; they implicitly guide 'politicians both in defining policy problems and in selecting appropriate solutions' (Smith, 1989: 107). Culture serves as an institutionalized, historically accumulated 'toolbox' that both renders shared reality comprehensible and within which discourses are politically contested (Wittgenstein, 1958). However, highlighting the national specificity of new poverty terminology is not to suggest something 'essentialist' or unchanging about national cultures. Nor is it to claim that cultural categories are themselves sufficient causes of poverty. If discourse reflects deeper national patterns and cultural rules, the construction of new social realities is still contested. Terms for the new poverty are symbolic resources in political conflicts which may result in social change.

While the social construction of new poverty discourses tends to be nationally specific, terms like 'underclass' and 'exclusion' are used in many national contexts. However, when a poverty discourse is imported, it acquires different connotations consistent with national cultures, histories and ongoing symbolic conflicts. Thus, while social scientists have devoted considerable effort to defining and measuring terms like 'exclusion' and 'underclass', their very ambiguity is of interest here. The same term may connote different things in different political cultures.

Historically grounded cultural explanations do not conform to strict causal logics. It is difficult to explain a change, say, the rise of a new poverty discourse, with something as enduring as culture. Rather, culture identifies a relatively permanent 'boundary condition' that constrains behaviour and belief by defining possible alternatives *within* a given cultural context (Greenstone, 1993). Such cultural explanations can pursue at least two strategies. One is *comparative* analysis, examining how different national cultures address similar realities. Contrasting political cultures or national 'paradigms' help explain the predominance of one new poverty discourse over another. Because conceptions of social belonging vary across nation-states, terms which might be translated the same or have the same general object take on discrete nuances, meanings and practical references in different countries (Miles, 1992: 19). The second approach is *political* analysis of conflicts within the bounds of a culture. Deconstructing names for the new poverty illuminates real symbolic politics in a way that goes beyond the now-conventional observation that ideas are interested. Although few today would deny that terms like the 'underclass' are value-laden (Gans, 1991; Morris, 1989), poverty discourses are not easily predicted from the social positions of those using them. Rather, the same discourse may have contested interpretations in the same national context, depending upon contending political ideologies. Political analysis reveals the meaning of poverty terminology for political actors within each national context.

This chapter argues that national paradigms and political cultures associate names for the 'new poverty' with other ideological 'keywords' (Williams, 1976). For example, 'exclusion' rhetoric is dominant in France partly because the term's connotations derive from the dominant French Republican ideology of *solidarisme*. When the term is used outside France, its meanings change. In contrast, the term 'underclass' is embedded in liberal and conservative ideologies of citizenship, consciously rejected by French Republicans, that historically helped legitimate many aspects of British and especially American social policies. American poverty discourse takes place within liberal ideological parameters, pitting Lockean *laissez-faire* liberals against communitarians. However, both France and Britain, unlike the US, also have a tradition of working-class politics that provided a social democratic justification for welfare state institutions. Accordingly, social democratic conceptions of the 'underclass' and 'exclusion' impart contested nuances to these terms, particularly with a rhetoric of social rights that resonates with a significant segment of the British and French, but not the American, public (see table 5.1).

Table 5.1   National comparison of ideological influences on new poverty discourses

	France	*USA*	*Britain*
Republican	dominant	minor	weak
Social democracy	minor	weak	dominant
Liberalism	weak	dominant	dominant

'Claimsmakers' frame new social problems by selectively drawing upon national paradigms and political cultures (Stafford and Ladner, 1990; Best, 1995). Politicians, intellectuals and the media choose from the repositories of national symbols and values those metaphors that legitimized earlier social policies to render new social realities comprehensible and to win support for new initiatives. This is well illustrated with the names of social policies designed to combat the new poverty. In France, these policies often have the terms 'insertion', 'integration', 'cohesion,' and 'solidarity' in their titles. British and American policies often refer to 'enterprise' and 'community'. 'Citizenship' is also invoked in the UK. Indeed, new poverty discourse becomes intelligible when contrasted with national paradigms of collective responsibility and integration.

REPUBLICAN SOLIDARISM AND FRENCH EXCLUSION DISCOURSE

The dominance of 'social exclusion' in French poverty discourse is intelligible in the context of Republican ideology. In official parlance, 'exclusion' is a 'rupture of the social bond' of 'solidarity'. This prototypical definition of 'social exclusion' can be found in the publications of the Commissariat Général du Plan (CGP) which has recognized the state's responsibility to nourish 'social cohesion' (Fragonard, 1993; CGP, 1992; Nasse, 1992; Foucauld, 1992a, b). 'Solidarity' is a distinctive notion of national integration that, after a century of political upheaval, helped legitimate the Third Republic (Ashford, 1986: 48) and, after the hiatus around the Second World War, the Fifth Republic's reconstructed institutions (Gaffney, 1991). Although some now speak of a crisis of Republican ideology and institutions, its values are shared by the wide centre of the French political spectrum (Hoffman, 1963; Hollifield, 1994; Mendras and Cooke, 1991).

Republicans sought a 'third way', reconciling socialism and state responsibility with liberal and humanist concerns for individual rights and fulfilment. In contrast with Lockean liberal or 'Anglo-Saxon' notions of the social contract based on political or market relations, Rousseau, Durkheim and other French thinkers emphasized a specifically 'social bond' (*lien social*) between the state and the poor (Farrugia, 1993). 'Solidarity' comes from society, which precedes the individual, thus justifying social protection policies. To achieve social integration, Republican solidarists, like Leon Bourgeois, attached great importance to cultural and moral as well as political and economic criteria of citizenship (Nicolet, 1982; Berstein and Rudell, 1992; Roy, 1991; Procacci, 1993; Ruano-Borbalan, 1993). They drew upon Revolutionary rhetoric about equality and fraternity and nineteenth-century working-class mutualism to incorporate the working class politically and to develop a rational, secular morality of rights and duties underlying the French welfare state (Hatzfeld, 1989; Chevalier, 1984).

Indeed, the expression *l'Etat Providence* (welfare state) suggests how a laic state displaced the church in social provision. French Republicans were less concerned than American and British liberals about checking government power. Pressured from both political extremes by preindustrial and emerging industrial social forces, French liberals were predominantly state-building reformists (Ashford, 1986: 79). Flanked on their right, French Republicans stressed public assistance over private, mostly Catholic charity and developed aggressively civic and laic Republican institutions. Since reactionary conservatism threatened the Republic, liberals and conservatives did not join political forces over time as they did in Britain and the US. Indeed, throughout the twentieth century, Republicans have periodically struggled with an *intégriste* (organic), racist–chauvinistic (xenophobic, anti-Semitic) and cultural (Catholic) counter-conception of citizenship whose anti-Republican rhetoric of the 'dangerous classes' – as violent, uncivilized, unassimilable, dependent on the state, and segregated in 'ghettos' (Guillaumin, 1991) – referred, in turn, to communists, European immigrants and, today, third world migrant workers (Chevalier, 1984; Balibar, 1991a; Noiriel, 1988; Ruano-Borbalan, 1993). Indeed, the *Front National* prefers a discourse of 'immigration' to one of 'exclusion', one that has occasionally pressured right- and left-wing parties into 'Republican Front' alliances.

Yet French Republicans see a tension between segmental institutions, subcultural pluralism and particularism, on the one hand, and national unity and the common good, on the other. The Revolution abolished the feudal *corps intermédiaires*; the Republic later defined voluntary associations as *établissements publics*, submitting them to state regulation (Ashford, 1986; Rosanvallon, 1992). Whereas American and British liberals consider mediating institutions like voluntary associations, churches and subcultures to be private and free from state interference, the universalist, centralized, egalitarian, laic, assimilationist and unitary French state defends the superior interests of the nation – the general will – as against those of communes, religions and ethnic groups which are not constitutive of the nation (Nicolet, 1982). At the turn of the century, the state incorporated immigrants and the poor into the working class and the nation as citizens, but did not assign a positive role to cultural minorities (Chevalier, 1984; Balibar, 1991a; Noiriel, 1988). Indeed, while French sociology has well-developed theories of social classes and movements, it lacks a theory of group relations or of society as comprised of groups (Touraine, 1990; Body-Gendrot, 1993).

Compared to the liberal stress on rights in the American Declaration of Independence, France's Declaration of the Rights of Man and the Citizen placed more emphasis on the duties of citizens. Under *les moeurs republicaines*, individual citizens are less bearers of rights than participants in a communal 'civility', a public life of fraternity (Rosanvallon, 1992). The schools, the army and other Republican institutions actively 'assimilate' cultures into a single, distinctive conception of citizenship and national civilization. Such moral unity and equality also demands laicity. Thus, in France, 'pluralism' is often conflated with an 'Anglo-Saxon' model of 'multiculturalism', most recently, in conflicts over Islam and ethnicity (Barrou, 1993; Hollifield, 1994). Since Republicanism gave the French a strong sense of who is included in the nation, it is not surprising that the term 'exclusion' has a special resonance in France. In Paul-Marie de la Gorce's words, *les exclus* are the 'pariahs of the nation'.

France's distinctively Republican poverty discourse not only drew selectively on liberal and conservative themes, but also on socialist thought. Such a history makes clear why France, unlike the US and Britain, never demarcated a clear boundary between the working and 'dangerous' classes (Touraine, 1991; but see Chevalier, 1984). 'Pauperization' was largely considered a 'working-class' problem, reflecting industrialization and an unequal division of the social product. As the working class was politically incorporated through recognized representatives, parties and unions claimed to speak for the working poor. Thus, during the *Trente Glorieuses* of full employment, one heard more about social 'inequality', 'unemployment' and 'low pay' than about 'poverty'. The term 'poverty' mainly designated the low standard of living of the unskilled *couches populaires* or an urban, spatial or housing problem confined to the slum dwellers of the *bidonvilles* and *cités d'urgence* (Paugam, 1993). Catholic radicals, like Abbé Pièrre and Père Joseph Wresinski, who founded France's homeless movements, assisted the small 'subproletariat'. Except for the extreme right, 'the poor' never became a distinct stigmatized social group in France.

The term 'poverty' was rarely used in political discourse because it had a pejorative, paternalist, even reactionary connotation incompatible with Republican citizenship. Before 1980, there was 'no poverty debate in France, no major poverty lobby, let alone any official anti-poverty programme' (Sinfield, 1980: 93). Before 1988, the country had no official poverty line, not to mention a universal minimum income (Paugam, 1993). Even today, there is no consensus about how to count the 'excluded' (Castaing, 1995b). In sum, French politicians, officialdom and academia largely neglected the subject of poverty as such until the last decade. Instead, politicians, activists, officials and journalists referred to the poor in vague terms. One of these was *les exclus*.[2]

It was not until the economic recovery of the late 1970s that 'exclusion' was identified as the social problem of the new poverty. The 'excluded' became *les oubliés de la croissance* (Stoleru, 1977; Donzelot and Roman, 1991). By the mid-1980s, both the right and the communist opposition blamed the Socialist government for rising unemployment, inequality and what they called 'the new poverty' (Paugam, 1993). In response to the opposition's discourse and fearful of losing the new middle classes to the New Left parties, the Socialist government reached back to the older discourse of 'solidarity' (Jensen, 1991). The term 'exclusion' referred both to the rise in long-term and recurrent unemployment and the growing instability of social relations (*liens*): family breakup, single-member households, social isolation, and the decline of class solidarity based on unions, workplaces and the working-class neighbourhood and social networks. It encompassed not only material but spiritual and symbolic aspects long emphasized by the New Left. Exclusion was seen as a rupture of the social and symbolic bonds that should attach individuals to the society (Xiberras, 1992). But if 'exclusion' conflicts with the ideals of 'integration', 'cohesion' or 'solidarity', the dynamic process of achieving these goals is called 'insertion'. Insertion is as difficult to define as exclusion.[3] It usually implies making room beside others, placing side by side, or making a space for oneself (Nasse, 1992; Body-Gendrot, 1993: 88). It regulates the *lien social* and responds to threats to 'social cohesion' (Paugam, 1993). Illustrating the Republican mix of liberal and socialist ideas, one observer defined insertion as 'the dynamic process by which an individual in a situation of exclusion acquires and finds a recognized place in the heart of the society while internalizing the social functions whose mastery ensures autonomy' (Delahaye, 1994: 245).

In France, 'exclusion' is addressed with 'insertion' policies, like the widely popular guaranteed minimum income, *Revenu Minimum d'Insertion.* Whereas narrowly economic American and British 'workfare' tries to change individual behaviour, RMI recipients must agree to an 'insertion' project of 'social utility' ranging from a job to participating in local associations. Unlike the 'Anglo-Saxon vision of insertion based on levels of consumption' (Delahaye, 1994: 265), insertion into a workgroup or local *cité* benefits both the society and the unemployed individual. Rather than passively receive benefits, the excluded actively construct solidarity.

Presidential candidates of both the Republican right and the left strongly support the RMI and the battle against exclusion. Indeed, both Mitterand and Chirac financed insertion programmes with a dedicated surcharge, the 'solidarity tax on fortunes' of the rich. Similarly, both right and left governments have raised minimum wages since 1981. France's tax and transfer programmes are not only consensual, but more effective in redistributing income than those in Britain or the US (O'Higgins, Schmaus and Stephenson, 1990; Castles and Mitchell, 1991). Thus, a 'welfare reform' like that currently contemplated by the American Congress is unthinkable in contemporary France. For example, when in 1991, Jacques Chirac commiserated with a French worker about 'the noise and the stink' of an African immigrant with 'three or four wives, twenty kids, who gets 50,000 francs in social transfers without working', he evoked a theme reminiscent of Reagan's 'welfare queen' and Thatcher's 'scroungers' on the dole. However, his remarks were almost unanimously condemned as factually false and racist. Appeals linking welfare, minorities and deviance run up against the limits of the distinctively French Republican consensus. Since social policies are widely supported and racial codewords are hallmarks of the French extreme right, it becomes clear why the French have avoided the term 'underclass' and use 'social exclusion' instead.

Contesting Republican Exclusion Discourse

Although Republican conceptions of exclusion dominate in France, they are not the only ones. Even within France, it is difficult to provide a simple definition of exclusion because its meaning is contested in symbolic politics. When ideological paradigms conflict, practitioners speak from 'incommensurable viewpoints' and use the same language to mean different things.

At the non-Republican extremes of the political spectrum, exclusion discourse is rejected altogether. For example, the FN won considerable support after 1983 by linking immigration to the conservative populist issues of crime (*insécurité*) and national identity. With anti-immigrant rhetoric drawing on the multicultural theme of a *droit à la différence* (see Silverman, 1992; Balibar, 1992), Le Pen has pressured the Gaullist RPR to take more radical positions on immigration in order to prevent their voters from defecting to the FN (Brubaker, 1992). On the far left, many French intellectuals also reject the term 'exclusion' as an official category of the political class and an ideological 'subterfuge, a way of escaping analysis' (Baudrillard, 1970–95). Both Castel (1995: 442–3) and Balibar (1992: 156) caution against the term 'exclusion' because 'no one is outside the society.' Those excluded from the market have nowhere else to go, and immigrants are already integrated into French social structures. Exclusion discourse evades class conflict, unemployment and exclusion from citizenship (Jensen, 1991; Verdes-Leroux, 1978).

However, symbolic politics *within* the Republican 'universe of political discourse' (Jensen, 1991) imbues the term 'exclusion' with different meanings. Political actors carve out constituencies by using a consensual term to represent an alternative interpretation of reality. If it is difficult to be in favour of exclusion, there is disagreement about its dimensions, causes and policy implications. For example, the new egalitarian and multicultural urban social movements of the New Left adopted an 'exclusion' discourse with different connotations. Although they oppose both the FN and the Republican parties, these movements are not strictly social democratic in that they speak less about social class than self-determination, human rights, and 'social action' for greater equality, political empowerment and a more tolerant, pluralistic, multicultural notion of French citizenship.

As successive social and political crises erupted in France during the 1980s, the meanings of exclusion and insertion expanded to encompass new social groups and problems, giving rise to its diffuse connotations (Paugam, 1993; Nasse, 1992). First, in the early 1980s, 'insertion' policies shifted from a focus on the handicapped to 'youth in difficulty' (Nicole-Drancourt, 1991). Since then, young people, who are disproportionately unemployed in France, have held periodic demonstrations. Second, primarily cultural associations of young *beurs*, second generation North African immigrants from the housing projects of the *banlieues*, marched for a full, civic citizenship tied to residence (Body-Gendrot, 1993: 88).[4] Since 1985, nationwide movements, like SOS-racisme and France Plus, also mobilized mass anti-racist demonstrations in reaction to the FN. These groups felt 'excluded' not only from the 'France for the French' envisaged by the *Front National*, but also from universalist and nationalist Republican formulations of solidarity, citizenship and civic life (Mothé, 1991; Roy, 1991; Genestier, 1991; Etienne, 1987; Silverman, 1992). By the early 1990s, as a controversy arose over whether Muslim girls could wear a *foulard* in the laic state schools, the Republic was forced to re-examine its universalistic, assimilationist conception of immigrant 'integration' (Barrou, 1993; Body-Gendrot, 1993; Schnapper, 1991). The Haut Conseil à l'intégration (1991) developed an official immigrant 'integration' policy which retained the principal elements of Republican solidarity discourse, but sought an uneasy conciliation with multicultural meanings of integration demanded by immigrants, *beurs* and other social movements of the 'excluded'.

After a series of violent incidents on suburban housing estates, 'exclusion' discourse also encompassed the issue of the *banlieues*.[5] The interrelated rhetorics of immigrant integration, youth problems and economic exclusion became spatially fixed and deracialized. Although public discourse contained ominous evocations of 'the Bronx', 'ghettos' and violent American cities, equating the petty delinquency and minor disrepair of the French suburbs to problems in the racially and socio-economically homogeneous American ghettos was clearly hyperbolic.[6] Nevertheless, to combat 'urban exclusion', the socialists introduced numerous social and housing programmes with names invoking Republican *solidarité* and culminating in 1991 in a full-fledged Ministère de la Ville (see Linhart, 1992). Fighting 'exclusion' by targeting social policies on non-cultural categories like *cités* or *quartiers défavorisés* was perfectly consistent with Republican ideology.

Thus, symbolic politics expanded the many connotations of 'exclusion' in French public discourse. Indeed, the various New Left movements that held independent demonstrations during the 1980s – homeless activists, the unemployed, *banlieusards*, *beurs*, immigrant anti-racist associations, women's organizations, as well as unions and relatively privileged students – have recently built coalitions (for example, *Alerte, DAL, Droits*) and now demonstrate together against all forms of 'exclusion' (Castaing, 1994, 1995a).

Exclusion Discourse in the US

The embeddedness of new poverty discourse in national paradigms or political cultures becomes clearer when considering 'imported' poverty discourse. Three patterns are apparent. First, a term may be directly incorporated into national poverty discourse. Second, foreign terms may be used to contrast national situations, highlighting something distinctive about poverty in one's own nation. Or finally, and most frequently, a term may be used selectively, highlighting only some of the nuances or connotations it has elsewhere.

The term 'exclusion' is rarely used in American poverty discourse, strictly speaking. Although a few social democratic and communitarian intellectuals use the term like their British counterparts (Katz, 1989; Walzer, 1990; Goldberg, 1993), Americans on both sides of the political spectrum use 'exclusion' and 'inclusion' more metaphorically than ideologically (for example, Tucker, 1990; Weir, 1993).

Moreover, rare usages of the term almost always carry a racial connotation. Most commonly, Americans use it as an adjective, as in 'exclusionary zoning'. Very recently, the term 'exclusion' became central to affirmative action discourse (for example, Mills, 1995; Turner, 1995: 11; Williams, 1995). For example, Clinton argued that affirmative action addresses 'the systematic exclusion of individuals of talent' (Klein, 1995). Americans find it difficult to grasp the non-racial dimensions of social exclusion found in French poverty discourse. Even attempts to convey the French understanding of exclusion Americanizes it in the translation. For example, a newspaper article about the 1995 French presidential elections explained: ' "Les exclus" (the excluded) is what the French call the three million or more unemployed who with their children form a growing underclass, without hope of training or work' (Lewis, 1995: 4).

President Clinton also conflated the term with the 'underclass' giving it negative racial and urban connotations. Promoting his 'crime bill', he remarked about urban gangs, 'It's not an underclass anymore, it's an outer class.'

To appreciate Clinton's exclusion discourse, the term needs to be contrasted not with 'solidarity' but with 'community'. As a 'New Democrat,' E. J. Dionne observed, Clinton drew upon 'ideas variously classified as communitarian, social democratic, and small-r republican.' His 'New Covenant' tried to balance individualism and obligation, private lives and the public realm of citizenship (Elshtain, 1993: 122). When Clinton proclaimed that 'we have to rebuild the bonds of society' with 'community development banks' and 'empowerment zones', he referred not to *liens socials* between citizens and the state, but rather, to a revitalized 'civil society' – 'parents, churches and community groups and private business people and people at the local level' (*New York Times*, 22 October 1994).

American Republicanism, unchallenged by socialism, mutualism and left Catholicism as in France, has always been more liberal. American political culture is bounded by a *genus liberalism* – belief in private property, liberty or individual rights, and government by consent (Greenstone, 1993). Lockean 'humanist liberalism', which stresses negative liberty and instrumentalism, has dominated American political ideology and accounts for Americans' exceptionally underdeveloped welfare state and lack of class consciousness (Hartz, 1955). In contrast, a contending 'reform liberalism' emphasized positive liberties and the duty to develop oneself and to help others do so as well. Yet, it prescribed no vision of the good society nor charged the state with diffusing an official national culture. Unlike the French *patrie* with its intolerance of competing cultural loyalties, American national identity is 'nonexclusive', impersonal, anonymous and interested (Walzer, 1990).

Constitutional constraints on the state guarantee absolute, individual and unqualified rights, create an inclusive political framework for group co-existence and leave moral questions to active, virtuous citizens to work out in a pluralistic civil society (Greenstone, 1993; Glendon, 1991: 11–13).

Recently, American 'communitarians' have sought to resurrect the minoritarian 'civic republican' stream of American thought (Wolfe, 1989; Bellah et al., 1985; Taylor, 1995; *The Economist*, 1995). To overcome classical liberalism's excessive individualism, they call for mutual co-operation in private mediating institutions and voluntary associations to reinvigorate community sentiment, shared identities and meanings, and social cohesion (Mulhall and Swift, 1992). But communitarians also reject the 'Jacobin model' because it overemphasizes the civic, public sphere, banalizing real felt differences in the civil, private sphere (Taylor, 1995). American exclusion discourse thus takes on communitarian, not solidaristic connotations.

Exclusion Discourse in Great Britain

Whereas exclusion discourse is dominant in France and minoritarian in the US, 'there cannot in any real sense be said to have been a general debate concerned with "social exclusion" in the UK' (Room et al., 1992: (33–5). One reason British politicians rarely refer to 'exclusion' is that, while communitarianism has recently become popular in Britain, counterparts of Republican ideology had very little influence there. The few intellectuals using the term 'exclusion' usually acknowledge the influence of EU policy or European academic thought, particularly about immigration and race relations. Yet, 'exclusion' still changes meaning in translation. British concerns replace French solidarist connotations. In particular, exclusion is adapted to social democratic conceptions of the new poverty as class related. 'Solidarity' becomes 'citizenship'.

The preoccupation of British intellectuals with social class is not surprising, given the fact that British partisan struggle has tradition-ally been class oriented and centred on the extension of the welfare state. The Labour Party sought to represent the poor and unemployed as part of the working class. More recently, however, Labour has downplayed the discourse of class conflict and reached back to the inclusive rhetoric of citizenship. The social democratic formulation of citizenship as 'full and equal participation in the community' draws explicitly upon T. H. Marshall's (1950) classic formulation (see Klausen, 1995). The progressive extension of civil, then political, and finally social rights bestows equal status, making citizenship the basis of social integration in inherently conflictual capitalist societies. Although political equality, especially the franchise, serves to temper market and status inequalities, Marshall feared it may also legitimate them. Only the extension of full *social* citizenship through a redistributive welfare state could moderate economic inequality, 'abate' class differences and elevate the status of workers and their families. T. H. Marshall's 'vision of welfare as a fundamental right of citizenship was shared (to varying extents) by Butler, Beveridge and Bevan and provided the foundation upon which Britain's welfare state was constructed' (Smith, 1989: 175).

Yet, for Marshall, equality of citizenship rests on a shared social heritage, 'a direct sense of community membership based on loyalty to a civilization which is a common possession' (1950: 93). That this model originated in relatively homogeneous Britain and is most popular in the socially homogeneous nation-states of western Europe should not be neglected.

When British social scientists use the term 'exclusion' in discussions of poverty, reference is almost invariably to exclusion from Marshall's three dimensions of citizenship (Lister, 1990; Golding, 1986). Some scholarly analyses of the 'underclass' have also adopted the Marshal-lian understanding of the term 'exclusion' (Dahrendorf, 1985; Schmitter-Heisler, 1991). But while the idea of social class underlies this British exclusion discourse, it is sometimes defined in Weberian, rather than Marxist terms (Morris, 1994). Like Marshall's citizenship, Weber's conception of social closure (Parkin, 1974; Murphy, 1988; Rex, 1988) has facilitated easy movement between usages of the terms 'underclass' and 'exclusion'.

Whereas social class is a central concept in social democracy, the

Labour Party and British intellectuals have just begun to adjust to increasing diversity in styles of life and cultural values (Harris, 1987). Political challenges posed by immigrant minorities have called dominant constructions of national identity into question. Much as French Republicans rejected the 'Anglo-Saxon' model, notions of 'Britishness', 'Englishness' and the Commonwealth were constructed primarily in opposition to continental Europe and to France in particular (Kumar, 1994; Anderson, 1991; Colls and Dodd, 1986; Samuel, 1989). During the 1930s, to deal with anti-Semitism, Labour developed its own discourse of 'Britishness' as a 'political community' (Knowles, 1992). Yet Conservative and Labour ideologies remained 'predominantly class-derived, and usually account for racial phenomena by making use of existing formulae developed over many years in response to class demands' (Reeves, 1983: 247).

This lack of emphasis on 'race' in favour of class in public discourse, politics and social policy led most British analysts to import racial theories from abroad. Until recently, they drew extensively upon American race relations models and neglected European concerns like the history of immigration and the politics of racism (Miles, 1993: 11, 27; Solomos, 1993: 24). Europeans, it is said, examine 'the processes by which minority communities and migrant workers are often excluded from equal access to political institutions and are denied basic social and economic rights' (Solomos, 1993: 30). Thus, British scholars are now importing exclusion discourse from Europe to address racial inequality as well as poverty. However, they are borrowing selectively from social democratic and leftist, rather than Republican conceptions of the term, and highlighting national similarities. Rather than contrast exclusion to solidarity or community, they oppose it to 'citizenship'. For example, British racial segregation 'symbolizes black people's exclusion from some fundamental rights of citizenship': civil, political and social (Smith, 1989: 144). While often sensitive to French cultural particularism, British comparative analyses emphasize the commonalities between the French idea of the 'nation' and the British category of 'race' by stressing the tension between 'inclusive' egalitarian universalism and 'exclusionary' hierarchical cultural differentialism (Silverman, 1992). British sociologists still conceive of 'race' as an ideological dimension of class struggle differentiating groups of workers and permitting super-exploitation of minority 'racialized class fractions'. Miles (1993: 18), like Balibar, takes the view, 'there is a predominant class logic to the structure of exclusion, and racism is a secondary and contingent (although not unimportant) determinant.' In sum, British exclusion discourse has social democratic, class-based connotations.

LIBERALISM AND UNDERCLASS DISCOURSE

So many have noted that 'underclass' discourse resonates with nineteenth-century Victorian images of the poor – vagabonds, paupers, outcasts, inefficients and the dangerous classes – as well as relating to the 1960s 'culture of poverty' debate, that it seems unnecessary to expand on the point.[7] These accounts emphasize national continuity in stigmatized conceptions of poverty. For over a century, one can discern a process of 'word substitution' to describe the deviant, disreputable poor and those who, regardless of economic growth, worked intermittently or were unemployed over the long term. This discourse is grounded in liberalism, an ideology that has long shaped American and British conceptions of poverty and the social policies addressing it. Underclass discourse becomes intelligible when contrasted with three central liberal keywords: 'self-reliance', 'opportunity' and 'community'. Yet, like 'exclusion', the 'underclass' is a politically contested, ideological conception.

Many associate the promulgation of underclass discourse with the rise of the New Right. Over time, American and British liberals formed uneasy coalitions with conservatives by distinguishing between economic and social intervention by the state (Hall, 1988, 1979; Barker, 1981; King, 1987). American and British conservatives maintained the moral disapproval and victim blaming associated with dominant poverty discourses in these countries. Deviant values, they believe, lead to deviant behaviour. Since Burke, conservatives have stressed 'law and order', religious morality, traditional family relations and nationalism, values that the 'underclass' supposedly lacks. Popular understandings of the term 'underclass' turn on behaviours violating norms of British 'respectability' (Macnicol, 1986: 299) or 'mainstream' American culture. In contrast, these moral connotations of poverty were not popularized in France where anti-Republican conservatism and clericalism attributed deviance less to the poor than to those outside the *nation*.

The ideological distinctions between conservatives and liberals are worth keeping in mind because they tend to blur in British and especially American underclass discourse.[8] The 'underclass', like exclusion, takes the 'multi-dimensional perspective' found in pre-1960s poverty discourse (Mincy, 1994: 133, 123). By combining liberal and conservative criteria, the 'underclass' becomes a subset of the poor exhibiting *cumulative* deprivations. As the number of dimensions of deprivation or deviance considered rises, the smaller the 'underclass' becomes (Mincy, 1994), and, one might add, the fewer who need to be assisted. For liberals, the two most important dimensions are welfare dependency as a correlate of long-term formal labour market detachment and spatial segregation as a correlate of social isolation. These dimensions are consistent with Wilson's (1991) notion of the 'ghetto poor'. For conservatives, 'behavioural' connotations, particularly those of deviance and racial subculture, are more relevant. Taken together, the term 'underclass' imputes both a *class*ness or commonality to otherwise heterogeneous individuals (Macnicol, 1986; Kornblum, 1984) and an *inferiority* which heightens public perception of the poor's 'alterity' (Cook and Curtin, 1987). While most reviews of the 'underclass' literature subsume all these connotations – dependency, deviance, racial and spatial – under the rubric of 'behavioral' definitions, and contrast them with 'structural' conceptions, here they are disaggregated to illustrate how the 'underclass' notion is embedded in national cultures and political ideologies.

Dependency

Although American 'underclass' rhetoric does differ from earlier poverty discourse (Stafford and Ladner, 1990; Mincy, 1994; Wilson, 1987), there is considerable continuity in national conceptions of poverty because the 'underclass' evokes values from the classical or *genus* liberalism that bounds American political culture and is one of the two dominant ideologies in British politics. While American 'reform liberals' contested the predominant 'humanist' or Lockean liberalism, British liberals considered their reforms as alternatives to 'socialism'. Thus, at the most general level, liberalism is at the origin of commonalities in recent American and British usages of the term 'underclass'.

Initially, American and British liberalism was strictly Lockean. In both countries, unlike France, liberals conceived of citizenship as a social contract. Entitlements to social assistance should be 'exchanged' for the exercise of civic responsibilities (see Mead, 1986; Janowitz, 1980; Glendon, 1991). Citizens are expected to work. Low levels of relief were designed to encourage 'enterprise' or a 'work ethic' and to discourage 'scrounging', 'shirking', 'cheating', 'shiftlessness' and spurious claims of incapacity. They also conveniently kept wages and taxes low. As illustrated by the principle of 'least eligibility' and official absolute poverty lines based on subsistence costs, public assistance set a low floor under wages (Walker, 1990; Spicker, 1993: 49; Ruggles, 1990). Liberal contractual conceptions of citizenship also pervade justifications for American and British 'workfare' programmes. The emphasis on individual responsibility, duty and obligations over the rights of citizenship dominated American and British social policy reforms during the 1980s (Weir, 1993: 103; King, 1992: 238–9).

Thus, liberals have long argued that 'dependency' on public assistance discourages work. The contemporary prototype of this liberal perspective on the 'underclass' is Charles Murray (1984, 1990), who helped put the issue of welfare reform on the American agenda during the last decade. Murray blamed lenient 1960s social policies for rising poverty, which provided a rationale for eliminating the right to welfare in the US. Indeed, in the Republican Party's 1994 'Contract with America', welfare reform became the 'Personal Responsibility Act'. The same rationale – eliminating the 'poverty trap' or 'unemployment trap' that made public assistance more attractive than work – underlay comprehensive reforms of British Social Security and employment programmes during the mid-1980s. 'Regular diatribes against scroungers' stigmatized 'dependency' and promulgated a new morality of 'enterprise' (King, 1992: 225).

Since the nineteenth century in both the US and Britain, liberal commitments to limited government have tied the symbolic politics of poverty to minimum wages, welfare and taxes. Indeed, one of the other contractual duties self-reliant individuals exchange for rights is taxpaying. Whether working taxpayers should provide relief or welfare for able-bodied non-workers is central to liberal poverty discourse and calls the citizenship of poor or unemployed members of the 'underclass' into question. 'Real' Americans 'want to make good citizens out of the "underclass" by getting them a job and making them, too, earning members of the society' (Shklar, 1991: 96). In Britain, throughout the twentieth century, individuals who 'consumed public resources' or had 'contact with particular institutions of the state' were classified into a social problem group (Macnicol, 1986: 300, 315). Similarly, Conservatives equated immigrants and blacks with 'the archetypal welfare recipient . . . a somewhat greedy member of the underserving poor and as personally responsible for his own lowly economic position' (Reeves, 1983: 158).

Although Locke construed liberty as freedom *from* the state, market failures and concern to create a national 'community' later provided a liberal rationale for social intervention. As 'unemployment' was recognized as a social problem beyond individual control (Topalov, 1994; Burnett, 1994), negative rights were supplemented by positive ones; the right *to* a minimum of resources would 'liberate' individuals to contribute to the moral and political 'community'. J. S. Mill, Lord Acton and L. T. Hobhouse provided the liberal justification for more generous state assistance to the poor (Green, 1992). Like American 'reform liberalism' but unlike French Republicanism, that perspective rejected socialism but accepted limited public intervention.

Once it was accepted that labour markets produce cyclical unemployment, contributory social insurance programmes also seemed justified. They were constructed in terms compatible with contractual obligations of citizenship, with workers having 'earned' their benefits. Once unemployment insurance was available, the 'undeserving poor' narrowed to those who were *persistently* unemployed or poor. Indeed, the 'underclass' almost always refers to the 'persistently' poor (Aponte, 1990): those who are out of work or on welfare for long periods of time or whose families may have also shared this fate. Yet, both American and, to a lesser extent, British social policy maintained a dual system of welfare in which non-workers, whether receiving insurance or means-tested benefits, were suspected of malingering (Morris, 1994).

Individualism

In individualistic America, large majorities, including the poor, believe the main causes of poverty are individual shortcomings. Most believe individuals 'have an obligation to take care of themselves' (Cook and Curtin, 1987). In the US, these liberal principles are often taken for granted, but in class-bound Britain, they are proclaimed. As the Home Secretary, Douglas Hurd, stated in 1987, 'We believe in individualism . . . the ladders of opportunity in our professions, in our industries, in our public sector, are open for all to climb.'

Yet the 'individual-as-cause thesis' (Aponte, 1990: 132–3) has two variants. While conservative definitions of the underclass stress deviant values and behaviour, liberals conceive it as a subset of the poor with the 'handicaps' imposed by a 'disadvantaged' background. Liberals did not overcome feudal privilege only to discover centuries later that characteristics ascribed at birth determine individual destiny. Thus, the underclass lacks 'human capital' or the equal opportunity to overcome one's family, subcultural or group-based 'socialization'. For a hundred years, a major focus of British and American stratification research, with its methodological individualism, has been the inter-generational transmission of poverty and welfare dependency, a concern which is still prominent in American and British 'mobility' and 'status attainment' models (Macnicol, 1986; Duncan, 1986; Hill et al., 1985). The consistent finding that many 'enterprising' individuals do escape their 'underclass' origins attests to the openness of liberal societies without challenging existing institutions or the comfortable position of the middle class. Conversely, if few individuals have multiple disadvantages and if dimensions of disadvantage are poorly associated over time, then it is possible to limit the import of a stable under*class* (Jencks, 1991). In so far as racial or other group inequalities persist, 'equal opportunity' and 'civil rights' laws should be sufficient to combat 'discrimination' against individuals. However, like Republicanism, liberalism is universalistic and rejects group rights. Liberals explicitly omit race from their underclass definitions.

Community

Liberal 'underclass' discourse is suffused with concerns to help individuals realize their potential. But since liberalism also emphasizes the strict separation of public and private spheres, it is not the government or employers so much as 'communities' that should play this role. 'Community', like the 'underclass' and 'exclusion', is itself a contested 'keyword'. Not only do French Republicans rarely use the term (Body-Gendrot, 1993), but also they actively dislike communities because they are exclusive (Plant, 1978; Calhoun, 1980; Silver, 1991). Yet, in Britain and the US, community 'seems never to be used unfavorably and never to be given any positive opposing or distinguishing term' (Williams, 1976: 66). Thus, while the names of French social policies evoke solidarism for their legitimacy, the names of American and British urban policies appeal to 'community'. While communitarians contrast 'community' to 'individualism', however, classical liberals contrast it with the state. Community belongs in the free sphere of civil society. It is based on common interests and values. Its expressions include primary and secondary groups, voluntary associations and 'networks' of friends and family.

Correspondingly, the underclass literature is markedly microsociological. Liberals spatially locate 'underclass' individuals in immediate residential localities or 'communities'. The absence of personal, face-to-face contact between the poor and the non-poor causes 'mainstream' Americans to exaggerate the differences between themselves and the underclass (Cook and Curtin, 1987) and isolates the ghetto poor from black middle-class resources, role models and values (Wilson, 1987, 1991). Whereas local interaction in ghetto 'communities' once exerted 'social control' over the ghetto poor, the exodus of the black middle class weakened 'mainstream' norms. Job contacts disappeared and institutions crumbled. This 'social isolation' produced inner city 'pathologies'. Thus, if ghetto 'culture is a response to social structural constraints and opportunities' (Wilson, 1987: 61), merely living near poor people has 'concentration effects'. When economically marginal individuals interact with others like themselves, deviant behaviour itself becomes normative, enticing even 'decent' and 'mainstream' neighbours.

However mixed the evidence in support of Wilson's theory (Mincy, 1994; Massey and Denton, 1993; Stern, 1993; Reed, 1991; Stafford and Ladner, 1990); it has helped to revive 'community studies' as the study of central city neighbourhoods (Newman, 1992; Cohen and Dawson, 1993). Indeed, this is not the only way in which Wilson's argument is permeated with the liberal assumptions of the Chicago School and human ecology about interaction, small groups, natural areas, social disorganization, assimilation and the relationship between outward migration and social mobility (Reed, 1991: 29). Although Wilson's theory may be social democratic in other respects, the roots of Chicago School sociology in liberal pragmatism and progressivism are well documented (Feffer, 1993; Safford, 1987, Silver, 1990). It would be ironic if the new urban sociologists, after rejecting this older paradigm, were to unwittingly embrace some of its underlying liberalism through the adoption of 'underclass' discourse.

Deviance

The liberal connotations of the 'underclass' become clearer when contrasted with conservative emphases on deviance, race and space. Conservatives do not define the 'underclass' as a subset of the poor. Rather, it consists of a 'certain type of poor person defined not by his condition . . . but by his deplorable behavior in response to that condition' (Murray, 1990: 68).[9] In brief, the underclass is deviant. It violates the norms of morally constituted, private 'communities'. For example, since Americans 'don't know how to make up for the lack of a community that rewards responsibility and stigmatizes irresponsibility', Murray (1990: 33) proposed a variation on the *droit à la difference*: letting 'communities with different values' run their affairs differently. Although most ethnographic and social psychological studies in the US find that the attitudes and aspirations of the 'underclass' do not differ much from those of other Americans (Cook and Curtin, 1987; Newman, 1992), conservative underclass discourse downplays 'the fact that many of the poor are individuals whose strong endorsement of mainstream values has *not* relieved their poverty' (Morris, 1989: 130).

Deviance-based definitions of the underclass assume 'a clear consensus around values and norms and deviation from them' (Stafford and Ladner, 1990: 144). Yet, across the political spectrum (Ellwood, 1988; Sawhill, 1989; Wilson, 1987: 6–11), 'mainstream' ideals often consist of taken-for-granted 'homespun verities' (Reed, 1991) whose content needs to be made explicit. A closer look at what passes for 'mainstream' values reveals that each nation makes reference to its own ideals of social membership. The normative criteria by which the 'underclass' is judged are themselves contested social constructions. For example, 'mainstream American values' are predominantly liberal. Just as the 'underclass' consists of individuals whose behaviour 'inhibits social mobility, influences children, and imposes costs on society' (Ricketts and Sawhill, 1988; Mincy, 1994), mainstream conduct apparently does the opposite. Since liberals consider not holding a job or receiving welfare to be deviant, American citizens are considered those earners and taxpayers who support their families and contribute to the 'community'.

This what Americans usually mean by 'middle class', and it too is a term central to American symbolic politics. Indeed, since Jefferson, Jackson and Tocqueville, the emphasis on equality of opportunity led most Americans to consider themselves of 'middling condition' (Wiebe, 1985: 322). The 'central, and largely unchallenged, image of American society' is that the middle class 'will eventually include everyone' (Bellah et al., 1985: 119). Unlike Britain, the dominant conception of the US is not of a class society, but one with an 'imperial middle' of individual strivers and self-improvers from which only the very rich and the very poor are excluded (DeMott, 1990). Thus, the 'underclass' is 'excluded' from America. They 'are all that a true American should not be – unconforming, illegal and unemployable' (Keith and Cross, 1993: 11).

It is in this cultural and behavioural sense of the mainstream as middle class that the American 'underclass' is a 'class'. While in Britain 'the notion of an underclass can be incorporated rather easily into traditional sociological frameworks focused on a class-based stratification system' (Morris, 1989: 130), belonging to the American middle class is more than an economic status (but see Mincy, 1994: 133). It also implies a certain cultural conformity and a pattern of consumption that extends well into the working class and even the working poor. Indeed, that a foreign observer, Gunnar Myrdal (1963), coined the term 'underclass' to refer to structural unemployment illustrates the point. Myrdal's conception relied on a social democratic notion of 'class' not widely accepted in the US. Organized labour and class consciousness remained weak compared to the group loyalties, local communities and pervasive individualism derived from liberalism. Consequently, his definition is rarely used in American underclass discourse. As Touraine (1990: 240) notes, the 'roots of American intellectual and political culture are in the eighteenth-century; the roots of European culture in the nineteenth.' While social class played a major role in French and British thought, the cohesiveness and integration of social groups are central questions in the United States.

Race

The weakness of working-class consciousness and the dominance of middle-class culture in the US is partly attributable to the American heritage of slavery, legal segregation and racial discrimination. In some respects, the 'mainstream' middle class is constructed in such a way as to exclude most African-Americans. Indeed, if residential segregation is any guide, American whites are more reluctant than Europeans to admit racial minorities and especially African-Americans of any class into the national community (Massey and Denton, 1993). Underclass discourse is pervaded with racial 'code-words'. While both Murray and Wilson do not define the 'underclass' in racial terms, they do often use blacks in their empirical illustrations. Moreover, race-neutral definitions of the American underclass result in a population that is disproportionately African-American (Kasarda, 1992; Jargowsky and Bane, 1990).

While contemporary American and British conservative discourse rarely contains biological references to race, racial categories are often used in a cultural sense. By emphasizing deviance, conservatives can talk about race without explicitly referring to minority groups. It is no coincidence that former KKK Grand Wizard David Duke campaigned for LA governor by complaining about the 'welfare underclass'. Although British race relations reflect the vestiges of a different history of colonialism and immigration than those in the US, British parliamentary debates also 'deracialized' racial discourse through 'sanitary coding' and 'imaging' (Reeves, 1983). While the term 'underclass' was rarely used, racist ideas or awareness were communicated to the public with 'seemingly aracial' terminology, linking welfare, urban politics, poverty and riot with blacks. Under the Conservatives and especially Mrs Thatcher, debates over successive immigration and nationality acts served to reconstruct Englishness, 'replacing the language of race with the euphemism of culture' (Smith, 1989: 128; Barker, 1981). Racist discourse simultaneously frightens and reassures 'through a vocabulary of coded panic terms: "loony leftism", "wilding", illegitimacy, drugs, and perhaps paradigmatically, "the underclass", notwithstanding Wilson's attempt to free the concept from these oppressive meanings' (Keith and Cross, 1993: 15). However, due to the dominance of social class in British politics, policy 'measures conceived of for racial minorities were transmuted into general policies for the socially disadvantaged as a whole' (Reeves, 1983: 254).

The Urban Underclass

In a context of residential segregation, 'spatial' keywords are themselves often used as 'racial' codewords. In the US, the rural, immigrant, and white poor are rarely included in the 'underclass', partly because they are more spatially dispersed. Cultural constructions of spatial categories, like racial ones, tend toward dualism. Just as Americans tend to treat those of 'mixed race' as black or white, the urban–rural contrast is stark, even though 'ghettos' are confined to certain urban or suburban neighbourhoods. White and black, mainstream and deviant are culturally projected onto the city's core and the periphery with clear buffer zones between them. Thus, 'sameness and otherness rule spatial relations' (Goldberg, 1993).

Distance is not spatial or geographical, but social. The *'urban* underclass', the *'ghetto* poor', the *banlieues* are the Other. They are 'over there', 'someone else's responsibility', 'out of sight, out of mind'. Indeed, even in France, where immigrants are a small percentage of suburbanites, are unevenly distributed across suburban municipalities, and are nationally diverse, the blanket label of the *banlieues* provided an apparently race-neutral term for social distance (Silverman, 1992: 107).

Yet the contrast between the 'inner city' and the poorer French 'periphery' is instructive. Britain and the US share a cultural preference for the 'pastoral' and an anti-urbanism associating cities with degeneration, disease and danger. Simply residing in an area with 'underclass' symptoms has become a definitional criterion of membership (Wilson, 1991; Ricketts and Sawhill, 1988), as if neighbours' problems are contagious. This theme is muted in France where *terroir* is associated with anti-Republicanism and the city with civilization.

The urban dimension of the underclass has liberal connotations as well. The liberal emphasis on social mobility was also an aspiration to move outward: in the US, to the frontier; in the UK, to emulate the landed gentry. In the 'Anglo-Saxon' tradition of 'community-based' development (Abou Sada et al., 1994: 9), specifically 'urban' policies allow liberal governments to target poor 'areas' without explicitly recognizing the groups living there. 'Collective consumption' functions associated with the underclass – housing and the physical environment, schooling and youth problems, and policing and crime – are considered 'community' concerns, and so are more decentralized in the US and Britain than in France. However much softened by ubiquitous references to 'community', urban discourse about 'ghettos', 'inner-cities', 'the homeless', 'law and order', 'delinquency', 'school leavers', and 'dropouts' divide the poor from others by place of residence. The urban dimension of underclass discourse spatially fixes social disadvantage, racial difference and deviance.

While liberals and conservatives emphasize different dimensions of the 'underclass' – with liberals stressing dependency and isolation and conservatives, deviance and race – urban discourse encompasses them all. Indeed, the first popular uses of the term 'underclass' associating urban poverty, race and deviance appeared after the New York City blackout riots in 1977 (Aponte, 1990). In Britain, too, after two waves of racial violence in the 1980s, 'once-discrete panics (over race, immigration, crime, welfare, fraud, and so on) have been absorbed into the imagery of the inner city, wherein blacks are blamed for a variety of urban ills' (Smith, 1989: 140). As in France, these riots gave new impetus to 'urban' policies. However, targeting deprived *places* has been an inefficient way of targeting *people* in need. In Britain particularly, 'most poor people do not live in poor areas and most of the people in poor areas are not poor' (Spicker, 1993: 70). Yet 'urban' policy is not only intended to address deprivation, but also, implicitly, concerns about racial tensions and law and order.

In sum, the embeddedness of the 'underclass' in liberal and conservative ideology helps account for the widespread use of the term in the United States and its intelligibility in Great Britain. 'Underclass theory . . . serves a profoundly ideological purpose. At a stroke, it reasserts conventional morality, spotlights the visible as wicked and justifies the cessation of welfare' (Keith and Cross, 1993: 13). In both countries, liberal ideology has long shaped national conceptions of poverty as dependency and isolation as well as the social welfare institutions designed to address it. Conservative ideology, by constructing and defending national and racial cultures, maintain the cultural stigma long associated with poverty. 'Within subgroups of political opinion the "underclass" represents a near-classic example of what Edelman refers to as "public language", a language through which "people can communicate . . . when they sufficiently share norms that they need not be explicit about premises and meanings . . . a term that implies the rest of the cognitive structure without calling attention to it" ' (Morris, 1989: 131).

Contesting American Underclass Discourse

None of this is meant to suggest that 'underclass' discourse is uncontested by the American and British left. Just as terms like 'exclusion' are 'sufficiently general to accommodate a variety of (frequently conflicting) interpretations, the "underclass" can likewise serve many masters when the question of why certain people remain poor is raised' (Morris, 1989: 132). Social democrats and the left wing of the Democratic Party rejected the term 'underclass', considering it too vague and politically loaded to be of much use (Gans, 1990c; Kornblum, 1984). They criticized Wilson for neglecting the capitalist 'overclass' (Walker, 1990), institutional racism, the white middle class, rising earnings inequality, and the less benign social control functions and discriminatory policies of the state.[10] At a time when the Republican Party was dismantling programmes to help African-Americans, and former organizational allies of African-Americans – unions, the courts, the Democratic Party, the welfare bureaucracy – were declining (Weir, 1993), Wilson was blamed for underestimating racism, overestimating pathological behaviour, rejecting black community development, and opening the door to conservative connotations of the 'underclass' (Stafford and Ladner, 1990; Massey and Denton, 1993).

In academic circles, these critics were apparently persuasive. In the US, 'few researchers now use the term *underclass*' (Mincy, 1994: 131). By 1991, even Wilson repudiated the term 'underclass' for the 'ghetto poor'. However, many European intellectuals consider Wilson a social democrat because he stressed 'structural' or 'economic' causes of the 'underclass' and hence, social class over race. He also proposed an apparently race-neutral 'hidden agenda', one explicitly called 'social democratic', designed to court white working-class support. And by arguing for a right to decent employment, he offered 'a European notion of social rights with an American twist' (Weir, 1993: 102). Thus, while the American left repudiated the term 'underclass', the British left adopted a selective understanding of it.

Contesting British Underclass Discourse

Like the term 'exclusion', politicians and the media rarely speak explicitly about the 'underclass' (see Ormerod and Salama, 1990). Even Charles Murray has conceded that 'British intellectuals still disdain the term' (1990: 3). British sociologists are aware of the 'underclass' concept's American origins, but when adopting the term, draw more upon its social democratic than its liberal and conservative connotations. While Americans stress *under*, the British stress *class*. Racial inequality is downplayed. And, like British 'exclusion' discourse, treatments of the UK 'underclass' increasingly link it to the social rights of citizenship.

The earliest usages of the term 'underclass' reflected British sociologists' long-standing preoccupation with working-class conservatism or *embourgoisement* and a lively Marxist–Weberian controversy over the nature of social class (Giddens, 1973: 217–20; Rex and Tomlinson, 1979; Solomos, 1993: 20). Indeed, a major theme in British analyses is whether the 'underclass' is distinct from the working class (Macnicol, 1986). Stressing class boundaries and typologies, a central focus of research is whether the new poor, the long-term unemployed, or benefit recipients have a distinctive class consciousness or subculture (Runciman, 1990; Smith, 1992; Gallie, 1993, 1988). For example, Dahrendorf (1988, 1985) argued that the long-term unemployed are too dispersed and heterogeneous to be described as a 'class', whereas Rex's (1986: 57) underclass is 'a quasi-group with a distinct class position and status weaker and lower than that of the working class' (1986: 74).

British discussions of the 'underclass' also make reference to T. H. Marshall's conception of citizenship. As early as the mid-1960s, Titmuss (1965) argued that the 'problems of the underclass in our cities' required positive discrimination within a universalistic welfare state. Recent discussions emphasize the loss of civil and social citizenship rights guaranteed by the welfare state and grounded in class politics (Dahrendorf, 1988: 153–5; Rex, 1986: 74; Field, 1989: 15). Yet, sometimes the underclass is defined to include anyone dependent on state subsidies (Willetts, 1992: 49).

Race, in contrast, is treated as incidental to British underclass discourse. However, as blacks resisted being portrayed as 'a "malignant wedge" in the inner city whose identity was incompatible with the label "British" and was the object of the law and order campaign central to moral authoritarianism' (Smith, 1989), some began to see race as an autonomous, if ideological and contested social construction around which to mobilize new urban social movements (for example, Hall, 1979; Centre for Contemporary Cultural Studies, 1982; Gilroy, 1987; Solomos, 1993; Keith and Cross, 1993). However, social class remains the material and economic base of these struggles. When race enters into 'underclass' discussions *per se*, the primary concern is whether blacks constitute a reserve army that divides the working class, a class faction that cheapens labour (Sivanandan, 1990).

Since Marxism and Fabianism tend to reduce race to class, 'underclass' definitions that accord racial inequality some autonomy usually draw on Marshall and Weber. For example, Rex (1986, 1988) argues that, unlike minorities who 'gained full rights in the society', the black British underclass, 'instead of forming an inert or despairing social residue, organizes and acts in their own "underclass" interest often relating themselves to colonial class positions' (1986: 69, 74). This contrasts with the American underclass, defined as those who failed to become 'property-owning', 'economically self-supporting' individuals in an 'open, status-seeking society'. Perhaps ironically, Rex attributes this definition to Myrdal, the most social democratic and least cited theorist of the American underclass.

French Underclass Discourse

As one would expect from the dominance of Republican ideology, the French media and politicians rarely use the term 'underclass'. Most explicit references to it are made by social scientists distinguishing American or British sociological usages from the French situation of exclusion (see Herpin, 1993). Some Republican thinkers explicitly reject the translation of 'exclusion' as 'underclass'. For example, a CGP publication indicated that '*Outsider* should be the adequate English expression for "*exclus*" rather than *undergroup* or *underclass*' (Nasse, 1992: 119).

Rare usages of the 'underclass' in France import only selected connotations of the term. On the one hand, left-wing sociologists tend to conflate the meanings of the 'underclass' and 'exclusion' since they restrict both terms to a structural, economic interpretation. The interchangeability of these terms implies that global restructuring is producing national convergence. For example, those associated with a social action or social movements approach to exclusion (Touraine, 1991, 1992) usually adopt the class-oriented 'underclass' definitions of Myrdal, Wilson and Wacquant rather than those of American liberals or conservatives. Research focuses on whether, with the decline of local working-class life, de-industrialization has created a French *substrat social, welfare class* or *sous-class* among immigrants or in the *banlieues* (Dubet and Lapeyronnie, 1992: 227; Lapeyronnie, 1993: 252–5; Wieviorka, 1991). For example, Castel (1995: 424) argues, 'there is not in France – in any case not yet – an *underclass* constituted on an ethnic base, although there is an ensemble of socially disqualifying characteristics, a low economic level, an absence of social and cultural capital, a stigmatized habitat, censured ways of life, etc. to which ethnic origin could be added.'

On the other hand, the French media, with Hollywood's help, have imported conservative and multicultural images of the 'underclass' by reporting on a selective set of American urban problems associated with minority communities and deviance: gangs, crime, riots and drugs in the 'ghettos'. Since the 'Anglo-Saxon' countries are popularly used as France's 'anti-model' (Crowley, 1992), the press uses terms like *sous-classe permanente* (Stehli, 1991: 49) and *class subalterne* (Romero, 1991) to warn of the possible fate of the *banlieues*. Particularly after a series of violent urban incidents in 1991, the suburban *cités* were portrayed as 'types of ghettos, collecting a population that accumulates many social handicaps: unemployment, foreign origin, youth, lack of skill' (*Le Monde Diplomatique*, 1991).

Despite attempts to qualify such comparisons (for example, Wacquant and Body-Gendrot, 1991), the Bronx of *Bonfire of the Vanities* and films like *Fort Apache: The Bronx* became a metaphor for French urban problems. Even President François Mitterand deplored the *banlieue* violence by declaring: 'Pas de Bronx en France!' On the other side of the political spectrum, Gaullist Michel Noir (1992: 23), then Mayor of Lyon, described the 'soulless ghettos that ring French cities and occupy America's inner cities' as 'fearsome factories generating exclusion, indifference, and racial violence'.[11] As one commentator lamented, the left has served up 'the ready made discourse of exclusion that the stone throwers repeat before the cameras. The right prefers bare repression that reassures honest people but generally aggravates the problems' (Joffrin, 1991: 58). Nevertheless, it is exceptional for French politicians from the Republican parties to use such rhetoric. Typically, they have sought new ways for the state to intervene in the *banlieues* and conciliate minorities.

CONCLUSION

This chapter has interpreted new poverty discourses through the lens of nationally specific political cultures. Even when these discourses are imported, they change meaning to fit dominant national paradigms.

But these long-standing national preoccupations are also politically contested. As the 'neo-institutionalists' observe, political actors use myths and symbols that 'antedate them and are widely shared' as 'instruments of interpretive order' that create and confirm coherent interpretations of reality. But symbolic politics are 'also a strategic element in political competition' which 'transforms more instrumental behavior and is transformed by it' (March and Olsen, 1984: 741–4).

Indeed, discourses about the new poverty are addressed less to the poor themselves than to a broader political audience. The new poor are rarely asked what they want to be called; their agents often reject any label at all as stigmatizing or dehumanizing. As the analysis showed, political and intellectual 'claimsmakers' usually define, objectify or 'typify' social problems. Selecting symbolic discourse from national paradigms, they set the parameters of dispute, the terms of engagement and the rules of the game in social policy conflicts. If they successfully legitimize their definition of a social problem, it is then institutionalized in social programmes. As Topalov (1994: 192) argues, 'To enunciate "problems", establish causalities, classify populations and prescribe solutions are inseparable moments of the same discourse.' Scholarly classifications necessarily 'evoke prescriptions for action and conflicts between actors'.

Because the power to name is a political resource, activists leading movements of the poor are keenly aware that insisting upon sympathetic labels helps build the political coalitions necessary to reform social policy, just as their opponents use stigmatizing labels to isolate the new poor from potential allies. To name groups is to draw social boundaries. To speak of a 'new poor' distinguishes it from the 'old poor' and often downplays continuities. Similarly, to identify the 'new poverty' as 'multidimensional' portrays it as different from, or more than, mere economic deprivation. This may afford opportunities to 'reform' social policies in a conservative direction. First, by redefining some people as 'not poor', the new poverty can be strictly confined to a highly differentiated set of individuals with multiple handicaps. A rhetoric that narrowly conceives of the new poverty as cumulative disadvantage, affecting only a subset of the poor, makes it easier to target policies on the most disadvantaged categories and then, through stigmatization, reduce even this limited support (Room, 1990).

Second, a multi-dimensional poverty directs attention to 'non-economic' – for example, urban, racial, ethnic, family, welfare – causes of deprivation. In this way, political discourse can introduce 'wedge issues' into the social policy debate that accelerates the 'class de-alignment' noted in analyses of recent electoral behaviour (Inglehart,

1990; Inglehart and Hochstein, 1972; Dalton, 1988; Dalton, Flanagan and Beck, 1984). Indeed, comparing new poverty discourses across national contexts reveals a common dynamic in symbolic politics. There is a marked partisan struggle in British, French and American politics for the support of working people who are situated just over the boundary line of some conceptions of the new poverty. They too have nationally specific names: *couches populaires*, working-class conservatives, Reagan Democrats. Polls also indicate widespread anxiety about losing one's socially accepted or customary style of life (André, 1994; Quirk and Dalager, 1993). To build the coalitions necessary to address the new poverty while still protecting the working class, political discourse must avoid pitting these social strata against each other.

Thus, constructing a poverty discourse is an exercise in symbolic politics. Selecting among the dimensions of the new poverty is crucial in the struggle to win allies for or against the interests of the new poor. In order for the idea of the new poverty to produce meaningful social change, it should be culturally constructed in a way that evokes broadly consensual symbols that historically legitimized earlier social policies in each nation-state or can cement new coalitions with the non-poor. An alternative discourse might emphasize how economic changes have created a widespread vulnerability to downward mobility and a relative poverty of 'deprivation'. Restructuring has not only produced the cumulative deprivations emphasized in some new poverty discourses but also affects, in one respect or another, a large number of people from many social strata. Emphasizing these commonalities may rebuild the coalition between working people and the new poor.

NOTES

1   Whereas the old poverty primarily referred to lack of income, the 'new poverty' is considered multidimensional, encompassing many deprivations. Whereas the old poverty reflected cyclical downturns or chronic labour market vulnerability, the 'new poverty' is an outcome of recent structural change that displaces not only populations traditionally considered 'poor' but members of most social classes. And the social policies of post-war Western welfare states designed to address the old poverty do not adequately protect those at risk from the new poverty. Core universalist and contributory programmes assumed that most working people have a uniform life cycle, career pattern and family structure, but the proliferation of heterogeneous 'special needs' and demands for differentiated services have swelled the numbers in means-tested benefit and categorical service programmes (Immergut, 1993;

Room, 1990). In some cases, the 'new poor' are ineligible for any form of public assistance. Whereas the older political logic of inequality and class conflict made interests in the workplace, neighbourhood and family consistent with partisan demands on the state, the political logic of the new poverty pits those permanently out of work against those with employment, citizens against immigrants, dominant ethnicities against minorities, the well educated against the illiterate, married against single people, generation against generation. It fragments constituencies in space. And because of the new poverty's individualized quality, many of the excluded are isolated from one another, hindering mobilization or representation (Foucauld, 1992a; Touraine, 1991, 1992a).

2 For early uses of 'exclusion', see Klanfer (1965), Verdes-Leroux (1978), Lenoir (1974).

3 One content analysis found that the term was often used synonymously with 'integration' (Barrou, 1993). The Commissariat Générale du Plan (1993) decided that insertion is a 'pluridimensional concept'.

4 These 'ethnic communities' mobilized after the right of association was extended to foreigners in 1981, and were fuelled by the Maastricht Treaty proposal to allow foreign residents to vote in local and European elections.

5 The first impetus came after the Les Minguettes riot in 1981, but peaked after incidents in Vaulx-en-Velin, Sartrouville and Mantes-la-Jolie in 1991.

6 French juvenile delinquency has been largely attributed to high unemployment and discrimination (Wacquant, 1993, 1992a; Dubet, 1987; Dubet and Lapeyronnie, 1992; Lapeyronnie, 1993). Only 17 of the 546 French *developpement social des quartiers* (DSQ) neighbourhoods have a majority of foreign inhabitants. While *'ouvriers'* represent 43 per cent in the average DSQ area, many of the neighbourhoods are occupationally mixed as well (Castellan, Marpsat and Goldberger, 1992).

7 Examples include Katz (1993, 1989), Reed (1991), Macnicol (1986), Morris (1989), Stafford and Ladner (1990), Morris (1994), Keith and Cross (1993), Castel (1995).

8 While liberals think of the poor as rational decision makers who prefer the greater incentives of welfare and tax evasion to legal employment, conservatives see the poor as morally deficient. Whereas liberals historically rejected paternalist, religious charity and favoured niggardly public support, if any, conservatives focused on the moral reform of the needy, often with punitive means. Whereas liberals conceive of 'community' as an interacting interest group, conservatives conceive of it as a morally integrated *Gemeinschaft* whose norms the underclass rejects. Whereas the liberal personification of the American underclass is the 'welfare queen', the conservative one is 'Willie Horton'.

9 More precisely, Murray's discussion of the British underclass synthesizes liberal and conservative concerns. Whereas receiving benefit was once condemned, the penalties and stigma declined in the 1960s and 1970s.

With social security reform, 'moral standards' decayed, and illegitimacy, violent crime and labour force withdrawal rose. This concern with 'aberrant behavior' is not the only similarity between Murray's and Wilson's discussions of the 'underclass.' Neither defines it in terms of race, and both see it resulting from concentration effects. Murray notes, 'the key to an underclass is not the individual instance but a situation in which a very large proportion of an entire community lacks fathers, and this is far more common in poor communities than in rich ones' (p. 13).

10   Indeed, the pervasiveness of liberalism means that Americans rarely acknowledge the role of state policy and corporate capitalist practices, rather than impersonal markets, in reinforcing the urban, racial and other contextual causes of 'underclass' symptoms.

11   Noir added that 'urban issues . . . have suffered for their association with the political left . . . and urban sociologists . . . viewed with mistrust by politicians and urban dwellers alike as exclusionary characters, forever babbling about the interdisciplinary and the complex.' Predictably, given Americans' stress on the deviance and racial connotations of the English term 'underclass', a translation of this essay appeared in the *New York Times* just after the Los Angeles riots.

Part II

The Underclass Debate in a Comparative Approach: Ethnicity, Class and Culture

6

From 'Underclass' to 'Undercaste': Some Observations About the Future of the Post-Industrial Economy and its Major Victims

Herbert J. Gans, Columbia University, New York

When in 1963 Gunnar Myrdal took an old-fashioned Swedish word for 'lower class' to describe a new American 'underclass', little did he know what immense effects his brief, seemingly offhand, new conceptualization would have on America's view and treatment of the poor. Indeed, had he known, I am sure he would have chosen another term, if only because some subsequent distortions of his idea ignored his crucial insight into the future of the US economy and those whom he saw as its newest victims.

My chapter is devoted to some observations about that insight 30 years after the publication of his new concept, and about two other topics: variations in how the victims of the post-industrial economy are chosen in different countries; and cross-national variations in the definitions and uses of the term 'underclass'. But before discussing these topics, a brief history of what happened to Myrdal's concept in America is in order.

CHANGES IN MYRDAL'S UNDERCLASS

Myrdal used a new term because he wanted to show that challenges to the then affluent American economy were creating 'an unprivileged class of unemployed, unemployables and underemployed who are more and more hopelessly set apart from the nation at large and do not share in its life, its ambitions and its achievements' (Myrdal, 1963: 10). Myrdal had already glimpsed what we now call the post-industrial economy, and had noticed that because it would require fewer workers, others would in effect be forced to the margins of the labour force in a new and permanent way.

Myrdal supplied enough detail about his concept to indicate that for him it was *structural*: the people he was describing were economic victims. However, one year later, the term has already developed a racial association (Kahn, 1964), albeit from a liberal activist who was concerned, like Myrdal, with joblessness. Leggett (1968), writing at the end of the 1960s ghetto disorders, continued both the leftist and the racial connotations of the term, and in fact saw the black underclass as having a revolutionary potential.

Four years later, however, a Chicago social worker specializing in youth and gangs and his co-authors warned in the conservative journal *The Public Interest* about the arrival of a 'dangerous' black underclass (Moore, Livermore and Galland, 1973). They began the intellectual and ideological transformation of Myrdal's term, and by the end of the 1970s, thanks in part to Oscar Lewis's writings about the culture of poverty and Edward Banfield's about the 'lower class', American journalists had turned 'underclass' into a *behavioural* term. In this new version, it referred to poor people, again mostly black, who behaved in criminal, deviant or just non-middle-class ways (*Time Magazine*, 1977; Auletta, 1982).

Although sociologists such as William J. Wilson (1978, 1987) and social workers, for example, Douglas Glasgow (1980), continued to define the black underclass in a basically Myrdalian fashion, the journalistic tide flowed strongly toward the behavioural definition, helping thereby to turn it into the popular American term it is today. In its behavioural form, 'underclass' is also the successor to such earlier terms as 'pauper', 'tramp', 'feebleminded' and 'shiftless', becoming the latest idiom in a venerable general category: the undeserving poor.

Soon after journalists initiated the change in Myrdal's term, some American social scientists and intellectuals, black and white, began to criticize and then to reject the term altogether. The first to reject it was Robert Hill (1978), then research director of the Urban League, but the major wave of rejections came only a decade later, among others by Katz (1989), Gans (1990a) and Wilson (1991). Still, many social scientists have continued to use the word 'underclass', but mainly as a structural term, while the behavioural definition seems to be used more frequently by psychologists and economists, particularly conservative ones.[1]

CROSS-NATIONAL VARIATIONS IN ECONOMIC VICTIMS

Several chapters in this book, notably the one by Hilary Silver, stress the importance of looking at the victims of the post-industrial economy in countries which vary economically, politically and socially. One analysis must examine who is chosen for victimization, how and why and by whom, dealing also with diverse ways in which people are victimized. Since race, religion and ethnicity, together with age, gender and arrival in the country, seem to play major roles nearly everywhere in the selection of economic victims, one question is: which of these social constructs is/are chosen and why.[2] Race, however defined, often seems primary, as Norman Fainstein reminds us in his chapter in this volume, and it may be no accident that just one year after Myrdal invented a colour-blind concept for America's newest economic victims, it was already applied mainly to blacks.

Given the centrality of the behavioural definition of 'underclass' in American life, a parallel cross-national study must look at which economic victims are stigmatized with this label, and by whom; and which economic victims escape the stigma and the punishments that accompany it. This is part of a larger subject: how do societies and their economic, political and other decision makers and institutions 'choose' victims, as well as targets of blame, for various harmful activities, such as coal-mining and other dangerous work, wartime combat, mental illness, addictions and the like. Since all of these are often correlated with poverty, an analysis of the larger subject may also shed light on non-economic factors in how all economic victims are chosen. And, needless to say, such studies are not complete without looking at the ways in which economic and other victims are protected from material deprivation as well as stigmatization by various welfare state institutions developed in different countries.

NATIONAL DEFINITIONS OF THE UNDERCLASS

My second topic is the terminological one with which I introduced the chapter. Several authors in this book call attention to national variations in definitions of underclass (see Morris, Silver and Wacquant in this volume; see also Fainstein, Gordon and Harloe,

1992: chapter 1 and pp. 259–61). What I find worth studying as well are the patterns by which countries take concepts from other countries, in order to understand in which countries new, and particularly stigmatizing, terms for the poor may depend on foreign exports. As far as I can tell, Anthony Giddens (1973: 112) was the first European sociologist to import the concept of underclass from the USA, citing John Leggett's definition for this purpose, although one must not forget that the American term was invented not by an American, but by a Swedish – really a multinational – scholar.[3] Later, other American social scientists brought their structural conceptions of the underclass to Europe; and why and how these were accepted, rejected or altered is worth looking at in the context of various differences between the USA and European societies. Although this set of events could also be analysed as another instance in the Americanization of European social science, one would need to ask first whether any American input was necessary, given the lively British debate over the concept since the 1970s. (And this in turn would suggest the question of why the British were the first in Europe to use 'underclass' widely.)

The same kind of analysis deserves to be carried out for behavioural definitions of the underclass; which countries have adopted them, and which ones have not – and why. For example, Charles Murray (1989) exported the behavioural underclass to England, and its impact, or lack of it, could be studied. More important, one needs to ask which countries have avoided stigmatization of their long-term jobless and why, which ones have resorted to racial and ethnic terminology, or to the general stigmatization of all poor immigrants rather than to old or new labels for the undeserving poor. But then one must also ask how such countries labelled their indigenous economic victims.

Moreover, any proper study of stigmatization labels might begin historically, comparing the usage of the term 'underclass' with the usage of earlier terms with much the same intent. Such a study would have to cover many centuries and even several millenniums, for while the term 'undeserving' dates only from Victorian England, England stigmatized a variety of economic victims with other terms in prior centuries. Most European countries – as well as nations on other continents – had blaming terms of their own over the centuries; and before then so, surely, did ancient societies. However, archaeologists have not yet begun to unearth clay tablets, papyri, scrolls, etc. including such terms.

As far as the import of the American term 'underclass' is concerned, the research would have to deal with how Europeans handle the distinctive American tradition of racial discrimination and oppression that is part of the American concept. The behavioural American term is distinctive in another way; it is, in some respects, a product of the extensive role that American journalists play in the creation of new terminology and of popular sociology, which reflects at the same time the limited influence of professional American social scientists on journalists. It is hard, at least for an American, to imagine that European journalists would feel free to drastically alter the meaning of a social science term developed by a world-famous scholar like Myrdal.

THE UNDERCLASS AS AN EXCLUDED STRATUM

My final, and most important, theme returns to – and extrapolates into the future – the critical element of Myrdal's original definition: that a set of workers are being forced to the economic margins of the economy. By now, the post-industrial economy has developed considerably beyond what it was in Myrdal's time. As many writers have pointed out, more jobs have been lost to the computer and to other kinds of machinery – as well as to cost-cutting conglomerates and multinationals – and more jobs in developed countries have moved to lower-wage nations that are now part of the new global economy. In addition, manufacturing and service industries that rely largely on a small number of highly trained workers have replaced manufacturing ones using very large numbers of semiskilled or unskilled workers. While some of the latter have found new jobs in the service sector, these tend to be low-wage. Finally, the end of the cold war also presages the reduction of another major manufacturing activity in a number of national economies.

As a result, every developed country has seen changes in the amount and types of employment: notably the increase in badly paid work, in part-time and flexible employment (voluntary and involuntary), and in the growth of the informal economy with its legal and illegal parts – although what is legal and illegal is, like part-time employment, to some extent a function of national policies and politics.[4] Finally, every country is facing increases in the length of joblessness, in the number of young people and others who have never worked, and in the number also of middle-aged people who, having lost their jobs, will probably never work full-time again for the rest of their lives.

In fact, advanced capitalism may now be advancing to the stage where ever fewer workers will be needed to achieve ever higher productivity, at least as economists usually define it. Consequently, the worker marginalization Myrdal observed 30 years ago seems rapidly to be turning into worker *exclusion*. Indeed, if current trends continue, someday unknown numbers of people will never be included in the formal labour force to begin with, and may spend all or part of their work lives in the informal labour market, and in keeping themselves busy in other ways the rest of the time.

Presumably the informal labour market is not independent of the formal one, however, and will eventually also suffer from the shrinkage of the latter. When people have fewer jobs or less steady work, they also have less spending power, thus further shrinking both the formal and informal economies. Despairing poor people may spend more on alcohol and drugs, but either they, or the victims of crime from whom they get the needed money, will be spending less overall. In the end, then, workers could be excluded also from the informal labour force (for example, Pahl, 1984: part 2).

If these trends come to pass, and no one can predict whether they will or not, they may also bring into existence a stratum of people which is literally and quite visibly a structural underclass. Not only will it be located at the very bottom of the class structure, but it will also be excluded to a significant degree from significant contact (however defined), other than that involving kin, with the rest of that structure.

Although most formulations of the behavioural underclass concept, as of its predecessors through the ages, have treated the people assigned to it as *déclassé*, literally this is obviously impossible. By definition, a class structure includes everyone in the society, even those whom many would prefer not to include. Moreover, as long as those at the bottom of that structure have some economic, social or cultural functions (Gans, 1995: 91–102) to perform in the rest of the society, they cannot be totally excluded. Even the people who make up the reserve army of labour and work just enough to depress wages for regular workers are a part of the economy. Once they stop working, however, they are excluded from the economy, and at that point it is doubtful whether they can still perform the wage-depressing and other functions of the reserve army. Even so, some will always have non-economic relations – and probably even off-the-books economic ones – with others in the society, for no exclusionary measure is completely enforceable.

Economic exclusion of the kind I have been hypothesizing is something new in modern economies. For example, it goes far beyond Wilson's conception (1987: chapter 6) that the underclass is *socially* isolated – that others of higher status move away from it and give up contact with it. American poor people also suffer from what I think of as *institutional* isolation: the practice of stores, banks, churches and other commercial and public facilities moving away, even if their intent is to escape low profitability or slum conditions rather than, or more than, the people. But economic exclusion is worse than social or institutional isolation.

Whether Wilson's concept of social isolation is empirically valid is still being studied, and most likely the data will show varieties and degrees of social – and institutional – isolation. Even if working-class and middle-class blacks can move away from poor areas, some may still retain ties to relatives and friends who are among the persistently jobless and poor. These social ties may be strained by differences of income and class, and by the inability or unwillingness of the more fortunate to help the less fortunate. Only as at last resort do the former cut social ties with the latter, just as only as at last resort do the families of drug addicts reject their addicted kin. But once people are totally out of the economy, it is possible that friends and even relatives may desert them.

So too may the American 'safety net' and the European welfare state desert them, especially when labour force exclusion increases significantly in number and duration. Two questions suggest themselves: will societies have enough money to support the excluded, and will they want to? How long will taxpayers, other voters and politicians from the various classes pay for financial support in lieu of work income – and when will they cut back or even stop?

If past US history is any guide, the greater the level of poverty and joblessness, the more the poor and the jobless are labelled as undeserving. Presumably this happens in part because as poverty worsens, a larger number of poor people resort to crime and departures from various kinds of non-mainstream behaviour patterns. The poor may in fact be perceived as becoming more criminal and deviant even when the actual rates of crime and deviance do not change.[5] However, taxpayers deal with the rising economic pressure on them by deciding – probably not even deliberately – that the poor are increasingly undeserving. For example, the stigmatization of American welfare recipients has continued and worsened even though their family sizes have declined, and their benefits as well as absolute numbers have been reduced.[6] And once people are labelled as undeserving, the voters are less willing to help them, at least in the USA.[7]

However, much of what is known and even more of what is speculated about is based on a short period of economic exclusion.

While dropping out or being pushed out of the labour force is on the increase, the sharply rising levels, for instance for young US blacks, date back only to the 1970s (Wilson, 1987: 43), and we do not know yet what happens over a longer period and when it involves several other population groups. For example, many of the young men who are no longer, or were never, in the labour force have children, but the data on what fate awaits these children remain inconclusive. Warnings from conservative and other quarters that many of the children growing up in single-parent families are psychologically or socially doomed need to be taken with a grain of salt. However, even if these children grow up properly and with only minimal hurt from welfare and stigmatization, it does not mean that there will be jobs for them in a shrinking labour market, and so they may be excluded anyway.

Moreover, what if rates of labour force non-participation spread beyond the 'displaced' former workers of the mainstream economy and the minority populations, where they are still heavily concentrated today, in the USA at least: will the polity, in a majoritarian and racist society like the USA, react when whites become victims in large numbers? So far, young whites in America have not yet been barred as extensively from the work-force as in several European countries. If the US economy begins to follow the European pattern, will their distress result in increases in unemployment insurance and welfare benefits, and to the higher levels which many western European countries have been paying? And when will the economy run out of money, even if the political will is there to tax the rich, big corporations and even affluent jobholders?

At the present time, it is too early to tell how both the excluders and the excluded will react to lifetime or multigeneration economic exclusion. Since we still know so little about the people who have become an excluded population over the last 20 years, we cannot know whether they will be angrier, or more depressed and passive, or more energetic about creating legal or illegal work for themselves in the informal economy as their exclusion from the formal economy lengthens. Nevertheless, it is difficult to see how long an economy, society and polity can function, even at minimal levels, if they include one or more generations of people who are kept out of the labour force because there is no work for them.

JOB CREATION AND WORKSHARING

There is no point in developing this kind of worst-case analysis further, since both the future of economic exclusion and its possible consequences are now not only unknown but unknowable. Instead, I will end with a brief analysis of some basic policy themes.

Only a century ago, American writers suddenly began to publish utopian novels, several of which, including the most famous (Bellamy, 1888), argued that machines would replace people for much of the dirty, strenuous and other unpleasant kinds of work. Now that we are in some respects moving toward this state of affairs and see that it also leads to mass unemployment and poverty, it looks far less desirable, but discussion of possible solutions is only just beginning.

In America, at least, deliberate job creation has not had much political support since the Great Depression, although the cold war was at times used for this purpose. Specialized job creation and other policies to make the overall economy more labour intensive would seem relevant in an economy shifting to so-called service jobs, but it too has not been much discussed as a strategy against joblessness. Indeed, even a modern version of the New Deal's massive resort to job creation through public works was almost never talked about by the Clinton administration despite its election campaign promises to create new jobs; and any possibility of action ended, at least for the moment, with the right-wing Republican Congressional victory of 1994.

The idea of *worksharing*, of reducing the workweek or workyear or worklife so that the available work can be shared among more workers, was proposed in America in the late nineteenth century, and again briefly during the Great Depression, but not since then (Gans, 1990b). In the 1990s, worksharing is slowly but surely being mentioned as a desirable policy by academic and other writers on the Left, and even a few union officials – and this despite the fact that American labour unions have generally opposed worksharing in the twentieth century. Many European countries have actually begun to implement a very modest worksharing policy, however, and slowly but surely, western European employers are moving towards the 35- or 36-hour week. Conversely, American firms have found it more profitable to fire some workers and put others on overtime. As a result, worktime is rising in some parts of the American economy even as it declines in other parts – and in other countries.

In theory, worksharing might one day be a major solution, but any significant reduction in worktime would also mean a decline in worker income, with obvious political discontent to follow. The only viable solution is some form of income redistribution and even a universal minimum income grant, so that work need no longer bear the burden of being the sole source of income for most people. However, a politically painless or even feasible method has not yet been designed anywhere.[8] Even so, in some long-distant future, worksharing accompanied by a basic income grant for everyone seems the only viable solution, not only for the USA and western Europe but for the entire global economy.

Nevertheless, a more realistic projection of today's politics in the USA – and in some European countries with conservative governments – would suggest a very different long-term scenario: economic exclusion with minimal welfare, accompanied by formal as well as informal methods of isolating the excluded from the rest of society as much as possible. To the extent that those sentenced to such a fate are racially, ethnically or otherwise different from an actual or constructed majority, that majority is apt to support its government in driving the excluded into greater hardship.

Thus, if present trends were to be extrapolated toward a worst-case analysis, it would be for a society in which a majority or plurality hold decent, satisfying or at least reasonably secure jobs, and the rest are condemned to varieties of low-wage, insecure involuntary part-time and sporadic work – with an ever rising number sentenced to virtual or total labour force exclusion. By that time, perhaps the excluded will have figured out whether and how to construct their own economies.

Societies in which large numbers are excluded from the economy now exist in parts of the third world, although usually the excluded have some access to an agrarian alternative which keeps them alive except during famines and wars or civil wars engaged in by the militaristic dictatorships often found in such societies.

Whether 'developed' countries could slide 'backward' to a version of so-called third world status is a question that needs to be debated so it can be prevented. In theory it does not seem empirically impossible, even though the outcome would be different in many respects from today's third world models. Indeed, the third world metaphor is as out of place in this discussion as is 'underclass', for workers driven out of the post-industrial economy are in a very different economic, political and social position from the underemployed peasants and labourers of the third world.

The chapter by Enrica Morlicchio in this book presents a seemingly more tolerable form of occupational exclusion, but whether Naples, which has long suffered from what she calls an 'under-equilibrium' and which is distinctive in many other ways, could be a model for American or other European cities, is hard to say. In fact, one of America's great virtues has been to encourage poor people to maintain high aspirations, and even expectations, for the future, but this virtue, which is less often found in societies in which poverty has existed unabated for centuries, also has its drawbacks. As a result, poor

Americans who cannot or do not want to reduce their aspirations run the danger of high rates of depression and other mental illnesses, and may be unable or unwilling to cope with under-equilibrium.

FROM UNDERCLASS TO UNDERCASTE

If the third world metaphor does apply to first world nations, those excluded from the post-industrial economy who are now described as a structural underclass might turn into an *undercaste*, a population of such low status as to be shunned by the rest of the society, with opportunities for contact with others of higher status and upward mobility even more limited than those of the people today described as an underclass.

In the USA, as elsewhere, caste has a racial connotation, and until the civil rights movement and legislation of the 1960s, blacks were for all practical purposes a caste. They still are so in some respects today, but there is nothing inherently racial about caste position. While it is likely that, judging by past evidence, anyone economically or socially condemned to caste status will be viewed as different in skin colour or religion, 'culture', 'moral worth' or some other newly constructed characteristic can also be used to exclude people and place them in an undercaste. For example, most poor young black men in America, and in some communities even poor white men, will enter adulthood with a police arrest record in their files. This can easily function as a permanent stigma that can be used to assign them to a 'criminal' undercaste. One should not underestimate the ability of societies in severe economic difficulties to find ways to sentence some people to caste status in one or another fashion.

A CONCLUDING CAVEAT

I write about an 'undercaste' with some hesitation, for the term has the same defects as 'underclass'. The latter may have had some useful political shock value when it was a newly minted liberal or radical term. However, underclass and undercaste are umbrella terms, and the umbrella is open to anyone who wishes to place new meanings, or a variety of stereotypes, accusations and stigmas under it. Consequently, once the shock value wears off liberal or radical terminology and stigmatization processes gather steam, the basic defect of any form of alarmist terminology will again become apparent. For this reason alone, the best terminological 'policy' for social scientists is not to invent any new terms unless absolutely necessary, and to stay with very specific old ones whenever possible. In the economy of the future, no one can predict either the full range of its economic victims, or their stigmatization and the labels with which that stigmatization will be expressed.

NOTES

1 For a more detailed history of the term and its usage, see Aponte (1990) and Gans (1995: chapter 2).
2 A prior question is how these categories are defined, or constructed, and whether and how they are stigmatized, since stigmatized populations seem to be chosen for economic victimhood more readily than others.
3 Actually, the *Oxford English Dictionary* credits the first use of the word 'underclass' to a Scottish socialist, John Maclean, but he wrote about a revolutionary class overcoming domination.
4 The US picture is complicated further by the reliance on new immigrants in place of or to replace higher-wage workers, as well as blacks. This is, however, not a new phenomenon; it can be traced back at least to the Nova Scotians who came to the northeastern US early in the nineteenth century.
5 In that case they may even be arrested for crimes, or stigmatized for deviant behaviours, of which they are innocent.
6 The seemingly never-ending pressures for further reductions in welfare payments will worsen all these conditions. Changing the legal status of welfare from a federal entitlement to a block-grant funded programme would result in catastrophic consequences.
7 American public opinion polls have long found that people are eager to do something about poverty and to help the poor, but that eagerness disappears when the word 'welfare' is used in the questioning.
8 In the USA, it has not yet even been discussed in academic or policy circles since the fears of the 1960s about 'automation', but a number of European institutions and scholars raised the issue with the beginning of rising joblessness in the mid-1980s. For a review see Van Parijs (1992).

7

A Note on Interpreting American Poverty

Norman Fainstein, Vassar College

I would like very briefly to make some observations about poverty in the United States, initially by noting how we Americans are talking about the subject, and then by examining some recent objective evidence. On the level of discourse, the good listener is struck immediately by a crazy symphony, from which one can disentangle at least three rather discordant themes. The most amplified of these, benefiting as it does from the force of political power and money from conservative foundations, is being orchestrated by Congressional Republicans under the batons of the Speaker of the House, Newt Gingrich, and the Senate Majority Leader, Robert Dole. Their 'Contract with America' interprets poverty as the inevitable outcome of moral decay (hence the need for a return to 'family values'), reinforced by profligate and misguided governmental intervention (hence the need to shrink the welfare state, and particularly to wean the 'welfare dependent' into the labour market through a politics of 'tough love'). The discourse of the politically empowered Right has drowned out the half-hearted support of the Clinton administration for an industrial policy by concentrating obsessively on the undeserving poor, who will be forced to work and to behave properly by a judicial combination of the discipline of the labour market and the penal system. The popular leitmotif of the Republican Right, written most clearly in its direct attack against affirmative action and other racially sensitive programmes, is that the majority of 'middle-class' Americans have paid too long for the wrongdoing and dependency of black people. The less popular subtext is that economic growth requires the freeing of business from government fetters, particularly from those which restrict the natural efficiency of the market economy in determining the price of labour and the distribution of income.

The second theme has been trumpeted by social scientists, particularly sociologists, who specialize in the study of poverty. Its main melody presents variations on poor people of colour who are concentrated in urban ghettos, who comprise an 'underclass', who are disengaged from the regular labour market and engaged in unacceptable behaviour, ranging from producing children through consuming drugs to committing murders. Even though many studies have shown that the so-called underclass comprises only a small minority of the poor, the bulk of research money and discussion has been concentrated on examining the attributes and behaviours of those poor people whom other Americans find the most visible and threatening fragment of the low-income population (see Fainstein, 1993). Analysts go to great lengths to show that the 'persistently poor', who are concentrated in 'underclass communities', pose a distinct social problem, qualitatively different from people who merely have low incomes and live impoverished lives. Thus, Robert Mincy, after carefully delimiting the underclass to a small minority of the poor, laments the fact that

> the term *underclass* does not appeal to everyone. The rhetoric and controversy of the 1980s make it impossible for some observers to focus on the concept's straightforward connection, through earnings and occupational structures, to terms like *middle class* and *lower class*. More important, individuals who do not participate in the labor force and other residents of communities that pose barriers to labor force attachment may also reject the term *underclass* as too pejorative. Such a response makes it more difficult for community leaders to use the results of underclass research in community-based solutions. (1994: 134).

'Community leaders' *should* be concerned about a terminology that places one fraction of the poor – many members of which no doubt labour in the enormous informal or illegal economy – outside of the class structure, while simultaneously ignoring the majority of the poor who are just 'lower class' working stiffs. The family of terms like 'underclass' and 'ghetto poor' – along with their European kin, like 'socially marginal' and 'excluded' – function to deflect attention from the dynamics of economic and political processes which generate and reproduce the very populations and places which appear to lie under or outside of capitalist systems.

At the same time as Americans are being Doled the Gingrich contract, and the poverty establishment continues, perhaps through inertia, on its underclass tack, an increasing scholarly literature, mainly written by economists, is emphasizing labour market segmentation, wage differentials and income inequality. This third theme has been gaining in strength for a decade now. So, Mincy's previously cited discussion of 'The Underclass' appears as a chapter in a major anthology (Danziger, Sandefur and Weinberg 1994), which broadly and rigorously examines both macro-economic processes and government policy as bases for poverty. Levitan and Shapiro (1993) have come out with a new edition of their popular *Working but Poor: America's Contradiction*, and other scholarly works have greatly enriched our understanding of the intersection between the labour market, class structure, race and governmental policy (see Levy and Murnane, 1992; Peterson and Vroman, 1992; Danziger and Gottschalk, 1993; Carnoy, 1994).

Perhaps surprisingly, the media have also been thinking about inequality and its implications for America, though these discussions are infrequently connected to other articles which concern themselves with inner cities, ghetto poverty, urban crime and racial conflict. The cover story of *Business Week* (15 August 1994) bannered the headline, 'Inequality. How the Gap between Rich and Poor Hurts the Economy'. This lengthy article not only showed startling growth in earnings inequality in the US compared to western Europe, but also dismissed the contention that other countries paid the price for greater equality in either unemployment or slower growth. In an almost surrealistic conclusion – given the close ties of the journal's publishers to free-market capitalists and the Republican Party – the authors lament: 'of course, the US can't simply copy what other countries do. But [Richard] Freeman and others argue that it can adapt many European methods to the American context. There's no sign, however, that this is likely to happen anytime soon' (*Business Week*, 1994: 82).

Similarly, the headlines of the centrist and influential *New York Times* have been calling attention to the fact that uncontrolled growth of inequality is not a natural consequence of economic competition in *fin de siècle* world capitalism: 'Gap in Wealth in US Called Widest in West. New studies on the growing concentration of American wealth and income challenge a cherished part of the country's self-image. They show that rather than being an egalitarian society, the United States has become the most economically stratified of industrial nations' (*New York Times*, 1995a: 1). 'America's Opportunity Gap.

America's Jeffersonian ideals of equality and its reputation as a land of opportunity have been battered recently by evidence of a widening gulf between the rich and the poor. And now a growing body of research is showing that, at the same time, it is becoming more difficult to move into the economic élite' (*New York Times*, 1995b. Sec. 4, p. 4).

It would be naive to think that the facts are speaking for themselves in this last discourse, which has not even become dominant in the social sciences, much less begun to affect popular thinking and political conflict. But clearly we have here a core of scholars and journalists who have touched down to American reality, and whose work and views might potentially grow in influence. Strong evidence, if not money and power, favours their side.

Let's take a look at some of it. Table 7.1 allows us to describe general trends in inequality and poverty from the end of the 1970s to the most recent year for which data are available, 1993. The Gini ratio measures dispersion of incomes, and varies between 0.000, a situation of total equality among households, to 1.000, a situation when all income would be concentrated in a single household. The Gini ratio has increased monotonically by more than 40 points, or 10 per cent, over a period in which median real household income declined from $32,143 to $31,241. From these data we know that the median family grew poorer and that incomes become more unequally distributed. But who were the winners and losers?

The answer is obvious from the next panels, which relate the changing shares of income strata at the top, middle and bottom of the American class hierarchy. The top 5 per cent gained the most in before-tax income, increasing its share from 16.9 per cent to 20 per cent; the top quintile further improved its position; the middle quintiles declined; and the poorest fifth of the population grew substantially poorer. By 1993, the average household at the very top (5 per cent) received 22 times the annual income of a similar household at the bottom (20 per cent); in 1979 the ratio had been 16. After-tax income distribution followed a similar pattern. A Congressional study, using sophisticated models, showed that the top 1 per cent of families cornered the bulk of the income growth of the Reagan eighties, increasing its share from 8.4 per cent to 13.4 per cent, with most of the rest going to the next stratum at the top. Low-income households lost badly, while the middle declined as well (see table 7.1 references).

The cause of this redistribution upward was an enormous leap in executive compensation along with a sharp reduction in earnings at the bottom of the wage ladder. The next panel shows that the percentage of full-time, year-round (FTYR) workers with earnings

Table 7.1 Economic inequality in the United States, 1979–1993

	1979/80	*1984/85*	*1988/89*	*1992/93*
Gini ratio of household income	.403	.417	.429	.447
Shares of aggregate household income (%)				
Top 5 per cent	16.9	17.6	18.9	20.0
Top 20 per cent	44.1	45.6	46.8	48.2
Middle 60 per cent	51.7	50.5	49.4	48.2
Bottom 20 per cent	4.2	3.9	3.8	3.6
Shares of aggregate after-tax family income (%)				
Top 1 per cent	8.4	11.2	12.8	13.4
Top 5 per cent	19.7	23.5	25.2	25.7
Bottom 20 per cent	5.4	4.4	4.3	4.3
FTYR workers with poverty-level earnings (%)				
All workers	12.1	15.9	16.3	18.0
25–34-year-olds	8.8	13.1	17.0	18.4
Persons in poverty (millions)				
All	26.1	33.3	31.6	39.3
White	17.2	22.9	20.7	26.2
Black	8.1	9.2	9.3	10.9
Poverty rate (%)				
All	11.7	14.2	12.9	15.1
White	9.0	11.4	10.1	12.2
Black	31.0	31.3	30.7	33.1

Source: US Bureau of the Census, *Current Population Reports* – 'Studies in the Distribution of Income', Series P60-183 (1992), Table 1; 'Income, Poverty, and the Valuation of Noncash Benefits: 1993', Series P60-188 (1995), Fig. 1, Table D-4; 'Money Income of Households, Families, and Persons in the United States: 1991', Series P60-180 (1992), Table B-3, US House of Representatives, Committee on Ways and Means, *Overview of Entitlement Programs, 1991 Green Book* (US Government Printing Office, 1991), Appendix J, Table 27

below the official poverty line (about $13,000 in 1992) increased by 50 per cent from 1979 to 1992. In America, it is ever more possible to be fully employed in the formal economy and to live in poverty; and economic deterioration has been even more devastating among just the cohort of younger workers likely to start families. Moreover, other data from the same Census Bureau study show that the sharp increase in poverty-wage employment affects every age, racial, gender and educational grouping. Even among male college graduates, the percentage with poverty-level earnings doubled, from 3.1 per cent in 1979 to 6.3 per cent in 1992.

If a substantial fraction of 'fully' employed workers are poor, it is also the case that about half of all those who are poor work at least part time in the official economy (Levitan and Shapiro, 1993: 20). In fact, the reality of who is poor, using the rather restrictive definitions of the government, is strikingly different from the impressions conveyed explicitly by the discourse of conservative politicians, and implicitly by students of the 'underclass'. Two-thirds of all poor people in America are white (and that proportion changes little if we parcel out the Hispanic component). But nearly all research is devoted to the one-third of the poor who are black, only some of whom meet the various criteria proposed to define an underclass. One reason for the concern about the black poor is obviously the greater incidence of poverty among blacks, where the poverty rate has hovered at just over 30 per cent. Yet the rate among whites, although lower, has increased substantially in the last decade, an unsurprising consequence of growing inequality in the labour market (rather than of some kind of cultural or communal illness).

Perhaps the black poor are more interesting than the white because they are contained within our cities and ghettoized into the poorest parts of them. Almost 80 per cent of poor black people live in metropolitan areas, and 36 per cent in impoverished neighbourhoods. The more numerous white poor are less visible, being white, and more dispersed; only 3 per cent of them live in poor city neighbourhoods, and more than a third reside in the countryside (Jargowsky, 1994: table 1). The urban black poor are the stuff of the nightly television news in every region of America. The white poor, who are dispersed in working-class city and suburban neighbourhoods, or who live in trailer parks and cheap motels on the metropolitan outskirts, are of little interest to anyone. They are mainly politically inactive, sometimes racist and xenophobic in their attitudes, and threatening only as individuals. The facts about poverty, and we have here only touched the surface, suggest that neither the conservative nor the 'underclass' themes in the current discourse are particularly helpful in capturing the American reality.

Increasingly, scholars and public officials in Western Europe have studied poverty in America and tried to tease out its lessons for their own societies. This book is itself a testament to the quality of that work. Yet correctly reading the American scene – with its peculiar political processes, dominant *laissez-faire* ideology and racial dimension – is not an easy matter. Adding to the difficulty is the fact that all such readings are politicized. A favourite approach of those on the responsible European left is to exaggerate the horrors of the American ghetto, from which the government has allegedly withdrawn completely, and then to contrast that situation with the much more responsible behaviour of European welfare states. The imagery employed bears an uncomfortable resemblance to the long-extant picture of 'darkest Africa', and the racial difference between the European lower class and the American always lurks just beneath the official text of the comparison.

I want to close this note on American poverty by cautioning against such a reading. Right now the American situation is qualitatively different from the European; most obviously, the European states are more active in securing the economic position of the most dependent parts of their populations. Race is less important in Europe, and residential segregation of the poor in deteriorated central city districts less common. But, as we have seen, most of the American poor are white and do not live in such neighbourhoods either. In fact, this is even true of the black poor: most live in neighbourhoods that are relatively heterogeneous in class composition; lessons drawn from the worst neighbourhoods in the Chicago ghetto cannot be generalized to the US as a whole (Fainstein, forthcoming).

What should be emphasized about poverty in the United States is that it is a result of exactly the economic polarization which dominates world capitalism at the present moment. Poverty, both here and in Europe, is not a condition; it is a process. The poor are not 'excluded' from the capitalist economy, they are simply the most exploited part of the labour force. Their marginal existence functions to keep down the price of labour throughout the system and to augment returns on capital. Only the state, under political pressure, can create the conditions which mitigate this tendency. The important point, then, is not that our poor differ from yours, but that our politics is different. As long as this holds true, poverty in America will remain harsher than in Europe, and our cities – and, less known to you, our countryside – will remain more violent places.

8

Dangerous Classes: Neglected Aspects of the Underclass Debate

Lydia Morris, University of Essex, Colchester

My choice of title for this chapter is in part intended as a reminder of the fact that the idea of the 'underclass', or its various equivalents, has been recurrent throughout recent history. 'Dangerous classes' was a term commonly used in the nineteenth century to refer to a population on the margins of society, perceived as a threat to social order. The idea thus serves as a comment on the contemporary significance of the underclass debate, and the reasons for its current political force. I want to open this paper by looking at the concept of the underclass as a sociological problem, asking what the idea is being used to achieve, both in sociological terms and in terms of public perceptions of social cohesion. To understand this we need to consider the social context in which the idea has taken hold.

The main point of significance I would identify is a growing instability of two traditional building blocks of British and American social life; one being full-time employment for men, and the other the nuclear family household, though we will later introduce a third, the nation-state. Both British and American society is based on assumptions about a division of labour producing a particular combination of work, family and welfare. Over the last three decades the fit between them has gradually become dislocated and much of the underclass debate revolves around where the explanation (or blame) for this dislocation lies. In particular, attention has focused on rising male unemployment, and rising single motherhood, both argued to be linked to aspects of welfare provision, and there has been some suggestion that the two phenomena are interrelated. Certainly doubts have been raised about the stability of two key social institutions.

In some ways the notion of the underclass, and the public attention it has attracted, can be seen as an exercise in conceptual containment. Rather than revise our understanding of social organization to accommodate a number of rather complex changes, some explanation or analysis is sought which leaves the social world as we understand it more or less intact. In Britain the policy of 'Back to Basics' was a symptom of the same unease and search for containment. The predominant view in the underclass literature defines a group which rejects the norms and values of mainstream society, and the evidence cited for this argument is state dependency, denial of the work ethic, the failure of morality, and the rejection of family norms, often also argued to be linked with criminality (for example, Auletta, 1982). A popular usage of the concept of the underclass groups these disparate features together into a residual category, located 'outside' of a society which remains cohesive and free from internal challenge.

The creation of a category of outsiders in the face of a threat to social order is by no means new, and the precursors of the concept of the underclass are interesting in this respect. For Malthus (1806) it was the redundant population who reproduced irresponsibly, without the means of survival; for Marx and Engels (1850) the lumpenproletariat, apart from the real working class, described in pejorative terms as the scum of the earth, the depraved element of all classes; for Mayhew (1861) it was the social outcasts – a race apart, a wandering tribe, with a repugnance towards civilization and a psychological incapacity for steady work. This idea of a race apart was also echoed in the eugenics movement and its attack on the degenerate hords who threatened social stability (for review see Jones, 1980). Even Booth's (1902) path-breaking work which revealed poverty in sections of the working population still claimed to identify a group incapable of improvement who degrade whatever they touch. A vocabulary of contagion is common to much of this work; the idea that certain sections of the population can contaminate society's more respectable members. The behaviour of the 'polluting' group was also usually felt to be underpinned by some moral incapacity, manifest in criminality, sexual licence, work avoidance and dependence on charity or the state.

Certainly a distinction between the worthy and the unworthy runs through the history of British and American provision for the poor, and the argument underlying present debate is that the welfare state has been over-generous, and is abused by many. The common assumption is that state provision has created a culture of dependency which has undermined the work ethic, and has been damaging to the stability of the nuclear family. The notion of the underclass thus hinges upon two different types of distinction; position in the system of production, conventionally the basis of 'social class' location, and position in relation to the state, and society more generally, in other words, civic status (Lockwood, 1987). Much of the sociological commentary on the 'underclass', however, has emphasized the former at the expense of the latter. Our understanding of the civic dimension of the underclass debate is best advanced through the idea of social citizenship, and the questions of social inclusion and exclusion which it implicitly raises.

CITIZENSHIP

In Britain there was an interesting watershed at the time of the Beveridge Report (1942), when for a brief period it was thought that the creation of the welfare state under these proposals would mark a turning-point. There was optimism about what Marshall (1950) terms the guarantee of social inclusion through social citizenship, defined as 'full membership of the community'. This idea of social inclusion stands as a counterpart to the notion of the underclass – a term designating social, material and moral exclusion, and referring to a condition which it was thought the British welfare state under the Beveridge Plan would eradicate.

One position on the political left has tried to appropriate the term 'underclass', arguing that the welfare state has failed in its aims, that the commitment to full employment was never strong enough, social provision for the unemployed was never adequate, and the administration of the system was always punitive. But the dominant rhetoric comes from the right, where we can see the underclass debate as bred of a moral panic about the unravelling of the work/family/welfare nexus. Thus we find a condemnation of the alleged culture of dependency, which argues that the welfare state has gone too far, and turns state dependence into a badge of exclusion rather than a guarantee of inclusion. The right to social inclusion has increasingly been called into question, and linked to the condemnation of a culture of dependency is the growth of a literature stressing social obligations above social rights (for example, Mead, 1986), the major obligation being to work for a living. This turns the original promise of citizenship upside-down, and is based on the view that the state dependent must be compelled to give something back to society.

The situation in America, as compared to Britain, differs in important details, most notably because the history and structure of welfare provision in the two countries has been sharply divergent (at least until recently). Crucially there is no 'as of right' provision for unemployed men ineligible for the contributory insurance benefit. Whilst both countries operate a contributory system of Unemployment Benefit, there are growing numbers of workers who do not qualify; a result of rising unemployment and increasing insecurity. In Britain the means-tested Income Support fills this breach, but there is no US equivalent. There the major means-tested benefit has been directed towards families with dependent children (AFDC) – and this has usually meant single mothers. Since 1989 this benefit has been available in all states to homes with dependent children in which there is an unemployed father present, but there are tight conditions attached. The main recipients have overwhelmingly been single mothers, and certainly not young unmarried or childless men, who have no automatic right to benefit.

The functioning of this benefit (AFDC) is at the heart of an American literature arguing that welfare provision has undermined the institution of the family and the work ethic. In this literature, state dependency is one defining feature of an underclass made up of single mothers, with young males living on the criminal fringe but assumed to have oblique access to welfare for which they are not themselves eligible, through these women. It should be added that this is perceived to be an overwhelmingly black life-style. The central character in this debate is Charles Murray (1984), who argues on the basis of rational choice theory that young women are better off living independently on their welfare cheques than throwing in their lot with the father of their children, hence the argument that welfare has undermined the institution of the family; these single mothers then foster a culture of the underclass which reproduces the pattern in the next generation, a culture which takes a hold because of the absence of a viable male role model. It is this alleged cultural reproduction of the underclass which is presented as the evidence of a rejection of the mainstream values of society.

The counter-position is taken up by William Julius Wilson (1987), who argues that the high proportion of single mothers is to be explained by structural factors producing high levels of male unemployment, together with the high mortality and incarceration rates of young blacks. The pool of marriageable men is thus argued to be far too low for the nuclear family household to be a viable option, having been undermined by the disadvantaged position of poor black men in the labour market. Murray and Wilson appear to agree, however, on seeing single parenthood as anomalous, and at least by implication holding up the nuclear family household as the ideal. For Murray the central issue is an ethical one, concerning correct upbringing and maintenance of the work ethic; for Wilson it is economic, with structural change in the economy undermining the viability of traditional gender arrangements.

GENDER AND THE UNDERCLASS

I would like at this point to examine the gender subtext to this debate, for although gender differentiation permeates the substance of discussion of the underclass it is rarely made explicit in analysis. Murray sees the absence of a male role model in the family unit as central in explaining the alleged growth of the 'underclass', and seems implicitly to suggest that the underclass is made up of men, but is reproduced by women. The task of socialization is thus firmly located in the family unit, and the generation of a subculture of the underclass is said to emerge because the single mother has failed in that duty. This leaves the women's status ambiguous, though if the underclass is defined in terms of state dependence, then those living on welfare are placed firmly inside the criteria of membership.

There have been varied responses to this situation:

1   one is the feminization of poverty argument (for example, Bane, 1988), which argues that women are being forced to carry the burden of society's poverty, and that better provision should be made for them;
2   the other more dominant view is that some work requirement is necessary for single mothers, both as a deterrent to welfare dependency and presumably to foster the work ethic in their children (for example, Mead, 1986).

We see quite clearly here a social control dimension to welfare, but which oddly seems not to address the real concern expressed in the debate which centres on the alleged withdrawal of young men from the labour force. It is ironically a solution which, at least in traditional terms, brings women's work role and family obligations into conflict.

There is in fact a more fundamental problem here, for an understanding of which we must return to the issue of social citizenship or social inclusion. Citizenship is a concept of the public sphere, and as such it is shaped by traditional gender roles which associate men with the public sphere and women with the private sphere (Pateman, 1989). To address the issue of women's social citizenship we have to address the work/family conflict faced by many women, and most dramatically by single mothers.

In both Britian and America the foundations of welfare were in support of traditional roles. AFDC was intended: 'to release from the wage earning role the person whose natural function is to give her children the physical and affectionate guardianship necessary . . . to rear them into citizens capable of contributing to society'. And for Beveridge: 'The ideal social unit is the household of man, wife and children maintained by the earnings of the first alone.' In neither case does this set of expectations any longer apply, but nor has a viable alternative been fully established in terms of work, family and welfare arrangements.

In relation to the underclass, single mothers and social inclusion, perhaps there is an argument to say that traditional gender roles no longer apply, that a majority of women are now in paid employment and single mothers should be no exception to this trend. It still remains to consider the employment options which are generally available to most low-skilled women in Britain and America, and which account for the rise in recent years of married women in the labour force. Wages available to most women are not adequate for family maintenance (see Jencks, 1992; Brown, 1989), especially where employment opportunities are confined to part-time work – increasingly the case in Britain; work constructed on the assumption of women's domestic role. The corollary of this is that many married women are working for a secondary wage, viable only because there is another wage in the household; not only for a secondary wage, but in secondary employment – low paid, insecure and designed for cheapness and disposability. For many women, limited employment opportunities, together with mothering obligations, necessitate some kind of dependency – either on the state or on a husband.

Thus the gender-related issues which arise from the debate about the underclass partly stem from unresolved questions about the sexual division of labour in society. Women's position in the household, and particularly the situation of single mothers, raises a number of problems for conceptions of social inclusion. As welfare dependents they become stigmatized members of the underclass, failing in their role of socialization. Their weak position in the labour market, which is partly the result of gender segregation, means they are for the most part unable to earn sufficient to be self-supporting, and full-time employment would anyway conflict with their mothering role. It is hard to see what full social inclusion would look like for these women, and without some reassessment of the sexual division of labour in society this will continue to be the case.

Women's full social inclusion would involve the breakdown of gender divisions in the private sphere, or the removal of much private labour into the public sphere. The underclass debate evades these issues by marginalizing the status of single mothers; single mother-hood is presented as a moral issue, and as a departure from the norms and values of mainstream society. Yet the breakup of the nuclear family household is happening at the centre of society; changes to household structures and the decreasing viability of marriage as a lifetime condition are far more far-reaching and more centrally placed in society than the underclass debate has ever suggested. So too is a dependent status for women.

Recent developments in the conceptualization of social citizenship have increasingly, as we have seen, placed at least as much emphasis on obligations as on rights, the prime obligation being work as a means to independence (see Pateman, 1989), and not, ironically, the care of the next generation of citizens. This places women in an ambiguous position; either they earn their 'public' citizenship rights by their own paid employment, or they perform their 'private' family obligations and remain dependent. This conflict can only be resolved by either a redistribution of the 'private' obligations of unpaid labour, or by some acknowledgement of the 'public' service such labour performs, or by increasing state involvement in the 'private' obligation to care for children, alongside fundamental labour market reform. The current situation, however, leaves individual women in something of a dilemma, especially if the fathers of their children are unwilling or unable to fulfil their traditional role. These women become the new 'undeserving poor'.

Thus, the underclass debate stigmatizes women's dependency in the context of a tradition which has constructed women as dependent. This tradition has been challenged but not overcome, and is still maintained by beliefs about appropriate gender roles, beliefs about the significance of motherhood, and also by the disadvantaged position of most women in the labour market. For single mothers the dilemma is particularly clear; as benefit dependents they are stigmatized members of the 'underclass', and as such are failing in their distinctively 'female' role of socializing the next generation. It is argued that the children in such households suffer from the absence of a breadwinning role model, and yet the weak position of the majority of sole mothers in the labour market prevents them from easily assuming this role themselves. Even were they to do so this would raise the problem of childcare, and more generally of whether they were meeting their traditional obligations as a mother. One response to this complex of problems has been strongly to reaffirm the strengths of traditional arrangements, but a more radical alternative states that any solution to the impasse over women's rights to social inclusion can only be achieved by a fundamental and far-reaching review of many taken-for-granted aspects of social life.

What we are currently witnessing is a breakdown in the family/ work/welfare nexus on a number of fronts: employment for men is in decline, the nuclear family is in decline, and the use of welfare to fill the breach is increasingly under political challenge. Yet women with children have no easy route to independence, because of their principal role in childcare and their limited labour market opportunities. The public anxieties surrounding these issues have been captured by the rhetoric of the underclass, which by isolating and stigmatizing single mothers seems to offer at least a containment of the problem. That problem, however, pervades the whole of a society which is undergoing some renegotiation of the organization of work, family and welfare. The nature of that change cannot be understood through a focus on a residual group, argued to be inadequately socialized, and without whom it is believed the problems will go away.

MIGRANT LABOUR AND THE UNDERCLASS

The problem discussed so far has concerned the decreasing viability of two traditional social institutions; the nuclear family household, and the male principal earner. It was also suggested, however, that a third institution is under challenge; that of the nation-state. In addition to the male unemployed and single parents there is a third group with a precarious claim to social inclusion; migrant workers, and particularly illegal migrants. The distrust awakened by the 'stranger' is apparent in popular responses to migrant labour in eighteenth-century England, with settlement regulations designed to protect parishes against the costs of the wandering poor. Where migration occurs across national boundaries these issues are all the more salient, and necessarily involve questions of citizenship and the social rights which follow from citizenship.

An obvious example concerns the circumstances and conditions of migration across socio-political boundaries, the place of the new arrival in the social and economic structures of the receiving 'community', and the rights of this individual to the resources and protections the 'community' conventionally offers to its citizens. As we shall see, the acceptance of migrant labour is often designed to be partial, to take the labour without conferring the rights of membership. Carens (1988) has considered the philosophical roots of such issues in the context of Mexican migration into the United States, though a particularly topical case of the negotiation and renegotiation of these matters arises, as we shall see, in relation to migration into the European Union.

'The conventional moral view is that a country is justified in restricting immigration whenever it serves the national interest to do so' (Carens, 1988: 207). The question commonly arises in contemporary society in relation to concern about accelerating demands upon the welfare state. The usual fear is that large-scale immigration will undermine the will and the capacity to support the institutions of the welfare state. However: 'almost all of the illegal immigrants and many of the legal immigrants are unskilled people eager to find jobs of any kind and prepared to accept difficult, unpleasant work at rates of pay that are low by American standards because these jobs are much better than whatever work (if any) they can find in their native land' (Carens, 1988: 210).

Certainly jobs of the kind filled by migrant labour in the States offer terms and conditions which fail to live up to the promise of full participation in the accepted standards of life for US citizens; they do not rival even the precarious existence available outside of employment, and can be filled only by workers with origins outside of that 'community' of expectations. Illegal immigrants are particularly vulnerable in this respect, and Carens goes on to argue that: 'the existence of such a vulnerable, exploited underclass is incompatible with the goal of creating a society in which all members are regarded as having "equal social worth" and equal social, legal and political rights.'

Where the supposed outsiders have in fact been recruited to perform the least rewarded and most poorly paid tasks by another society then their exclusion from the full rights of membership in that 'community' is on dubious grounds. The situation is further compounded if the 'outsider' can be deemed to be in some other sense foreign, that is, to be of different racial or ethnic origin. The receiving 'communities' may then object to their presence in defence of their common identity and distinctive way of life. It was argued above that the notion of the 'underclass', with its connotations of social exclusion has as its counterpart that of social citizenship, defined by T. H. Marshall as 'full membership of a community', for purposes of civil, political and social rights and duties.

Marshall's treatment of citizenship has been argued by various writers (Yuval-Davis, 1990; Held, 1989) to be deficient in a number of ways, notably through an emphasis on social class as the main social differentiator, and through an implicit confinement to the nation-state.

Yuval-Davis takes up this point and problematizes the notion of 'community': 'it assumes a given collectivity . . . [not] an ideological and material construction, whose boundaries, structures and norms are a result of constant processes of struggles and negotiations, or more general social developments. Any dynamic notion of citizenship must start from the processes which construct the collectivity' (1990: 3).

The issue of community membership needs therefore to be brought to the forefront in a manner which Marshall fails to address. Thus Held argues: 'while it is the case that national sovereignty has been most often the victor when put to the test, the tension between citizenship, national sovereignty and international law is marked, and it is by no means clear how it will be resolved.'

Traditional concepts are thus argued to be undermined by: 'the dynamics of a world economy which produces instabilities and difficulties within states and between states and which outreach the control of any single "centre" '.

The construction of a labour supply with a particular, inferior, relation to the nation-state and therefore with limited claims to membership of the 'community' which that state represents is one particular instance of this dynamic. It poses a knot of problems for the relationship between the construction of an underclass, the status of outsider, and claims to social rights, which welfare provisions are inadequate to solve. In fact, access to welfare is one of the central issues in the denial of full membership to the migrant worker and there have been a number of different ways of restricting these rights. The presence of this population, however, offers support to the view that there are jobs available for those willing to work, and that welfare dependents thus constitute an 'underclass' in another sense; optional withdrawal from the labour market. These problems have long been identified in North American society (for example, Mead, 1986), but are currently emerging in a very particular context in the European Union.

THE CASE OF POST-WAR EUROPE

In several industrialized states of western Europe foreign citizens make up 10–15 per cent of the labour force (Hammar, 1990: 1). The origins of migrant labour are by no means confined to those countries included in membership of the European Union (EU), and there are particular questions which have recently arisen concerning inward labour migration. In the post-war period European countries adopted different means of controlling their migrant labour but the broad picture is the same for all; particular populations of workers were channelled into an extremely vulnerable labour market position, with very limited rights in their country of employment. This then was the European equivalent of the Chicago labour force in the US. Moore (1977) identifies three categories of migrant worker; foreign workers (that is, non-EC nationals), ex-colonial workers and illegal migrants, to which we can add the ambiguous category of asylum seekers. All of them, argues Cohen (1987: 113): 'characteristically enjoy less favourable civil, legal and political status. Their family life is limited or prohibited, their housing is inferior, their rights as employees are often markedly worse than indigenous workers, while in most European countries they are disenfranchised and unorganized in trade unions.'

These workers were typically seen as part of a reserve army of labour (Castles and Kosak, 1985) – and sometimes termed an 'underclass' – through which the industrialized countries of Europe exploited the cheap, mobile and disposable labour of migrants from the third world or southern and increasingly eastern European migrants. They were thus excluded from full social (and often legal) citizenship.

The common pattern is confinement to a narrow range of low-status, insecure jobs which would otherwise be difficult to fill, and which are often subject to fluctuations in demand. Like Chicano labour in the US these workers are employed because they are willing to work on terms unacceptable to indigenous labour, and mainly lacking citizenship rights they are held at an immediate disadvantage, intended to be easily expendable. The rights and status of foreign workers show some variation between countries, and are directly related to the differing style and intensity of attempts to control their presence. By the early 1970s, however, almost all of the receiving countries faced the problem of control, and began to seek ways of limiting or dismissing their foreign workers. A number of ways of doing so were introduced, some of which were inherent in the original terms under which migrants were allowed into the country concerned. The principal uses of migrant labour in the post-war period had been intended to be temporary, though countries differed in the nature and rigidity of the mechanisms established to permit control of the situation; the guest-worker systems of Germany and Switzerland being arguably the most severe, and these countries were more successful than the other countries in reducing their foreign work-force in the period after 1973 (Gordon, 1989: 22).

In brief, countries with access to a colonial labour force could exploit this source (Britain, France and Holland), while others relied on some form of guest-worker system (Germany, Belgium and Switzerland):

> jobs filled by these workers were ones which were less acceptable to the indigenous work force. Immigrants were disproportionately employed in jobs which required arduous physical effort, had poor working conditions, had little security and in some instances their employment was subject to seasonal variation and redundancy. These features of the work experience were common to ex-colonial labour and guest-workers alike. (Nanton, 1991: 192)

Similarly Gordon (1989) argues that although there is considerable variety in the uses to which migrant labour is put – growing low-level service sector jobs, or jobs in a declining manufacturing sector, 'they are mostly destined for routine manual work at the bottom of the occupational hierarchy' (p. 17). The particular patterns of employment in different countries will reflect 'varying forms of discrimination and closure in the indigenous labour market', but to much the same end.

The general trend has been away from the guest-worker pattern, which proved hard to sustain, and towards much more permanent settlement, though with migrants holding inferior formal and informal status in a majority of countries. Their rights are often restricted, especially politically, they can be threatened with deportation for transgression of their conditions of residence, and they occupy a distinctly inferior position in the social and occupational structure. They are also denied free access to the wider labour market of the EU. Even where migrants have made the transition to citizenship, or in other cases arrived as citizens, this has not guaranteed full social inclusion. Allen and Macey (1990: 388) make a distinction between nationality and citizenship which, they argue, 'strikes at the very heart of the concept of citizenship as including civil, political and social rights embedded in institutions'.

There has been some kind of racist response to the immigrant population in almost all of the countries considered, and access to social resources remains limited. A second generation is now growing up for whom there is no place in the labour market but who have no real ties with their parents' country of origin. Thus the need for labour reserves in the post-war labour boom, usually to fill the jobs rejected by the 'host' population, has created an 'underclass' of a particular kind, often ethnically and racially distinct, in inferior employment and increasingly unemployed, and often denied both formal and social citizenship. A precarious claim on social resources or the need for employment as a condition of residence can force them into work which full citizens of the receiving country would probably reject.

Even where migrants have gained full citizenship, discrimination severely limits their prospects.

There has of course been some debate about the suitability of a terminology of exclusion for migrant labour, such as sub- or lumpen-proletariat (Castles and Kosak, 1985), terms arguably equivalent to the notion of the 'underclass'. As part of the work-force, can migrants correctly be termed an underclass? Migrant labour has, however, clearly been used to perform a particular function in terms of the labour needs of industrialized economies which leaves the migrant in a precarious social and economic position, and many of the issues which arise in connection with the underclass debate apply to them; labour market disadvantage, social exclusion and stigmatization. Their position inevitably raises questions about what constitutes membership of a social and economic 'community' and under what circumstances and by what mechanisms the rights to such membership can be denied. These questions are just now arising in a new context, in relation to what has been termed 'Fortress Europe'.

A EUROPEAN PROBLEM

The circumstances discussed above combine to pose an interesting challenge to the concept of European citizenship and European integration. The right of free movement of labour in the EU raises particularly interesting questions given that migration into Europe from non-EU countries is much greater than movement between EU countries. The long-term trend in migration has meant a shift in the balance between European and third world migrants such that the latter group make up over 40 per cent of the minority populations of Britain, France and Germany (Castles, 1984: 89).

> The northern Member States realized too late that the workers they had imported from Turkey and North Africa in the sixties and early seventies did not come only to work and then allow themselves to be sent back home afterwards. They came as guest-workers and became immigrants ... the result is: vulnerable groups of immigrants, uncertain about their future, dreaming of returning to their country of origin but knowing that they and their children no longer have a future there. Often too, living with the bleak prospect of lack of work and in poverty. (Hoogenboom, 1992: 42)

One feature of the 1980s has been the unprecedented number of asylum seekers, who in 1985 exceeded foreign workers. Whilst they are commonly denied work permits they will inevitably join the numbers of clandestine labour. There has also been extensive reunification of the families of guest-workers, marking their transition to permanent settlers; there has been considerable illegal immigration into southern Europe, mainly from North Africa, which could even equal legal migration; there has been a re-emergence of the guest-worker system, for mainly skilled workers; and there has also been the beginning of a flow of migration from eastern Europe – numbers of between 4 million and 8 million are anticipated over the next few years (Migration News Sheet, 1991). In Germany workers from the east have begun to displace the Turkish labour force (Baldwin-Edwards, 1991), and similar patterns could emerge elsewhere in Europe.

A high level of illegal migration into southern Europe is largely the result of proximity to underdeveloped countries where demographic pressures are pushing people to seek access of some kind to the more developed economies of Europe. In the southern countries immigration control is much weaker and the coastal border vulnerable to illicit entry. There is also a large informal sector in the economies of the south which offers a range of opportunities to illegal entrants. Throughout the 1980s there have been various regularization programmes with differing degrees of take-up in Spain, Italy and France which have been introduced alongside penalties for both employers and workers who continue to operate illegally.

The shift towards third world migration has accelerated to the extent that in 1990 there were 13 million legally settled non-Europeans in the 12 countries of the EU (Nanton, 1991), and 15 million non-EU nationals (Allen and Macey, 1990: 378): 'an estimated 60 per cent of [foreign citizens] settled in France and 70 per cent in Germany and the Netherlands are citizens of countries outside the EC. This foreign population comprises a predominance of North Africans in France, Turks in Germany, Turkish and Moroccan communities in the Netherlands, and Moroccans in Belgium' (Nanton, 1991: 191).

The point at issue is whether freedom of movement across borders within the EU should be extended to legally resident non-EU nationals. Potentially, the immigration decisions of one country would have an ultimate impact on those of another. The member states differ, however, both in terms of the nature and structure of their economies, and also the nature of their policy and their degree of practical control over immigration. As we noted above, the countries of the south have higher levels of clandestine migration, and this has in part been dealt with by offers of regularization. Are these regularized migrants then to be granted freedom of movement within Europe, and would selective restriction be consistent with the Community's aims of equal treatment and social justice?

Under the banner of defence of sovereignty many of the more prosperous countries of Europe wish to defend their borders, and therefore their resources from the presence and claims of 'outsiders'. Collaboration on the basis of a European Union has so far come into conflict with the right to decide on membership of and access to the national 'community'. A final agreement on free movement for non-EU nationals would mean that the greater accessibility of southern European countries to third world migrants, and particularly the regularization of clandestine labour, would ultimately affect the populations and resources of the more developed (and richer) countries of the north. One of the fears which underlies resistance to this situation is that it opens up the possibility of 'social dumping'. Free movement of labour in an integrated market would mean that states with high unemployment or low social welfare provision could effectively export their unemployment to states with jobs to offer or with better welfare provision.

One way to prevent this would be to establish a social dimension to the single market, of the kind represented by the Charter of Social Rights, which is not at present legally binding. By standardizing terms and conditions of employment, minimum wages, equal treatment by gender and race, social security systems and rights, etc. national barriers to labour mobility could be removed without the fear of social dumping (Roche, 1992: 215). But this would also limit the degree of exploitation of foreign labour in a way which would not suit employers, and would confer full social citizenship upon the migrants, something which has so far been resisted. This, of course, is one of the reasons for the desire for a strict and standardized policy on immigration, but should this be achieved there will still be a reluctance on the part of some countries to accept the consequences of the previous immigration policy of others; a resistance to conferring social citizenship upon migrants who they would never have allowed across their borders. These questions are all the more pressing given the breakup of the eastern bloc, and the emergence of new nations in the east, many of which think the solution to their problems lies in entry into Europe. If they are not received into the EU as nations, their populations will as individuals seek their own way in.

THE UNDERCLASS AND SOCIAL CITIZENSHIP

As with single parents, a full understanding of migrant labour clearly rests upon an appreciation of their civic status in relation to social inclusion and social support, alongside their structural position in the labour market. In other words, it should take into account the two dimensions of structured inequality referred to earlier; that of civic status, and that of position in the labour market. On the one hand are questions of formal and informal citizenship, claims to state resources, social perceptions of the status of dependence, and the standards of living achievable by this means. On the other hand are rankings by skill, prospects of employment, vulnerability to unemployment, and the terms and conditions under which an individual worker can still be expected to labour.

In this chapter I have considered two particular groups – single parents and migrant workers. In fact, both of these groupings incorporate a very heterogeneous collection of individuals, but at the extremes of disadvantage both face particular problems in achieving social inclusion; in the one case these problems stem from the sexual division of labour in society, and in the other from inter-national divisions of labour. Single mothers have a precarious claim to social citizenship because of the constraints their domestic obligations place upon their fuller participation in society, while migrant workers are constrained by their lesser claim to society's resources and opportunities by virtue of their national, cultural and 'racial' identity. Both groups are subject to a set of circumstances which result in less than full social inclusion; circumstances which can only be explained in terms which lie outside the existing framework of the underclass debate.

It could, however, be helpful to this debate to include analysis which takes in much more than the position of the unemployed and/or state dependent, and considers the structuring and distribution of different types of employment in terms of broad social groupings. If accomplished alongside a consideration of the foundation and conditions of social inclusion, such analysis could do much to change the terms of debate from a focus on the residual category of the 'underclass' to a reconsideration of how sociologists think about social structures.

9

Space and Race in the Post-Fordist City: The Outcast Ghetto and Advanced Homelessness in the United States Today

Peter Marcuse, Columbia University, New York

Space and race play a new role in the dynamics of urban poverty in the United States today. The outcast[1] ghetto, the ghetto of the excluded, is one product; advanced homelessness, the peculiar homelessness of technologically advanced societies, is another. Both reflect a new process of exclusion from the mainstream of society. Both are part of a broader pattern that makes up the post-Fordist city:[2] a pattern of division, of quartering, in which gentrification for some accompanies ghettoization for others. The post-Fordist city results from four linked processes: technological change, internationalization, concentration of ownership, and centralization of control. Space and race determine how these processes will impact their victims, and that impact will be mediated through historic differences in spatial and racial patterns. Looking at that process of mediation suggests whether developments in the United States and western Europe may be expected to converge in the coming years: whether the outcast ghetto and advanced homelessness in the United States are harbinger of what is to come in Europe and elsewhere.

The organization of this chapter reflects the above argument. The first section argues that the ghetto in the US today is an outcast ghetto, differing in its definition and role from the historic black ghettos: it is today a ghetto of the excluded and cast out rather than of the subordinated and restricted. The evolution of the black ghetto and ethnic enclaves is crucially different, the role of the state in the contemporary process of ghettoization, and the spatial configuration of the ghetto, are also new in the post-Fordist city in the United States, New York City being an example.

The second section describes advanced homelessness: again, how it is differentiated from the homelessness of prior years both in quantity and in quality, and how state policy has reinforced its role for those of the excluded not 'sheltered' in the ghetto.

The third section, on the new spatial divisions of the post-Fordist city, summarizes the argument about the divisions of the post-Fordist city which have produced both the outcast ghetto and advanced homelessness: a process of quartering, in which increasing gentrification for those benefited by the transition to post-Fordism is linked to increasing ghettoization of those victimized by that transition, with increasing instability, tension and conflict in the spaces between.

The fourth section spells out, with a simple model, how this process of victimization is mediated through the uses of race and space, and what determines the cost to the victims, in the public as well as in the private sphere.

Throughout, one point needs emphasis, even though it may not be explicitly repeated in every context: what is new is only partially new.[3] Ghettos have existed at least since Venice in the fifteenth century, homelessness in the literal sense was more prevalent in the Middle Ages than today, racism is hardly new, spatial divisions within the city antedate Roman times, and so on. Thus some of the causes cannot be new, and some of the remedies are likely to be ones often suggested before but never carried out. It is easy to forget that fact in the fascination with what is new. But policy responses cannot only be to what is new; they must also address more long-standing and deeper-seated roots. The focus here is nevertheless on what is new because problems cannot be dealt with in general, but only in their specific and concrete settings, and those settings, together with the precise way those problems are manifest today, rather than earlier, must be understood for effective analysis. The chances are that a thorough remedy will involve some cures that are old and some that are new.

THE GHETTO, THE ENCLAVE AND THE STATE

Much has been written about ghettoization in the United States recently, but little deals historically with the qualitative change that the ghetto has undergone in the transition from the Fordist to the post-

Fordist city. In two of the best recent books, the focus is more on the persistence and intensity of segregation and ghettoization than on changes in its character (Massey and Denton, 1993; Goldsmith and Blakeley, 1992). Most see the ghetto in the United States as strictly a phenomenon of African-American residence;[4] others link the ghetto with the Latino *barrio* (Goldsmith and Blakley, 1992); that there have been recent changes in the relative role of African-American and other spatial concentrations of ethnic/racial groups is little explored. The focus here is on what is different about the African-American ghetto of today from earlier ghettos in the United States, or the historic ghettos of other countries: on the *outcast ghetto*.

The Outcast Ghetto

William Wilson has explored the consequences of ghettoization more than its specific causes; he lays stress, among immediate causes, on the out-migration of middle-class blacks from older areas of racial concentration in the 1970s as a result of the fair housing successes of the civil rights movement of the 1960s, arguing that it left behind a new form of ghetto that produced what he first called the 'underclass', and more recently called the 'ghetto poor'. Wilson begins his explanatory account of the new ghetto with the major economic and social changes summarized later in this chapter, but the direct explanation for changes in the role of the ghetto are narrower issues of demographics and population movement. And others have argued that the out-migration he references is largely a chimera, and that middle-class blacks remain segregated within black ghettos as much as poor blacks (see Fainstein in this volume; Massey and Denton, 1993).

The term 'hypersegregation' might be used to describe the new stage in the development of the United States ghetto, but that is not how it has generally been used. It has rather come into use to differentiate, in purely quantitative terms, areas of extreme differentiation on one or more scales.[5] Loïc Wacquant in this volume alternatively suggests the term 'hyperghetto' for a 'reconfigured, decentred and spatially differentiated ghetto' (p. 267). The suggestion flies directly in the face of the more conventional definition of the ghetto, which in its extreme form is given by Massey and Denton as

> a set of neighborhoods that are exclusively inhabited by members of one group, within which virtually all members of that group live. By this definition, no ethnic or racial group in the history of the United States, except one, has ever experienced ghettoization, even briefly. For urban

blacks, the ghetto has been the paradigmatic residential configuration for at least eighty years. (Massey and Denton, 1993: 18–19)

The two definitions raise exactly opposite problems. Massey and Denton's ignores a central feature of any full definition of the ghetto: that it stands in an inferior position to the society around it. Any 'group' – a term left undefined in the definition[6] – may be considered to live in a ghetto; thus one could have a ghetto of movie stars in Beverly Hills, or of the elderly in retirement communities. And the definition suggests no change in the basic nature of the ghetto over time. On the other hand, the strength of the definition is that it makes the spatial aspect of the ghetto paramount.

Wacquant's definition, by adding 'hyper-' to ghetto, does indeed suggest that something new is happening. But it drops precisely the spatial component; if a ghetto can be 'decentred', it no longer refers to a place or set of places, but rather to a set of persons.[7] But it also makes, precisely because of that switch, an important positive contribution: it emphasizes the unifying characteristic of the ghetto as the relationship of a set of persons, a group, to others, to the society at large.

The post-Fordist ghetto is a 'new ghetto'[8] in that it has become an outcast ghetto, a ghetto of the excluded, rather than more generally of the dominated and exploited, or of the marginal.[9] It builds on the oldest characteristic of the ghetto. I use here as a working definition of the ghetto in general:

> a ghetto is an area in which space and race are combined to define, to isolate, and to contain a particular population group held to be inferior by the dominant powers in society.

The outcast ghetto adds a new dimension, a specific relationship between the particular population group and the dominant society: one of economic as well as spatial exclusion.[10] That has not historically been true; in Richard Sennett's (1992) fascinating account of the origins, in 1516, of the ghetto that added the word to the language,[11] the ghetto of Venice, it is clear that Jews left the ghetto each morning to transact business in Venice, returning to the ghetto only in the evening, and were an essential part of the Venetian economy. Indeed, there was a significant number of non-Jews who came into the ghetto each day to work or on business; in 1638, one account has it, 4,000 Christians worked in Jewish factories there. It is not an outcast ghetto; indeed, it had precisely two characteristics that distinguish the older ghetto from the new outcast ghetto: ties to the mainstream of economic life in the outside society, and internal resources (partly as a consequence) permitting its residents to draw strength from their very ghettoization. Thus, Sennett says: '[the story of the Jews of Venice] is the story of a people who were segregated against their will, but who then made new forms of community from their separateness and who acquired an interest, as social actors, in being segregated.' Those in the ghetto are separated, indeed, and held inferior by the construction of the ghetto; but they remain a key part of the larger society, and are not being cast out of it.

This sense of being a part of society, of being artificially separated spatially from that of which they are economically and socially a part, can be seen in Robert Weaver's definition, given at what was perhaps the last moment that full integration of blacks into United States society seemed a practical goal, immediately after the end of the Second World War:

> the modern American ghetto is . . . not, as the ghetto of old, an area which houses a people concerned with perpetuation of a peculiar (and different) culture.[12] It is no longer composed of black people almost all of whom are too poor to afford decent shelter. The Negro ghetto of today is made up of people who are American to the core, who are a part of the national culture and who share a common language with the majority of Americans . . . Its inhabitants are better prepared and more anxious than ever before to enter the main stream of American life. Residential segregation, more than any other single institution, is an impediment to their realization of this American Dream. (Weaver, 1948: 7)

Kenneth Clark's description of the ghetto 17 years later already presents a darker picture:

> the dark ghetto's invisible walls have been erected by the white society, by those who have power, both to confine those who have no power and to perpetuate their powerlessness. The dark ghettos are social, political, educational, and – above all – economic colonies. Their inhabitants are subject peoples, victims of the greed, cruelty, insensitivity, guilt, and fear of their masters. (Clark, 1965: 11)

Clark wrote of the ghetto presciently, just at the point where its character was beginning to change. The powerlessness that was no part of the feeling of Weaver's ghetto – and certainly not of Harlem, the capital of black America in the 1920s (see Johnson, 1925; Osofsky, 1968) – becomes characteristic by the late 1960s, but still in an integrationist context. Clark had after all given key support for the plaintiffs in the school desegregation cases that outlawed the formal segregation of public schools in 1955. The ghetto colonies are linked to the colonizers, the masters have an interest in, profit from, the work of the subject peoples. That has changed in the post-Fordist city. Those in today's black ghettos are not productive for their masters; their masters get little benefit from their existence. As far as the dominant society is concerned, most residents of the new ghetto are only a drain on public and private resources, a threat to social peace, fulfilling no useful social role. They are outcasts; hence an outcast ghetto 'defines, isolates, and contains' its victims.[13]

Figures tell part of the story. A solid recent study of Philadelphia, for instance, shows that, in 1980, 47.5 per cent of blacks living in the ghetto were on public assistance; 17 per cent of men aged 25–44 were unemployed, 33.3 per cent were not in the labour force (Jargowsky, 1994: 248) and 44.3 per cent of black families were single parents (Jargowsky, 1994: 246). Figures on rates of incarceration through the judicial system, on victimization by crime, on drug abuse, on failure to complete 12 years of schooling, could be cited endlessly. But, beyond the figures, the composition of the outcast ghetto differs from its predecessors and from the immigrant and ethnic enclaves noted below, in the crucial area of social organization also. Loïc Wacquant has described some of the key characteristics of the outcast ghetto elegantly; he speaks of 'lack of social potency . . . low organization density . . . the massive inferiority of its resident institutions . . . de-solidarizing effects . . . an impossible community, perpetually divided against [itself]' (1993: 372).[14]

The difference from the earlier descriptions of Harlem in, say, the biographies of Adam Clayton Powell, is clear. Or compare the older descriptions of Jewish Brownsville with a contemporary one, or Michael Gold's picture of the Lower East Side with Janet Abu-Lughod's (1993). Wacquant similarly distinguishes the 'European worker's space'.

A peculiar irony accompanies the evolution of the outcast ghetto. As its residents are more and more cast out, marginalized, unemployed and unwanted by the dominant forces in society, their internal cohesion is weakened, but the importance of place to them may even be strengthened. As real economic bonds, bonds of a common and viable education, cultural life, work and community building, are eroded, the bonds of a common residential area increase. Thus, even if the internal organizational structure of Harlem appears weakened, its residents' turf allegiance is strengthened – defensively, it is true, and as a last resort, perhaps, but nevertheless the allegiance is strong.

A comparative dimension suggests the difference between the old and the new ghetto. If 'ghetto' is the generic term and 'outcast ghetto' is the appropriate term for the new ghetto, the opposite traditional model of the ghetto might be called the *ghetto of exploitation*. The extreme form of the ghetto of pure exploitation is the labour camp. The concentration camps of Nazi Germany add a strong, in most cases a primary, component of political control, but to the extent that they were used as a source of forced labour they represent exploitation in its harshest form, functionally equivalent to slavery. On a smaller scale, the barracks for workers without residence permits in Moscow in the Stalinist era, the dormitories for foreign workers in East Germany, the tolerated squatters' colonies on the other side of the Mexican border for workers paid substandard wages for work in the United States, represent the same phenomenon. So do migrant labour camps in California or Florida. The homelands and segregated townships of South Africa are the extreme example; their purpose was to house a large part of the necessary labour force, reduce the costs of maintaining it (reduce the 'social reproduction cost of labour') and keep it under tight control (Marcuse, 1995a). Spatial segregation is sometimes the beginning and basis for the exploitation, sometimes an additional opportunity to reinforce exploitation, sometimes only its inevitable by-product, but in all cases the involuntary spatial segregation is linked to the exploitative work relationship. In the outcast ghetto, not exploitation but exclusion is the heart of the matter.

The Enclave and the Ghetto

Not every contemporary space of racial or ethnic concentration is a ghetto, as I use the term here, however, and the differences are crucial for historic understanding and for public policy. The issue of immigrant 'ghettos' has become a high visibility one recently, in part through more detailed looks at the complexities of Los Angeles and its riots, in part through work on specific immigrant enclaves, especially of Cubans in Miami. An understanding of the difference between the black ghettos and immigrant enclaves in the United States today is an important one both for analytic clarity and for policy, for the assumption that blacks should behave like immigrants, that black ghettos ought to be steps towards self-organization and upward mobility as immigrant enclaves are thought to be, plays a major role in attitudes towards blacks. Its ultimate expression is blaming the victim: 'if Koreans can do it, why can't blacks; its their own fault if they don't.'

I use the word 'black' in the following discussion, rather than 'African-American', to emphasize the point;[15] while African-American emphasizes a positive ethnic identity linked to a country or continent of origin, and thus establishes a basis for identity, a link to cultural tradition, and a claim for equality of treatment that has strong positive value, the issue here is rather the relationship with the dominant group(s). For that purpose, African-American suggests a similarity with Korean-American or Italian-American that is misleading. Blacks are not immigrants, and their position is markedly different from that of many other 'hyphenated' groups.[16]

The spatial patterns reflect the difference. Map 9.1 shows the distribution of the black population in New York City; its concentration is striking. Map 9.2 shows the distribution of the white population; there is slight overlap at the edges, but none at the centres of concentration. Map 9.3 shows the distribution of the Asian population; it has similar areas of concentration, but also shows much dispersion. It overlaps with areas of white occupancy, but not with areas of black. The Asian pattern is more that of a set of enclaves; the black reflects ghettoization in its harshest form.

Enclave is indeed the word used for those areas in which immigrants have congregated which are seen as having positive value, as opposed to the word 'ghetto', which has a clearly pejorative connotation. Historically 'ghetto' can indeed have a positive aspect; Sennett speaks, for instance, of the ghetto as 'a space at once a space of repression and a space of identification' (1992: 40), and people have pride in Harlem at the same time as they condemn segregation. By the same token, 'enclave' has a negative aspect; its original use, derived from 'enclosure', was to designate part of a city or country surrounded by foreign territory, and typically referred to an imperial enclave in a colonial country. It was thus both dominant and defensive; it suggested power, but also fear and limitation.[17]

While both 'enclave' and 'ghetto' thus are two-sided concepts, 'enclave' is here used to describe those spaces given a primarily positive meaning, 'ghetto' those with a predominantly negative meaning. It is important to remember: all spaces of concentrated homogeneous minority population share some characteristics of a ghetto and some of an enclave. The single voluntary/involuntary distinction is not definitive either, for all voluntary actions are in part involuntary, that is, chosen from an involuntarily restricted range of possibilities. Pure types do not exist. And indeed even some of what are conventionally called Jewish ghettos were in their origins perhaps better designated as enclaves, clearly enclaves as well as ghettos.[18]

Immigrants have historically first settled in separate communities defined by their national origin, forming enclaves providing mutual support and an orientation to the new land. Perhaps because such communities have always been seen as voluntary and transitional, their characteristics are not normally considered in the context of

1 dot = 50

Map 9.1 The distribution of the black non-Hispanic population in New York City

1dot = 50

Map 9.2 The distribution of the white population in New York City

1 dot = 50

Map 9.3 The distribution of the Asian population in New York City

ghettoization or segregation. It was assumed workers employed in them earned less than they would have if they had been in the mainstream work-force, that they submitted to super-exploitation because they saw it as a likely way out of the enclave and into the mainstream. In many cases the immigrant networks in fact supported the first entry of immigrants into contact with the mainstream, for example, Korean grocery stores in non-Korean neighbourhoods, Chinese restaurants catering to a non-Chinese clientele.[19]

The discussion about 'ethnic enclaves' of today makes a different point (see also here in Logan et al., chapter 10). Those today under discussion differ from earlier immigrant landing places in that those in the new enclave confined their economic activity to within the enclave itself, but earned more than their compatriots, otherwise similarly situated but living outside of the enclave and employed outside it. This was the finding of Portes and Bach (see Portes and Stepick, 1993), studying the experience of the Cuban community in Miami. They speculated that there was a productive attenuation of class relationships within the enclave, in which ties of ethnic solidarity resulted in employers providing training, skills and upward mobility in return for initially lower wages:

> ethnic ties suffuse an otherwise 'bare' class relationship with a sense of collective purpose . . . But the utilization of ethnic solidarity *in lieu* of enforced discipline also entails reciprocal obligations. If employers can profit from the willing self-exploitation of fellow immigrants, they are also obliged to reserve for them . . . supervisory positions . . . to train them . . . and to support their . . . move into self-employment. (Portes and Bach, 1985: 343)

One might quarrel with 'collective purpose' as a component of class relationships, and there have certainly been arguments about the validity of the empirical findings (see Waldinger, 1993: 445; Sanders and Nee, 1987). More to the point here, however, is the relationship between ethnic enclaves[20] and the ghettoization of blacks.

The issue is whether the black ghetto should be seen as an enclave, differing from the immigrant enclaves in degree but not in nature. The traditional answer has generally been an implicit 'yes', although recognizing (or stressing) that the difference in degree is vast, with residential segregation being the primary culprit (Massey and Denton, 1993: 2; Weaver, 1948; Logan, et al., 1994b: 12 and 16–17). And that answer is true, in part: there is an identity derived from the ghetto as a localized space, a special cultural development, a support for political leadership, economic gains from retailing and services that meet local needs, that is analogous to the positives claimed for immigrant enclaves. But the links between these pluses and the existence of separated spaces is more and more questionable for the black ghetto. Saskia Sassen says flatly that the 'recent development in immigrant communities . . . the expansion of an informal economy . . . contrasts sharply with the growth of an underclass in black neighborhoods' (1990: 484). Today's black ghetto is a ghetto, not an enclave, even if those confined to it are sometimes able to marshal strength from their very confinement.

To summarize: all 'separateness' is not per se invidious. David Harvey emphasizes particular forms of 'separation', or of separate cultural and local identity, as the basis for a resistance against processes of homogenization and suppression of individuality. Kenneth Frampton's conception of a desirable 'critical regionalism' goes in the same direction. The central distinction is whether the separateness contributes to subordination in a hierarchical relationship, or on the contrary supports resistance to incorporation into a hierarchy[21] or independence from it.

The State

Conventional economics would have it that people sort out where they wish to live by their personal preferences, and that the spatial pattern of a city results from the complex interaction of individual preferences, mediated through a housing market where, if supply and demand are in equilibrium, demand will determine residential locations. State action plays at most a secondary role in this scenario, perhaps reflecting cumulative personal preferences in zoning ordinances and building codes.

Such a description is remote from reality. The state's activity flows through every artery of the housing market. Indeed, the state's actions are needed for the most minimal market even to exist: the enforcement of the laws, the establishment of a currency, the judicial oversight over contracts, the forbidding of trespass, the regulation of nuisances, are all required before a private market in the commodity housing can function effectively. Not to speak of the provision of roads, sewers, utilities, water, policing, fire protection, transportation, zoning and building codes, parks, schools, and on and on. State action is sometimes spoken of as 'intervention in the housing market'; it would be more accurate to speak of the state as 'constituting the housing market'.

Segregation in housing and land uses is thus likely to be as much or more a product of state action as of atomistic individuals. The state is not acting autonomously, to be sure, responsive as it is to the distribution both of political and of economic power, but acting as the state nevertheless. Whatever the limits of the state's autonomy might be, any attempt to influence the facts of segregation, ghettoization, the casting out of whole groups from the primary and even the secondary labour market, must reckon with the state.

Slavery was of course legally enforced in a major part of the United States before the Civil War, and was critical in determining the locational pattern of blacks in the South. Patterns of segregation were different, but the extent of segregation relatively similar, in the North. Reconstruction did not change the patterns dramatically. Legal (state) enforcement of private restrictive covenants, private agreements to preserve segregation, remained in effect until *Shelley* v. *Kramer* in 1948; exclusionary zoning maintains that pattern in countless localities today. The pattern of white suburb and black inner city, the rich residential noose around the poor city slums, is the result, carrying with it a train of anti-metropolitanization sentiments, distorted control over state legislatures, discriminatory education, parks, security, enjoyment of environmental amenities, that characterized United States urban patterns from the outset.

The more recent history, since the Second World War, shows three distinct but overlapping phases, with a significant shift at the point at which one may begin to speak of the post-Fordist city. In the first, for the decade or two after the war, the state, through its urban renewal programmes, formally initiated programmes to restructure cities towards a greater support for service industries, away from heavy manufacturing, with a concomitant restructuring of residential locations for factory workers as opposed to more white-collar and upper-class households. The displacement caused by such action was one of the stimuli that produced the northern urban civil rights movement, and the urban riots of the 1960s. These in turn produced the integrationist second post-war phase. Black power grew, white support was substantial, civil rights legislation was passed, segregation was on the defensive.

But not for long. Nixon's counter-offensive put the state back on the side of conventional law and order, using force where necessary to quell protest. The crudeness of the Nixon policies was not, however, necessary. With the opening provided by the fiscal crisis of the mid-1970s (Marcuse, 1981: 330), the state stepped into the background, letting the market initiate and smoothing its path in the restructuring of the city. Gentrification on the one hand, deterioration, abandonment and increasing ghettoization, on the other, were and are the result. The turning-point reflects a shift in the balance of power between those claiming a wider distribution of the benefits of economic prosperity and those in dominant positions within the state and the economy resisting such claims. That turning-point parallels, indeed is a component of the transformation of urban life from a Fordist to a post-Fordist stage. Globalization in its modern form played a major role in facilitating that transformation; we will spell out the dynamics in the fourth section below; the changes in the state's role in the context of globalization are central.

The state's role in the constitution of the outcast ghetto, combining racial discrimination and class stratification in a spatial nexus that is today's city in the US, can be traced through a number of developments:

- state policies on public housing, of which Massey and Kanaiaupuni have said: 'Public housing ... represents a federally funded, physically permanent institution for the isolation of black families by race and class ... the presence of housing projects substantially increased the concentration of poverty in later years' (1993: 109 and 120);
- support for gentrification, through zoning, park 'upgrading', facilitating condominium conversions, concentration of public services and facilities (see Abu-Lughod, 1993);
- in cities like New York, focusing public policies *vis-à-vis* housing on 'divide and siphon' approaches, in which the poor are divided from the very poor and benefits of public policies intended for them are siphoned up to the middle class and beyond (Marcuse, 1988a: 8–11);
- locating undesired public facilities – jails, bus garages, sanitation plants, drug treatment clinics – only in poor and black neighbourhoods, skilfully using the NIMBY (Not in My Back Yard) syndrome to create what Vergara (1991: 3ff) has called the 'new ghetto';
- adopting Empowerment Zone legislation,[22] promoted by the Clinton administration as a key part of its housing and community development programme but likewise supported by the Reagan and Bush administrations, concentrating public subsidies in limited 'poverty' areas with a meaning of 'empowerment' quite different in the post-Fordist city than in its predecessors;[23]
- electoral redistricting and maintenance of an electoral system which minimizes the impact of minority votes in local, state and national legislative elections (Raskin, 1995: 16ff).

ADVANCED HOMELESSNESS

Advanced homelessness is that form of homelessness specific to the post-Fordist city. Homelessness may be seen in three historical perspectives, paralleling the divisions in the history of the spatial organization of cities.[24] They are divided by two great watersheds.

One comes in the nineteenth century, with the Industrial Revolution and urbanization. Previously there had been periods in which many more people were without adequate shelter; one thinks of the periods of agricultural depression in England, the Thirty Years' War on the continent, etc. With the nineteenth century and the Industrial Revolution, the first watershed, however, homelessness became more urbanized, and therefore more concentrated; and it became separated from its direct dependence on employment and other outside forces as the home itself became separated from the workplace.[25] The rise of capitalism, rather than the Industrial Revolution which followed it and brought it to maturity, is an alternate dating of this watershed, the displacement of rural workers by the enclosure movement being the beginning of 'modern' homelessness. In the period of industrial capitalism the main determinant of homelessness became the business cycle, short-term fluctuations in the level of economic activity; while in bad times homelessness was often severe, in good times it virtually disappeared.[26]

The second watershed in the history of homelessness occurred sometime in the 1970s, with the transition from the Fordist to the post-Fordist city.[27] Its presence is witnessed by both quantitative and qualitative changes.

Quantitatively, advanced homelessness is marked by a sudden and significant increase in the extent of homelessness. A few figures taken from the record in New York City are illustrative:

- The high point in the average night-time census of those being provided temporary shelter by New York City before 1990 was 10,000 persons, in 1936. The low point thereafter was 300 persons, during the Second World War. The figure did not exceed 2,000 persons again until 1978; by the winter of 1986–7, it reached 10,000.
- In 1978, New York City spent $8 million for operating costs and capital improvements for shelter services for single men and women, by 1985, that figure was over $100 million.
- Emergency shelter for families was first provided by the city in 1982; by 1985 it had reached $100 million also (New York City Human Resources Administration, 1984; New York City Mayor's Office of Operations, 1987).
- The number of stories in the the the *New York Times* on homelessness increased from four in 1979 to 302 in 1988 (Kirchheimer, 1989–1990).
- *Callahan* v. *Carey*, the court case which required New York City to house homeless single men, was brought in October 1979, and decided in August 1981; *Eldredge* v. *Koch*, which required the city to house single women, was decided in December 1982 (469 NYS2d 744); *MacCaine* v. *Koch*, which required it to house families, was decided in May 1986 (523 NYS2d 112).

These patterns are not unique to New York City; indeed, the latest national figures are startling. The 1990 census count of 459,215 is rejected by most commentators as grossly inadequate (US Bureau of the Census, 1990). The best figures previously available on a national basis are based on beds in shelters, and thus grossly undercounted the absolute number of the homeless; but they indicate that the figure doubled in the three years from 1984 to 1987.[28] A new study by a team of Columbia University researchers has now, for the first time, attempted to estimate, not the number of persons homeless on a single night, but rather the number of persons who have encountered homelessness at some point in their lives; that figure, on a nationwide basis in the United States, turns out to be 13.5 million people, 7.4 per cent of the total population! (Link et al., 1994).

The qualitative changes in homelessness, which suggest that there is really a substantive difference in the character of homelessness today that justifies a new name – *advanced homelessness* – are fourfold:

1   advanced homelessness is *not related to any recession* or downturn in the business cycle, it persists despite prosperity and upturns in the business cycle; it is present in periods of relatively full employment as well as periods of joblessness;
2   advanced homelessness is heavily *concentrated among blacks* in particular and the victims of racism in general;
3   the *spatial location* of the homeless is the subject of concerted state action (market pressures have always been in this direction), which seeks to remove the homeless from gentrifying neighbourhoods and from the location of mainstream business and to concentrate them in existing and expanding ghettos;
4   *exclusion, rather than integration*, has become a significant part of policy towards the homeless, joining a trend in housing policy in general, a trend also seen in welfare policy, criminal justice policy, and broadly in social policy.

On the first point, the independence of homelessness from the business cycle, the figures again tell the story:

• Recession years, officially so designated, were 1960, 1969, 1970, 1974, 1975, 1980, 1981, 1982; years of peak income were 1973, 1978, 1987. These ups and downs bear no systematic relationship to the ups and downs in homelessness, in particular to the sharp upswing that began in the mid-1970s, and has been largely continuous since then.
• The high-point in number of families below the poverty level, after the post-war years, was reached in 1959, with 8,320,000 families; the low point in 1973, with 4,828,000 families. After 1973, the number went up slowly until 1983, then began to decline slowly, just as the number of the homeless began shooting upwards.
• Those homeless are increasingly permanently homeless. The permanence of poverty for the very poor and the homeless is widely recognized. In earlier periods, it was always assumed, by economic analysts but also by the general public, that poverty was temporary (or deserved), and that

sooner or later anyone wanting to work would be able to do so again. This was very obvious in the Great Depression, for instance, when the poor were widely regarded as the 'submerged middle class'. No one would characterize the homeless in that way today.

On the second point, the racial character of homelessness, unfortunately no good historical figures are available. But one reads in vain through the literature of homelessness of the period before 1970 for any implication that the majority are black, or belong to any minority group. By contrast today, the best estimates in New York City are that over 90 per cent of the homeless are black or Hispanic.

On the third point, the use of space to isolate and neutralize the homeless (Marcuse, 1988b), government has seen to it (under pressure from private market forces) that there is both a push and a pull at work – a push out of spaces where the homeless are not wanted, and a pull into spaces no longer of concern to dominant groups in the city, specifically into the heart of the black ghetto.

On the pushing out side, the examples are legion. The most dramatic in New York was the clearing of Tompkins Square park, in the middle of an area targeted for gentrification, by mounted police in an assault in the middle of the night, destroying temporary shacks built by the homeless and assaulting many brutally (Smith, 1992; Abu-Lughod, 1993). The most expensive will probably be the Forty-Second Street Redevelopment Project, which proposes to use the tools of physical demolition and new construction to replace places frequented, among others, by the homeless, with new massive office towers in which their absence can be guaranteed. The most explicit is probably the funding by the Grand Central Business Improvement District's leadership of a programme for the homeless, the only condition of which is that the social service agency given the grant make certain that the homeless remain at all times invisible to the ordinary business users of the District. That approach replaces the earlier one, recounted graphically by Jonathan Kozol, in which the floors and entrance ramps of Grand Central Station were washed down with lye in the middle of the night to make sleeping on that surface impossible (Kozol, 1988). The most recent example is the closing of the Kenmore Hotel, only two blocks from the upscale neighbourhood of Gramercy Park, a large building accommodating over 600 largely formerly homeless people, raided by the police and closed down although conditions there were arguably better than in a number of other buildings in neighbourhoods whose residents had no power or pull with City Hall.

Pushed out to where? Vergara (1989) has coined the phrase 'the new ghetto' to describe the government policy of locating emergency and transitional homeless housing, AIDS facilities, half-way houses, drug rehabilitation programmes, homes for juvenile delinquents, all in concentrated portions of the ghetto. The market rationale is simple: these are the areas of housing abandoned by the private market, which is to say, in which the mainstream economy has no interest. Buildings come into city ownership when real estate taxes are not paid on them. They thus become city-owned, and largely empty. They are thus arguably the cheapest place to put the homeless, in dollar terms. And indeed that is where the homeless are put.

The spatial concentration of homelessness and poverty resulting from these policies creates a vicious circle: the more concentrated the poverty, the lower the level of public services, the greater the deterioration of the physical and social environment, the greater in turn will be the concentration of poverty and the physical, social and economic abandonment that accompanies it. At the governmental end, the policy is called triage (Marcuse, Medoff and Pereira, 1982: 33ff); the real estate economists call it the influence of neighbourhood factors on real estate values; if bankers do it, it is red-lining (Marcuse, 1979). Its consequences are what much of William Wilson's under-class discussion is about.

Exclusion, the fourth distinguishing characteristic of advanced homelessness, is part of a general trend in social policy which has not been seen, at least in overt form, in the United States since the New Deal, in other words, since the beginning of the welfare state here. The prototypical example is that of the HELP programme, initiated by Andrew Cuomo in New York with the full support of that city and state (Mario Cuomo, former governor of New York State, is Andrew Cuomo's father), and so well regarded in Washington, DC that Andrew Cuomo has been made Assistant Secretary of the Department of Housing and Urban Development in charge of community development activities. A central feature of HELP's programme relies on the insight that many homeless have problems in addition to the lack of housing, an insight with which it is difficult to quarrel. HELP thus does intensive 'intake interviewing', in which not only the range of problems a particular homeless person faces is investigated, but also his or her willingness to participate in prescribed programmes to deal with them: 'housing readiness programmes'. These in general require, as a condition of admission to solidly constructed if regimented 'transitional shelters', often built fortress-like in largely abandoned neighbourhoods, the willingness to submit to the discipline of those shelters: the keeping of regular hours, abstinence from drug use, essentially chaste behaviour within the shelter, submission to social work intervention. A reward for adhering to an agreement as to such behaviour is, at the end of the necessary period, often six months, referral to 'permanent housing', often in specially renovated buildings similarly in abandoned areas.

Exclusion is a feature of such programmes, both for those homeless participating and for those not participating. For those participating – at least for many, but studies of the longer-term living conditions of those involved are not (yet) available – the label 'homeless' is one that is attached to them not only during but after their participation. The 'permanent' housing they receive is 'homeless housing', an oxymoron if ever there was one (Marcuse and Vergana, 1992). They are, presumably permanently, relegated to the abandoned city (see below), excluded from the essential economic, social and political life of the city.

Exclusion is even more clearly the lot of those unwilling or unable to submit to the discipline of the HELP programme. What is to happen to them is not quite clear. As it is, many simply stay on the streets; they remain permanently, literally, homeless. Others go into the city's emergency shelter system in the worst weather, or when they are forced to, and otherwise stay on the streets. Many sleep on the floors, or on desks or chairs in the city's welfare offices waiting for something better.

Sympathy is not wasted on them in official circles; they are the 'voluntarily homeless', what historically were the 'unworthy poor'. The concern is to protect society from them, from the implications of their existence and their visibility and the problems their existence implies. It is a parallel to the concern that has built more places in prisons in the United States in the last ten years than in schools, that proposes absolute limits on welfare payments to poor people after a specified time as a means of reducing the welfare budget, that seeks to reduce health care costs by limiting those entitled to care. In general, policies in which state action for the exclusion (and, as we have seen, the spatial segregation) of a distinct group has become a key feature of a new approach to social policy in the post-Fordist city.

THE NEW SPATIAL DIVISIONS OF THE POST-FORDIST CITY

Both the creation of the outcast ghetto and the appearance of advanced homelessness are part of a larger pattern of development of the post-Fordist city, in which space has been used both to reflect and to reinforce deeper divisions. They can only be understood as part of a broader set of changes, in which areas of gentrification and wealth increase in size and change in location, ghetto areas grow and change in nature, working- and middle-class areas shrink, and the homeless are wanted in none. Space and race overlay on class to set the boundaries between these areas, these virtually separate cities within the city. The spatial and racial divisions parallel and accentuate economic divisions.

Spatial divisions in the city are certainly nothing new, historically. Never mind the slave quarters of ancient Athens and Rome, the ghettos of the Middle Ages, the imperial quarters of colonial cities, or the merchant sections of the trading cities of the mercantile era. At least from the outset of the Industrial Revolution, cities have been divided in a way quite familiar to us. Disraeli coined the phrase 'dual city' in the 1860s (Marcuse, 1989a), and even earlier Engels had described, in striking detail worth rereading today,[29] the differences between the back-alley tenements of the working class in Manchester and the bourgeois houses on the main streets in front of them.

Is the fact that cities today are not 'dual', but more like 'quartered', cities, new? (Marcus, 1974). The answer becomes clear if we recapitulate the argument about the patterns of the contemporary city briefly (Marcuse, 1989a; 1993: 355–65).

The *residential city* today[30] may be seen as divided roughly into the following quarters:[31]

- *luxury housing spots*, not really part of the city but enclaves or isolated buildings, occupied by the top of the economic, social and political hierarchy;
- the *gentrified city*, the city of those who are making it, occupied by the professional/managerial/technical groups, whether yuppie or muppie without children;
- the *suburban city*, sometimes single-family housing in the outer city, other times apartments near the centre, occupied by skilled workers, mid-range professionals, upper civil servants;
- the *tenement city*, sometimes cheaper single-family areas, most often rentals, occupied by lower-paid workers, blue and white collar, and generally (although less in the United States) including substantial social housing;
- the *abandoned city*, the city of the victims, the end result of trickle-down, left for the poor, the unemployed, the excluded, where in the United States home-less housing[32] for the homeless is most frequently located.

These divisions in the residential city are roughly paralleled by divisions in the *economic city*;

- the *places of big decisions* include a network of high-rise offices, brownstones or older mansions in prestigious locations, but are essentially locationally not circumscribed; it includes yachts for some, the back seats of stretch limousines for others, airplanes and scattered residences for still others;

- the *city of advanced services*, of professional offices tightly clustered in downtowns, with many ancillary services internalized in high-rise office towers, heavily enmeshed in a wide and technologically advanced communicative network;
- the *city of direct production*, including not only manufacturing but also the support of advanced services, government offices, the back offices of major firms, whether adjacent to their front offices or not, located in clusters and with significant agglomerations but in varied locations within a metropolitan area, sometimes, indeed, outside of the central city itself;
- the *city of unskilled work and the informal economy*, small-scale manufacturing, warehousing, sweatshops, technically unskilled consumer services, immigrant industries, closely intertwined with the cities of production and advanced services and thus located near them, but separately and in scattered clusters (Sassen, 1989), locations often determined in part by economic relations, in part by the patterns of the residential city (spatially, the overlap with the city of advanced services is substantial, for the service economy produces both high- and low-end jobs in close proximity to each other, for example, janitors in executive offices, etc.; see Stanback et al., 1981);
- the *residual city*, the city of the less legal portions of the informal economy, the city of storage where otherwise undesired (NIMBY) facilities are located, generally congruent with the abandoned residential city.

These spatial differences do not simply reflect, on the residential side, differences of 'life-styles' or 'special needs' (Marcuse, 1989b), nor do they arise from inevitable differences in 'consumer preferences'. On the economic side, they are not simply reflections of efficiency criteria, the need to reduce frictions of space to the utmost. To the contrary: they manifest and reinforce positions in a hierarchy of power and wealth in which some decide and others are decided for. As one progresses down in the scale in the quarters of both the residential city and the economic city in the United States, the proportion of black and Hispanic and immigrant households, and of women heading households, increases; race, class and gender create overlapping patterns of differentiation – invidious differentiation. The frequent formulations about increasing inequality do not hit the mark (Marcuse, 1993: 357), although they are true, for it is not deviation from some concept of linear or uniform distribution that defines the divisions, but the relations of the occupants of each division to each other: inequalities in a zero-sum game, in which the wealth and power of the one depends on the poverty and subordination of the other.[33] That is hardly a new insight, but global divisions of labour and movements of capital make it visible today on an unprecedented scale.

These patterns are spatial, but they are not rigid, in the old sense in which Burgess and Park tried to describe city structure. And their spatial pattern varies widely from city to city, country to country. Los Angeles, for instance, has a pattern I have described as fluid, separations as of oil and water together with walled enclaves, rather than the more clearly bounded and more homogeneous quarters of New York City (Marcuse, 1992a). But the spatial patterns are always there, if differing in intensity and sharpness. Initial work on the 1990 census in the United States has demonstrated that fact.[34]

What is new about what we witness today? This is, it seems to me, an important and under-debated question.[35] If the patterns are the same as in the nineteenth century, the causes are likely to be the same, and the solutions the same. The problem then lies with economic and social relationships that run deeply through the years. If, on the other hand, the patterns are substantially new, then new solutions necessarily need to be discovered (not that old problems may not also need new solutions). Since the answer, of course, is that the patterns are partially new, partially old, a greater attention to which particular aspects are new will help steer the strategies that may be addressed towards their improvement.

The specifically new aspects of the present divisions of space can, I think, be outlined concretely. They date from a turning-point somewhere in the post-war period,[36] a change that involves a shift from a Fordist to a post-Fordist society,[37] from a manufacturing to a service economy, from a national to a global organization of production, distribution and services, from a welfare to a post-welfare state, from modern to postmodern structures. I have used the shift from the Fordist to the post-Fordist city here as shorthand for these changes.[38] No exact dating of the shift should be expected, of course, but key quantitative measures suggest some time in the 1970s: manufacturing employment in the United States grew until about 1979, then began to decline (in major cities the decline began at least as early as 1970; see Sassen, 1990: 467–8). Christopher Jencks cites a sharp turn-around in the direction of change of the numbers of households living under the poverty level: declining from 13.7 per cent in central cities between 1960 and 1970, then increasing to 15.4 per cent by 1987 (1991: 7). The details of these developments are too well known to need repetition here.

The spatial changes that have accompanied these economic changes are, I believe, the following; they are the particular spatial characteristics of the post-Fordist city. They include:

1   The growth in the size of the gentrified city and the shrinking of others: *expanding gentrification.*
2   The growth in the size of the abandoned city: *increasing ghettoization.*
3   The dynamic nature of the quarters, in which each grows only at the

expense of the others: *tensions among quarters*, with displacement as the mechanism of expansion.

4 The importance which the identity of the quarter has in the lives of its residents: *the defensive use of space*, including the intensity of turf allegiance.

5 The walls created between quarters, and the intensity with which they are defended: *spatial barricades and spatial battles*.

6 The *role of government*, not only acceding to but promoting the quartering of the city in the private interest, fortifying both the gentrified and the abandoned city: the subsuming of the public interest under the private.

To take these points up one at a time:

Expanding gentrification. The linked pattern of expansion of the gentrified city and of the abandoned city, at the expense of the tenement and suburban city, have been described in detail elsewhere (Marcuse, 1985: 195–240; Smith and Williams, 1986). The economic logic underlying the changes, both on the labour market and the real estate market ends, is clear. Displacement of the poor by the rich is nothing new in history, but generally heretofore it has followed one of two patterns: either a gradual outward movement of the rich, sometimes displacing poor people in their way, as when the move up the West Side of Manhattan made possible by transportation improvements displaced squatters living near Central Park; or a leapfrog movement, in which settlements of poorer people are temporarily left in place, only to be squeezed out later, while the rich move beyond them, as in the development of Fifth Avenue leap-frogging over the garment district (Cardia, 1987, forthcoming).

Today, the pattern is different in at least two ways. First, it reflects not so much a shift in location of economic activity but a change in its composition. It is a gentrification of areas close to the centre, not a movement out or a leapfrogging. Second, it is not so much the result of expansion, of growth (although they may also be taking place), as it is of restructuring, existing populations shifting their location around – in particular, the professional and managerial and technical group-ings.

Gentrification, in the broad sense of the reclaiming of land in and near the central business district for the residences of the upper middle class, the professionals, technicians and managers, precedes ghettoiza-tion, abandonment and homelessness. It is an early harbinger of the post-Fordist city.[39]

Increasing ghettoization. The changing nature of the ghetto, the evolution of the outcast ghetto, has been discussed in detail above. Detailed quantitative discussion for the United States should be postponed till data from the 1990 census, now slowly becoming available, is subject to analysis. But several highlights can be observed from that data, using New York City as a case study.

In a number of 'underclass' discussions, notably some of those brought together by Jencks and Peterson (1991), it is argued that the 'underclass' is shrinking. It follows that the size of the abandoned quarters of cities, as here defined, should be shrinking, and so it is argued. But the argument is fallacious. It relies for its statistical measure on the use of the index of dissimilarity, a measure of segregation that is quite useful in presenting a gross comparative view of developments among different cities, but provides no measure either of the intensity of segregation nor its spatial pattern.[40] In the more detailed analysis by Jargowsky and Bane in the same volume, the figures for New York City are given. Using a definition of ghetto neighbourhoods – more than 40 per cent of the residents below the poverty line – that may well approximate the definition of the abandoned quarters of a city, they find that the number of residents of such neighbourhoods increased between 1970 and 1980 from 134,139 to 477,621. Similar results are presented for other major north-eastern and north-central cities, for example, Philadelphia goes from 49,657 to 127,134, Chicago from 74,370 to 194,338.[41]

The most recent figures from the 1990 census thus far available are too aggregated to be very illuminating. They suggest some declines, if small ones, in indices of segregation for many major cities, including Los Angeles, and increases, if small ones, in others, including New York City. Table 9.1 summarizes some of the figures.

Massey and Denton's conclusion is that 'segregation remains high and virtually constant' (1993: 223); other commentators point out that the pattern is consistent with an expanding ghetto, in which areas on the edge of expansion appear briefly and for a transitional period only statistically integrated.

Tension among quarters; displacement among them. In earlier periods, the expansion of residential areas for use by particular groups came out by a process of new settlement, the incorporation of new areas into the existing urban structure.

Displacement is perhaps a more central concept than gentrification here. Alan Murie highlights the displacement of working-class and poor council housing tenants by home owners of higher income and occupational status as council housing is privatized (Murie, 1991). The demographics of public housing in the United States have changed substantially over time, largely as a function of public policy, and many have left public housing when they would have preferred to stay. Restructuring rather than growth explains the changes.

Displacement is the conversion of a quarter from use by one strata/

Table 9.1   Indices of segregation for major US cities

Metropolitan area	1970	1980	1990
Boston	81.2	77.6	68.2
Chicago	91.9	87.8	85.8
Cleveland	90.8	87.5	85.1
Detroit	88.4	86.7	87.6
Los Angeles/Long Beach	91.0	81.1	73.1
Newark	81.4	81.6	82.5
Atlanta	82.1	78.5	67.8
Houston	78.1	69.5	66.8
Washington, DC	81.1	70.1	66.1
New York City	81.0	82.0	82.2

The table provides sample figures, looking only at black/non-black divisions; thus where segregation of Hispanics is significant, it distorts the results substantially (see Massey and Denton, 1993: 222). For Chicago, for instance, the white–Hispanic dissimilarity index was 61 in 1980 within the city, 64 in the metropolitan area, for Puerto Ricans the figure was 81 in the metropolitan area (Orfield, 1985). Treatment of Hispanics deserves a full discussion by itself, not attempted here.

class to use by another. The city, through policies of triage, up-zoning, allocation of public services, investment in infrastructure, and often directly by its housing policies, from the privatization of public housing to the sale of foreclosed units, if not directly by planned land acquisition and disposition directly as in earlier urban renewal, provides substantial impetus for the process. Displacement as the fundamental mechanism of expansion, propelled by the private market but shaped and accelerated by governmental action, is thus new in scope and effect.

The defensive use of space, intensity of turf allegiance. The symbolic importance of neighbourhood has increased dramatically in the last 40 years. Slum clearance schemes in the 1920s aroused negligible opposition on the grounds of turf. Geographically based community solidarity was the exception rather than the rule. That changed significantly in the US with the earliest redevelopment efforts, for example, Robert Moses in New York City. But even in the 1960s the hope of those displaced was still for integration, for better housing and better neighbourhoods, whether in the existing location or not. Both public policy and, although not uniformly, actual patterns of residence reflected these goals; segregation, at least in its racial form, diminished by many definitions.

Not only have the facts changed,[42] but the goals of most also. Neighbourhood has become more than a source of security, the base of a supportive network, as it has long been; it has become a source of identity, a definition of who a person is and where she or he belongs in society. The shift from workplace- to residence-based self-identification has been much discussed (Katznelson, 1984). Whether such residence-based self-classifications are consumption based or not, and what their relation to production-based identities is, remains much disputed; certainly there is a great deal of congruence between residential location and economic position, as our descriptions of the quarters of the city, summarized above, suggest. That the importance of neighbourhood in the equation is greater by a quantum leap than in earlier times seems hard to dispute; the intensity of turf allegiance is a new element in the urban (and perhaps as well the national) picture today.

Spatial barricades and spatial battles. Putting the new displacement dynamic and the new intensity of turf allegiance together, increasing divisions between quarters and increasing battles over residential turf become inevitable. Any week's worth of the *New York Times* issues disclose them: violent Afro-American versus Hassidic Jewish confrontations in Brooklyn; anti-gentrification marches on the Lower East Side; protests against high-rise rezoning for luxury units by the middle-class and yuppie-muppie upper West Side at the Trump development site; conflicts over the disposition of city-owned property for homeless accommodation in working-class and abandoned Harlem; passage of a Fair Share ordinance to deal with the apparently intractable problem of locating NIMBYs, an ordinance generally approved in theory but disregarded when it comes to any concrete issue, as recently in the location of homeless housing; and on and on.

Both the market and city government have sought walls between quarters that might avoid direct clashes; what they seek is more like barricades than boundaries. Rivers are of course natural boundaries: the location of a project such as Battery Park City, with water on three sides, provides a wonderful natural barrier against the intrusion of outsiders, and every architectural and policy means available is used to ensure the essential homogeneity and security of its residents. In other cases, redevelopment projects have formed boundaries; the history of the West Side Urban Renewal Project and the Morningside Heights Neighborhood Renewal Plan provide exemplary evidence. Turf conflicts are no longer simply among gangs, sports clubs or schools, or even simply along ethnic or religious and national lines. They are geographically based in distinct quarters, and divide ultimately along a few sharp cleavages – four/five are suggested here – as never before. Turf-based tensions and measures to avoid their explosion are a qualitatively new and pervasive phenomenon on the

New York City scene. The prevalence of barbed wire, and indeed the razor-edged wire developed by the United States army for military use after the Second World War, is a graphic and frightening symbol of the cleavages running throughout the city.

And not only New York City. The experience of southern California and many other places (Marcuse, 1994b) suggests that walls and fences are, not metaphorically but actually, an increasing part of the accepted everyday landscape in that Horatio Alger area of fluid boundaries (Leavitt and Goldstein, 1990; Marcuse, 1992b). New private cities are built with walls around them, policed by private security patrols whose permission is needed for access. Even in the public city, fences around developments are ubiquitous; whether it be luxury co-ops or public housing, each cluster wishes to be protected from intrusion by the outside. The scale of the phenomenon exceeds anything heretofore seen. Where 'defence of turf' was once a phrase used to describe only the conduct of street gangs, it today describes the conduct of the majority of the city's residents, the rich perhaps in even more extreme form than the poor.

The role of government. History here truly seems to move like the swings of a pendulum, but the swings are more variations on a theme than changes in direction. Before the twentieth century, both gentrification and ghetto formation were essentially private market results; the state may have ratified and facilitated but did not lead. For New York City the annexations of 1896 and the zoning ordinance of 1916 began an ever more active role for the state, culminating in the sweeping urban renewal schemes of Robert Moses in the 1950s and 1960s. Popular resistance to those measures forced a retreat, and briefly, during the heyday of the civil rights movement, the city, under John Lindsay, almost seemed to switch sides. But that did not last long; as the momentum of the civil rights movement abated, conservative national policy under Richard Nixon went on a counter-offensive. The fiscal crisis of the city gave legitimacy to that counter movement. State and market forces joined together in more sophistic-ated ways – what today is called public–private partnership, the private sector, however, leading the public – to define neighbourhood patterns. The form of state action has changed; its direction has not.

The divisions of the city, including their spatial manifestations, may be seen in three broad historical perspectives: one, the perspective of the history of organized society, in which hierarchies have always existed, and have always been reflected in space; a second, in which the particular divisions created by capitalism are reflected in the particular forms of the capitalist city; and a third, in which the particular magnitude and intensity and form of those divisions is affected by the transition from the Fordist to the post-Fordist city.

THE NEW PROCESS OF VICTIMIZATION

The pattern of division and exclusion described above is not inevitable, nor does it occur uniformly in all countries, not even all those in the same phase of societal development, for example, post-Fordism. Globalization has much to do with both the causes and the differences in results.

The processes of globalization, and some of their spatial impacts, have been extensively discussed in the literature, and are treated at greater length elsewhere in this volume. But globalization is sometimes treated as a single, uniform process, indeed sometimes as an inevitable and universal trend. For our purposes, it is worthwhile trying to disaggregate it, if crudely, to show its direct links to the process of victimization which lies at the heart of the new spatial order of the post-Fordist city.

From Globalization to Victimization

The economic changes that have taken place since about the early 1970s are by now well recognized. Often they are pictured as the inevitable result of technological changes: the development of automation, computerization, cybernetics, fast air transportation, etc. If that were so, there would be a big puzzle: why have these advances not led to greater health, welfare and prosperity for the mass of the world's peoples? Certainly human happiness has not grown at the same pace as technological progress; the benefits of that progress have been very unevenly distributed, so actors other than technology must be involved. And, indeed, they are.

As they affect cities, four linked changes are of key significance in affecting the distribution of wealth and power (Marcuse, 1996):

- changes in the *technological* aspects of the production of goods and the production of services;
- the growing interconnectedness – *internationalization* of the connections between certain sections of most cities and the outside world, with impacts on all quarters of the city;

- the *concentration* of control of the ownership and benefits of economic activity, manifest at all levels of economic activity: local, regional, national and international;
- the growing *centralization* of control of economic activity, shifting upwards from local to regional to national to global, with the locus of the highest centralization being a limited number of global cities.

While the first two of these changes might be expected to lead to greater prosperity for all those affected by them, the combination with the last two leads inexorably to changes in the distribution of wealth and power. The increasingly hour-glass (more realistically, bowling-pin) shaped configuration of the income distribution is by now well known (Jencks and Peterson, 1991: 7 and 254; Sassen, 1990: 477).

Recent studies of the results of the 1990 census in the United States reflect it, as does the discussion of the 'two-thirds' society in Germany (Häussermann and Siebel, 1987). The cause is in some part a change in the job requirements derived from changes in technical methods of production: a greater need for higher skills and a lesser need for lower skills. But that is only part of the picture, for there is no inherent reason why those with lower skills cannot be upgraded, and those at the top do not possess skills in as high a ratio to those of the unskilled as their incomes are to the incomes of the unskilled. The increasing differentiation comes not 'naturally' from technological change, but rather from the increasing concentration of control and of wealth derived from the increased bargaining power given those who control capital and the mobility of that capital, its internationalization. Concentration, internationalization and technological progress have thus in combination led to a drastic change in the balance of power between capital and labour, leading to the further enrichment of the former and the increased impoverishment of the latter, the second element in our model.

'Two-thirds society' hardly grasps the nature of that change, however, because it suggests a two-way division, lumping everyone in either one or the other of two extremes. That is not the case. I have suggested above a five-way division. Others have other, more complex, categorizations. The important point for present purposes is not just what the range of divisions in society is, but rather that there is an increasing division at the bottom, between what used to be called the 'working class' and those poorer than they, largely excluded at least from the formal economy, more and more often impoverished and even homeless. I desist from using the term 'underclass', for reasons eloquently argued elsewhere;[43] but the intuitive resonance the term has found suggests it refers to a widely perceived new reality. Let me substitute the term 'excluded'. I would then argue that the changes

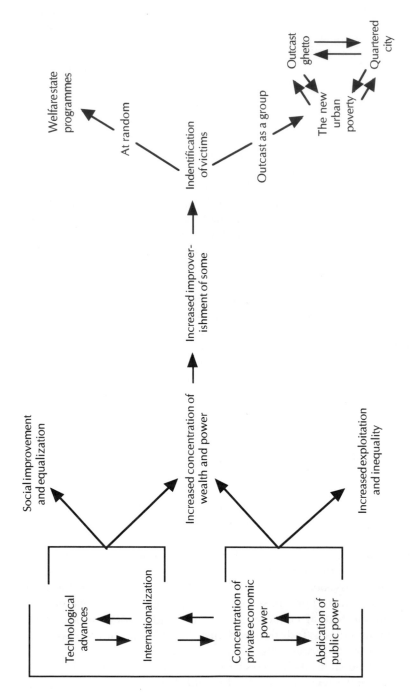

Figure 9.1 A model of the process of victimization

accompanying globalization have had different effects on at least five categories of people (directly paralleling the divisions noted earlier):

- for the owners of wealth and the wielders of power, increases in wealth and power;
- for professionals, technicians, managers, the owners of productive equities, the winners in the process of economic change, a large increase in numbers, and often in income and privilege, but accompanied by some insecurity as to status;[44]
- for the old middle class, civil servants, skilled workers, semi-professionals, a decline in numbers and a loss in status and security;
- for the old working class, a continuing erosion of the standard of living and decline in economic and political bargaining power;
- and, most important for our purposes, for the excluded and the marginalized, the victims of economic change, the very poor, squeezed more and more out of the mainstream of economic activity, presumptively no longer needed even as a 'reserve army of the unemployed', no perceptible long-term prospects of improvement through normal economic channels.

Just how and to what extent each group will be affected in these ways depends on the relationships of power and the related distribution of wealth among them and the manner in which each deal with the incvitable conflicts involved. In those conflicts, both space and race have played key roles in the United States.

The Mediation of Victimization Through the Uses of Race and Space

If victims are inevitably produced by the processes of globalization and the linked set of economic changes that lead from Fordism to post-Fordism then how those victims are treated becomes a critical question. It will be determined largely by how government will deal with them. That in turn depends on who they are, where they live, and how they act. Figure 9.1 suggests a general model of the process.

The identification of victims is a central determinant of the policies a state will follow in deciding how to treat victims. There are two polar choices, and reality will include some mixture of the two, in varying proportions, in any given society.

Sometimes victims appear to be identified by economic circumstances rather than by personal characteristics. They may be those who happened to work in one industry rather than another; they may be those who entered the job market at a particular time, and have less seniority or work experience; they may be those in one particular part of the country instead of another. They may thus appear to be people just like everyone else, and the majority may identify fully with them, sympathize with them, feel that, when they see them on the street, there but for the grace of God go I. That was, for instance, the situation in the United States during the Great Depression. To most observers, the happenstance of unemployment had nothing to do with the person: it was 'random'.

It is the situation that leads to a welfare state type of response. Such welfare state legislation as there is in the United States was in fact largely initiated during the Great Depression. Middle-class homeless families with children evoke much greater sympathy, and charitable contributions for them flow much more freely, than for single unemployed young black men. Unemployment benefits are much more easily passed in Congress than welfare benefits, because working and facing unemployment is a fear most people have to one degree or another, regardless of who they are. The more like the majority of the population the victims are, the better the treatment they are likely to receive.

If, however, victims can be *cast out as a group*, for example, by race, the situation is quite different. African-Americans in the United States, Turks in Germany, Algerians in France, Pakistanis in England, have all been stigmatized in the past; in the United States, certainly, there is a long tradition of oppression and racism from which African-Americans have suffered more than any other group, and have suffered regardless of their actual status in the work-force, in formal law, or in contribution. It is a stigmatization in this sense unconnected with class, although it increases the vulnerability to victimization by economic change particularly of working-class and young African-Americans, and of African-American women.[45]

Where such stigmatization has a historical basis or can be developed, repression and segregation are a readily available alternative to those in power for the treatment of the new victims, though this reaction would not be politically acceptable where the victims appear to be 'randomly' selected and 'just like everyone else'. The tendency to stigmatize victims is an old one – to differentiate between the deserving and the undeserving poor. The welfare state is an expensive and unpopular approach with many. If increasing stigmatization can save money by justifying repression without risking loss of social control, then it is an alternative likely to be chosen.

The possibility of *spatial separation*, that is, ghettoization, increases the likelihood of repressive treatment of the victims of change dramatically. Gunnar Myrdal, remarkably, laid out the scenario succinctly 50 years ago: '[racial segregation creates] an artificial city

. . . that permits any prejudice on the part of public officials to be freely vented on Negroes without hurting whites' (Myrdal, 1944: 618; Logan and Molotch, 1987).

The ultimate point is arrived at when victimized and segregated become identical. Is that not the ultimate implication of William Wilson's shift from 'underclass' to 'ghetto poor'? By equating the two, spatial location becomes the defining characteristic by which the victims can be identified. It must be remembered that, in the United States context, 'race' and 'ghetto' are inseparable concepts. A non-ghetto or non-racial underclass is a theoretical possibility[46] not considered important for discussion, the outcast is defined by his/her connection with the outcast ghetto, even if the casting out is from the mainstream economy.

It is the history of racism that makes the extreme of spatial ghettoization possible in the United States. Yet the tendency towards the spatial segregation of outcasts exists even in the absence of racism, if in significantly attenuated form. Wacquant speaks of 'territorial fixation and stigmatization' of the marginal, of a 'stigma of place', of 'penalized spaces' (Wacquant, 1994b: 8). Marginalization and then exclusion, created as a result of economic relationships, become transmuted into spatial ones: 'social polarization through the field of collective consumption' (Kesteloot, 1994: 2).

The identification of the victims of the particular form of economic change now taking place will thus help determine how those victims are treated by government.

The treatment of the victims by the state permits two options. The state may ameliorate the position of the victims through welfare benefits and attempt to integrate them into the dominant activities of society. Or it may repress and impose rigid external control, effectively excluding the victims from social or economic participation. While both can be, and often are, used together, they are conceptually and politically very different. Economic outcasts may or may not be made political outcasts.

Welfare state benefits are expensive. Paid for by taxes, taxes which those in the upper echelons of the economic hierarchy would always rather minimize, and which those in the lower echelons can generally be counted on to resist as well, the welfare state redistributes resources from one segment of society to another. Those who believe it is *their* resources that are being redistributed will always tend to oppose welfare state policies. One might well argue that welfare state benefits become only a means of last resort to deal with the problems of the victims of economic change. It is a means adopted only when the alternative, repression and exclusion, is for particular historical circumstances not feasible, as when the threat of social unrest is real, or when economic conditions make welfare ultimately profitable, as in the Fordist compromise.

Repression, legal to forceful, exclusion, in some form or other is a characteristic of all societies to date, whether it is in the blatant forms adopted by dictatorships using concentration camps or death squads or in the more refined form of criminal proceedings, and prison terms (Foucault, 1977). In modern democracies such repression is legitimated as provoked by certain types of acts not seen as targeted at a particular group. Yet in the United States today we have the highest number of prison inmates per capita of any developed country in the world, and those who fill our prisons are overwhelmingly African-American. Almost all were very poor at the time of their arrest and trial. The concern about rising rates of criminality suggests that the response of repression through incarceration is likely to be an ongoing and even growing one. The calls for law and order that resulted in the election of a former criminal prosecutor like Rudolph Giuliani as mayor of New York City is another symbol of the increasing reliance on repression as a cure for the social problems created by economic change.

Segregation couples exclusion with a wider form of repression; ghetto walls function in ways similar to prison walls as a restraint on a population. I have elsewhere dealt extensively with the reality and the metaphor of walls within the city as reflective of the hierarchical divisions of a society (Marcuse, 1994b). Such walls can range from the old cliché of the railroad tracks that divided the 'good' part of town from the 'bad', to the modern superhighways that separated and divided the riot-torn areas of Los Angeles from their middle- and upper-class neighbours, or Chicago's public housing from its CBD. Sometimes they are only walls of distance, separating a particular community, a particular suburb perhaps, from the rest of its region. Segregation, as I am using the term here, is involuntary, forced on a population by those with more power than it. It is a form of confinement, a form of repression. It is another possible answer to the problem of what to do with the victims of economic change: segregate them, confine them, repress any danger they may cause to others.

The repressive, exclusionary, approach to the victims of economic change has ramifications up and down the line of the economic hierarchy. For the line between the working class and the excluded is a fluid one; if the segregation of the excluded is to be legitimated by reference to the negative characteristics of those excluded, the working class will seek to separate itself from them. But so will the middle class; and seeing the fluidity of the line separating common workers from the excluded, the middle class will seek to separate itself from both. Both those at the top of the hierarchy and the professionals, technicians and managers directly responsible to them will also be concerned about their separation from those below; in seeking their own security, they will, and do, attempt to differentiate themselves and separate themselves from all below. The pattern of a quartered city is a result.

Between these two polar responses (welfare state or repression) to the growing number of victims of economic change, I suggest that the identification of the victims that will bear the social costs of economic change will primarily determine the response, and I suggest that the presence of historical patterns of racism and spatial segregation will substantially increase both the extent and the depth of exclusion that result.[47]

NOTES

1   In chapter 11 here, Loïc Wacquant also uses this term with the same meaning.
2   A slightly misleading phrase, for no city more than 20 years old is *just* a post-Fordist city; one of the glorious facts of city life is that every city carries its past into its present. The built environment and the human traditions of a city are always a combination of the old and the new. The phrase should always be 'the city in the post-Fordist era'; the shortened version is used simply for convenience.
3   Enzo Mingione, in the first chapter of this volume, deals with this point explicitly. I have discussed it in more detail in Marcuse (1993: 355–65).
4   Massey and Denton, for instance, define the ghetto (see below) in such a way that they can say: 'no ethnic or racial group in the history of the United States, except one, has ever experienced ghettoization, even briefly' (1993: 19).
5   See the complex definition of Massey and Denton (1993: 74), and their discussion in Massey and Denton (1989). See further Jencks and Peterson (1991).
6   'Neighbourhood' likewise remains undefined. The problem is important not only for purposes of measurement – changing the scale of the unit, the neighbourhood, changes the results of the Index of Dissimilarity substantially, for instance – but also substantively. Ronald van Kempen, for instance, raises the question of what to call a situation where Chinese make up only 10 per cent of a given neighbourhood, but all Chinese in the city live in that neighbourhood. That certainly sounds like an exclusion of Chinese from all other neighbourhoods, and I would be surprised if looking at 'neighbourhood' on a smaller scale did not reveal an area in which Chinese were the large majority.
7   I have taken Wacquant's suggestion, made in a footnote, out of context to make my point. He is in the text explicitly concerned with 'the

dilapidated racial enclaves of the metropolitan core' and sees them as, among other things, clearly spatially defined.

8   The term is hardly original; but we are concerned here with specifying more precisely what is new, and why. Camillo Vergara, in a number of writings, has used the term to denote a ghetto created by government, in part through the concentration of public actions locating specific groups, for example, the homeless, drug-dependent populations, in concentrated areas which clearly become even more ghettos than they generally were before. His point is valid and useful, but I use the term 'new' in a broader sense here. See Vergara (1991).

9   Christian Kesteloot (1994) suggests that 'the growing importance of exclusion over marginalisation' is a key characteristic of the present phase.

10 'Institutionalized' is added to the definition by Van Amersfoort: a ghetto is 'an institutionalized residential area in which all the inhabitants belong to a single ethnically, racially or religiously defined group and all members of this group live in this area . . . "institutionalized" means that the inhabitants did not choose their dwelling or residential area themselves: they were to some degree coerced by society . . . by law or . . . by subtle discrimination.' Quoted in Van Kempen (1994: 3). It is thus apparently intended to be synonymous with 'involuntary', and an implicit component of the definition in the text. Were it to mean either 'with its own institutions' or 'created by formal institutions of the dominant society' it would raise other questions.

11 Sennett (1992). In Sennett's etymology, at p. 11, 'ghetto' comes from the Italian for foundry, from *gettare*, to pour, because the location of the first Venice ghetto was on an island that comprised the old foundry district of Venice. That etymology differs from the much more tepid one of the *Oxford English Dictionary*, which derives the word from the Italian for 'boundary'.

12 Such a ghetto is here called an enclave; see below. The next sentence suggests Weaver did not consider the earlier black ghetto an enclave either.

13 Thus the more striking historical analogy for the outcast ghetto is the leper colony rather than the medieval Jewish ghetto.

14 He warns, properly, against converting this description to a normative one, arguing that the ghetto has indeed a 'specific social order', but a 'socio-fugal' one.

15 Following Herb Gans's logic (1991: x): 'African-American . . . is a term that seems to me to emphasize an ethnic heritage, and thus to de-emphasize, if not intentionally, the racial issues inherent in the term black.'

16 For instance, the labour force participation rate (largely the euphemistic opposite of the unemployment rate) for blacks in the United States in 1990 was 63 per cent, compared to 65 per cent for the total population, 67 per cent for all Asian Americans, 71 per cent for Thais, 72 per cent

for Asian Indians, and 75 per cent for Filipinos (US Department of Commerce, 1993).

17 There are indeed other uses of 'enclave' which stress the 'positive' or 'voluntary' character to the exclusion of the negative. See, for instance, Andrew Vernoy's definition: '[An] enclave is an enclosed sector of the city, usually fairly small, that uses its separation from the rest of the city as a means to increase its potential land rent differential' (1993: 4). It is a usage, in real estate terms, related to the broader and richer concept of the 'citadel' introduced by John Friedman more than ten years ago.

18 Indeed, the first known legal segregation of Jews was in Speyer, where the bishop 'in order to attract Jews to the city and thus "add to its honor," gave them the right to have a separate residential quarter where "they might not be readily disturbed by the insolence of the populace" '.

19 The literature is replete with descriptions of such enclaves: Dahya discusses Pakistanis in Bradford, England, Suttles Italians in Chicago, for example.

20 Not all concentrations of those with a common ethnic background are enclaves, in the predominantly positive sense in which the word is used here. John Logan and his colleagues (1994b) point out, for instance, in a detailed analysis of the Los Angeles metropolitan area, that Japanese, Chinese, and Korean enclaves are significantly different in their economic structure than areas of concentration of Mexicans or Filipinos.

21 Rolf Kuhn (1985) has made the point eloquently, and illuminated my own understanding of it, in his discussion of the role of 'equality' and differentiation in socialist housing policy.

22 Omnibus Budget Reconciliation Act of 1993: 'Empowerment zones, enterprise communities, and rural development investment areas', part I, title XIII, chapter I, subchapter C.

23 Among the best short critical discussions are those of Ed Gramlich, prepared for the Center for Community Change and the Coalition for Low Income Community Development, both in Washington, DC. For my own comments on the New York City application and the politics behind it, see Marcuse (1994a: 20–1).

24 Both Hopper and his colleagues and Hoch and Slayton present excellent histories of homelessness, on which any extended discussion of the points here made would have to rely. They do not, however, break out the turning-points in quite the manner suggested here.

25 For a fuller discussion of the change to the contemporary concept of the 'home', see Blackmar (1989).

26 This period is explored in greater depth in Hopper (1983); the implications of a non-historical treatment are spelled out in Marcuse (1988b: 69, 97).

27 In Europe, Brian Harvey (1994), President of FEANTSA, the European association of national organizations working with the homeless, dates the recognition of the changed nature of homelessness to the early 1980s.

28 To over 1 million homeless at some time during 1987 (Burt, 1991: 33).

29   See Marcus (1974) for an excellent new discussion, comparing Engels's account to the much less perceptive accounts of his contemporaries.

30   I use as the model the major United States cities, but I believe the pattern is international, if with differences in scale and intensity.

31   See Marcuse (1989a, 1991). 'Quartered' is used both in the sense of 'drawn and quartered' and of residential 'quarters', although there are also essentially four of such quarters, the very wealthy not being bound by any specific spatial configuration as to where they live. For slightly different approaches, also however differing from 'the dual city' formulation, see Mollenkopf and Castells (1991), especially the Introduction and Conclusion, and Wallock (1987).

32   For the concept of 'home-less housing' and discussion of its location, see Marcuse and Vergara (1992).

33   Keil puts the underlying dynamic succinctly: 'Citadel functions produce . . . ghetto labor markets and living conditions' (1994: 152).

34   See, for instance, for New York City, the work of Andrew Beveridge, and for Los Angeles, the work of Paul Ong, for instance, Ong and Lawrence (1992).

35   For one of the few explicit discussions, see Fainstein and Fainstein (1990). On the uniqueness of the gentrification process, Chris Hamnett has commented that 'it can be seen as constituting no more than an historically and spatially specific manifestation of a set of more general transformation processes' (Hamnett and Randolph, 1986). The question, of course, is for what purpose the line between 'general' and 'specific' is sought to be drawn.

36   A growing number of economists see 1973 as a watershed year in conventional economic terms: productivity, for instance, grew at an average annual rate of 2.5 per cent from 1948 to 1973, then dipped to 0.7 per cent from 1974 to 1991 (Peterson (1994) citing also Lester Thurow and Robert Heilbroner).

37   Alain Lipietz defines Fordism as (a) based on Taylorism plus mechanization, resulting in mass production, for which wage workers would be the major market, (b) a market undergirded through Keynsian state policies co-ordinating economic activities and supporting aggregate demand, in which (c) unions recognized as representing the interests of workers secured long-term security of employment and steadily increasing incomes. He argues that there are many forms of 'post-Fordism', not just a single one based on flexible specialization replacing mass production. His argument is consistent with that presented here. For a brief summary, see Leborgne and Lipietz (1994).

38   I know that this fudges some major questions, the largest of which is the extent to which the transition from the earlier to the later pattern results in qualitatively new forms of social relations, or 'merely' new forms of relationships that have existed for a substantial period of time, and are inherent in capitalism as such. Further, there is a strong functionalist, if not deterministic, element in much of the discussion about post-Fordism.

I tend to agree with the comment of Rustin that: ' "Post-Fordism" is better seen as one ideal-typical model or strategy of production [rather] than as a valid totalizing description of an emerging social formation here and now.' Nevertheless, it is a better term than 'post-industrial' since industry is still firmly with us, if in different forms and locations than before, or 'postmodern', which, in addition to its other problems, is better developed in cultural than in economic or political or policy terms. 'Post-Fordist' does convey a type of change, and a rough time-point, in certain leading economies, and I use it to indicate the period commencing with that change.

39   It was first commented on by Ruth Glass in 1964 (Glass, 1964: xiii–xlii). It is in some ways an extension, but by other means, of the redevelopment programme of the Housing Act of 1949 and the urban renewal provisions of the Housing Act of 1954. Its full consequences were delayed in their impacts by the popular protests against public displacement that make Caro's account of Robert Moses so fascinating (Caro, 1974), and then by the civil rights movement itself. In the end, however, the gentrifiers were, at least temporarily, the stronger. Increased ghettoization and homelessness are its results.

40   The index calculates the percentage of a population group that has to move in order for the proportion in each subunit (generally, census tract) to be equal to the proportion in the unit as a whole (generally, the city). Thus 100 is complete segregation, 0 is uniform mixture. But the index says nothing of the pattern of segregation, that is, whether all more segregated subunits are concentrated together or scattered, and it says nothing about the degree of concentration, that is, whether there are many partially segregated tracts *or* a few very segregated ones. Nor does the index reflect differences in the absolute size of the populations being compared; thus it cannot tell us whether the ghetto is expanding, only whether it is more concentrated or not.

41   The reason southern cities do not show similar changes may have to do with southern to northern migration; for western cities, census definitions (her calculations use SMSA data) may have an impact on the results. Again, careful analysis of the 1990 data should be revealing.

42   See the preliminary results of Andrew Beveridge of Queens College (1992).

43   Most notably by Gans (herein, chapter 6), who recognizes the need for a structural definition but rejects 'underclass' as being increasingly linked to a behavioural one. Other authors have their own definition of 'underclass', and the debate over definitions is not very useful here. For practical purposes, Nick Buck's definition, elsewhere in this volume, is quite adequate: 'that part of the population with no stable relationship to legitimate employment'.

44   The most recent account of the increase in income and wealth for this group – although blurring it with the next – is Bok (1993). He points out that J. P. Morgan 'considered it a matter of principle that no CEO in his

companies earned more than twenty times the lowest-paid worker –
compared to 200 times or more today'. See review by Richard Parker,
1994: 28.

45 Norman Fainstein, in several recent articles and herein (chapter 7), has
gone further than most in disentangling the racist elements in the present
urban context in the United States.

46 See Gans's comment on the use of the term, going back to Myrdal,
defining underclass by structural economic position, rather than by race
or space.

47 For a case study of the forces that have influenced the outcome in
Australia, see Marcuse (1995b).

10

Minorities in Global Cities: New York and Los Angeles

John Logan, Richard D. Alba
and Thomas L. McNulty,
State University of New York at Albany

New York and Los Angeles are the two largest metropolitan centres in the United States, with more than 30 million residents.[1] Though they are sometimes thought of as opposites, as examples of the old and the new American city, we will emphasize their similarities. They are both global cities, in part because they play key roles in international markets and production systems (Sassen, 1991). Of equal importance, and perhaps more consequential for the organization of everyday life in these places, is their position in global population movements. Both owe their size to international migration streams that also make them extremely diverse. As shown in table 10.1, New York's total population grew only slightly during the 1980s. It actually lost nearly a million non-Hispanic white residents, but its Hispanic population grew by about a third and its Asian population more than doubled. Los Angeles grew in the 1980s. While its white and black populations remained nearly unchanged, it added about 2 million Hispanics and more than 700,000 Asians.

The exploding diversity of these urban regions creates a multiethnic society, where there is not one minority but instead there are several. This diversity is not even very well captured in the four categories used in table 10.1. 'Hispanics' in New York have historically been predominantly Puerto Ricans, but today they also include large numbers

Table 10.1   The racial and ethnic composition of the New York and Los Angeles metropolitan areas, 1980 and 1990

	New York		Los Angeles	
	1980	*1990*	*1980*	*1990*
Non-Hispanic whites	11,532,000	10,647,000	7,032,000	7,230,000
	69.6%	62.3%	61.8%	50.2%
Blacks	2,643,000	2,886,000	1,037,000	1,157,000
	15.9%	16.8%	9.1%	8.0%
Hispanics	1,997,000	2,704,000	2,728,000	4,715,000
	12.0%	15.8%	24.0%	32.7%
Asians	374,000	850,000	567,000	1,274,000
	2.2%	4.9%	4.9%	8.8%
Total population	16,546,000	17,087,000	11,364,000	14,376,000

of immigrants from the Caribbean (for example, Dominicans), and Central and South America. LA's Hispanics, by contrast, are predominantly Mexican. Among Asians, the largest numbers are Chinese, Korean, Japanese, Filipino and Indian – people speaking different languages, with different national identities and cultures, and even different patterns of incorporation into the US economy. Finally, the black population includes a growing proportion of immigrants, especially in New York where there are now large Jamaican and Haitian communities. Although it has been said that the old ethnic divisions among whites of European origin have been diminishing (Alba, 1990), new divisions constantly emerge.

Our purpose here is to probe the relationship between race and social resources in this multiethnic system. American sociology long sought to encompass all minorities within the historical metaphor of the melting pot: the experience of gradual but full incorporation into mainstream society. Recently two new models have been put forward to account for the visible survival and even reinforcement of minority communities in major cities. These are the underclass and ethnic enclave models. Both models embrace important aspects of assimilation, though the underclass model shows that some fall outside its reach and the enclave model suggests that autonomy is a precondition for a group's upward mobility.

The underclass model was developed by Wilson (1987) with the black ghetto in mind, although others (Tienda, 1989) have applied it to Hispanics. Wilson argues that certain inner city neighbourhoods have suffered the convergence of two processes: rising unemployment due to regional de-industrialization and the failure of community resources (including both public and private institutions). These neighbourhoods now house a residual pocket of blacks with the lowest income, the least prospects and the poorest chances of moving onward. These are collapsing neighbourhoods, where economic constraints are reinforced by a way of life (including welfare dependence, illegitimate births and street gangs) that further divides the underclass from mainstream society (see also Logan and Molotch, 1987, on the community dimension of ghetto life).

The underclass model shows a sensitivity to the linkages between labour and housing markets, hypothesizing that it is the combination of marginality in the labour force with segregation into communities with few social resources that creates an underclass. However, Wilson believes that the same society that leaves some of its members without hope is also open to assimilation of most persons – even most blacks. Surprisingly, although the underclass is mostly black, race itself has little to do with Wilson's model. Indeed, he suggests that it is the upward mobility of the growing black middle class, and its exodus from the inner city, that deprives underclass neighbourhoods of the class diversity, role models and black social institutions that once sustained ghetto life.

Wilson's rejection of the importance of race, with his implicit acceptance of assimilation as the appropriate model for working-class and middle-class blacks, has been attacked by Fainstein (1993: 401), who argues that class 'may actually be declining in significance' for blacks. Massey, basing his claim on studies of residential patterns, argues that it is residential segregation that creates underclass neighbourhoods, not a new mobility of the black middle class (see especially Massey, 1990; Massey, Gross and Shibuya, 1994). Nevertheless, discussions of the underclass now dominate sociological discourse on race and the city.

The second new model, that of the ethnic enclave, builds mainly on the experience of urban immigrants. The concept first emerged in Portes's analysis of the Cuban community in Miami, which has grown to nearly half the city's population (Wilson and Portes, 1980; Portes and Bach, 1985). Cubans, it was argued, had managed to create a semi-autonomous economy in which Cuban entrepreneurs and workers controlled not only the sectors that serviced their co-ethnic population, but also key institutions in manufacturing and finance. Portes acknowledges the obstacles to Cuban immigrants' full integration into the mainstream economy, where they face disadvantages associated with language, culture and skills that are either not transferable or (in the case of professionals like doctors and lawyers) not certified. But he hypothesizes that they can achieve upward mobility in the enclave labour market comparable to what natives find in the primary sector of the economy, and he suggests that residential mobility will naturally follow.

The original studies of the Cuban enclave in Miami have been supplemented with numerous Asian case studies: of the Chinese in New York, San Francisco and Los Angeles, and the Koreans in New York and Los Angeles (Sanders and Nee, 1987; Zhou and Logan, 1989; Model, 1992). These communities have much in common: they include large and spatially concentrated minorities, renewed at a rapid rate through new immigration from non-English-speaking countries, and with a highly visible small business component. They represent the 'new migration' into the United States since 1965, particularly from Asia and Latin America. Their apparent success suggests that there may now be favourable conditions for development of enclaves by other groups and in other parts of the country.

The enclave model posits that immigrants' concentration in *barrios* of the inner city can be an economic resource, both a source of cheap labour for ethnic entrepreneurs and a market for their products, and perhaps even a basis for networks of supply and distribution among ethnic firms (Wilson and Martin, 1982). In some cases ethnic firms in the United States receive financing (through family networks or other mechanisms) from their countries of origin, and they may also serve as distributors for goods produced in those countries. In other words, there may be a global dimension to their operations. But this line of thought appears not to have much relevance for American blacks, who are still a source of low-wage labour outside the primary labour market, principally for enterprises controlled by non-minority owners. Afro-Americans have a low rate of self-employment outside of the underground economy, suffering unequal access to capital and to jobs that might otherwise provide the requisite experience for entrepreneurship (Light, 1984). It is well known that a large share of retail stores in Afro-American neighbourhoods are owned by outsiders, giving rise to the characterization of the black experience as one of 'internal colonialism' (Blauner, 1972).

How do these various groups fare in the labour and housing markets of New York and Los Angeles? We take as a starting point the existence of a hierarchy of groups in terms of education and income. Table 10.2 summarizes this hierarchy for the two regions using three simple indicators from 1990: attainment of college education, median household income and (to focus on a more specific aspect of the income distribution) poverty. In both regions, whites have the highest average income and the lowest proportion of families below the

Table 10.2 Indicators of socio-economic status of racial and ethnic group members in the New York and Los Angeles metropolitan areas, 1990

	New York			Los Angeles		
	College[a]	Income in dollars[b]	Poverty[c]	College	Income in dollars	Poverty
Non-Hispanic whites	30.4	44,574	4.0	27.6	41,544	4.8
Blacks	13.1	26,179	19.5	14.9	26,625	18.5
Hispanics	9.5	24,189	25.4	6.3	28,891	18.3
Asians	42.8	40,493	10.2	37.1	40,724	10.7
Total population	25.8	38,445	9.1	22.0	36,711	9.8

[a]Percentage of persons aged 25 and above with some college education.
[b]Median income of households.
[c]Percentage of families below the poverty line.

poverty line. Their educational level, however, is surpassed by Asians, despite the large number of recent immigrants among them (these immigrants may account for the larger number of Asian than white poor). At the other end of the spectrum, blacks and Hispanics fall well below the regional average in both New York and Los Angeles.

We want to explore the structure of the markets that produce these outcomes. Is the low income level of blacks and Hispanics attributable simply to their lack of human capital, or is the labour market organized in ways that make these groups more vulnerable to unemployment or underemployment? We ask a similar question with respect to neighbourhoods. Is the segregation of blacks and Hispanics from whites and their location in poor neighbourhoods attributable to their lesser human capital – that is, their lack of resources to compete in the housing market? Or is the housing market structured in ways that deny opportunities to some minorities?

Although we ask a similar question about both markets, our approach to each is distinct. With respect to labour markets, we are especially interested in the racial patterning of business ownership and in evidence that ethnic ownership results in better employment opportunities for co-ethnics. With respect to housing markets, the evidence of residential segregation is already quite convincing. Our contribution here is to link segregation to inequalities in community resources available to group members, and to evaluate the degree to which residential disparities are due to racial group membership. In both analyses, we focus on multiple groups: non-Hispanic whites, non-Hispanic blacks, Hispanics and Asians. Among Hispanics we single out Puerto Ricans in New York and Mexicans in Los Angeles for special attention, and we focus on the largest Asian group in each region, Chinese in New York and Japanese in Los Angeles.

THE ETHNIC ORGANIZATION OF LABOUR MARKETS

Two characteristics of enclave economies are especially relevant to our interest in racial divisions. The first is the contribution enclaves may make to the economic standing of various minority groups: we want to know whether blacks, Mexican Americans or any Asian groups have established their own niches in business ownership. The second is the impact that these enclaves may have on relations among minority groups. The key feature of an ethnic economy is that it is bounded by race, ethnicity or national origin. It rests fundamentally on *co-ethnicity of owners and their employees*.

In their seminal article on Cubans in Miami, Wilson and Portes (1980) identify enclave participants simply as Cubans who have a Cuban employer. Co-ethnicity is at the heart of the advantages that they believe enclave entrepreneurs have over their competitors, providing them a 'privileged access to markets and sources of labor . . . [and] the reciprocal obligations attached to a common ethnicity' (Wilson and Portes, 1980: 315). It is presumed that minority entrepreneurs create job opportunities for fellow group members – jobs that may not require English language facility, in which workers are protected from discrimination based on their race/ethnicity, and in which it is possible to learn the skills and develop the networks that would facilitate an eventual move into self-employment. Bailey and Waldinger (1991) argue, in fact, that the ethnic enclave is essentially a 'training system' that would be too risky to sustain without the guarantees provided by ethnic ties between employers and employees. In their research on New York City, Bailey and Waldinger (1991: 48) note that every major minority group 'has a marked concentration in one or two industries. And since access to ethnic networks is based on particularistic criteria, and job information and assistance comprise scarce resources, the creation of the specializations involves a process of boundary creation and maintenance, restricting members of other groups from jobs or occupations within the niche' (see also Waldinger, 1986–1987).

If indeed ethnic enclaves constitute training systems, they represent a double barrier to other minorities: they lack access not only to opportunities for small business ownership (and therefore to capital accumulation), but also to entry-level jobs in sectors of the economy

Table 10.3 Economic sectors in which various racial/ethnic groups are over-represented as owners (or as owners and workers), New York and Los Angeles metropolitan areas in 1980

Metropolitan area	Agric/manufacturing industries	Service/trade industries	Number in 1000s
Non-Hispanic blacks in New York		*private households*	1813.8
Non-Hispanic blacks in Los Angeles		*trucking* *personal services*	925.8
Puerto Ricans in New York		*food stores*	877.9
Mexicans in Los Angeles	*agriculture* *electrical*	*construction* *repair services*	1643.2
Chinese in New York	*apparel* food products	*eating places* transportation private households personal services hospitals social services	129.0
Japanese in Los Angeles	*agriculture* *printing* apparel wood products	*food stores* *eating places* auto/gas sales retail *repair services* hospitals education services personal services	117.2

Italicized sectors are those in which the group is over-represented as both owners and workers. In other listed sectors, the group is over-represented only as owners.

dominated by other groups. The first step in our analysis, then, is to evaluate the New York and Los Angeles economies in terms of evidence of ethnic enclaves.

Table 10.3 lists the economic sectors in which various racial/ethnic groups are over-represented (see Logan, Alba and McNulty, 1994a, for a complete description of the methodology used here). This table includes non-Hispanic blacks, Puerto Ricans in New York, Mexicans in Los Angeles, Chinese in New York and Japanese in Los Angeles. Whites are not included because they are over-represented as owners in so many industry sectors, more than 30 in each region. Because they are also over-represented in the work-force of many of these sectors, it seems possible that their control provides privileged access to employment. Following the terminology applied to new immigrant groups, we might well describe whites as having a most highly developed enclave economy, though we usually think of it as simply the 'mainstream' economy with no ethnic identifier. The 'white' enclave is mostly based on key services: communications, financial/ real estate, business services, entertainment, elementary and second- ary schools, social services and professional services (including law and engineering). These services are expanding rapidly in both regions, and white control of these sectors appears to offer them an important advantage in the labour market. Whites are also predomin- ant as owners in most sectors of manufacturing, but they are rarely over-represented as workers in these sectors.

Turning to the groups listed in table 10.3, the first finding is that blacks (in either region) and Puerto Ricans are rarely over-represented as owners. Mexicans are found disproportionately as owners in agriculture, which may reflect Mexican labour contractors to some degree. Otherwise they are not dissimilar to blacks and Puerto Ricans. A closer look at the distribution of Mexicans in the work-force shows one difference, however. They are a key part of the labour force in some manufacturing industries, especially in apparel manufacturing and furniture making, where they are employed predominantly by people of other ethnic backgrounds. Although manufacturing is declining nationally, and its share of total employment even in Los Angeles is falling, the absolute number of manufacturing jobs is increasing in this region.

Asian entrepreneurs are less numerous than are whites, but they have strong concentrations in retail sectors associated with food: food products, food stores and eating places (that is, restaurants). And in several cases these are matched by over-representations as workers, hinting that Asian food stores and restaurants practice some degree of ethnic exclusivity in hiring. Chinese in New York and Japanese in Los Angeles are found disproportionately as owners in apparel manufac- turing (as are Koreans in these regions).

These Asian enclaves have a weaker economic base than do whites: apparel and textiles are the least capital intensive and lowest paying sectors of manufacturing, and eating and drinking places have a lower average wage than any other industry sector in this analysis. Yet they are strong relative to the other minorities considered above. And they extend in various ways unique to each group. For example, the Japanese have a historic niche in agriculture as both owners and workers, and the Chinese are over-represented (although to a lesser degree than in their core sectors) as owners in several other manufacturing and services sectors. (On another important ethnic economy in Los Angeles, organized by Koreans, see Light and Bonacich, 1991).

RESIDENTIAL SEGREGATION

Aside from the racial structuring of the labour market, we believe that the next most decisive arena of inequality is in the region's housing market. But our emphasis here is not specifically on housing itself – rather, our concern is with the community context in which people live. The neighbourhoods in which whites, blacks, Hispanics and Asians live are not equal. Some offer their residents superior access to those community resources, like schools or personal security, that enhance the quality of life. Others, abandoned by both public facilities and private business and left behind by previous residents with better opportunities, do not. At the low end of this spectrum is the underclass neighbourhood which is at the core of Wilson's (1987) model of inner city poverty. We measure those differences here as the median income of households in the neighbourhood; other aspects of the income distribution, such as the proportion below poverty, would yield similar results. The income of neighbourhood residents is an indicator of other local resources: higher income neighbourhoods tend to have better schools, lower rates of crime, better public services, and social networks that indirectly offer residents better access to a whole range of other kinds of resources.

We begin with an overview of the differences among groups in their place of residence. Our data, from the 1980 Census of Population and Housing, are for census tracts, which are intended by the census to be relatively homogeneous areas of about 4,000–6,000 inhabitants. Non-Hispanic whites live in tracts which have on average a median income of about $22,000 in both regions. Among minority groups, Asians are the most advantaged (differences among Asian nationality groups are relatively small, except that New York's Chinese live in surprisingly poor areas, reflecting the concentration in Manhattan's Chinatown). Hispanics and blacks live in the least desirable areas, with average incomes about one-third less than the average neighbourhood of non-Hispanic whites. New York's Puerto Ricans rank even below blacks, but all Hispanic groups in Los Angeles live in somewhat better neighbourhoods than do blacks.

It might be expected that these disparities are partly due to differential suburbanization, since in most parts of the country the

Table 10.4   Median income (in dollars) of census tracts where the average group member lives, New York and Los Angeles metropolitan regions in 1980

	New York		Los Angeles	
Racial/ethnic category	Metro	City	Metro	City
Non-Hispanic white	21,861	17,175	22,146	21,359
Non-Hispanic black	12,674	11,151	14,275	12,072
Hispanic	12,442	10,969	16,235	14,478
Mexican	14,644	11,770	15,975	14,327
Puerto Rican	11,087	10,051	17,574	15,721
Cuban	15,116	13,713	17,407	16,557
Asian	17,933	14,804	20,038	16,684
Japanese	22,717	19,078	21,196	17,914
Chinese	16,235	13,846	20,814	16,247
Filipino	18,795	15,695	19,400	16,007
Korean	20,094	16,088	19,943	16,750

central city has a much higher proportion of minorities and lower average income level than the surrounding suburbs. This pattern is also found in New York and Los Angeles, but it does not account for much of the difference in neighbourhood standing between whites and others. Table 10.4 also presents the averages for central city residents. Surprisingly, in Los Angeles the central city census tract in which the average non-Hispanic white lives is nearly indistinguishable from the typical suburban white person's place of residence: its average income level is not even $1,000 less. Central city whites in Los Angeles are highly segregated and therefore sheltered from a 'city' social environment.

If disparities in where people of different races live are not simply a matter of city versus suburban residence, what does account for them? Social scientists have recourse to two quite distinct theories to explain residential segregation. The first emphasizes personal characteristics that happen to be associated with race: differences in socio-economic standing and in cultural background that are themselves the real reasons for unequal residential outcomes. This is the model represented by the metaphor of the 'melting pot', referred to above (see Massey, 1985). People are sorted into different parts of the metropolis, from this perspective, simply according to criteria of needs, preferences and affordability. Segregation by race or ethnicity is understandable as a temporary phenomenon: new immigrants, constrained by unfamiliarity with the mainstream language and culture, may settle together, but such settlements will be undermined by eventual assimilation and educational or occupational mobility of many group members. In the market for better locations, persons with higher socio-economic status naturally do better; those who buy homes are in different locations than renters. These are the choices underlying neighbourhood change, as people respond to the opening up of new areas and the physical deterioration of others.

Following this reasoning, one would predict that most group differences in location could be accounted for by differences in average socio-economic status and assimilation to American culture. Controls for these characteristics should leave only negligible net differences between groups, at least among the more affluent. This is implicitly the view espoused by Wilson (1987), who believes that a growing black middle class has succeeded in gaining access to better locations.

An alternative view has emphasized enduring institutional barriers which effectively limit minority residential mobility. This perspective is best represented by the literature on dual housing markets experienced by blacks and, according to some studies, Hispanics (Henretta, 1984; Krivo, 1986; Alba and Logan, 1991). Segregation between blacks and whites remains high despite decades of change in both black socio-economic status and the legal order. Based on this literature, one would predict that locational differences between groups could not be attributed to compositional differences. After controlling for all relevant predictors of location, there would remain net differences reflecting the status hierarchy of racial groups, with whites at the top and blacks at the bottom. For example, as has also been found in status attainment research, whites might receive a larger payoff than blacks from educational achievement.

These two models offer contrasting hypotheses about locational patterns within *any* part of the metropolis. They are likely to apply unequally to various minority groups. Massey and Denton (1987, 1988; see also Denton and Massey, 1988; White, Biddlecon and Guo 1991), for example, find important differences between the segregation patterns of Asians, blacks and Hispanics. In all regions of the country, in cities and in suburbs, blacks are most segregated from whites, while Asians, despite the recency of their immigration, tend to be least segregated (see also Farley and Allen, 1987). Beyond these differences in level, segregation appears to respond differently to assimilation and socio-economic variables in the three groups. According to these studies, black–white segregation is resistant to socio-economic improvement, in contrast to the more varied profiles of Asian and Hispanic segregation. But the locational patterns of the main Hispanic groups in our regions, Puerto Ricans and Mexicans, seem to be more similar to blacks than to Asians.

To evaluate these models of residential outcomes we apply the method developed by Alba and Logan (1992; see also Alba and Logan, 1993, Logan and Alba, 1993) to estimate individual-level regression equations from files provided by the decennial Census of Population and Housing. The Census Bureau releases data separately for individuals (the Public Use Microdata Samples, which generally do not include information on place of work or residence below the county level) and for geographic units (the Summary Tape Files). Our method allows us to estimate ordinary least-squares regression models as if we possessed a single data file at the individual level that contained characteristics of place of residence as well.

Our analytical model views the income level as a desirable feature of a community, one of the characteristics that serves to locate it in a hierarchy of places. The model can be expressed formally as follows:

$$Y_j = a + b_1X_{1ij} + b_2X_{2ij} + b_3X_{3ij} + \ldots$$

where Y_j is a measure of community status, X_{1ij} is the household income (or another human-capital variable) for individual or household i in community j, X_{2ij} is English-language ability (or another assimilation measure), and X_{3ij} represents other (possibly control) variables, such as household configuration or age. The model is estimated for individuals, separately for each racial/ethnic group. Communities are operationalized here as census tracts.

As already noted, one primary data source for this study is a Summary Tape File (4A) from the 1980 Census of Population and Housing. This file provides extensive data on the demographic, socio-economic and housing characteristics of racial/ethnic group members by tract of residence. STF4A reports separate information for seven groups, identified on the basis of the race and Hispanic origin questions on the 1980 census. We use the data for four groups here – whites (including Hispanic and non-Hispanic persons), blacks (also including both Hispanic and non-Hispanic persons), Hispanics (including white and black Hispanics) and Asians.[2]

We estimate the effects of several predictors of spatial outcomes that are important to both the assimilation and stratification models: age and education of the household head, family income, and housing tenure (Bianchi, Farley and Spain, 1982), the marital status of head of household and presence of children (Parcel, 1982). Our selection of predictors was guided by these prior studies. We have represented all of the independent variables in categorical form, as dummy variables

Table 10.5 Estimated median income (in dollars) of place of residence for racial/ethnic group members with given characteristics, New York and Los Angeles metropolitan areas in 1980

	Poor immigrant[a]	Poor native[b]	Affluent native[c]
New York			
Non-Hispanic white	12,471	15,037	34,525
Non-Hispanic black	9,692	8,706	20,636
Puerto Rican	9,554	12,428	27,392
Chinese	9,511	9,861	28,890
Los Angeles			
Non-Hispanic white	13,567	15,538	34,062
Non-Hispanic black	9,428	9,818	23,931
Mexican	11,746	15,331	29,082
Japanese	12,540	13,715	29,902

[a] A person aged 25–64 with income under $5,000, less than a high school education, home renter, who arrived in the US within the previous five years and speaks English poorly.
[b] A person aged 25–64 with income under $5,000, less than a high school education, home renter, who was born in the US and speaks only English at home.
[c] A person with income above $75,000, college education, and homeowner, who was born in the US and speaks only English at home.

(for, say, the nine categories of household income), rather than as interval scales. This is because the data source provides information only in categories, and it would introduce error into the analysis to transform them into interval scales.

Table 10.5 provides a summary based on the regression equations estimated separately for every racial/ethnic group. Based on these equations, we have calculated the predicted value of the community's median household income for three specific kinds of individuals, whom we describe as 'poor immigrant', 'poor native' and 'affluent native'. These reflect the extreme values of individuals' socio-economic (income, education and homeownership) and social (nativity and language) characteristics.

Table 10.5 provides some support for the assimilation model. Higher socio-economic status (the comparison between where poor natives and affluent natives are predicted to live) invariably has a strong impact on place of residence. This is, of course, natural in a market society. And in most cases there is a clear disadvantage for recent immigrants who do not speak English well (the comparison between poor immigrants and poor natives). Even controlling for socio-economic resources, native whites (in both regions), Puerto Ricans (in New York) and Mexicans (in Los Angeles) live in higher income places. The differences are much smaller, however, among Asians, and native blacks actually suffer a disadvantage in New York (where black immigrants, such as Jamaicans, tend to live in somewhat better conditions). These findings mean residential mobility through 'acculturation' cannot be taken for granted.

There are also indications in table 10.5 of housing market inequality. Remember that the predicted values in this table are for persons with given individual characteristics, and it would be difficult from within the assimilation paradigm to account for any group differences. Yet clearly whites are advantaged: in every comparison and in both regions they live in better places than comparable Asians, Hispanics or blacks. Blacks are similarly disadvantaged: in every comparison except one, they live in worse places than comparable persons of other races. Other minorities do not fit so neatly into a hierarchy of groups, but they are typically midway between whites and blacks. For example, poor Chinese in New York, regardless of immigrant status, live in very low-income neighbourhoods, but affluent Chinese do much better (if not as well as whites) in the housing market. Note that although Japanese in Los Angeles were shown on average to live in places with only about $1,000 lower income than whites (table 10.4), the gap is about $2,000 among persons classified as poor natives, and reaches about $4,000 among affluent natives. This suggests that what appears to be nearly equality between these two groups is due not to equal residential processes but rather to the high average socio-economic standing of individual Japanese in this region. Thus our analysis reveals a little-known aspect of the Asian situation that is quite different from the 'model minority' image: some Asians in Los Angeles do apparently experience a degree of disadvantage, possibly due to discrimination, in the housing market.

Finally, we point out how the disparity between blacks and whites changes according to the social mobility of individuals. The most useful comparison is between the poor and affluent native categories, because as we have seen 'immigration' has a distinctive impact for blacks. In New York, the gap in predicted community income grows from a little over $6,000 for persons at the lowest socio-economic level to nearly $14,000. In Los Angeles, it grows from about $5,700 to over $10,000. Put another way, even the wealthiest blacks are disadvantaged relative to comparable whites, and in absolute terms they are the *most* disadvantaged.

CONCLUSION

We conclude that both the labour market and the housing market are structured in ways that work to the disadvantage of blacks and some other minorities in the New York and Los Angeles metropolitan areas. The evidence is incomplete, but here are the directions in which it points.

First, non-Hispanic whites have a powerful position in the regions' economies, as reflected in both the extent of business ownership and the kinds of businesses in which ownership is concentrated. The enclave economies of Chinese and Japanese residents include a smaller number of sectors of ownership, and their common element is their foundation in textiles/apparel and in food stores and restaurants. These are also the sectors in which they apparently take advantage of an ethnic labour market (except that the Japanese in Los Angeles probably do not employ many Japanese workers in apparel), cutting their costs of operation and restricting employment opportunities for other minorities. These sectors are characterized by low levels of capitalization and low wages, but they do offer a foothold in the economy for these Asian groups. Blacks, Puerto Ricans and Mexicans have little recourse to entrepreneurship and we would guess from our data that they rarely can rely on co-ethnic owners for employment. Whether Mexican labour concentrations in several manufacturing sectors (where they surely work for employers of other ethnicities) help to compensate for the lack of an ethnic enclave is a question that we cannot answer here. Groups compete, and they compete unequally, for advantage in the labour market.

In housing also we find white advantage: whites are located in the better neighbourhoods of the metropolis, and this is only partly because of their higher average level of individual resources – whites have a built-in advantage over other groups. Asians on average live in better neighbourhoods than other minorities, although their success is mostly attributable to their high socio-economic status (they do not live in the same kinds of neighbourhoods as do comparable whites). The net result is that whites and Asians tend to be sheltered from the community-level problems confronted on a daily basis by blacks and Hispanics.

The gap in community resources faced by Hispanics is to a large degree due to compositional differences between whites and Hispanics. Hispanics are strongly disadvantaged by foreign birth and unfamiliarity with English, far more strongly than any other group. Because so many Hispanics are recent immigrants, this disadvantage affects a large portion of this group's members. A further issue for Hispanics, as we have documented elsewhere (Alba and Logan, 1993), is that many are black. And the evidence of housing discrimination against blacks is especially clear: at best, the predicted value of neighbourhood income for a black person is three-fourths the predicted value for a white with the same background.

These findings have some bearing on the underclass and enclave models that are now being applied to American cities. Like both of these models, we posit some linkages between the labour and housing markets in which minorities compete. Their geographic concentration in certain neighbourhoods can be either an obstacle (in the case of blacks, Puerto Ricans and Mexicans) or a stepping stone (in the Asian cases) to economic security. Their communities, depending on how they are organized and the public and private resources that they make available to residents, can immobilize or energize people. The urban location of racial and ethnic groups, in our view, is not simply a consequence of the groups' social standing, but also a substantial causal force.

Where we part with the underclass and enclave models is in the premise of each that there is a 'way out' of minority disadvantage. According to Wilson, the underclass represents an unusual coincidence of lack of individual and community resources, relevant only to the poorest city residents. Our data suggest a different reading, that blacks, Puerto Ricans and Mexicans all lack an entrepreneurial class, and that they all – and especially blacks – experience a segmented housing market that leaves them in disproportionately poor communities. While the extent of problems faced by the underclass is extreme, the underclass should be seen as a symbol of racism that cuts a much wider path through the metropolis.

We are less certain of how to interpret these findings with regard to the enclave model. Certainly an ethnic economy generates opportunities for group members, though some recent analyses have demonstrated that the opportunity structure within the enclave is more generous for owners than for workers (Sanders and Nee, 1987). Our principal reservation is the limited extent of enclave development in both New York and Los Angeles, where Asian minorities have established dominance in relatively marginal economic sectors, a bare echo of the white economy or even of the unique Cuban economy in Miami. It would require a leap of the imagination to suppose that small business could offer similar opportunities to blacks, Puerto Ricans and Mexicans, given their low average levels of education and lack of capital. And we note that neither the Chinese in New York nor the Japanese in Los Angeles, despite their entrepreneurialism, are achieving residential mobility commensurate with their class positions. Successful enclaves may be an exceptional mode of immigrant incorporation, rather than a model for many groups to follow.

In a pathbreaking book over 30 years ago, Glazer and Moynihan looked forward to the time when their racially divided New York would 'in the end be an integrated city – or rather something even better, a city where people find homes and neighbourhoods according to income and taste, and where an area predominantly of one group represents its positive wishes rather than restricting prejudice' (Glazer and Moynihan, 1963: 65). The evidence reviewed here for New York and Los Angeles suggests that these global cities continue their historic function of accepting diverse populations from around the world. But neither the housing nor the labour market in these regions meets the criterion of openness anticipated by Glazer and Moynihan. The racial structuring of access to business ownership, jobs, and neighbourhoods divides these urban regions today, and we have found no reason to predict that even the next 30 years will undermine this pattern.

NOTES

1   As we analyse it here, the New York region includes the entire New York/New Jersey Consolidated Metropolitan Statistical Area with the exception of the portion found in Connecticut. It includes four 'primary' metropolitan areas in New Jersey and four in New York. Los Angeles is defined here as the Los Angeles–Long Beach CMSA, which includes Los Angeles, Orange, Riverside, San Bernardino, and Ventura Counties.

2   The number of census tracts for which group data are available in STF4A differs somewhat for whites, for Hispanics, for blacks and for Asians. Data are not reported for tables based on individuals when there are less than 30 group members residing within the tract. Complementary suppression (designed to prevent indirect inference of suppressed data) is another source of data loss. Despite these missing data, more than 95 per cent of the region's population is covered by the following analyses.

11

Red Belt, Black Belt: Racial Division, Class Inequality and the State in the French Urban Periphery and the American Ghetto

Loïc J. D. Wacquant,
University of California, Berkeley;
Centre de Sociologie Européenne

Two interconnected trends have reshaped the visage of western European cities over the past two decades. The first is the pronounced rise of multifarious urban inequalities and the crystallization of novel forms of socio-economic marginality, some of which appear to have a distinctly 'ethnic' component and to feed (off) processes of spatial segregation and public unrest. The second is the surge and spread of ethno-racial or xenophobic ideologies and tensions consequent upon the simultaneous increase in persistent unemployment and the settlement of immigrant populations formerly thought of as guest-workers or colonial subjects.

The structures of this 'new poverty' (Marklund, 1990) are far from being fully elucidated but their empirical manifestations present a number of clear commonalities across national boundaries. Long-term joblessness or precarious occupational attachment, the accumulation of multiple deprivations within the same households and neighbour-hoods, the shrinking of social networks and slackening of social ties, the open proliferation of distressed 'street persons', and the inade-quacy of traditional forms of social insurance and public assistance to remedy or check hardship and isolation: all of these can be observed, to varying degrees, in all advanced societies.[1] Similarly, there is today throughout the continent growing concern over the development of

'European racism' and renewed theorizing about its historical or functional linkages to immigration, the crisis of the national order, and various facets of the ongoing post-Fordist economic transition (for example, Balibar, 1991b; Miles, 1992 and 1993; Wieviorka et al., 1994).

The coincidence of new forms of urban exclusion with ethno-racial strife and segregation has given prima facie plausibility to the notion that European poverty is being 'Americanized'. Consequently, many European scholars (though by no means all) have turned to the United States for analytic assistance in an effort to puzzle out the current degradation of urban conditions and relations in their respective countries. Hence the transatlantic diffusion of concepts, models, and sometimes ready-made theories from recent (and not-so-recent) American social science.[2] This is visible in the worried and confused public discussion in France – and in other countries such as Belgium, Germany and Italy – about the presumed formation of 'immigrant ghettos' in degraded working-class neighbourhoods harbouring low-income housing tracts known as *cités*. It can be detected also in the spread of the notion of 'underclass' in Great Britain and in its smuggling into the Netherlands to address the strain put on citizenship by the emerging concatenation of joblessness, ethnic discrimination and neighbourhood decline.[3] Such conceptual borrowings, however, stand on shaky analytical grounds inasmuch as they presume exactly that which needs to be established: namely, that the American conceptual idiom of 'race relations' has purchase on the urban realities of Europe – leaving aside the question of whether conventional American categories (or newer concepts such as the mythical notion of 'underclass') pack any analytical power on their own turf to start with.

The best way to answer, or at least productively reframe, this question is through a systematic, empirically grounded, cross-national comparison of contemporary forms of urban inequality and ethno-racial/class exclusion which (a) does not presuppose that the analytical apparatus forged on one continent should be imposed wholesale on the other and is sensitive to the fact that all 'national' conceptual tools have embedded within them specific social, political and moral assumptions reflective of the particular history of society and state in each country (see Silver herein); (b) attends consistently to the meanings and lived experiences of social immobility and marginality; and (c) strives firmly to embed individual strategies and collective trajectories into the local social structure as well as within the broader national framework of market and state.

This chapter is part of a larger attempt to contribute to such a comparative sociology through an analysis of the social and mental structures of urban exclusion in the American 'Black Belt' and the French 'Red Belt' (Wacquant, 1992a, 1992b, 1994b, 1995b). 'Black Belt' is used here to denote the remnants of the historic 'dark ghetto' (Clark, 1965) of the large metropolis of the Northeast and Midwest of the United States, that is, the dilapidated racial enclaves of the metropolitan core that have dominated recent public and academic discussions of race and poverty in North America.[4] The expression 'Red Belt' refers not simply to the townships of the outer ring of Paris that form(ed) the historic stronghold of the French Communist Party but, more generally, to the traditional mode of organization of 'workers' cities' in France (Magri and Topaloff, 1989; Fourcault, 1992), anchored by industrial male employment, a strong workerist culture and solidaristic class consciousness, and civic incorporation of the population through a dense web of union-based and municipal organizations creating a close integration of work, home and public life. It is in such peripheral working-class neighbourhoods that urban inequalities and unrest have coalesced, making the question of the *banlieue* perhaps the most pressing public issue in the France of the 1980s.[5]

The analysis that follows uses data from a variety of primary and secondary sources and combines observations drawn from censuses, surveys and field studies of the American ghetto and the French *banlieue*. On the French side, I concentrate on the Red Belt city of La Courneuve and its infamous public housing concentration called the Quatre mille (after the nearly 4,000 units it originally contained). La Courneuve is an older, Communist-governed, northeastern suburb of Paris with a population of 36,000, situated midway between the national capital and the Roissy-Charles de Gaulle airport, in the midst of a densely urbanized, declining industrial landscape. On the American side, I focus on the South Side ghetto of Chicago and in particular on the neighbourhood of Woodlawn, where I conducted ethnographic fieldwork in 1988–91. The South Side is a sprawling, all-black zone containing some 100,000 inhabitants, the majority of whom are unemployed and live under the official federal 'poverty line'.

I presented elsewhere a detailed sociography of both sites which highlighted a number of parallel morphological traits and trends.[6] In summary, both locales were found to have a declining population with a skewed age and class structure characterized by a predominance of youths, manual workers and deskilled service personnel, and to harbour large concentrations of 'minorities' (North African immigrants on the one side, blacks on the other) that exhibit unusually high levels of unemployment caused by de-industrialization and labour market changes. This comparison also turned up structural and ecological differences suggesting that the declining French working-class *banlieue* and the black American ghetto constitute two *different socio-spatial formations*, produced by different institutional logics of segregation and aggregation and resulting in significantly higher levels of blight, poverty and hardship in the ghetto. To simplify greatly: exclusion operates on the basis of colour reinforced by class and state in the Black Belt but mainly on the basis of class and mitigated by the state in the Red Belt (Wacquant, 1992b: 98–9), with the result that the former is a racially and culturally homogeneous universe whereas the latter is fundamentally heterogeneous in terms of both class and ethno-national recruitment.

The purpose of this chapter is to flesh out some of the invariants and variations in the social organizational and cognitive structures of urban exclusion by contrasting four dimensions of daily life salient in both the French *banlieue* and the black American ghetto, though, as we shall see, with significantly discrepant inflections, degrees of urgency and socio-political dynamics. I move from the more comparable to the more dissimilar, starting with the powerful territorial stigma that attaches to residence in an area publicly recognized as a 'dumping ground' for poor people, downwardly mobile working-class households and social outcasts. The second dimension, crime and insecurity, is of central importance not only as a major determinant of the quality of life but also because it feeds stigmatization and crucially affects local housing and economic conditions. The third, closely related, dimension of organizational density and diversity concerns the provisioning of the basic needs of residents and impacts their sense of inclusion in or isolation from the broader society. The fourth and last section takes up the question of the social divisions and bases of conflict operative in stigmatized neighbourhoods of concentrated poverty in France and the United States, and briefly considers the different social mechanisms that fuel urban tension and ethno-racial hostility in the two settings.

TERRITORIAL STIGMATIZATION: ROOTS, EXPERIENCE AND EFFECTS

Any comparative sociology of the 'new' urban poverty in advanced societies must begin with the *powerful stigma attached to residence in the bounded and segregated spaces*, the 'neighborhoods of exile'[7] to which the populations marginalized or condemned to redundancy by the post-Fordist reorganization of the economy and state are increasingly being relegated. Not only because it is arguably the single most protrusive feature of the lived experience of those assigned to, or entrapped in, such areas but also because this stigma helps explain certain similarities in their strategies of coping or escape and thereby many of the surface cross-national commonalities that have given apparent validity to the idea of a transatlantic convergence between the 'poverty regimes' of Europe and the United States.

'It's Like There's a Plague Here'

Because they constitute the lowest tier of that nation's public housing complex, have undergone continual material and demographic decline since their erection in the early 1960s, and received a strong inflow of foreign families from the mid-1970s on (Barrou, 1992), the *cités* of the French urban periphery suffer from a negative public image that instantly associates them with rampant delinquency, immigration and insecurity. So much so that they are almost universally called 'little Chicagos', both by their residents and by outsiders.[8] (Revealingly, two other labels commonly used to denote the degradation and presumed dangerousness of French *cités* are 'Harlem' and 'the Bronx'.)

To dwell in a Red Belt low-income estate means to be confined to a branded space, to a blemished setting experienced as a 'trap' (Pialoux, 1979: 19–20; Bachman and Basier, 1987). Thus the media and its inhabitants themselves routinely refer to the Quatre mille as a 'dumpster', 'the garbage can of Paris' or even a 'reservation' (Avery, 1987: 13), a far cry from the official bureaucratic designation of 'sensitive neighbourhood' used by the public officials in charge of the state's urban renewal programme. In recent years, the press of stigmatization has increased sharply with the explosion of discourses on the alleged formation of so-called *cités-ghettos* widely (mis)represented as growing pockets of 'Arab' poverty and disorder symptomatic of the incipient 'ethnicization' of France's urban space (Wacquant, 1992a).

It should be noted, however, that the Quatre mille does not exist *as such* in the perceptions of its residents. The indigenous taxonomies the latter use to organize their daily round distinguish numerous subunits within the large estate which in effect has only an administrative and symbolic existence – though it has real consequences. What appears from the outside to be a monolithic ensemble is seen by its members as a finely differentiated congeries of 'micro-locales': those from the northern cluster of the project, in particular, want nothing to do with their counterparts of the southern section, whom they consider to be 'hoodlums' (*racaille* or *caillera* in the local youth slang), and vice versa. 'For the residents of the Quatre mille, to change building sometimes means to change lives' (Bachmann and Basier, 1989: 46; also Dulong and Paperman, 1992). Yet it remains that *cité* dwellers have a vivid awareness of being 'exiled' to a degraded space that collectively disqualifies them (Pétonnet, 1979: 211). Rachid, a former resident of the Quatre mille, gives virulent expression to this sense of indignity when asked about the eventuality of moving back into the project: 'For us to return there, it would be to be insulted once again. *The Quatre mille are an insult* . . . For many people, the Quatre mille are experienced as a shame.' When the interviewer inquires about the possibility of salvaging the housing project through renovation, his answer is no less blunt:

> To renovate is to take part in shame. If you agree to play this game, then in a way you're endorsing shame. We've come to a point of no return where you got no solution but to raze the whole thing. Besides the people here agree there's only one solution: 'Gotta blow it up.' Go and ask them . . . When you don't feel good inside, when you don't feel good outside, you got no jobs, you got nothing going for you, then you break things, that's the way it is. The shit they're doing trying to fix the garbage disposal and the hallway entrance, the painting, that's no use: it's gonna get ripped right away. It's dumb. It's the whole thing that's the problem . . . You gotta raze the whole thing. (cited in Euvremer and Euvremer, 1985: 8–9)

For Sali, another North African youth from the Quatre mille, the project is 'a monstrous universe' seen as an instrument of social confinement by its inhabitants: 'It's a jail. They [second-generation residents] are in jail, they got tricked real good, so when they get together, they have karate fights against the mail boxes and bust everything up. It's all quite easy to understand' (1985: 9; also Bourdieu, 1991a: 12–13). The verbal violence of these youths, as well as the vandalism they invoke, must be understood as a response to the socio-economic and symbolic violence they feel subjected to by being thus relegated in a defamed place. Not surprisingly, there is great distrust and bitterness among them about the ability of political institutions and the willingness of local leaders to rectify the problem (Aïchoune, 1991; Jazouli, 1992).

It is hardly possible for residents of the *cité* to overlook the scorn of which they are the object since the social taint of living in a low-income housing project that has become closely associated with poverty, crime and moral degradation affects all realms of existence – whether it is searching for employment, pursuing romantic involvements, dealing with agencies of social control such as the police or welfare services, or simply talking with acquaintances. Residents of the Quatre mille are quick to impute the ills of their life to the fact of being 'stuck' in a 'rotten' housing project that they come to perceive through a series of homological oppositions (*cité*/city, us/them, inside/ outside, low/high, savage/civilized) that reproduce and endorse the derogatory judgement of outsiders.[9] When asked where they reside, many of 'those who work in Paris say vaguely that they live in the northern suburbs' (Avery, 1987: 22) rather than reveal their address in La Courneuve. Some will walk to the nearby police station when they call taxicabs to avoid the humiliation of being picked up at the doorstep of their building. Parents forewarn their daughters against going out with 'guys from the Quatre mille'.[10]

Residential discrimination hampers job search and contributes to entrenching local unemployment as inhabitants of the Quatre mille encounter additional distrust and reticence among employers as soon as they mention their place of residence. A janitor in the *cité* relates a typical incident in which he helped new tenants contact firms by telephone only to be told that there was no longer any position open whenever he revealed where he was calling from: 'It's like there's a plague here,' says he in disgust (in Bachmann and Basier, 1989: 54).[11] Territorial stigmatization affects interactions not only with employers but also with the police, the courts and street-level welfare bureaucracies, all of which are especially likely to modify their conduct and procedures based on residence in a degraded *cité*. 'All youths recount the change of attitude of policemen when they notice their address during identity checks' (Dubet, 1987: 75), for to be from a *cité* carries with it a reflex suspicion of deviance if not of outright guilt. A high-school student tells of being stopped by subway controllers in the Paris metro: 'We took out our identity cards. When they saw that we were from the Quatre mille, I swear to you! They went . . . they turned pale' (in Bachmann and Basier, 1989: 65).

'People Really Look Down on You Because of Where You Come From'

In America, the dark ghetto stands similarly as the national symbol of urban 'pathology', and its accelerating deterioration since the racial uprisings of the mid-1960s is widely regarded as incontrovertible proof of the moral dissolution, cultural depravity, and behavioural deficiencies of its inhabitants.[12] The journalistic reports and academic (pseudo) theories that have proliferated to account for the putative emergence of a so-called 'underclass' in its midst have accelerated the *demonization of the black urban (sub)proletariat* by symbolically severing it from the 'deserving' working class and by obfuscating – and thereby retroactively legitimating – the state policies of urban abandonment and punitive containment responsible for its downward slide (Wacquant, 1992c: 115–22 and 1994b; also Katz, 1989; Gans, 1992).

Today, living in the historic Black Belt of Chicago carries an automatic presumption of social unworthiness and moral inferiority which translates into an acute consciousness of the symbolic degradation associated with being confined to a loathed and despised universe.[13] A student from a vocational high school on the city's South Side voices this sense of being cut off from and cast out of the larger society thus:

> People really look down on you because of where you come from and who you are. People don't want to have anything to do with you . . . You can tell when you go places, people are looking at you like you are crazy or something. (in Duncan, 1987: 63)

The defamation of the ghetto is inscribed first in the brute facts of its physical dilapidation and of the separateness and massive inferiority of its institutions, be they public schools, social agencies, municipal services, neighbourhood associations or financial and commercial outlets (Wacquant, 1994b; Orfield, 1985; Monroe and Goldman, 1988). It is constantly reaffirmed by the diffident and contemptuous attitudes of outsiders: banks, insurance companies, taxis, delivery trucks and other commercial services avoid the Black Belt or venture into it only gingerly; kith and kin are reluctant to visit. 'Friends from other places don't want really to come here. And you yourself, you wouldn't want to invite intelligent people here: there's markings and there's writing on the wall, nasty, whatever', says an unemployed mother of three who lives in a West Side project. Children and women living in public housing in the inner city find it difficult to evolve personal ties with outsiders once the latter learn of their place of residence (Kotlowitz, 1991).

Desmond Avery (1987: 29), who lived in both the Cabrini Green project in Chicago and in the *Quatre mille*, remarks that residential discrimination is at least as prevalent in the Windy City as in the Parisian periphery. Ghetto dwellers are well aware that living in a stigmatized section of town penalizes them on the labour market: 'Your address, it's *impression for jobs.*' Residing on the South Side, and even more so in a public housing project whose name has become virtually synonymous with 'violence and depravity', is yet another hurdle in the ardous quest for employment. A jobless woman who lives in the ill-reputed Cabrini Green housing development remarks:

> It's supposed to be discrimination, but they get away with it, you know. Yes, it's important where you live. Employers notice, they notice addresses, when that application's goin' through personnel, they are lookin' at that address: (worried tone) 'Oh, you're from *here*!?'

Over and beyond the scornful gaze of outsiders and the reality of exclusion from participation in society's regular institutions, the thoroughly depressed state of the local economy and ecology exerts a pervasive *effect of demoralization* upon ghetto residents. Indeed, the words 'depressing' and 'uninspiring' come up time and again in the description that the latter give of their surroundings. Moreover, two-thirds of the inhabitants of the South Side and West Side of Chicago expect that their neighbourhood will either stay in the same state of blight or further deteriorate in the near future; the only route for improvement is to move out, to which nearly all aspire.

The possibility of accumulating resources in preparation for upward mobility is further eroded by the predatory nature of relations between residents and by the pressure toward social uniformity which weighs upon those who try to rise above the poverty level common to most inhabitants of the area: 'They won't let you get ahead. Stealin' from you and robbin' you and all that kinda thing', laments a 27-year-old machine operator from the far South Side. Given the inordinate incidence of violent crime (examined in more detail below), living in a ghetto neighbourhood also entails significant physical risks and, as a corollary, high levels of psychic stress which tend to 'drag you down' and 'wear you out'. No wonder that life in the Black Belt is suffused with a sense of gloom and fatality, a social *fatum* that obstructs the future from view and seems to doom one to a life of continued failure and rejection (Monroe and Goldman, 1988: 158–9, 273; Kotlowitz, 1991; Wacquant, 1992d: esp. 56–8).

An Impossible Community: How Stigmatization Breeds Dis-integration

Paradoxically, the experiential burden of territorial stigmatization weighs more heavily on the residents of the French *banlieue* than it does on their counterparts of the American ghetto, in spite of the fact that the latter constitutes a considerably more desolate and oppressive environment (Wacquant, 1992a). Three factors help account for this apparent disjuncture between objective conditions and the subjective (in)tolerance of those who evolve in them.

First, the very idea of relegation into a separate space of *institutionalized social inferiority and immobility* stands in blatant violation of the French ideology of unitarist citizenship and participation in the national community, an ideology fully embraced and forcefully invoked by youths from the Red Belt, especially second-generation immigrants of North African origins in their street protest and marches of the past decade (Jazouli, 1992).[14] By contrast, the colour line of which the black ghetto is the most visible institutional expression is so ingrained in the make-up of the American urban landscape that it has become part of the *order of things*: racial division is a thoroughly taken-for-granted constituent of the organization of the metropolitan economy, society and polity.[15]

Second, residents of the American ghetto are more prone to embracing a highly individualistic ideology of achievement than are their counterparts of the French *cités*. Many if not most adhere to the social Darwinistic view that social position ultimately reflects one's moral worth and personal strivings so that no one, in the long run, can be consistently held back by his or her place of residence.[16]

A third and most crucial difference between Red Belt and Black Belt is found in the nature of the stigma they carry: this stigma is only residential in the former but jointly and inseparably *spatial-cum-racial* in the latter. The French *banlieue* is but a territorial entity which furthermore contains a mixed, multiethnic population; it suffices for inhabitants of the Quatre mille or any other *cité* to hide their address in order to 'pass' in the broader society. No readily perceptible physical or cultural marker brands them as members of the Red Belt and use of simple techniques of 'impression management' (Goffman, 1963) enable them to shed the stigma, if only temporarily. Thus adolescents from poor Parisian *banlieues* regularly go 'hang out' in the upscale districts of the capital to escape their neighbourhood and gain a sense of excitement. By traversing spaces that both symbolize and contain the life of higher classes, they can live for a few hours a fantasy of social inclusion and participate, albeit by proxy, in the wider society (Calogirou, 1989: 64–9). This 'consciousness switch' renders more intolerable the idea of permanent exclusion and the outcast status associated with consignment to a degraded *cité*.

Residents of the American Black Belt are not granted the luxury of this dual 'awareness context'. For the ghetto is not simply a spatial entity, or a mere aggregation of poor families stuck at the bottom of the class structure: it is uniquely *racial formation* that spawns a society-wide web of material and symbolic associations between colour, place and a host of negatively valued social properties (Pettigrew, 1971: 91–2, 179–82). The fact that colour is a marker of identity and a principle of vision and division that is immediately available for interpretation and use in public space and interaction (Feagin, 1991) makes it nearly impossible for inner city dwellers to shed the stigma attached to ghetto residence. For instance, they cannot casually cross over into adjacent white neighbourhoods, for there 'the sight of a young black man evokes an image of someone dangerous, destructive, or deviant' (Monroe and Goldman, 1988: 27; Anderson, 1991: esp. 163–7), so that they will promptly be trailed and stopped, nay systematically harassed, by police. More generally, unless they offset their low caste status by a competent outward display of the symbols of middle-class (white) culture, blacks are always by definition presumed to be ghetto dwellers and of low class provenance.[17]

Ghetto blacks in America suffer from *conjugated stigmatization*: they cumulate the negative symbolic capital attached to colour *and* to consignment in a specific, reserved and inferior territory itself devalued for being both the repository of the lowest class elements of society and a racial reservation. In a race-divided society such as the United States where all spheres of life are thoroughly colour-coded (Terkel, 1992), and given the low chances of escaping the ghetto, the best one can do is make a virtue of necessity and learn to live with a stigma that is both illegitimate and unacceptable to French working-class youths of the Red Belt *cités*.

Yet the main *effect* of territorial stigmatization is similar in both countries: it is to stimulate practices of internal social differentiation and distancing that work to decrease interpersonal trust and undercut local social solidarity. To regain a measure of dignity and reaffirm the legitimacy of their own status in the eyes of society, residents of both *banlieue* and ghetto typically overstress their moral worth as individuals (or as family members) and join in the dominant discourse of denunciation of those who 'profit' from social assistance programmes, *faux pauvres* and 'welfare cheats'. It is as if they can gain value only by devaluing their neighbourhood and their neighbours and by castigating the latter as undeserving. They also engage in a variety of strategies of social distinction and withdrawal that converge to undermine neighbourhood cohesion.

These strategies of stigma management take three main forms: mutual avoidance, reconstitution and elaboration of 'infra-differences' or micro-hierarchies, and the diversion of public opprobrium onto scapegoats such as notorious 'problem families' and foreigners, or drug dealers and single mothers.[18] In the French *cité*, residents commonly insist that they are there only 'by accident' and carp about the waste of public resources allocated to those who, 'contrary to them', do not genuinely need assistance. Similarly, in Chicago's ghetto, residents disclaim belonging to the neighbourhood as a network of mutual acquaintance and exchange, and strive to set themselves apart from what they know to be a place and population of ill repute. This 41-year-old nurse from the West Side neighbourhood of North Lawndale, one of the most destitute in the city, speaks for many of her peers of both Black Belt and Red Belt when she says:

> Hell, I don't know what people [around here] do, I guess I'm pretty much on my own. I don't associate with people in the neighbourhood; I mean I speak to them, but as far as knowing what they're about, I don't know.

To sum up, residents of the French *banlieue* and of the American ghetto each form an *impossible community*, perpetually divided against themselves, who cannot but refuse to acknowledge the collective nature of their predicament and who are therefore inclined to deploy strategies of distancing and 'exit' that tend to validate negative outside perceptions and feed a deadly self-fulfilling prophecy through which public taint and collective disgrace eventually *produce* that which they claim merely to *record*: namely, social atomism, community 'disorganization' and cultural anomie.

DELINQUENCY, STREET VIOLENCE AND THE SHRINKING OF PUBLIC SPACE

French working-class *banlieues* and American ghettos have this in common, that they are publicly regarded as dangerous places where delinquency and crime are prevalent, where the rule of law applies but very imperfectly, and that one should shun if at all possible. Yet, they differ sharply in the intensity and frequency, degree of social embeddedness, and nature of the criminal or illegal activities they harbour, as well as in the impact that these and other forms of street violence have on the organization and flow of daily routines. To anticipate: in La Courneuve, the main problem is a feeling of insecurity rooted in the ecology of the neighbourhood and fuelled by petty youth delinquency; on Chicago's South Side, actual physical danger suffuses everyday life and creates an oppressive climate of tension and fear that has caused the virtual disappearance of public space.

Youth Delinquency and the Feeling of Insecurity in La Courneuve's Projects

Following a handful of highly publicized incidents, the *cité* of the Quatre mille has, like many of its counterparts in the Parisian periphery and in the suburbs of Lyon and Marseilles, earned the reputation of being a 'no-go' area plagued by rampant crime and ruled by bands of lawless youth. Outsiders readily identify it as a 'bad' neighbourhood to be avoided; it is rumoured that police dare not enter it; some residents of the project themselves insist that theirs is a tough and risky environment (*ça craint*). This familiar media image,[19] however, bears only a tenuous relation to the quotidian reality of the estate.

While it is true that groups of young men engage in street fights and in occasional muggings and vandalism, and that internal social relations evidence a notably higher recourse to physical violence than would be common among the middle class,[20] it is in fact quite safe to walk through the Quatre mille, including at night, and one can go about freely in and out of buildings, as there is much public life around them. In the municipal park immediately adjacent to the project (a three-mile by one-mile expanse of grass and shrubbery), one can spot families out for picnics, joggers and cyclists, adolescents playing a game of pick-up soccer, children flying kites and couples walking their dogs in the early evening.[21] People who work in the vicinity routinely cross project grounds to reach the adjacent metro station, which is packed with commuters at rush hours. Those who hold jobs inside the Quatre mille express exasperation and disbelief at the idea that their place of employment puts them in physical jeopardy.

Car and motorcycle thefts, petty robberies and larceny are the most common crimes in La Courneuve. In a normal year, there is not a single homicide in the entire city. For instance, in 1983 and 1984, the most serious incidents were 18 armed robberies, none of which resulted in deaths. The town has a total police force of only 140 and rates for various crime categories are barely above the national average and compare favourably with those of many more reputable cities: for instance, the figure of 10.8 break-ins per 1,000 inhabitants lags well behind that for Paris (25.6). Residents can mention no major incident of racial or ethnic violence since the death of little Toufik in 1983[22] – the mere fact that the latter made national headlines and stands out in the collective memory is indicative of its anomalous character.

The practice of *dépouille* (the stealing of jackets and shoes under threat of force) has become more common over the past decade but it occurs mainly between local adolescents and very seldom involves the use of arms. Tension is perceptible between the police and young men and fights occasionally break out during public balls and other outdoors events but this happens in working-class cities throughout the country at popular celebrations such as the Fourteenth of July.

'They don't escalate into violence because the associations are well represented, they handle that pretty well', avers a public official who works inside the Quatre mille. The episodic violent outbursts that attract disproportionate media attention are generally well circumscribed and targeted, singling out the police and the private security guards of local stores in retaliation for what local youths consider unfair, brutal or disrespectful treatment.

Yet there is, among residents of the project as in many other *cités* of the French urban periphery, a widespread and deeply entrenched feeling of insecurity and distrust (Avery, 1987: 110; Dulong and Paperman, 1992: 58) generated by increasing petty delinquency and by the depressed and depersonalizing setting of the estate in which heterogeneous populations come in daily contact.[23] As a result, many inhabitants of La Courneuve opt to equip their homes, cars and shops with alarm systems; some elderly residents even carry gas canisters, though they seem to be a minority. Drugs – not physical violence – is viewed as the number one item on the agenda of public safety in the Quatre mille. The basements of most buildings have been condemned to prevent youths from hiding in them to consume illegal substances and it is not hard to spot petty dealers when they work the vicinity of the local supermarket. But the drug trade in La Courneuve pales in intensity, volume and sophistication when compared to its counterpart in Chicago. Street-level distribution is intermittent and involves primarily small quantities of opiates and marijuana rather than 'hard' drugs such as heroin or derivatives of cocaine, though the latter are not unknown.[24]

Though it has risen noticeably in recent years with the increase in persistent youth unemployment, drug dealing remains a marginal activity which attracts unemployed school dropouts who are often themselves substance (ab)users and whose main concern is to generate sufficient income to support their own addiction. Its recent growth notwithstanding, the trade in La Courneuve is nowhere close to having evolved into a highly differentiated, self-sustaining economy generating cashflows in the tens of millions of dollars and allowing for durable careers outside the regular labour market, as in the inner cities of America. What is more, it has not spawned a specific 'culture' or complex of loose-knit but extensive networks of users and traders (Williams, 1992): in the *cité*, drugs are synonymous with social withdrawal, not with the individual pursuit of sensuous gratification and economic opportunity.[25]

Petty youth theft, drugs and alcoholism are the most common forms of delinquency in the degraded *cités*. Much of this delinquency is opportunistic and has a strong ludic or expressive dimension: its main purpose is to generate not so much money as 'action' and to vent the rage felt at being encaged in this bleak environment.

It may entail riding the train to Paris without paying, sneaking into movie theatres for free, stealing from stores (Calogirou, 1989: 120) or from schools and other public buildings, street larceny or acts of minor vandalism such as 'tagging' or destroying mail boxes – and, in more extreme cases, cars which are set on fire in a sort of inverted potlatch. It has more to do with 'getting a good laugh' than with entering into a criminal career (Dubet and Lapeyronnie, 1992: 135–6). Remarkably, residents of La Courneuve still establish a distinction between pilfering committed inside the estate and theft (*fauche* or *resquille*) committed outside. Thieves who prey on their 'own kind', that is, on neighbours and occupants of the surrounding buildings, are often reprimanded or excluded from networks of reciprocity.[26] Similarly, in the projects studied by Dubet (1987), residents hardly tolerate stealing within the community. This is in sharp contrast with the black ghetto, where internal predation is rampant and takes on radically more violent forms.

Street Violence and the Withering Away of Public Space on Chicago's South Side

Indeed, the level of physical insecurity reached in the ghetto neighbourhoods of the American metropolis is incomparable with that of French *cités*, or with that of other 'inner cities' anywhere in continental Europe or Great Britain. If the impact of delinquency on daily life in La Courneuve is felt mainly at the level of representations, open violence – including assault and battery, homicide, rape and shootings – has become so prevalent in the Black Belt that it has forced a complete restructuring of the fabric of daily life.[27]

Recent epidemiological reports indicate that homicide is now the leading cause of mortality among ghetto residents and that young black males face a greater risk of violent death walking the streets of America's urban core than they did fronting the battlefields of Vietnam two decades ago. The upsurge in the murder rate to levels comparable to casualties in a military engagement have prompted talk of a 'black male genocide' (Staples, 1987). Thus an overwhelming majority of the 849 homicides recorded in the city of Chicago in 1990 took place in the ghetto: according to a detailed FBI study, 'the typical 1990 murder victim was a black male, under 30, and killed by gunfire in the poorest neighborhoods' (*Chicago Tribune*, 1991). In the Wentworth police district which comprises the historic Black Belt of the South Side, 96 homicides were reported for a staggering rate approaching 100 murders per 100,000 residents, nearly 15 times the rate for the city's white bourgeois district of the northwest districts. A tactical officer from a local unit laments: 'We have murders on a daily basis that never make the news. No one really knows or cares.'[28] Police also complain that young criminals now routinely employ high-powered weapons such as sub-machine and automatic guns: 'Kids used to have bats and knives. Now they're equipped with better guns than we have' (1991: 14).

Dubrow and Garbarino (1989: 5) have compared the vicinity of public housing projects on Chicago's South Side to 'a war zone complete with noncombatants fleeing the front lines'. The most serious dangers cited by mothers living there are shootings, gangs and darkness in descending order, whereas mothers living in a demographically comparable neighbourhood in the suburbs mention kidnapping, traffic accidents and drugs as the most serious hazards faced by their children. In Woodlawn, as in most other areas of the city's Black Belt, residents commonly barricade their homes and apartments behind wrought-iron bars and gates; they tailor their daily round so as to minimize forays to the outside and to avoid public places and facilities and hurry inside at nightfall: 'I never go to Washington Park at night or without my gun. Why? If one of them punks jump on me, they gonna get some of my piece', intones an elderly informant. In the summer of 1991, the Mayor of Chicago, called upon by South Side residents to account for the fact that one cannot walk safely across public parks even in broad daylight, inadvertently conceded that gangs and drug dealers, not local government, control this section of the city when in exasperation he compared it with . . . Bogotta, Columbia – this was at the time when the Medellin cartel was terrorizing this city with firebombings and assassinations. In many areas of the South Side, public phones have been disconnected to prevent their use by drug dealers and train stations closed to entry in a last-ditch attempt to limit crime.

With the widespread availability and circulation of handguns and drugs, the street itself has become a sort of grotesque theatre of aggressive masculinity in which violent confrontation serves as the currency of honour and where the slightest pretext – a bump, a look, a cap turned the wrong side or the wrong colour jacket – can tip a routine impersonal encounter into a lethal display of brutality. 'Everybody in d'ghetto frustrated,' explains a 28-year-old former gang member from Woodlawn, 'so when you bump into a guy, (exagger-

ated, angry snarl) "nigga, I'mma kill ya!" *I'm serious*, tha's frustration.'
And he continues:

> You gotta be strong and learn how to survive. When you out there in
> d'street, some crazy guy might wanna jump on you and bust yo' head
> for no reason. You gotta know how t'protect yourself, how to survive. I
> always watch my back and I would kill to protect myself and my right to
> live. You gotta be a man, tha's the only way. Shiiit! sometime, I think *I
> was better off in jail*: it's worse out there now.[29]

Death is so much part of everyday life that the simple fact of reaching
adulthood is considered an achievement worthy of public acknowledgement. When asked what has become of their childhood friends,
the most frequent answers given by young men from the South Side
ghetto revolve around a fateful tryptic: going to jail, dealing drugs and
shot to death.[30] A janitor at a Woodlawn McDonald's restaurant
reflects: 'I seen people shot. I seen people killed. I seen a person *shot,
killed* that was standin' right next to me an' I felt that it coulda been
me an' hum, the best thin' that I need to do was change my
acquaintances.' The harshness of living conditions, the banality of
sudden death and the high incidence of incarceration also explain that
jail is perceived as continous with the ghetto, representing merely an
extension of life in the Black Belt.[31]

Philippe Bourgois (1989, 1992), who conducted five years of
fieldwork on the crack trade in New York's East Harlem, suggests that
the streets of the ghetto have become the breeding ground of a
veritable *culture of terror* that grows in functional relation with the
illegal street-level drug trafficking that dominates the booming
underground economy of the urban core. Regular open displays of
violence are a *sine qua non* of success in the ghetto informal sector in
which they are 'essential for maintaining credibility and for preventing
ripoffs by colleagues, customers and intruders.' Indeed, reinterpreted
in the logic of this irregular economy, such violence may be seen as a
'judicious case of public relations, advertising, rapport building, and
long-term investment in one's "human capital development"'. The
need to cultivate this culture of terror − so as to generate income, to
intimidate others or simply to preserve some degree of individual
autonomy and physical integrity − extends well beyond those who
partake in the drug trade, with the result that it 'poisons interpersonal
relationships throughout much of the community by legitimizing
violence and mandating distrust' (Bourgois, 1989: 631–2, 635).

In the French *cité*, delinquency is a source of (considerable)
annoyance rather than (ubiquitous) danger. Public violence is limited
and remains embedded in local patterns of sociality: it is a 'form of

regulation applied to intensive social practices, a moment of sociability in which physical force is asserted . . . as the foundation of repute' (Laé and Murard, 1988: 20). In the American ghetto, crime is more economic than ludic and violence is pandemic because of the dominance of the informal economy over the wage-labour sector and the breakdown of public institutions, and both are largely disarticulated from local social relations, save those that pertain to the partially autonomous microcosm of the gang as a quasi-institutionalized social predator or informal entrepreneur (Sánchez-Jankowski, 1991; Padilla, 1992). These sharply divergent patterns of violence, in turn, point to the different organizational contexts of the *banlieue* and the ghetto and to the different forms and levels of social control that these provide.

INSTITUTIONAL ISOLATION VERSUS ORGANIZATIONAL DESERTIFICATION

An important characteristic of isolated enclaves of persistent poverty is the extent to which they harbour the institutions designed to fulfil the basic needs of their residents and incorporate them into the surrounding society. Here again, at the level of experience, Red Belt and Black Belt are somewhat similar: both are perceived as organizationally lacking and the residents of each deplore the dearth of key organizations needed to contribute to the community's functioning and well-being.

Yet, objective comparison yields another notable transatlantic contrast: the French *cité* is the home of a plethora of grass-roots and public services due in good part to ramifying state intervention,[32] while the ghetto has experienced an accelerating process of organizational desertification caused largely by state abandonment (Wacquant, 1992c and 1994b). More specifically, it will be suggested that La Courneuve suffers from an over-penetration of state agencies and public organizations which tend to atomize and isolate their users, whereas the South Side has weathered the *withdrawal* and near-total breakdown of public institutions.

The Paradox of Organizational Density and Institutional Isolation in the Red Belt

Though the perception of its inhabitants (as well as of public authorities) is that the Quatre mille is a 'void' lacking even the most basic amenities, dominant institutions are far from absent from the project. Of the city's ten public kindergarten and thirteen primary schools, twelve are located inside the estate, and two of La Courneuve's six high schools sit right alongside the *cité*. Health and social services are also well represented within the housing complex; major facilities such as the Municipal Health Centre, the Centre for Social Services, and six nursery schools financed by the *département* of Seine-Saint-Denis are right at the residents' door. Additionally, eight major administrative offices are located inside the estate, including the regional Social Security (that is, health, welfare and family assistance) administration, a state Income Tax outlet, a Centre for Information on Women's Rights, and the headquarters of the local HLM (low-income housing) authority.

The roster of cultural facilities located inside the Quatre mille is no less extensive.[33] It comprises the Houdremont Cultural Centre (inaugurated in 1977), which houses the National Conservatory of the Region as well as music and popular dance workshops; the Centre for the Dramatic Arts and its acting school with an 800-seat auditorium; a neighbourhood House for Youth (*Maison des Jeunes*) and a public library; a youth club offering sporting, artisanal, cultural and academic programmes; a government-sponsored public 'Computer workshop' (with 100 members and 22 microcomputers in 1987) and a city-run Crime Prevention Club. Several 'Leisure Centres' keep some 2,000 pupils busy on Wednesdays when school is out, and during the evenings and academic holidays. Finally, three religious facilities, a Catholic church as well as a Protestant church and a Jewish temple, are located inside the project, while a small Jehovah's Witness group actively recruits in it.[34] As Avery (1987: 31) notes, 'social structures of communication are plentiful.' Beyond the numerous associations and clubs, there are posters on most walls, and graffiti and inscriptions in *verlan* – the slang of youth from working-class *banlieues* – cover many buildings.

Yet there is, relative to the large teenage population – nearly half of the *cité*'s dwellers are not 20 years old – and the high unemployment level, a great paucity of sporting and recreational facilities, with the consequence that teenagers have no place to congregate and spend time together as a group. The sole movie theatre of the project closed down in 1973 because it was losing too much money and being degraded. Numerous stores, including the project's only fast-food outlet, and the Yuro theatre went out of business in the early 1980s owing in part to nagging petty crime and vandalism that raised insurance costs, in part to depopulation which reduced the carrying capacity of the local market and also because the remaining customers have taken to shopping in larger, cheaper supermarkets located in surrounding cities. Only a couple of bars remain and they close early at night to avoid trouble. The commercial centre of the main tower, which services the southern cluster of the *cité*, contained 27 shops in business in 1986 but fewer than a score five years later. Apart from the bakery, the newspaper and magazine store and the local pharmacy, sales are slow at local businesses. Thus the atmosphere of the Viniprix, the last food mart in operation, is characteristically impregnated with a slight feeling of anxiety, and shopkeepers are downright depressed about the commercial prospects of the neighbourhood.

The high density of formal organizations of the project notwith-standing, local and state officials openly speak of the inefficiency and indifference of public institutions in *cités* such as the Quatre mille. In good part, this failing of public services is due to the stigma that bears on being assigned to a Red Belt city and its loathed public housing estates. An official from the Prefecture of Ile-de-France confesses: 'There's no glory in being appointed in the Seine-Saint-Denis: for a civil servant, to be sent there is tantamount to being punished, like being put on hold.' Moreover, the organizations that exist are often geared more to the middle-class needs and values of those who conceive and administer them than to the requisites and requests of the population they are supposed to serve. And, in many areas, they are largely unable to meet demand because of the high concentration of socially and economically 'fragile' families in need of multiple forms of assistance (Simon, 1982).[35]

This translates into the congestion of public services, which causes residents to spend much of their time waiting in lines and manœuvring the intricacies of local street-level bureaucracies. This, in turn, makes the project over into what Avery (1987: 176) describes as

a zone of impossibility where everything becomes strangely heavy and complicated, even services that ordinarily have nothing to do with social problems: a post office, a bank, a supermarket where people stand in line somberly, where everything seems to operate as if in slow motion, where employees no less than customers display a vaguely martyrized expression. What is at first merely a specific problem turns into a generalized atmosphere.

The lack of efficiency and co-ordination between the myriad public and semi-public organizations implanted in and about the Quatre mille is compounded by the notion that many of their long-term users eventually develop, that one is 'owed' assistance and services, a notion which may inspire passivity and apathy among the most dis-possessed.[36] Ultimately, the structural inability of these programmes, and especially of the local schools, to offset the crumbling of traditional means of political representation and claims-making of the working class and to deliver, or lead to, what matters most to inhabitants of the *cité* – a secure job and the stability of life that comes with it – nourishes discontent and turns them into yet additional mechanisms of exclusion in the eyes of the *cité*-dwellers (Balazs and Sayad, 1991). *Dependency and dissatisfaction thus form a vicious cycle* in which each reinforces the other. The prevalence of public-sector institutions, and especially of welfare agencies, also accentuates the negative reputation of the locale, thereby fuelling the spiral of stigmatization and sociofugal strategies that decrease social integration and aggravate internal dissension – enough to have prompted some cities to refuse to participate in the state's Neighbourhood Social Development plan to avoid having their worst areas publicly labelled 'sensitive neighbourhoods'.[37]

Paradoxically, then, the over-representation of state agencies and facilities in the Red Belt *cité* relative to other formal organizations contributes to further stigmatizing the neighbourhood and to increasing the sentiment of isolation and discontent among its residents. Yet, at the same time that they complain over the ubiquitous interference of the state in their lives, they continually demand more of it in the form of expanded crime control (including tougher repression of delinquents), social programmes, and public aid (Dubet, 1987: 249, 260–6). The French state thus finds itself in a Catch-22 situation where the more it intervenes in the *banlieue* to stem public disorder, the more glaring its inability to remedy the underlying economic marginalization of its residents and the more it is called upon to provide social compensation, only to fuel further recrimination and protest.

Organizational Desertification and the Debilitation of the Public Sector in the Ghetto

Since the early 1970s, the ghetto neighbourhoods of Chicago and of other major cities across the United States have weathered not only a sharp rise in joblessness and poverty due to the restructuring of central-city economies (Wilson, 1987) but also, and in marked contrast to France's poor *banlieues*, a deep and wide retrenchment of the public sector. Brutal cuts in federal funds for urban and community development, the steady erosion of welfare payments, the shrinking of unemployment coverage, regressive tax schemes, and state and city policies of 'planned shrinkage' have combined to unravel the web of programmes that had helped sustain inner city (that is, poor minority) residents since the days of the Great Society, resulting in a drastic degradation of the remaining public facilities and in the rapid decomposition of the organizational fabric of the ghetto (Wacquant, 1994b: 242–5, 258–64). What is more, the city's own development efforts have been harnessed to reinforcing private investment, providing downtown corporate services and attracting (or retaining) white, professional and managerial households in the centre and north side of town, at the cost of abandoning the ghettos of the West Side and South Side to continued decay.[38]

Because of grievous shortages of finances and manpower, public authorities can provide neither minimal physical security, nor effective legal protection, nor the routine municipal services that are taken for granted by residents of neighbourhoods outside of the historic Black Belt. On Chicago's South Side, the police service comes woefully short of fulfilling its mission for want of the means to heed all requests for intervention. Patrol officers in the Wentworth district answer calls for crime without interruption from the moment they begin to work till the end of the day; yet the district frequently runs out of cars and has to 'simulcast' 'in-progress' calls in the hope that, somewhere in the city, a detective will be available to respond.[39] The criminal justice system is similarly overwhelmed by the staggering growth of crime: prosecutions have jumped from 13,000 in 1982 to 18,000 in 1987, forcing an overflow of cases into four suburban courts; the city jail is so overcrowded that in 1988 alone, over 25,000 criminals had to be released on their own recognizance for lack of space to accommodate them. No wonder many ghetto dwellers think twice about relying on the state and choose instead to take justice into their own hands (Kotlowitz, 1991: 47, 225, 233).

The same is true of public health. In the past decade or so, most of the neighbourhood public health facilities of the South Side have closed down. Like half a dozen others, the Woodlawn Community Hospital fell into bankruptcy in the mid-1980s because of lagging and insufficient Medicaid reimbursements and the inadequate (or non-existent) health care coverage of its poor clients; it was then razed to make room for a segregated elderly public housing complex which has imported more poverty into the area. And, since the University of Chicago Hospital pulled out of the city's emergency care network in 1990 to safeguard its profitability, victims of serious injury and trauma who cannot supply proof of enrolment in a private health insurance plan must be ambulanced nearly ten miles away to the decrepit and overburdened Cook County hospital. Today, the South Side has not a single health facility which provides prenatal health services to uninsured mothers-to-be and no drug rehabilitation programme readily accessible to those without the means to pay for it.

The parlous state of housing – not to mention streets, bridges, train tracks and sewers – in the Black Belt is equally revealing of its abandonment. Whereas in La Courneuve and other Red Belt *cités*, city and state have been conducting a sweeping urban rehabilitation programme designed to improve housing conditions and revamp public services, Woodlawn is blighted by thousands of abandoned buildings, burnt out or boarded up, and thousands more are run down, improperly heated and structurally unsound. In addition, there has been virtually no construction or renovation in the neighbourhood since the 1950s, even though close to half of its housing stock has been destroyed through arson and dereliction in the past three decades (Wacquant, 1995b). Most of the churches which used to form the organizational backbone of Chicago's 'Bronzeville' in its heyday (Drake and Cayton, [1945] 1962) have also closed down. Those that remain are, for a majority of them, small and fragile organizations with only a handful of members and cramped facilities, if not 'store-front' operations whose existence hinges on the tireless activity of their individual founders. They still attempt to make up for the glaring lack of governmental services by organizing pantries to feed the hungry, setting up shelters for the growing ranks of homeless, and running drug counselling programmes, job banks, literacy campaigns, and community clean-ups or social gatherings. But their most pressing problem today is survival in the face of dwindling attendance and sagging resources.[40]

No organization is more emblematic of the degree of institutional debilitation and political abandonment suffered by Chicago's ghetto than public schools (Kozol, 1991: 40–82; *Chicago Tribune*, 1992). First, the Chicago public education system has become a veritable *academic reservation* for poor minorities as whites and middle-class families fled into the private school system or outside the city altogether: over seven in ten of its students come from families living under the federal poverty line and nearly nine in ten are black and Latino. Second, ghetto schools are typically plagued by ageing and overcrowded facilities, undertrained and underpaid teachers, and outdated and grossly insufficient supplies. Most establishments lack staff, desks, boards, space and even adequate bathrooms; they often have no library, no working photocopying machine, no science lab and no chemical supplies; the textbooks they use, if they are lucky to have enough of them, are frequently outdated rejects from suburban schools – recently students in a history course were found to be using a book in which Richard Nixon was still the country's President. There is virtually no counselling (the DuSable high school at the heart of the South Side has one counsellor for over 420 students, compared to one for 20 to 30 pupils in affluent suburban public schools) and no programmes to ease the transition from school to work. For the large majority, college is out of the question since most establishments do not offer college preparatory classes and students are massed in vocational tracks anyway.

Finally, much of the day's energy must be devoted to tasks that have little to do with teaching and learning. At the Fiske elementary school in Woodlawn, only two blocks away from the University of Chicago's business school (but outside of the perimeter of operation of the latter's lavishly staffed private police force), the priorities of the daily round are first to feed children so that they do not fall asleep or act aggressively during classes because of hunger, secondly to provide physical security for the pupils and staff by means of a militia of parent volunteers who patrol the school grounds throughout the day with baseball bats. To complete this picture, Woodlawn has no high school, no museum, no movie theatre or other cultural facilities, and the only library of the neighbourhood is both grossly underequipped and under-utilized, limping along with a miserly budget which does not allow it to reach out into the community.

It is *as if public policies were designed to further debase public institutions and to encourage exit into the private sector* by all those who can leave the sinking ship of the ghetto and *its separate and unequal facilities*. Thus city and state leaders as well as business associations have consistently resisted, or even lobbied against, tax increments needed to improve education for children of colour and the poor. Reagan's Secretary of Education labelled Chicago's public schools 'the worst in America' (*Chicago Tribune*, 1992) but dismissed demands for more funding and social services from the federal government.[41] As a result of the erosion of its tax base, the city's public school system receives $90,000 less per pupil over his or her academic career than the (equally public) school system of the rich northern suburbs of Chicago. 'We can't keep throwing money into a black hole', declared Governor Thompson in 1988, in an expression with telling racial overtones, when asked to justify the refusal of his administration to funnel additional monies to Chicago's public schools to correct this egregious inequity. Incredibly, not one of the city's last five mayors sent his (or her) children to a public school and well under half of the system's teachers have enrolled theirs in it. As an alderman candidly puts it: 'Nobody in their right mind would send [their] kids to public school' (Kozol, 1991: 53).

The retrenchment of public authority from the ghetto is at once a component and a major determinant of a wider process of *organizational desertification* that has virtually emptied the Black Belt of its formal institutions. Thus the number of businesses operating in Woodlawn has been cut from 700 in 1950 to about 100 today. Whereas the neighbourhood used to have banks, large hotels, department stores, movie theatres and light manufacturing, today the remaining commercial establishments are comprised mainly of liquor stores and small lounges, laundromats and beauty parlours, fast-foods and family-owned eateries, a smattering of currency exchanges, an assortment of thrift stores, and cheap clothing and furniture outlets, most of which are operated by Asian or Middle-Eastern entrepreneurs and their kin. It is no exaggeration to say that, in much of the Black Belt, the regular, wage-labour economy has been superseded by the irregular and often illegal street economy. This twofold withdrawal of state and market explains the social destitution and the warlike atmosphere of the ghetto (Wacquant, 1992c). For they have debilitated the proximate means of formal and informal social control through which most illegal and criminal behaviour is ordinarily checked (Sullivan, 1989) and 'urban disorder' held in abeyance (Skogan, 1988).

In the manner of a magnifying prism, then, La Courneuve and Woodlawn reveal the contrasting weaknesses of the respective political structures and state policies that mould them by determining the institutional articulation of colour, class and place. In the Red Belt, highly conspicuous public institutions weave a much-needed safety net and contribute significantly to increasing social control; but red tape and bureaucratic cacophony also induce apathy and stoke collective frustration; the very (short-term) responsiveness of the political system seems even to encourage urban protest. In the Black Belt, the collapse of public authority and public institutions is the leading cause of systemic physical and social insecurity and of the decomposition of the neighbourhood's organizational fabric, which in turn stimulate individual strategies of internal predation or outmigration that further aggravate neighbourhood conditions.

SOCIAL VISION AND DIVISION IN GHETTO AND *BANLIEUE*

We have seen that the nexus between territorial stigma, insecurity and public abandonment is highly distinctive in the Black Belt by virtue of the racial isolation inflicted upon blacks in America. This is reflected in the caste consciousness and cleavages that structure life in the ghetto, where the dichotomous division between blacks and whites is all-encompassing. In the Parisian Red Belt, by contrast, the dominant opposition pits not native French residents and immigrants but youths versus all others. Though foreigners and especially families of North African descent have become more concentrated in peripheral Red Belt *cités* since the shutting off of legal immigration in 1974, the French *banlieue* remains a highly heterogeneous universe in which racial or ethnic categories have little social potency.

American Apartheid and Dichotomous Racial Consciousness

As a result of the historic experience of two centuries of slavery followed by one century near-total racial separation and multifarious forms of discrimination, many of which persist into the present, Afro-Americans have carved out a rich expressive culture which provides them with a distinctive set of practices, idioms and signs through which to construct themselves and to impart meaning to the world about them (Levine, 1977; Jones, 1985; Abrahams, 1970).[42] The United States is unique for having what Orlando Patterson (1972: 28) calls a 'classificatory racial system' in which 'anyone who is not completely white and has the slightest trace of black ancestry is considered black.' Strict application of this rule of 'hypo-descent' has blocked the emergence of a socially recognized mixed-blood or mulatto category despite the widespread intermixing of the black and white populations, resulting in an unbridgeable division between them. As might be expected, that particular social fiction called race forms the pivotal axis around which the Afro-American cultural matrix revolves. The inflexible, dichotomous racial boundary that whites have imposed on blacks across society, most visible in the enduring spatial segregation between the 'races' and exceedingly low interracial marriage rates, finds its expression in forms of consciousness anchored in a rigid 'us/them' opposition between blacks and whites mirroring the objective caste relations that have historically prevailed between them.

Race is inscribed everywhere in the ghetto: in the objectivity of space and of the separate and inferior institutions that entrap its population, as well as in the subjectivity of categories of perception and judgement that its residents engage in their most routine conduct. Indeed, caste consciousness in the Black Belt is so ubiquitous and suffusive as to go without saying – so much so that it can go unnoticed even by careful observers because, precisely, it is embedded deep in what Alfred Schutz (1970) calls the 'natural attitude' of everyday life.[43] In the Black Belt, racial categories have an immediacy and pervasiveness that make them central cognitive tools. For instance, the first characteristic of a person conveyed, if implicitly, in mundane conversation is whether or not he is 'a brother' or she 'a sister'.

The fact that most residents of the ghetto have little occasion to interact on a one-to-one basis with whites (and, increasingly, with middle-class blacks) further increases the perceptual omnipresence of colour. Kotlowitz (1991: 161) tells the story of a child living in a project on Chicago's West Side who, at age ten, 'began to wonder aloud about being black. "Do all black people live in projects?" he asked his mother. "Do all black people be poor?" ' I am the only white friend that the young black men I met during my three years of fieldwork in a Woodlawn boxing gym ever had. Even blacks who managed to move into nearby white areas (such as the 'integrated' neighbourhood of Hyde Park) report feeling out of place and being subjected to intense monitoring and continual suspicion by people around them. 'Once a nigger, always a nigger' is the saying they invoke, with bitterness if not anger, to explain the reticence of whites fully to accept their presence.

That residents of the Black Belt should take the colour line for granted is not surprising given that their life is almost entirely self-contained within the racially uniform world of the ghetto and, for many of them, in a small section of it: their street, block or 'stomping ground' of the immediate vicinity. The white world 'out there' remains largely unknown, for it is virtually inaccessible, save via the mass media or state instruments of surveillance.[44]

> The Man, it was said, owned everything worth having and wouldn't let black people get in the door. But they practically never saw a white face except on TV and the innocent suburban lives depicted there . . . were as distant from their own as Mars from Earth. Their cityscape was nearly all black, except for a few bureaucrats, teachers, and cops, and they rarely left it, a trip to the [downtown] Loop, for most, was a major expedition. Thirty-ninth street, that's your world . . . The rest was *they* world, a white world with different codes of speech, dress, and conduct. (Monroe and Goldman, 1988: 100)

So powerful is the racial prism through which ghetto residents see the world that those of them who manage to climb up the class structure and leave the Black Belt are widely perceived as trying to 'become white' and as 'traitors' to their community – irrespective of the fact that nearly all of them end up moving into all-black neighbourhoods elsewhere in the city or in segregated suburbs. Class differences among blacks thus find themselves couched in the idiom of race. An unemployed young man from Woodlawn rails against the teachers, business people and police who fled the area since his teenage years in those terms: 'Everybody tryin' *be white*, try to git behin' a white person, movin' in a white neighborhoo': "I'm the only black *livin' in my neighborhoo'* " – (disbelieving) they be braggin' about that, I'm serious! (chuckles) "I'm the *firs' black out there!*" I said, boy, you sick here! *Bleachin' they skin*, I'm like boy! *Normal seekin' the abnormal*, that's what it is.'

As long as the residential and interactional structures of 'American apartheid' (Massey, 1990) persist, the dichotomic opposition existing between whites and blacks in objective reality has every reason to continue to be replicated in consciousness. And there is little chance that other principles of vision and division might challenge the supremacy of 'race' in everyday life.

Jeunes des Cités *Against the Rest of the World*

If there is a dominant antagonism that runs through the Red Belt *cité* and stamps the collective consciousness of its inhabitants, it is not, contrary to widespread media representations, one that opposes immigrants (especially 'Arabs') and autochthonous French families but the cleavage dividing youths (*les jeunes*), native and foreign lumped together, from all other social categories. Youths are widely singled out by older residents as the chief source of vandalism, deliquency and insecurity, and they are publicly held up as responsible for the worsening condition and reputation of the degraded *banlieue*. Avery (1987: 112) reports that

> the bands of youth that congregate in the stairways [of the Quatre mille] are a favourite topic of conversation: 'They bust the lightbulbs so we can't see what they do,' says one. 'They shoot drugs in broad daylight,' 'they sit there and smoke reefers all night long,' 'they piss in the stairwells,' 'we don't like to encounter them at night, we are prisoners of our own apartments.'

Mixing fact with fiction, such accusations are based on the reality that youths are demographically pre-eminent in projects like the Quatre mille and that they typically take over the streets and the few public spaces available, including building hallways and porches, which makes others feel they are misappropriating a collective good for their own particular uses.[45] Whether founded or not, these grievances invariably portray young people either as themselves troubled or as generators of trouble. Bachmann and Basier (1989: 100) point out that, in La Courneuve, 'in every incident, youths are both the cause and the victims of violence in the *cité*: they stand way out in the foreground.'

For their part, youths from stigmatized Red Belt neighbourhoods feel that they are being subjected to a pervasive pattern of anti-youth discrimination which prevails both inside and outside their estate. They complain that governmental programmes and public authorities neglect them, reject their queries and input, and promise much but deliver little or next to nothing of value to them; that police harass them or subject them to unwarranted suspicion and surveillance; and that adults more generally fail to recognize their plight, concerns and aspirations. But, most of all, youths assert that none of the above accord them the recognition and *respect* they feel entitled to: ' "We don't exist, nobody sees us." "They treat us like rats" ' (Lapeyronnie, 1992: 11). The burning rage that many experience at being durably shut out from employment and at being denied the individual dignity that comes with economic self-sufficiency finds an outlet in a nihilistic discourse glorifying predation and violence as a means of access to the sphere of consumption and which, for want of being able to put a face on the mechanisms that exclude them, fastens on the police as the target of enmity (Dubet, 1987: 80–9; Jazouli, 1992: 148–9).

Because the findings of the researchers who have investigated tensions in the housing projects of the degraded *banlieue* up close are strikingly at odds with the vision that has come to dominate media and public debate, they are worth quoting at some length. Avery (1987: 21), for instance, 'never observed during [his] years in La Courneuve . . . situations of open racial intolerance, of blatant collective scorn' of the kind he witnessed on Chicago's West Side or in a British working-class city where he previously resided. Though 14.5 per cent of the electorate of La Courneuve voted for the xenophobic National Front in the 1986 legislative elections, he insists that 'there is no racist climate here, habitually. I find on the contrary a lot of mutual respect and solidarity in the daily life of the *cité*' (Avery, 1987: 21–2). In an isolated working-class project in the western suburbs of Paris, Calogirou turned up slightly more 'ethnicized' forms of perception of space: separate sections of the estate and specific buildings tend to be identified, and referred to, by the assumed racial or ethno-national membership of its most visible tenants. None the less, 'tolerance is the most widespread attitude' and 'those who establish national or religious restrictions in their network of friends are far and few' (Calogirou 1989: 144).[46] For youths from these projects, personal characteristics override 'ethnic' membership and they often use humour to deflect the derogatory denotation of racist insults, for example, by turning such terms as 'dirty nigger' (*sale nègre*) into joking terms of address.

Group Intermixing, Collective Trajectory and 'Racial' Tension

What explains the muted character of racial or ethnic consciousness in the working-class estates of the Red Belt in spite of the growing presence of immigrant families into the most degraded housing projects of the urban periphery – their representation in La Courneuve doubled between 1968 and 1982 to reach 22 per cent – and the expanding place accorded the theme of racism in the public sphere as the 1980s wore on? Three reasons may be adduced briefly.[47]

First, as noted above, Red Belt *cités* are very heterogeneous ensembles in terms of their ethno-racial recruitment. No *banlieue* is the exclusive or even predominant 'turf' of a particular group, as there is no 'ordered segmentation' (Suttles, 1968) of space in France and immigrant families are rather widely distributed across neighbourhoods, with the exception of select locales monopolized by (higher class) natives. French *cités* are not ghettos if by that we mean a racially and/or culturally uniform socio-spatial formation based on the forcible relegation of a negatively typed population to a specific territory (Wacquant, 1992a and 1992b). Their make-up typically brings together a majority of French native families and a mixed grouping of households from 15 to 50 different nationalities and more.

True, residents of foreign descent are disproportionately represented in the Quatre mille compared to their national or regional weight (around 30 per cent compared to 11 per cent nationwide, and upwards of 40 per cent in the southern cluster of the project). But this results from their skewed class composition, *not* from the ethno-racial segmentation of the housing market. As in Great Britain, what ethnic concentration exists in the French *banlieues* is 'essentially a function of the social position of the populations involved' (Lapeyronnie and Frybes, 1990: 154), that is a by-product of the much lower distribution of immigrant families in the class structure. Nor do the poorest and most destitute Red Belt neighbourhoods overlap closely with the *cités* containing the largest proportions of foreigners, as the thesis of 'ghettoization' would imply.

This mixing of populations is decisive in accounting for the overwhelming likeness in the experiences and strategies of Red Belt youths of native French and North African background, a point made most effectively by Dubet (1987: 326; also Bourdieu, 1991a: 8):

> In no group did youths introduce immigration as a fundamental cleavage of relations among themselves in a given neighborhood. Never,

in the *cités* where we went [three of them in the Parisian Red Belt, a fourth in the suburbs of Lyons], did youths talk in terms of 'us,' immigrant youths, and 'them,' French youths, and conversely. Relations and friendship ties are multiethnic. This does not necessarily derive from antiracist beliefs; it springs, rather, from the basic fact that, since their childhood youths have had the same experiences in *cités* which are not racial ghettos. These youths attend the same schools, have the same leisure activities, and go through the same 'horseplaying' and misdeeds. There are no bands or gangs formed along the immigrant versus French cleavage, nothing comparable to the English 'skinheads' or to Chicago's 'Spanish Cobras.'[48]

Secondly, Le Pen's recent electoral surge notwithstanding, racial or ethnic differences do not constitute *legitimate* principles of construction of social reality in the French tradition of nationhood. The historical institutionalization of French citizenship as a state-centred, territorial community, as opposed to a community of descent expressed in cultural terms as prevails in Germany, for instance (Brubaker, 1990), has – thus far – prevented ethno-racial categories from becoming the organizing medium of social perceptions and relations, by blocking their usage as bases of social mobilization and political claims-making in the public sphere. The timid attempt to conscript the *Beurs* (second-generation 'Arab' immigrants) into a distinct voting 'pressure group' during the 1986 legislative campaign could make no headway against a party system and electoral regime structurally designed to erase all intermediary affiliations.[49]

Thirdly and most importantly, second-generation immigrants from the Maghrib, on whom the recent 'moral panic' on *intégration* has fastened, are in spite of everything fast assimilating into French society. They have largely adopted the cultural and behavioural patterns of the French and have failed to form a distinct 'community' constituted around their unique cultural heritage (Lapeyronnie, 1987; Jazouli, 1992). Indeed, they and the leaders of their associations 'forcefully reject any idiom of [ethnic] specificity and assert that the problems they pose are quintessentially French and social' in nature (Dubet and Lapeyronnie, 1992: 143).[50] Not only are most second-generation 'Arabs' being rapidly assimilated culturally; a variety of empirical indicators also reveal an overall improvement of their social position and living conditions, in spite of their much higher unemployment rate and lower income than native French households.

There is no evidence thus far that the spatial separation of so-called Arabs has risen. On the contrary, the increased presence of North Africans and other immigrants in HLM *cités*[51] represents not a status decline on the housing market but a material improvement over a previous situation of genuine segregation into shabby 'guest-workers' wagon-estates' run by the special housing authority of SONACOTRA and illegal 'shanty towns' (*bidonvilles*) that were much more isolated and dilapidated than are today's low-income housing projects (Sayad, 1975; Barrou, 1992). The immigrant population is also becoming more similar to the native one in terms of occupational distribution, family size, and other demographic characteristics such as fertility and mortality. Intermarriage rates with autochthons are rising steadily, especially among females of North African descent who have higher upward mobility rates than their male counterparts via the school. Scholastic inequality between ethno-national groups in France has likewise decreased since the 1970s and students of foreign origin have augmented their representation at all levels of the educational system. What is more, the higher they climb up the academic ladder, the better their results compared to those of native French children. In fact, differences in academic achievement between them are negligible once class origins are controlled for (Bastide, 1982).

This is not to gainsay the cruel reality of joblessness, social isolation and discrimination that weighs disproportionately on a growing number of immigrant urban youths, nor the undisputable ascent of venomous expressions of xenophobic enmity loudly echoed on the national political stage. It is to suggest that, unlike in America where hostility and violence are fed by the *deepening* spatial and social schism between poor blacks (and other minorities) and the rest of society, urban unrest in the French periphery is fuelled by the *mixing* of ethno-national categories – especially in housing and schools – and by the *closing* of the economic, social and cultural distance between immigrants and the stagnant or downwardly mobile fractions of the native working class stuck in the *banlieue*.

In contrast to the black (sub)proletariat of the American metropolis, then, North African families of the French urban periphery are not uniformly travelling on a dark journey to the nether region of social space. Contrary to the claims of Hollifield (1991: 141), they are not in the process of forming a distinct 'Muslim underclass' – whatever that may mean. Rather than signalling the crystallization of properly ethnic cleavages in the French city, the seemingly 'racial' animosity and simmering tension observed in the *banlieues* over the past decade are expressive of the *social* crisis brought about by persistent un(der)employment and by the spatial conjugation of educational exclusion, housing blight and poverty in areas where native and immigrant working-class families compete over diminishing collective resources in the context of the breakdown of the traditional mechanisms that used to translate such conflicts into class demands in the realm of politics.

CONCLUSION

The purpose of this chapter has been to uncover some of the similarities and differences between the 'new urban poverty' in France and in America as it is locally structured and experienced by those whom the term (or its equivalent) has come to designate in these two countries. Rather than compare national aggregate statistics on income, standards of living or consumption patterns, which often measure little more than properties of the survey bureaucracies and procedures which generate them and take no account of the specific welfare-state and socio-spatial environments in which individuals and groups actually evolve in each society, I have proceeded by way of a contextualized examination of four master aspects of life in a stigmatized neighbourhood of concentrated poverty: territorial in-dignity, crime and insecurity, institutional ecology and embeddedness, and salient social divisions.

Drawing out the organizational and cognitive texture of everyday living in the Parisian Red Belt and in Chicago's Black Belt, how the residents of these blighted areas negotiate and experience social immobility and ostracization in 'the ghetto' – as social myth in one case and enduring historic reality in the other – highlights the distinctively racial dimension of inner city poverty in the United States and the critical role played by the state in the differential 'stitching together' of colour, class and place on the two sides of the Atlantic. It also points to the uncertainty in the process of collective identity formation in the Red Belt caused by the demise of traditional agencies of class formation.

Whether France and America converge or continue to differ in the future with regard to the social and spatial patterning of inequality in the city, there can be little doubt that racial separation, where it prevails, *radicalizes* the objective and subjective reality of urban exclusion. And that state retrenchment, whether it occurs by omission or commission, through brutal withdrawal or slow erosion, only serves to intensify the cumulation of dispossession and to exacerbate the destructive consequences of socio-economic marginality, not only for those upon whom it is imposed and for their neighbourhoods, but for the broader society as well.

NOTES

This chapter is based on research supported by the Urban Poverty and Family Structure Project at the University of Chicago, the Joint Center for Political and Economic Studies, the Society of Fellows of Harvard University and the Russell Sage Foundation. It benefited from the comments and criticisms of participants to the 1992 ISA conference on 'Comparative Trends in Urban Inequality' at UCLA, to the Workshop on Citizenship and Social Policy at Harvard University's Center for European Studies, and to the Conference on 'Democracy and Difference in France and the United States' held at the New School for Social Research in November of 1993.

1 For a sample of discussions of the 'new poverty' in England, France, Italy, the Netherlands and the United States respectively, see Townsend, Corrigan and Kowarzick (1987), Paugam (1991), Mingione (1991b), Engbersen (1989) and Wilson (1994).

2 For instance, in France, the early Chicago School has become quite fashionable in some quarters (to wit, the translation of Wirth's *The Ghetto* and the translation of a selection of writings by the fathers of urban ecology), in spite of the fact that its paradigm is near-unanimously regarded as obsolescent after the devastating theoretical critiques of the past two decades (Gottdiener and Feagin, 1988; Walton 1993). Even more strangely, to give conventional analyses of urban migration and violence a veneer of glamour and audacity, other French scholars have imported from the United States the trendy rhetoric of 'postmodernism' which American social scientists believe originates in France!

3 On the swirling debate about 'ghettos' in France, consult, for instance, Vieillard-Baron (1987 and 1994), Touraine (1991) and Désir (1992), and see Wacquant (1995a) for a synopsis; a detailed critique of this 'moral panic' can be found in Wacquant (1992a and 1992b). Discussions of an 'underclass' in Britain and the Netherlands (where the term means something quite other than what it implies in the United States) can be found in Smith (1992) and Morris (1994), and in Engbersen et al. (1993).

4 I purposely leave aside the thorny question of whether, or rather in what sense, segregated working- to upper-class black neighbourhoods located outside the traditional 'Bronzeville' may be said to be part of a reconfigured, decentred and spatially differentiated ghetto or 'hyper-ghetto'.

5 On the historical formation of the Red Belt, read Stovall (1990); on its crisis and decomposition, Dubet and Lapeyronnie (1992). Jazouli (1992) recounts the rise of the *banlieue* as a public issue while Breton (1983) offers an insider's account of the distinctively workerist atmosphere of life and culture in the exemplary Red Belt town of La Courneuve.

6 See Wacquant (1995b) for a more detailed presentation of the data, sources and a number of important methodological and theoretical caveats.

7   To borrow the title of a recent study of the French *banlieues* by Francois
     Dubet and Didier Lapeyronnie (1992: 114) who write: 'The world of the
     cités is dominated by a feeling of exclusion which manifests itself first of all
     in the themes of reputation and scorn. The various *cités* are hierarchized
     on a scale of infamy that affects all of their aspects . . . and each one of
     their residents. There is a veritable stigma of the *cités*.'

8   For example, Dubet (1987: 75), Laé and Murard (1985: 7–8) and Dubet
     and Lapeyronnie (1992: 115). Bachmann and Basier (1989: 86, 97) open
     their study of the image of La Courneuve in the public mind on a chapter
     entitled 'Chicago, Varsovie, New Delhi, La Courneuve'. They mention
     that, as early as 1971, the former owner of what was at the time the only
     movie theatre of the city created a furore by publicly comparing La
     Courneuve with Chicago. In 1983, city policemen found it necessary
     explicitly to remind journalists that 'La Courneuve is not Chicago, let's
     not exaggerate.'

9   'Why do we get thrown in jail? That's because of the *cité*; you feel inferior
     to others, you're not like the others: the others, they have pals in the city,
     parties, a clean house where, if you do something, water doesn't get in,
     the walls don't crumble down. You immediately have a reputation when
     you come from the *cité*. As long as the person doesn't know where you're
     coming from, it's alright, but once you've told her, you feel embarrassed,
     you dare not speak' (cited in Pialoux, 1979: 23).

10   In every *banlieue*, there exists a fine hierarchical gradation of disrepute
     among the various projects whose manipulation calls for skilful stigma
     management. A youth from a *cité* in Northern France relates (in
     Bourdieu, 1991a: 11): 'It's kind of funny when you talk with, say, girls
     who live in a *cité* that's a little bit cleaner, more . . . You tell them "I live
     at the Roseraie" . . . They leave, that's it. That's why, that's no good.
     Then you got to rap them hard.' His friend adds: 'Then they think you're
     a criminal.'

11   This pattern of discrimination is not a phenomenon of the 1980s; it is
     virtually coextensive with the existence of the *cités*, as noted by Colette
     Pétonnet (1982: 147) in fieldwork conducted in the early 1970s:
     'Shopkeepers and employers prove reluctant towards a population whose
     reputation is spreading and charged with a miserable and vile content.
     Youths complain: "We can't find any jobs. As soon as we say that we live
     there, that's it! The boss answers: We'll write you later." ' Pialoux (1979:
     22) made similar observations in another Red Belt town in the late 1970s:
     'We the youths of the *cité*, we are separate [*à part*], it's like for work: in T.,
     you tell them about the *cité*, they kick you right out the door. Me, I don't
     say *cité* of C. no more, I say number 70 on S. Avenue. Even in Paris, they
     know it, the *cité* of C.'

12   Outsiders typically 'view the ghetto as a mysterious and unfathomable
     place that breeds drugs, crime, prostitution, unwed mothers, ignorance,
     and mental illness' (Anderson, 1991: 167). For the white ethnics of
     Brooklyn, the nearby ghetto is an opaque and evil reality to flee, a 'jungle

infested by dark-skinned "animals" whose wild sexuality and broken families def[y] all ideas of civilized conduct . . . "They steal, they got no values . . . [I]t's the way they live. They live like animals" ' (Rieder 1985: 25, 26). For more or less euphemized scholarly versions of this vision, see, *inter alia*, Banfield (1970), Jencks and Peterson (1991: for example, 3, 96, 155–6), and Mead (1992).

13 For proof that this is not unique to Chicago's ghetto, see Wilkinson's (1992) perceptive ethnographic account of territorial stigmatization in a mixed black and Puerto Rican public housing project in Roxbury in Boston.

14 This is due to their swift cultural assimilation into French society, the absence of any credible idiom of ethnicity in the discursive repertoire of French politics (Lapeyronnie, 1987; Wacquant, 1995a) and, ultimate irony (or revenge) of history, to their enduring belief in the universalistic 'civilizing' capacity of the French school system inherited from the colonial era.

15 Numerous academic theories (beginning with the ecological paradigm of the early Chicago School) have buttressed this view by presenting the formation and persistence of segregated and sharply bounded ethnic–racial neighbourhoods as 'natural' products of the 'race relations cycle' and other putatively universal urban dynamics which are in fact highly specific to American society. The demand to 'rebuild the inner city' (rather than *dissolve* it) by progressive politicians and minority leaders after every major urban disturbance (such as the South Central Los Angeles uprising of May 1992) reveals the extent to which the racial segmentation of the city is taken as an inexorable given.

16 This is in keeping with the dominant American belief about inequality and opportunity in general (Kluegel and Smith, 1986: chapter 3). Duncan (1987: 89) shows that ghetto residents of the South Side area of Kenwood assess their success and failures almost exclusively in personal terms. One of my informants from Woodlawn gives a hyperbolic formulation to this view: 'Well, everybody can survive in this country. There's so much food around. You can eat out of garbage cans or go to some restaurant and ask for the left-overs. *If someone starve in this country, it means that somethin's wrong with him.* He weak and maybe he don't deserve to survive.' Research has shown time and again that 'middle-class misconceptions about the motivation of the poor are often held by the poor themselves' (Williamson, 1974: 634).

17 As Lewis Killian (1990: 10) writes: 'To most whites, actually accepting blacks as residents of their neighborhoods seems to mean that drug-ridden welfare recipients from the ghetto will be on their doorsteps tomorrow.'

18 See Paugam (1991: 193–205) for a cogent discussion of these strategies. Numerous quotes could be adduced here. One will have to suffice: 'In this world of negative social homogeneity, the manipulation of gossip aims at "overclassing" oneself and "downclassing" others . . . Foreigners

are, according to dominant discourse, responsible for the degradation of the neighborhood, for crime, and for the lack of jobs . . . and for the devalorization and stigmatization of the *cité* . . . The fantasical negation of relations of neighboring becomes a necessity' as does 'the stigmatization of others for their low education and the exaggeration of one's educational abilities. To demonstrate one's adherence to dominant norms is crucial', which leads to creating the 'maximum distance between oneself and other families' (Calogirou, 1989: 17, 21–2, 41). On this point, see also Pétonnet (1979: 220–234), Gwaltney (1980: 121–6), Kotlowitz (1991), and Wilkinson (1992).

19   See Bachman and Basier (1989) for a fuller analysis of the media construction of the Quatre mille and Dulong and Paperman (1992) for an examination of the production and effects of 'discourses of insecurity' fastened around the degraded *banlieues*.

20   Mauger and Fossé-Poliak (1983) have shown that patterns of collective conduct involving an open assertion of 'rough' masculinity (including public drinking, ostentatious use of foul language and street fighting) expressive of working-class values and sociability are often misperceived as dangerous delinquent behaviour by outside (that is, middle-class) observers. The same socio-cultural patterns among black Americans has often been erroneously interpreted as evidence of a 'ghetto-specific' culture (for example, Hannerz, 1969), though they have been found to prevail also among white and Latino working-class adolescents in both England and the United States (for example, Sullivan, 1989; McLeod, 1988; Willis, 1982; and Foley, 1990).

21   Amart's (1987) data on use of the park shows no major difference between the Quatre mille and other public parks in adjacent municipalities.

22   Toufik was a child of North African descent who was accidentally gunned down by an older tenant exasperated by noise on a hot summer night. The event made the front page of national dailies and prompted President Mitterrand to visit the Quatre mille within days to dramatize public condemnation of the killing and to announce a speeding up of state policies of urban renewal.

23   This is characteristic of isolated French public housing projects in general: 'Petty delinquency is a component of the feeling of insecurity: fear of being broken into or of having one's car stolen, fear of being mugged on the street, in parking lots, in the metro. It is fairly common to lump together youths and criminals as well as immigrants and criminals' (Calogirou, 1989: 39). See also Pinçon (1982), Bachman and Basier (1989) and Dubet and Lapeyronnie (1992).

24   Youths from the French *cité* typically establish a sharp differentiation between 'grass', which they view as a non-addictive form of recreative intoxicant similar to alcohol, and 'powder', considered highly addictive, destructive and symptomatic of personal pathology.

25   The kind of 'open-air' drug supermarket scene described by Bourgois

(1992) in East Harlem is completely unthinkable in the French context, as is the conspicuous trade of cocaine and Karachi I observed in many sections of Chicago's South Side.

26 In the *cité* of Blanchard studied by Laé and Murard (1985: 15–16) in Rouen, early death (from diseases and ill health) is banal and 'takes the appearance of a fate . . . The perspective of an early passing jumbles all phases of life. The cruelly felt paucity of jobs coincides with this vision of a life cycle deployed over twenty years at most.' But, again, violent death is extremely rare and the most serious crimes involve stealing or battery, not murder. Larceny and car theft are the prototypal delinquent acts at Blanchard but they are condoned to the extent that they are committed outside of the estate: such petty crime brings into the latter additional resources which immediately enter networks of reciprocal exchange.

27 For a fuller portrait and analysis of crime and violence and their impact on life in the ghetto, see Wacquant (1992d, 1994b), Bourgois (1992), Sullivan (1989), Kotlowitz (1991) and Skogan (1986).

28 According to several informants and a variety of converging reports, an unknown but not insignificant number of murders are never reported, even to the police, because the bodies do not turn up or because residents fail to inform authorities of these deaths for fear of reprisal or plain habituation. A young man from South Shore (near Woodlawn) whom I interviewed on the topic summed up his reaction to witnessing shootings thus: 'I just turn my head and don't look.'

29 Kotlowitz (1991: 236) describes how a mother of four living in a West Side housing project 'couldn't stop thinking of [her son] Terrence [just sentenced to eight years of detention]. She tried to rationalize his imprisonment. It would be good for him to get off the streets, to get away from the drugs and the shootings. If he were out there, he might just get in more serious trouble.'

30 Of the black men raised at the heart of the historic Black Belt, Monroe and Goldman (1988: 269, emphasis added) write: 'They were all successes in their way, *victors by the mere fact of being alive* with some change in their pockets and a smile for a new day.' In the neighbourhood of Kenwood, a few blocks east towards Lake Michigan, killings reached such frequency by the mid-1980s that 'kids' interviewed by Duncan (1987) started 'a serious discussion as to whether it was possible to live past thirty.'

31 'Doing time didn't scare Honk; it wasn't much worse than living in the projects, and in the joint, unlike the street, they fed you free . . . The ghetto and the Graybar Hotel, his new address, were otherwise pretty much the same' (Monroe and Goldman, 1988: 123, 154). See also Kotlowitz (1991: 112, 236).

32 Also, voluntary organizations have grown throughout French society more generally in the 1980s (Mendras and Cooke, 1991) and immigrants' associations have proliferated since legal restrictions on their creation and scope were lifted by the Socialist government in 1981.

33   This partial census is based on various city documents as well as on field observations. A fuller list of the organizations active in the Quatre mille as of the mid-1980s is in Avery (1987: 52–4 and 56).

34   As of 1987, the mosque, which opened in 1982, was attended by an average of 30 believers daily. The Catholic church had 50 regulars at mass and around 160 children enrolled in bible classes. The Jewish temple welcomed an average of 60 worshippers daily; an estimated 1,200 Jews reside in the *cité*. The Jehovah's witnesses numbered around 120 (Avery, 1987: 53).

35   Also, the distribution of public infrastructure and amenities in the Greater Paris area mirrors the spatial patterning of class segregation (Pinçon-Charlot, Préteceille and Rendu, 1986).

36   'The long duration and permanence of public aid leads ['target populations'] to consider them as an eternal flow, as something owed to them' (Laé and Murard, 1985: 61); see also Jazouli (1992: 121–2) on job assistance for youths, and Paugam (1991: 107–16) on the moral career of the 'professional' *assisté*. The same is much *less* true in the American ghetto where no public aid recipient is secure in his or her status due to the highly repressive organization of the welfare bureaucracy and the routine implementation of administrative procedures expressly designed to deny or roll back claimants' access to public resources (for example, Kotlowitz, 1991: 80, 103). Not to mention that welfare payments are woefully inadequate even for sheer survival (Edin, 1991; Wilkinson, 1992: chapter 2).

37   For two evaluations of the 'perverse' effects of some of the urban policies implemented by the French state in the 1980s, see Jazouli (1992: 115–35) and Bonetti, Conan and Allen (1991). For an 'insider' account of the bureaucratic maze (and mess) thereby created, read Bourdieu (1991b); a suggestive analysis of the 'institutional bad faith' that frames the bureaucratic intervention of the French state in declining public housing enclaves can be found in Bourdieu et al. (1993: 245–7).

38   'Commercial districts, housing, and infrastructure away from the center of Chicago have suffered from long-standing neglect, whose magnitude serves to justify continued inattention' (Squires et al., 1987: 168).

39   Kenneth Clark's (1965: 86) observation of 30 years ago on Harlem remains apposite today: 'The unstated and sometimes stated acceptance of crime and violence as normal for a ghetto community is associated with a lowering of police vigilance and efficiency when the victims are also lower-status people. This is another example of the denial of a governmental service – the right of adequate protection – which is endured by the powerless ghetto.'

40   Christmas mass at the Church of Santa Clara in Woodlawn in 1989 recorded an attendance of under two dozen (including out-of-town guests and foreign visitors such as myself and my fiancée), less than a tenth of the average attendance at its weekly soup kitchen. In the nearby neighbourhood of North Kenwood, a church that attracts 20 to 30

parishioners on Sunday is considered successful (Duncan, 1987: 8). The sharp decline of churches is also visible on Chicago's West Side (Kotlowitz 1991: 143).

41 The erosion of federal funding and the inequities of local financing of urban public schools and their effect on the educational chances of poor minorities are discussed in Kantor and Brenzel (1993).

42 The fact that Afro-American culture, blending elements from the Old and New Worlds, has long been 'rendered historically inarticulate by scholars' (Levine, 1977: ix) and continues to be grossly misunderstood (if not wholly negated) by contemporary analysts wedded to antiquated functionalist conceptions of culture as a unitary set of 'shared norms and values' or mechanical 'adaptations' to objective conditions, or yet to positivist modes of reasoning which reduce culture to a 'variable' (whose 'effect' is somehow to be 'partialed out' and weighed – preferably statistically – against those of 'race' or 'space') does not obviate its existence and structuring potency.

43 The ubiquity of racial consciousness among Afro-Americans is amply documented in the 'self-portrait of black America' assembled by John Langston Gwaltney (1980) and in the interviews of Chicago residents on the topic compiled by Terkel (1992).

44 'For many young men at Horner,' a housing project on the city's West Side ghetto, 'their only contact with the world outside their own immediate environs is the courts' (Kotlowitz, 1991: 226).

45 'What is it that people reproach youths? That they occupy squares, that they sit on benches or on the steps in front of stores . . . that they stay there talking, laughing, making a racket.' Youths, on the other hand, see 'the street as a mere place of well-being, a neutral ground' (Calogirou, 1989: 36–7; also Bourdieu, 1991a: 12). For an excellent analysis of how the mixing of diverse groups with different cultural and social outlooks breeds conflict over the use of public resources in French low-income housing, see Pinçon (1982).

46 Indeed, Calogirou (1989: 93, 96, 98, 101, 115, 131) goes on to show that these networks systematically cut across ethnic boundaries and nationality groupings. Pétonnet (1979: 224) also emphasizes that, 'in the *cité*, there is no ethnic hierarchy. There are only interpersonal hierarchies.' On the rejection of the 'immigrant/native' dichotomy in the mundane practices and representations of youths in a *cité* in northern France, see Bourdieu (1991a).

47 No claim is made that these three factors provide an exhaustive explanation for the low social potency (as distinguished from salience) of ethno-racial divisions in the French Red Belt; they are simply those that most obviously separate the latter from the American ghetto at the present time. A fuller analysis (precluded here by limitations of space) would have to include a historical sociology of the bases and effects of the work of *class-making* carried out by the trade union movement and other left-wing organizations which have traditionally 'melted' immigrants into

French society by incorporating them into a unified, ethnically blind, working class.

48   Recapitulating a decade of research on the topic, Dubet and Lapeyronnie (1992: 128) conclude: 'Young French people and immigrant youths experiencing the *galere* [drifting] are all equally uprooted, they do not oppose each other in terms of culture and differences. Their common experience is that of a composite, mixed-breed (*metis*), unstable universe in which local ties are more meaningful than national or ethnic roots.' When we're in the street,' says one youth, 'we are all brothers: it's the family spirit.' It is revealing that, unlike their American counterparts, rap bands from the French popular *banlieue* are typically pluri-ethnic or *Black-blanc-beur* as they like to say (that is, mixing blacks, whites, and North Africans).

49   Thus, while Islam, with perhaps as many as 3 million believers, has undergone spectacular expansion and adaptation to French society, its expression is relegated to the private sphere where it functions as a cultural framework for the protection or reconstruction of personal identity in a way that is broadly compatible with social integration (Kepel, 1987).

50   Because populations from the Maghrib are socially diversified, ethnic identity among them is largely defensive, and community organization 'weak and conflict-ridden' – and in good part sustained by funding from the French state. 'Composed of highly assimilated youths', North African associations are 'rarely homogenous and are not organized on an ethnic basis. They are first and foremost the expression of a given neighborhood or *cité*' and 'do not eventuate in political action' (Dubet and Lapeyronnie, 1992: 100, 98).

51   In 1989, 74 per cent of North African families had access to public housing compared to about 45 per cent a decade earlier (Barrou, 1992: 128). Segregation is more liable to occur *within* the HLM (*habitation à loyer modéré* – public sector housing) estate, as foreign families find themselves assigned to the most isolated and decrepit suburban projects vacated by upwardly mobile French families, as opposed to the better maintained, central-city ones.

Part III

The Poor in Europe: Marginality, Exclusion and Welfare

12

Social and Economic Change in Contemporary Britain: The Emergence of an Urban Underclass?

Nick Buck, University of Essex, Colchester

Western European economies have experienced profound changes in the period since the mid-1970s. Common factors have affected most countries, including diminishing returns from economies based on mass production, instability in the financial systems, growth in service activities, a gradual shift in the economic centre of gravity towards the Pacific rim. While these factors may have been common, different countries and regions have experienced very different outcomes in terms of the impacts on patterns of labour demand, and more broadly in the restructuring of labour markets and social structures. These differences have depended in part on differences in inherited economic structure and in macro-economic performance, but they have also depended to a substantial degree on different state policies.

In the United Kingdom the process of economic restructuring has perhaps been more severe than in most of the rest of western Europe, and it has been combined with a political regime which undertook a thoroughgoing experiment in social policy to liberalize the operation of the labour market, and reduce the role of the welfare state to that of a minimum safety net. While this experiment may have been incomplete, there were substantial consequences from both economic restructuring and changes in social policy in the social structure of the UK. This chapter is concerned with a major component of this change, the substantial expansion in the numbers and proportion of the population in poverty and more particularly those marginalized from the labour market. The chapter aims in particular to examine how far the literatures surrounding the underclass and the new urban poverty provide a helpful set of explanations of change.

However, there are certain difficulties even in starting this exercise. The underclass literatures display a very wide and disorganized range of meanings attached to the term – a range which this chapter cannot make any attempt to cover. It focuses on two sorts of approach: those based around economic marginality and those based around spatial segregation and concentration. At least some of these approaches contain both structural and behavioural components. However, the paper does not address those, largely conservative, approaches in which the explanation for the emergence of the underclass is sought in behavioural responses to the welfare state (for example Murray, 1984, 1990). Refutations of such arguments depend on both political arguments and microbehavioural analyses which are beyond the scope of this chapter. It might, however, be worth observing in passing that the expansion of the population potentially described as an underclass in the UK has paralleled the attenuation of the role of the welfare state.

Quite apart from this variety of uses there are two problems in using the term in European analysis. The first problem is the degree to which it is politicized principally on the right, but also to some degree on the left. The use of the term carries with it a particular set of agendas. In summary it constitutes a new version of 'blaming the victim', and generally its use tends to imply that the explanation for problems lies with the pathological behaviour of those who experience them. Moreover by focusing on the exclusion of the underclass from mainstream society it disconnects their problems from those of other social groups. The second problem stems from the term's origins in the USA. It is clearly a chaotic concept within the American literature, and is politicized there also. It becomes even more chaotic in Europe where the main condition for its definition in the US (the black ghetto) does not exist on any remotely comparable scale. I will return to the question of the relationship between the potential use of the term in Europe and the US. However, the difficulties with the term suggest that we should be very cautious in using it unless we can specify coherently what it means. This chapter argues that we cannot do so in Britain at least.

There is another observation which is somewhat more general. This is that by focusing on the underclass, the marginal, the (new) urban poor, we need to ensure that we do not lose sight of the fact that their experience is a part of a social and economic process affecting the whole society. In Britain there have clearly been major changes in social structure and a polarization of life chances over the last two decades – these changes are related to processes of economic restructuring, de-industrialization, changes in the role of the state, perhaps changes in the workings of the family. The simplest definition of the group we are concerned with measuring is that group which has suffered worst out of these processes. We need to be sure that our definition of terms does not marginalize our group of interest from this process of change.

To stress again, this chapter is therefore not primarily intended as an overview of underclass theories and usages and their relevance for the UK. Rather, its main purpose is to describe the emerging patterns of social and economic exclusion in the UK, and to explore, firstly, how far these processes are leading to the creation of a single coherent excluded strata, and secondly, how far there is a distinctly different pattern of social exclusion in cities which would allow us to speak of a new urban poverty, or urban underclass in the UK. The reason for using the term 'underclass' is that it carries an implication that the group experiencing social and economic marginalization is expected to be characterized by homogeneity, stability and spatial segregation. This is an important hypothesis, though it cannot be claimed that the existence of an underclass, based on other definitions, is supported or refuted on the basis of the fate of this hypothesis.

DEFINITIONS OF THE POTENTIAL UNDERCLASS

The great increase in unemployment, and especially long-term unemployment, in the UK, as in other European societies, is well known. A number of recent sociological analyses of the UK have focused on the question of whether those who have experienced this unemployment, and particularly more extended unemployment, might be defined as an underclass. Heath (1992) using data from the British Social Attitudes Survey found no evidence that those dependent on social welfare benefits exhibited attitudes implying alienation from work or the traditional family. Gallie (1994) found that the unemployed, and particularly the long-term unemployed, experienced high levels of material deprivation. However, he found no support either for the 'conservative' view of the unemployed under-class as becoming unemployable as their values adjust to the lack of work, or the 'radical' view of the unemployed underclass as having political and cultural values distinct from those of the working class.

Morris (1993, also Morris and Irwin, 1992) examined employment histories, attitudes and social networks of different types of unemployed workers in a city in north-east England which had experienced a high level of long-term unemployment. She again concluded that while there were differences in degree in attitudes and networks between the long-term unemployed, the insecurely employed and those with more stable work histories, they were insufficient to justify treating any of the categories as a culturally distinct underclass.

This test of whether some potential underclass category shows sufficient distinctiveness from the mass of the working class to allow it to be described as a separate group has been the main basis for criticism of underclass theories in British sociology. Silver (1993 and herein) suggests the enquiry into how an emerging underclass fits into existing models of the class structure has been particularly significant in the British sociological discussions of the underclass, and reflects the dominance of the class paradigm. Runciman (1990) makes an explicit attempt to incorporate the underclass, defined in terms of dependency on state welfare, into a class schema. Other approaches, however, have tended to argue that observed difference in attitudes and behaviour from the working class are insufficient to lead to any modification of class schemas.

This chapter takes a somewhat different approach to the exploration of the place of the underclass in social change. Rather than focusing on the attitudes and values of a potential underclass, it starts at a rather earlier stage to explore the consistency of potential definitions of the underclass and the implied characteristics of a group defined on the basis of such a plausible definition – whether it would be characterized by homogeneity, stability and spatial segregation. It uses national level social survey data to undertake this analysis. The second important feature of this approach is the focus on household formation in the evolution of poverty and exclusion in the UK. As the chapter will demonstrate, their incidence in household types has been radically different. A focus, for example, on traditional married couple family types will miss most of the important processes at work. In a sense then this chapter provides some empirical evidence bearing on the issues discussed in the first half of Morris's chapter in this book. It shows how far the growing instability of employment and family life have led to changes which have been conveniently labelled as the growth of an underclass, but also that such a label serves to hide real processes.

Unemployment and labour market participation lie at the core of the approach to social and economic exclusion used in this chapter. The definition of a potential underclass is that part of the population with no stable relationship to legitimate employment (Smith, 1992). The basic unit of analysis is the household – and the potential underclass is defined as those working-age households which are not currently integrated into the labour market through one or more of their members.[1] Thus the chapter has nothing to say directly about, for example, criminal or related behaviour or definitions involving pathological attitudes and values. In addition, space has no part to play in the definition – the point is rather to explore whether, given this definition, distinctive spatial patterns can be found.

The rationale for using the household rather than the individual is that at least in principle it is a unit within which resources are shared (though see Pahl, 1989) and within which the labour market participation decisions of separate members are likely to interact. This is particularly critical for the analysis of women, since the nature of their labour market participation depends so heavily on their household situation, as Morris's chapter argues. For many purposes, state welfare systems also treat the family as the basic unit for the assessment of needs, resources and entitlements. It contrasts with the individual-level approach adopted by Gallie (1994), though his focus on attitudinal and psychological measures may make this more natural. It is difficult to see, however, how the household context can be ignored. The issue might be re-expressed by asking whether a cross-class household containing an underclass member is conceptually possible. The interaction pattern implied by common household membership would seem to run counter to the definition in terms of exclusion from interactions with non-underclass members.

However, this raises problems of how family or household labour market activity can be operationalized as a concept given that, except in family businesses, labour market activity is essentially an individual concept. The two solutions would be to treat one key individual as being dominant in the definition of the household's activity or to provide a measure which summarizes some or all household members' activities. The difficulty with couples is that to use a key individual without much fuller information on earnings potential and other measures of dominance than is usually available, would mean that the male partner will almost necessarily be selected. However, it is difficult to see why a couple household should be regarded as economically active if the husband is working and the wife is not, but not in the reverse situation. In this chapter, the economic activity of married couple households is defined on the basis of the more active of the partners whichever this is. However, the activity of working-age children does not contribute to the household activity definition. This may create some limited distortions, particularly in the case of older lone-parent families. It is probably in relation to young adults still living with their parents that the limitations of the household focus are greatest, and more specific study of this group is desirable.

Households with head or spouse aged 60 and over are excluded. Patterns of retirement dominate household economic inactivity above this age. While some early retirement represents experience of labour market exclusion, a large part reflects the possibilities following from growing pension entitlements. Those over pensionable age are completely excluded. However, it is clear from analyses of income distribution that pensioners, and particularly lone pensioners, contain one of the largest groups in poverty in Britain. To focus on these groups would, however, imply an overall focus of the chapter on poverty rather than labour market exclusion.

The structure of the labour market and the forms of state labour market regulation, particularly through the welfare system, will have an important bearing on the way in which labour market marginality and exclusion are manifested. The associations between welfare policy, labour market regulation and household formation have been discussed by Esping-Andersen (1990), who identified three different welfare state regimes with different consequences for inequality, and also for what he terms (1994) the outsider surplus population. Here, the most important variables would appear to be the level of labour market flexibility (that is, the rate at which poor quality jobs are created), the overall level of job growth, and the degree to which welfare and related policy permits or supports both exclusion from the labour market and incorporation within it for different demographic-ally defined groups. To make the last point more concrete, this refers, for example, to whether lone parents can receive social assistance unconditionally, or conversely whether there is support for childcare. It might also relate to policy towards labour market participation of those approaching retirement age.

What this means is that a definition of labour market attachment and detachment, and hence of a potential underclass or of urban poverty, appropriate to one country may not be appropriate in another. This raises questions of how we should elaborate our working definition of a potential underclass, that is, those families which do not have a stable relationship with legitimate gainful employment. At issue in particular are issues of stability and duration. It is not simply being pedantic to distinguish between a stable absence of relationship to legitimate employment and an unstable relationship with employment.

In this chapter the definition is based on long-term unemployment or non-participation. This means essentially those households where all adult members are either unemployed for more than one year, or are not looking for work. I exclude those households where members describe themselves as retired or sick or disabled, or as students. To be clear, this means that in a couple household where the husband is long-term unemployed but the wife is working, then the household is economically active and not part of the potential underclass.

This sort of definition might well not be appropriate in the United States, nor would it be relevant in another period in Britain when an analogous phenomenon may have existed: the so-called dangerous classes of Victorian cities – the problem of the perceived unemployability of a fraction of the population on the fringes of the casual labour market (Stedman-Jones, 1971). In the US the legacy of labour market flexibility and a very weak welfare system to support long-term unemployment was a high level of job creation, relatively low or negative growth in real wages, unemployment probably lower than in Europe, but more poor quality jobs and more people subsisting over a long period on very unstable jobs or marginal forms of employment. The new urban poverty in the US appears to be composed of a mix of unemployment and marginal or unstable employment, and Sassen (this volume) discusses some of the underlying causes of the growth of this poverty. In Europe, or at least northern Europe, on the other hand, in spite of some policies attempting to increase wage flexibility and to use unemployment as a labour market discipline, there have been parallel policies whose effects have been to preserve and enhance the standards of living of those in employment, by reducing the downward pressure on wages of excess labour supply, for example by encouraging early retirement. In Britain, at least, there have not yet been fundamental attacks on the right to long-term welfare benefits (except, importantly for 16- and 17-year-olds), and other forms of long-term withdrawal have emerged. There has, for example, been a substantial apparent growth in numbers not working because of long-term sickness. The consequence of this is that if we are to find an underclass in Britain it is likely to be constituted in different ways from that in the US, and to be characterized by persistent long-term unemployment, rather than occasional work or participation in non-legitimate forms of employment.

Issues of stability and duration, however, remain. They have both microsocial and macrosocial aspects. The important point here is that while cross-sectional evidence presents a static picture of an economically marginal population, there is underlying movement. Individuals and families move in and out of marginal states. It is important to underclass arguments that this group is rather detached from the remainder of the population. This means that the chances of moving into and out of this groups should be rather low. This presents substantial problems of measurement, which this chapter cannot readily address. As yet we have insufficient true panel data which could allow monitoring of patterns of very long-term continuous unemployment or very irregular employment and their consequences at the individual level. Early results from the British Household Panel Study show around one-fifth of very-low-income households experiencing significant income increases, sufficient to take them out of that state, over a single year. It also found somewhat less than one-fifth of lone parents forming partnerships in a year (Buck et al., 1994). Longer running panel studies in the USA have found that numbers in long-term poverty are small relative to the numbers observed in poverty in any single year (Duncan, 1984; Bane and Ellwood, 1986). This evidence is mainly introduced as a caveat to the data to be presented below. If we were to extend the observation period we would find fewer members of the potential underclass. As the observation period increased, however, we would find an increased number in very irregular employment.

However, we must also expect that patterns of labour market marginality will be significantly affected by changes in the national economy. There are two potential components to this, cyclical fluctuation and major structural change. The relationship between the size of the groups most marginal to the labour market and cyclical fluctuations is a critical indicator of how far they should be regarded as a distinctively excluded category. Thus if the size of the group fluctuates directly with overall cyclical fluctuations then it indicates that previous members are being drawn back into the labour market with economic growth, and thus at least a substantial part of the group remains integrated with economic and social change, and cannot be treated as an outsider population. On the other hand, if the size of the group is relatively immune to fluctuation, this suggests that distinct exclusionary factors are at work, and that members are not responding, or not able to respond, to economic growth.

The issue of the impact of structural shifts is complex. There clearly have been major differential impacts of change on specific industries, occupational groups and regions. This has clearly created some groups of redundant workers with limited prospects of re-employment, and areas where traditional patterns of labour recruitment have broken down. Moreover the value of skills and educational qualifications have changed in very differentiated ways, leaving some groups with a very weak labour market position. This certainly leads to a situation where in some localities there is a very acute problem of long-term unemployment – Morris's work cited above is concerned with such a locality. However, such locality factors do not provide an explanation for the mass of long-term unemployment and inequality. Rather different arguments, not pursued here at length, but see for example Esping-Andersen (1993), would imply that productivity changes and shifts towards a service economy have created an imbalance between labour demand and potential labour supply.

THE CHANGING PATTERN OF LABOUR MARKET MARGINALITY

This section presents evidence on the size of the potential underclass as defined above, its composition in terms of household types, and the pattern of change over the last 16 years. The following section uses more formal statistical methods to explore the relationships between labour market inactivity and potential causal factors.

Much of the analysis in this paper is based on a secondary analysis of the British Labour Force Survey micro data sets, for the years 1977 to 1993.[2] This is a large-scale national sample survey, carried out biennially up to 1983, and annually from then to 1991, and quarterly thereafter. One of its particular advantages for our purposes is that its basic sampling unit is the household, and it provides full information on all household members. It thus allows an analysis of the relationships between the labour market situation of different house-hold members, and of individual work situations in different types of family and household.[3]

Table 12.1 shows the estimated number of working-age households in the UK classified by household economic activity and household type. The term 'inactive' is shorthand to include the long-term unemployed and others not seeking work (except students, the retired and the long-term sick). 'Intermediate inactive' – unemployed or not seeking work for more than one year and less than two – are distinguished from the 'long-term inactive' – unemployed or not seeking work for more than two years. On this basis we find only slightly over 80 per cent of households with a reference person aged less than 60 where one of the principal potential earners is employed. Nine per cent, or more than 1.4 million households, are classified as inactive (even after we have excluded the early retired and the long-term sick). This is more than 2.5 times the number of households classified as short-term unemployed. Within the inactive group more than two-thirds are long-term inactive. It would therefore appear from these figures that processes of polarization between work-rich and work-poor households (see Pahl, 1988) have created a substantial

Table 12.1 Household activity status by household type, 1993 (for households with reference person aged 16–59)

Type	Working	Unemployed less than 12 months	Intermediate inactive	Long-term inactive	Total inactive	Retired, long-term sick, students
Single person	1,938,540	192,200	131,160	168,670	299,830	331,490
	70.2%	7.0%	4.7%	6.1%	10.8%	12.0%
Couple – no others present	4,993,180	163,880	122,450	179,200	301,650	103,810
	91.7%	1.5%	1.1%	1.6%	2.7%	4.0%
Couple – children under 16	4,993,180	163,880	122,450	179,200	301,650	103,810
	89.8%	2.9%	2.2%	3.2%	5.4%	1.9%
Couple with others	1,594,040	18,530	14,890	33,680	48,570	70,730
	92.0%	1.1%	0.9%	1.9%	2.8%	4.1%
Lone-parent family	472,460	84,400	129,760	437,600	567,360	50,510
	40.2%	7.2%	11.0%	37.3%	48.3%	4.3%
Other households	637,810	63,640	29,720	74,450	104,170	153,490
	66.5%	6.6%	3.1%	7.8%	10.9%	16.0%
Total	12,598,320	571,090	464,640	949,190	1,413,830	839,530
	81.7%	3.7%	3.0%	6.1%	9.1%	5.4%

stratum of households almost entirely marginalized from the labour market.

The table also shows extreme differences in labour market marginality by household type. Couple households are very unlikely to be long-term unemployed or inactive, especially those without children. Single-person households and other miscellaneous household types are somewhat more likely than average to fall into this category, but lone-parents households are distinctly more likely to be so. Very nearly half of all lone-parent households with children under 16 are classified here as long-term unemployed or inactive. The reasons for this discrepancy are not hard to find. The great majority of lone-parent households are female headed, and the low wages that the majority of women can earn, especially in part-time work, combined with the relatively high cost of childcare, as well as its low availability, place large economic barriers to work. The relationship of this outcome to unresolved questions about the sexual division of labour in society are discussed much more fully by Morris in chapter 8. Lone parents will figure large in the remainder of this chapter, but this does not equate lone parents with the underclass. Rather, it shows that labour market activity definitions will tend to include exceptional proportions of them in any definition of economic marginality. However, the distinction between lone-parent families and other household types is a fundamental fault-line within the economically marginal population. There is a lack of homogeneity between the two groups.

The implications of the relationship between household structure and economic exclusion may also be seen from table 12.2, based on Family Expenditure Survey data. This shows a measure of the proportion of households in poverty.[4] Here, figures for both 1979 and 1991 are included. The first point to note is that the proportion of households in poverty under this definition has doubled over this period. Because the measure is a relative one, this mainly reflects the substantial increase in inequality in the income distribution of the UK over this period. However, there is some evidence that over this period the lowest income groups have experienced an absolute fall in income. Once again the table shows the highest incidence of poverty amongst lone-parent families, and the proportion of this group living in poverty has risen almost in line with overall increases. By contrast, couple households generally show the lowest poverty incidence, with single-person households falling in between. The exception to this is the case of couple households with three or more children, which show substantial poverty rates (though these did not rise as fast as for other groups).

Table 12.2 Households in poverty, that is, below 50 per cent of median equivalent income (working-age households only)

	1979			1991		
	% of all households	% in poverty	% of all households in poverty	% of all households	% in poverty	% of all households in poverty
Single person households	11.3	15.9	19.0	17.2	25.1	22.8
Couple households with no others	19.3	3.2	6.5	17.7	7.0	6.5
Couple with 1 or 2 dependent children	39.8	5.7	23.9	28.5	13.0	19.5
Couple with 3+ dependent children	9.3	20.5	20.2	6.2	27.1	8.9
Other couple households	9.0	2.7	2.6	10.2	5.5	3.0
Lone-parent household	6.1	37.7	24.4	9.7	61.2	31.1
Other households	5.2	6.0	3.3	10.5	15.1	8.3
All working age households	100.0	9.4	100.0	100.0	19.0	100.0

Source: Family Expenditure Survey Micro data set 1979 and 1991

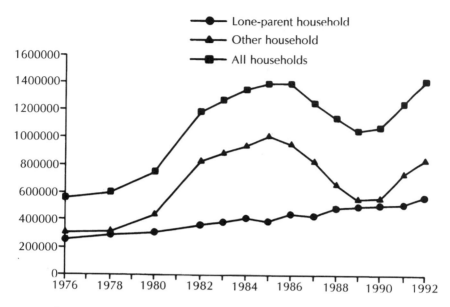

Figure 12.1 Long-term unemployed and inactive households

Returning to the inactivity measures, figure 12.1 shows the pattern of change in numbers of inactive households since 1977. The figure makes clear the distinctive trajectories of lone-parent households and other household types. Lone-parent households exhibit a reasonably steady upward trend in inactivity, while other household types exhibit substantial cyclical fluctuations overlaying some upward trend. Thus it would appear that structural factors are keeping lone parents out of the labour market, and they provide a gradually rising number of economically inactive households over the period since 1979, but are not substantially affected by the fluctuations in national unemployment. For all other household types, however, there clearly have been sharp fluctuations in numbers which relate closely to changes in unemployment. It is important to stress that there is not a simple circularity here – it would be possible for unemployment fluctuations to be affecting only the short-term unemployed, and not long-term unemployment and other forms of inactivity. Indeed this is what we would expect if we had a clear emergence of a distinct underclass – that it would not be affected by short-term cycles. If we translate these numbers into percentage rates we still find the substantial fluctuations in incidence, with some upward trend, for other household types. However, for lone parents we find that most of the upward trend reflects the growth in the total numbers of lone parents. There is some

Table 12.3 Change in household inactivity rates by household type, 1990–1993 (for households with reference person aged 16–59)

Type	Total inactive 1990 (%)	Total inactive 1993 (%)	% change in incidence of inactivity
Single person	9.2	10.8	+17.4
Couple – no others present	2.0	2.7	+35.0
Couple – children under 16	3.0	5.4	+80.0
Couple with others	1.7	2.8	+64.7
Lone-parent family	48.1	48.3	+0.4
Other households	9.3	10.9	+17.2
Total	7.0	9.1	+30.0

evidence of a response to changing unemployment up to the mid-1980s, but thereafter the incidence rates are relatively flat.

The implications of this can be seen in table 12.3, which shows changes in incidence of inactivity by household type between 1990 and 1993. There is barely any change at all for lone-parent households, growth broadly in line with overall change for single-person and other miscellaneous households, and growth substantially above the overall trend for couple households.

This section has three main conclusions. Firstly, over the last two decades there has been the emergence of a substantial number of households in the UK which appear, at least from cross-sectional data, to be only marginally attached to the labour market. These amount to around 10 per cent of all working-age households, containing around 3 million people. It thus constitutes a substantial policy problem. The second conclusion concerns the substantial role of household formation in the constitution of this group. Single-person households, and even more especially lone-parent households, make up a substantial proportion of this group. Finally, evidence on the changing incidence of labour market marginality over time and by household type suggests that this marginality is constituted in very different ways for different household types. For lone-parent households the marginality is essentially structural in origin and is relatively immune to the fluctuations of the national economy. For other household types, however, the incidence of marginality appears rather directly related to the fluctuations of the national economy. This is a macrolevel observation, rather than a microlevel observation, and it is not impossible that within this overall group there are subgroups whose inactivity is not affected by overall economic fluctuations.

Another important caveat to make here is of course that individuals switch between household types. Evidence of movement out of lone-parent status was cited above. The analyses of US panel data cited also showed that movements in and out of poverty are particularly associated with demographic events such as births, and partnership formations and separations.

Rather than pursuing these issues, which would require different types of data, the next section explores correlates of inactivity and in particular its spatial distribution.

CORRELATES OF LABOUR MARKET MARGINALITY

The introduction to this chapter did not discuss one major dimension of US conceptions of the underclass – spatial segregation. This was central to Wilson's seminal discussion (1987), and in subsequently (1991) shifting to the use of the term 'ghetto poor', he reinforced the spatial dimension. The important point of these arguments is not just that the potential underclass is spatially concentrated, or even segregated, relative to the remainder of the population, but that this segregation plays a part in constituting the underclass. Part of their isolation or exclusion from mainstream society is a spatial isolation and this reinforces economic marginality. There is in effect a process of cumulative causation. Of course, in the US this segregation interacts with and is reinforced further by the racial dimension to ghetto poverty. In Britain we do not find the same scale of inner city racial concentrations experienced in the US and it is clear that an underclass cannot be defined on racial lines in any way comparable to the US. However, Wilson's argument for the role of spatial segregation is not dependent only on race. It depends on the economic and social dislocations caused by the decentralization of economic activity and of middle and upper income groups. Such processes have equally been occurring in the UK, and other processes such as the decentralization of low-income population to relatively remote public sector estates could be argued to have parallel consequences.

In the UK there is not good spatially disaggregated data which could measure extreme economic marginality, but Wilson's argument does imply that there should be processes of cumulative causation in the ghetto, so that there should be higher levels of extreme economic disadvantage in the cities as a whole after controlling for background characteristics leading to disadvantage in all locations.

We would expect to find spatial concentrations of the inactive

Table 12.4 Logistic regression on probability long-term unemployed or economically inactive, 1989–1993

	All households	Lone parents	Couple households	Other households
Intercept	− 5.5370	− 2.9163	− 5.6112	− 3.6262
Single HoH	1.4321[a]	0.2503[a]		− 0.2414[a]
Divorced, etc. HoH	1.5275[a]			
Female HoH	0.5914[a]	0.5936[a]		− 0.0553
1 child	1.1055[a]		0.3653[a]	
2 children	1.3927[a]	0.5245[a]	0.5992[a]	
3+ children	1.9423[a]	1.1613[a]	1.2581[a]	
Age 16–19	0.2948[a]	1.7156[a]	0.4545[c]	0.0685
Age 20–24	− 0.0107	1.3282[a]	− 0.2428[b]	− 0.3418[a]
Age 25–29	− 0.2874[a]	0.8338[a]	− 0.6101[a]	− 0.4206[a]
Age 30–49	− 0.6863[a]	0.1477	− 0.8399[a]	− 0.4086[a]
Age 50–54	− 0.3329[a]	0.2291	− 0.3616[a]	− 0.2527[a]
No qualifications	0.5847[a]	0.6867[a]	0.4714[a]	0.5947[a]
Afro-Caribbean	− 0.0899	− 0.8703[a]	0.2469	0.2914[b]
South Asian	0.5109[a]	− 0.0688	1.0334[a]	0.3670[b]
Other, not stated	0.4806[a]	0.0061	0.8563[a]	0.3524[a]
Owned, outright	1.0593[a]	0.5687[a]	0.8492[a]	1.3089[a]
Public rented	1.9677[a]	1.2054[a]	2.5036[a]	1.7521[a]
Private rented	1.1064[a]	0.9152[a]	1.3790[a]	1.0312[a]
Sub-regional unemployment rate	0.0716[a]	0.0376[a]	0.0963[a]	0.0596[a]
Inner London	− 0.2176[a]	0.1803	− 0.3089[b]	− 0.2401[b]
Outer London	− 0.0118	0.1064	− 0.0705	− 0.0095
West Midlands	0.0703	− 0.0192	0.2325[c]	0.0766
Grtr Manchester	0.0609	− 0.1134	0.2219	0.1152
Merseyside	0.3456[a]	0.3595[a]	0.5513[a]	0.3441[a]
South Yorkshire	0.1957[b]	0.2139	0.3732[a]	0.1408
West Yorkshire	0.0892	− 0.3155[b]	0.4399[a]	0.1271
Tyne and Wear	0.0199	− 0.2155	0.1889	0.1003
Clydeside	− 0.1561[b]	− 0.1043	− 0.0887	− 0.0434
Rest of North	0.0001	− 0.1258[c]	0.1461[b]	0.0257
Northern Ireland	0.0873	0.3004[c]	0.0835	0.2418[c]
Inactive N	17786	8088	4830	4868
Total N	208801	16679	145741	46831
− 2 Log L (Cov)	38280.303	3865.550	9128.974	3699.212

[a]Significant at 0.1%
[b]Significant at 1%
[c]Significant at 5%

populations as defined above for a number of reasons which have nothing to do with the cumulative effects of spatial segregation. Broadly we may identify two major categories of explanation. The first is that there is an uneven distribution of the population with characteristics likely to lead to labour market disadvantage. There are variations in household structure, in the distribution of educational qualifications, in ethnic composition, and in the housing tenure distribution. Some of the causal connections between labour market disadvantage and these factors are ambiguous, and they may be in part consequences of past disadvantage. However, these factors are not subject to extreme spatial concentration and it should be possible to test for the independent effects of these factors and spatial location. The second set of factors relate to the state of the local economy. Variations in local unemployment are liable to lead to variations in the extent to which disadvantaging factors lead to extreme economic marginality (Buck and Gordon, 1987).

The logic of the argument here is that if we control for economic conditions and population characteristics then any remaining positive associations between area and inactivity should represent area-specific effects – cumulative causation. In practice it may be difficult to control for all possible economic and population characteristics. However, if, after controlling for what we can, area effects are only limited, then this suggests that cumulative causation effects are weak.

Regional analysis of the data used in the previous section suggest that there is some concentration of inactivity in urban areas, with proportions in London and other British conurbations of around 12 per cent, compared with around 7 per cent in the non-conurbation areas of England. This is hardly enough of a difference to suggest great segregation. In order to control for other factors, however, we present a logistic regression analysis with household economic inactivity as the dependent variable.[5] The models shown in table 12.4 are based on the households from the LFS data for the years 1989 to 1993 pooled together. This both increases the effective sample size, and ensures that there is some variability in the regional unemployment rates, making it easier to find region-specific effects.

The first column shows the results for all households. There are very substantial demographic effects. The first six variables (single and divorced head, female head, and number of children) are in effect distinguishing non-couple households and households with children from others and, unsurprisingly, given the results in table 12.1, are substantially significant.[6] The age coefficients are mainly negative, reflecting the fact the excluded category, household head aged 55–59, has a high probability of inactivity. Absence of educational qualifications increases the probability of inactivity, a consequence presumably of the way it weakens labour market position. Surprisingly, Afro-Caribbean households are not more likely to be inactive than white households once other factors are taken into account. However, this reflects in part differences in the demographic composition of black households – especially the higher proportion of female-headed households, which is already accounted for in the model. Asian and other race households do experience higher inactivity. There are very substantial tenure effects, with the highest inactivity rates experienced in public sector housing, particularly in contrast to owners with a mortgage, the excluded category. Private renters and those owning outright, however, do also experience above average inactivity rates. There is a very strongly significant effect of the regional unemployment rate. The size of this inactive group then does clearly respond to variations in the level of shorter term unemployment. Substantial area effects are found in models without the regional unemployment rate (not shown here), but these mainly disappear when this variable is included. Merseyside and South Yorkshire are the only conurbations where there appears to be some additional concentration of the inactive as defined here over and above that expected on the basis of population concentration and current unemployment. By contrast, Inner London has a significantly lower level than would be predicted on the basis of these factors. On this basis, the evidence for local urban cumulative effects is very weak.

However, as suggested in the previous section, the economic marginality of different household types appears to be constituted in very different ways, and it is necessary to explore the causal processes underlying marginality for these groups separately. Thus the second, third and fourth columns show equivalent models for lone-parent households, couple households, and other household types (mainly single person).

Some effects are relatively consistent across the household types, in particular qualification and tenure effects, though the latter are somewhat more extreme in the model for couples. Similarly the effect that more children increase inactivity rates is consistent across the lone-parent and couple models. Some of the other demographic factors are very different. In the lone-parent model it is younger households which are more inactive. However, in both the other groups there is a U-shaped relationship, with inactivity greatest at youngest and oldest age ranges. Amongst lone-parent households, the female and the single never-married have much higher inactivity rates. However, amongst other households without children, there is no significant gender difference, and it is the divorced and separated who experience higher inactivity. Race effects are also somewhat different. Afro-Caribbean lone parents are significantly less likely to be inactive than all other groups. Lone parenthood is much more prevalent amongst this population, which may mean that strategies for combining this state with paid employment are better developed. Amongst couple households the Afro-Caribbean population is not significantly different from the white population, but amongst other households, there are rather higher rates of inactivity.

Turning to the other measures, the inactivity of couple households appears to be much more sensitive to the regional unemployment rate than does that of the other two groups, especially the lone parents. This would be largely in conformity with the finding in the previous section of differences in association with cyclical movements in the economy. However, it should be pointed out that even after including area-specific dummy variables, the effect of the unemployment rate on lone parent inactivity is still highly significant, suggesting that there is a response to local economic conditions, and hence that this group cannot be seen as detached from economic processes. Specific area effects are generally very much weaker once regional unemployment rates are taken into account. For lone parents the only significant positive effects are in Merseyside and Northern Ireland. Amongst couple households, Merseyside, South Yorkshire and West Yorkshire have significant positive effects, though Inner London has a significant negative association. Amongst other households, Inner London again has fewer than expected inactive, and Merseyside and Northern Ireland have more than expected.

These results confirm that there are important spatial concentrations in the distribution of economic inactivity and marginality. There is a strong association with local unemployment, and a number of the other factors shown to be associated are themselves subject to spatial concentration (for example, the ethnic minority population). The strong associations with housing tenure also imply some considerable level of local spatial concentration. However, taking the country as a whole, none of these factors can be regarded as exclusive to inner cities or large urban areas, let alone to particular subdistricts within these areas. So while there is concentration of economic inactivity, if there were important processes of cumulative causation specific to urban ghettos, we would expect to see some persisting urban effects in the models shown here, unless these effects affected only very tiny proportions of the population.

However, the large urban areas do not display a consistent pattern of greater concentration of inactive and long-term unemployed households once their population composition and current economic situation are taken into account. With one exception, none of these areas are closely defined inner urban areas, and they include substantial suburban parts, though here we should still expect to be able to detect substantial ghetto effects at the conurbation level. The one exception, Inner London, which is narrowly defined and includes areas which are amongst the most deprived in the country, exhibits in most cases lower levels of inactivity than expected. Merseyside stands at the opposite extreme, with consistently higher levels of inactivity than expected even on the basis of its very high unemployment rate and unfavourable population structure. This is probably the area which experienced the weakest economic performance of any in the UK in the last two decades, and it is therefore perhaps an area where the cumulative effects of economic decline have manifested themselves in the most extreme economic marginality of a fraction of the population. With this important exception, the evidence presented in this section of the chapter does not support the notion of a substantial urban underclass characterized by high levels of spatial segregation, and reinforced by area-level processes of cumulative causation.

CONCLUSION

This chapter has shown that recent economic and social change in Britain has led to a large increase in the number of households experiencing long-term inactivity, and hence poverty. It has also shown that the group displays considerable heterogeneity, particularly in terms of its relationship with household formation. Indeed household formation processes appear to be at least as important as labour market processes in generating long-term inactivity. The evidence, however, does not suggest high levels of spatial segregation.

It is likely that if we moved towards a more coherent group defined either in terms of spatial segregation or social identity we would be defining a very much smaller group, and in the process of course ignoring the problems of the larger group, or, if the images are negative, tainting the larger group with the problems of the smaller. This is not of course to say that there have not been behavioural responses to long-term unemployment which may be regarded as pathological and tend to exacerbate the social isolation of some part of this group – this is a separate research issue, and it is important when addressing it to recognize that such responses are likely to affect only a small part of the potential underclass as defined here, and we should be very wary of using language which tends to generalize the phenomenon.

The chapter has focused on only one country, and in that sense it is difficult to draw firm comparative conclusions. However, the comparison with the ideal typical model of urban poverty in the USA suggests that differences in state welfare policy and in labour market regulation may lead to poverty and marginality being constituted in very different ways – participation in extremely unstable labour markets in the USA, very-long-term withdrawal in the UK. This clearly has implications for policy, but it also has methodological implications. We need to treat very seriously these differences in state policy in the analysis of urban poverty, and we need to be very cautious in translating definitions of marginality and exclusion from one society to another.

NOTES

1 See Buck (1992) for a more extended discussion of the definitional issues raised in this section.
2 The data from the Labour Force Survey were supplied by the Office of Population Censuses and Surveys through the ESRC Data Archive. Neither of these bodies bear any responsibility for the analysis reported here, or for the conclusions reached.
3 Its other major advantage is the very large sample size, in excess of 60,000 households since 1983, and more than 80,000 before then. In addition, because the analysis is based on survey data the results should not be contaminated by changes in the official unemployment benefit regulations. The response rate is high, around 80 per cent in most years. This is important because the potential underclass is undoubtedly less likely than average to respond to surveys. Results in this section are presented using weights which gross survey responses up to the national population.
4 The poverty definition used here is a conventional relative measure – households with equivalent income (that is, adjusted for household size and composition) below 50 per cent of median income. As in the previous analysis, only households with heads aged under 60 are included. Material from the Family Expenditure Survey is Crown Copyright, has been made available by the Central Statistical Office through the ESRC Data Archive and has been used by permission. Neither the CSO nor the ESRC Data Archive bear any responsibility for the analysis or interpretation of the data reported here.
5 Logistic regression measures the odds of being in a state relative to a control group. The results are presented as a set of regression coefficients which represent the log of the relative odds, for the relevant characteristic. Thus in table 12.4, the coefficient for a female-headed household is 0.5914. Exponentiating this gives 1.815, implying that female-headed households are around 80 per cent more likely to be inactive than male-headed households. Standard statistical significance tests can be applied

to these coefficients, and are indicated in the table by superscript letters a, b and c.

6   The effects of separate coefficients are additive in the logs, and therefore multiplicative in relative odds. Thus in this model a household headed by a single female with three or more children would be 54 times as likely to be inactive as a married couple household with no children.

13

The Social Morphology of the New Urban Poor in a Wealthy Italian City: The Case of Milan

Francesca Zajczyk, University of Milan

MILAN: A CONTRADICTORY DEVELOPMENT

During the 1980s, according to the Government Committee on Poverty and Marginalization (CIPE, 1985, 1992), there was a marked increase in poverty, both in relative and absolute terms. In 1983, 13.1 per cent of Italian households were classified as poor, while in 1988 the rate was 15.2 per cent. Poverty among elderly people decreased; on the other hand, children and minors were becoming poor with greater frequency, though the number of single-parent households was low and cannot be put forward as a cause. Southern regions still had a higher concentration of poor people. Despite the lack of disaggregated data to confirm the trend, we can say that poverty was shifting from rural areas (where it was located after the Second World War; see Braghin, 1978) to urban areas, where chronic poverty was found especially in Naples and Palermo as well in other southern cities and in the decaying suburbs of Rome, Milan, Turin and Genoa.

As far as we know from current research, it is not possible to say how much poverty exists in Milan (Zajczyk, 1995). In 1986, taking the number of social welfare recipients as a basis, it affected about 66,000 individuals (disadvantaged elderly people, drug abusers, outcasts, minors, etc.), which is 4.4 per cent of the resident population. An estimate of the real number was more than double this figure, that is, 180,000 (Campiglio, 1988)[1] or 12 per cent, which is close to the estimate based on income.[2] However, the situation is still far from resembling that in the US. If we restrict ourselves to extremely poor people, we find a fairly lower incidence of real outcasting, equal to a few thousand members of the resident population.

In sum, poverty in Milan seems to be less widespread than in other urban contexts; moreover, it is not increasing sharply nor is it concentrated in particular social or territorial groups. On the other hand, it has some features in common with advanced regions in Europe, such as the higher risk of becoming poor run by elderly people, but also the young, young adults and single-parent households whose family head is a woman. Poverty in Milan takes on a different form compared to the rest of Italy. As we can see from the last report on poverty in Italy (CIPE, 1995) and from the analysis of Naples by Morlicchio in the present volume, typical poverty in southern regions affects large families in which young people and women do not have paid work.[3]

Whatever the numbers affected by poverty, it represents a serious challenge. In order to meet it, a typological analysis will be of great help. In reality, it is less a matter of collecting numerical evidence than of identifying the critical factors in becoming poor and those unsatisfied needs and difficulties that reinforce the vicious circles and prevent effective reinsertion measures. The analysis of urban poverty in Milan is particularly relevant because the combined impact of the post-Fordist transformation in the labour market and a welfare system with low effectiveness and poor co-ordination has not resulted either in an increasing risk of becoming poor nor in an accentuated polarization of social conditions, as can be observed in other metropolitan areas in industrialized countries.

The aim of this chapter is to present a mainly typological interpretation of severe poverty in Milan through a quantitative and qualitative analysis of data from recipients of private and public social assistance, as well from the life histories of outcasts appearing in two recent reports.[4]

THE SOCIO-ECONOMIC AND DEMOGRAPHIC CONTEXT

The boundaries of metropolitan Milan are a matter of opinion for researchers and politicians (IReR, 1991; Ercole and Martinotti, 1988) given that it consists of numerous municipalities with no single overarching administrative or ruling body. Four to five million inhabitants live in the area, where the major part of Italian financial and entrepreneurial activities are concentrated, making Milan the most important global centre in southern Europe.[5] During the last 15 years, this metropolitan area has undergone a profound post-Fordist transformation in its occupational system, the main indicators of which are a decreasing employment capacity, especially in medium-sized and large manufacturing plants, and a simultaneous steeply differentiated increase in jobs in private services, a typical sign of global cities and post-Fordist economies (Sassen, 1991; see also the present volume). The municipality of Milan lies at the hub of the metropolis and it is to this smaller area that I refer in the rest of the chapter.

The post-Fordist transformation of the decade 1981–91 is confirmed by several indicators (Kazepov, Mingione and Zajczyk, 1995). Activity and employment rates were fairly high (44.7 per cent in 1991, which corresponds to an increase of 3.8 per cent in the decade 1981–91), especially for women (from 24.8 per cent to 34.3 per cent in the last 20 years). The tertiary sector absorbed the main part of the increase,[6] more in self-employed than salaried work, while employment in traditional industries decreased substantially (from 51.3 per cent in 1951 to 26.6 per cent in 1991). The weakening of the protective capacity of occupational transformations resulted in unemployment and the flourishing of precarious and low-income jobs. Although the overall unemployment rate decreased, young people became more disadvantaged in finding a tenured job. So that, in 1991, the unemployment rate among people aged 14–29 reached 12.2 per cent. It should also be taken into account that even though most of the young conclude their education at 18 or beyond, there is a sizeable quota of dropouts especially in the first two years after compulsory school (Massa et al., 1992).

Unemployment does not affect only the young nor it is solely a matter of delayed entry into the labour market. There is in fact a growing number of male adult labourers who have been deskilled by technological innovation, and are difficult to re-skill, so often both father and young adults in the family are unemployed (Saraceno, 1990). My evidence does not allow me to claim a definite linkage between being out of the labour market and poverty; however, as Mingione points out (see chapter 1), a strong positive correlation between rising unemployment and the growing number of people under the poverty threshold is evident (CIPE, 1995). Considering demographic indicators, the first important point is that since 1971

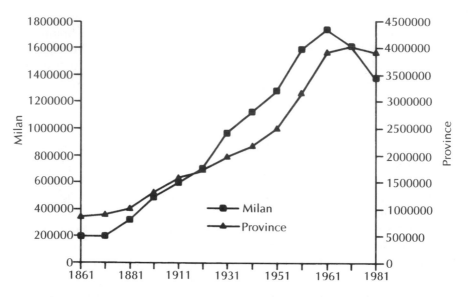

Figure 13.1   Resident population of Milan and its province (*Istaat*)

Milan has undergone a continuous decline in its resident population (from 1,723,118 in 1971 to 1,367,733 in 1991; see figure 13.1).

There are two main causes for this decline: the lower birth rate (Golini, 1994) and the migration of residents from the city to the hinterland (Martinotti, 1993). Figure 13.2 shows that the share of the youngest cohorts (0–14 years) has dropped dramatically, while the oldest (65 years and over) are a growing part of the total population, especially in the case of women.

The low fertility rate has had a direct impact on family size and typology. The average number of members per household fell from 3.1 per cent in 1951 to 2.3 per cent in 1991; however, during the last decade, alongside the traditional household – two parents and one or more children – other types of households have appeared. These consist of married couples without children – less often one parent and child – or single-person households, often widows over 66 on a low income or old age pension income – less often separated or divorced young people and never married people (see table 13.1).

Milan has the highest divorce and separation rate in Italy: in 1991, 8.4 per cent of married women were divorced compared to a national rate of 2.9 per cent. Being divorced increases the risk of becoming poor since legal procedures do not protect the wife and children financially during the separation process. *De facto* separations are even more

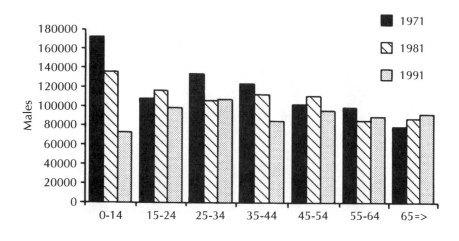

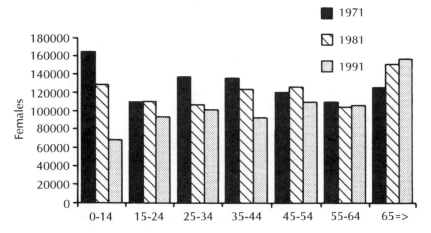

Figure 13.2 Resident population by sex and age (*Istat*)

numerous than legal ones so that the real extent of the phenomenon is wider than that reported by official statistics.

In addition, housing is a very problematic area, and it plays a stronger role in the sequence of becoming poor. While the average demand for rented accommodation has been higher than the national average (more than 40 per cent in comparison with 30 per cent on a national scale), the housing supply remained very low for many years, then suddenly increased. At the same time, however, high rents have been charged and a large number of evictions have taken place. Public housing has been in short supply and has been able to cover only a

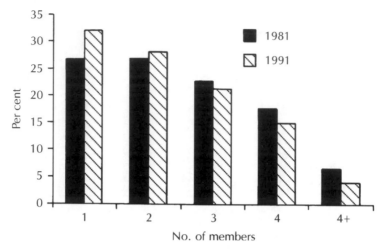

Figure 13.3   Number of members per family in Milan, 1981 and 1991
(*Istaat*)

Table 13.1   Loneliness rate by sex and age (percentage)

	19–25	*26–35*	*61–65*	*>66*
Men				
1971	3.8	5.6	6.8	10.3
1981	4.2	9.9	8.2	13.4
1991	8.7	19.7	12.9	20.6
Women				
1971	2.1	3.8	21.8	29.6
1981	3.2	6.8	27.4	40.5
1991	5.8	10.0	25.2	54.6

Source: Istat

limited proportion of those evicted. Further, the major part of the poor
are homeless: social welfare intervention does not ensure enough
income to rent a house; relatives or friends can often give only
temporary assistance; due to the fact that most of the poor have been
thrown out of their homes, they have difficult house-sharing experiences, do not succeed in renting a house and end up living in a hostel.

A final, less visible but no less dramatic, aspect of poverty in Milan
has to be taken into account: that is, the pauperization linked to the
decay of the suburbs, which suffer from the de-industrialization
process and the expulsion of low-income workers from the inner city.

Under the conditions sketched above, poverty remains relatively invisible apart from two exceptions: the homeless and non-EU immigrants, who are found mostly within the metropolitan area.

CAN THE POOR IN MILAN BE 'COUNTED'?

The chronic lack of reliable official statistics, especially at the territorial level of cities (Zajczyk, 1991), does not allow a quantitative outline of poverty. Consequently, the study of poverty in an urban context is generally carried out by analysing data from social assistance. Even though the social welfare system is relatively more effective in Milan than in the rest of Italy (Kazepov, Mingione and Zajczyk, 1995) it is deficient in organization and internal co-ordination, which causes interventions to be highly fragmented. Moreover, it is also characterized by poor co-ordination with private assistance bodies, preventing a more effective action against pauperization and in favour of reinsertion. The picture resulting from data provided by social assistance cannot be considered representative of the whole phenomenon: on one side, it should always be accompanied by a qualitative check in order to verify whether a social welfare recipient benefited from more than one kind of assistance; on the other, it cannot be assumed that everyone applying to the services is poor even if the application presupposes a condition of real need. Finally, there are others who do not apply at all because either they do not know assistance is given to people in need or they feel ashamed to ask for help.

> The lady was so worried; she felt uncomfortable making demands and minimized her problems. There was a stark contrast between her appearance of suffering and what she was saying, as if she could somehow manage . . . She does not ask for anything even though her condition has worsened . . . I think she should be helped to deal with her shyness in asking for aid. (A social assistance operator, Kazepov, 1995b: 66)

> Getting in touch with social welfare always makes Lidia feel uncomfortable; she does not like every time she asks for aid having to tell them 'a lot of things'. (A social assistance operator, Kazepov, 1995b: 66)

Whatever the quantitative dimension of poverty in Milan, the point is to try and indentify which conditions lead to poverty and, at the same time, which allow individuals to avoid it. In this perspective, it is of crucial importance to have an understanding of 'areas within which deprivation causes unbearable situations, which carry with them a gradual bio-psychological and cultural wasting away of women and men of various ages, the loss of their social bonds, homes, neighbour-hoods, towns and cities, the crisis of their habitat' (Negri, 1990: 31). For these reasons, a typological analysis of poverty which takes into account both structural features and individual biographies is fully worthwhile.

THE PLACES OF SOCIAL EXCLUSION

While Italy as a whole is strongly characterized by its territorial context, especially in terms of the north–south divide, this is not the case with Milan. Poverty in Milan is neither apparent nor confined to particular groups or situations. Although there are typical paths that are more likely to lead to poverty, it resembles more of a threat than a phenomenon affecting particular kinds of individuals who suffer the same condition and who are easily identifiable.

Three main territorial concentrations can be found which have already been identified by the social assistance system or where there is the risk of entering the path towards deprivation.

First, places where severe marginalization is found: first aid centres; temporary shelters for immigrants and the homeless; night shelters; housing and run-down areas where non-EU immigrants and homeless people live, mostly in the vicinity of the central railway station but also in the inner city, where they can find more structured aid (see black markers on map 13.1).

Secondly, deprivation is concentrated in central districts in which wealthy residences and working-class housing coexist (Zajczyk, 1992), and also decaying houses where the elderly live, sometimes waiting for official eviction to be carried out.[7] Worth noting is the position of these dwellings within the urban context: they were built in the 1920s and 1930s in formerly peripheral areas for factory workers, while they are now sometimes right in the inner city (see house markers on map 13.1).

Finally, the districts on the outskirts: hostels where former 1960s immigrants and low-income households live, where renting is cheaper but there is a long-lasting lack of public services – schools, transportation, hospitals, etc. – and leisure facilities. It cannot be said that these districts have undergone a process of 'gentrification'; and living in them multiplies the risk of social exclusion. The resulting picture is a mix of deprived and wealthy areas, where individuals characterized by different socio-economic conditions live side by side

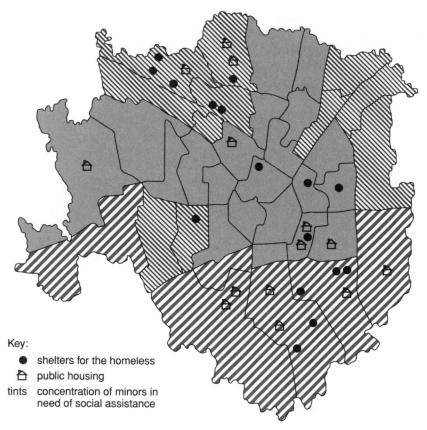

Key:

● shelters for the homeless

🏠 public housing

tints concentration of minors in
need of social assistance

Map 13.1 Municipality of Milan: location of hostels and working-class
housing; concentration of minors in need of assistance

(Frattini, 1994). Confirmation of this is given in map 13.1, which
shows, contemporarily, the concentration of minors in need of social
assistance in the various districts (grey and striped areas), the location
of hostels (black markers) and the location of working-class housing
(house markers).

A core area (grey) indicates a very wealthy socio-economic milieu
together with elderly people not yet expelled from the inner city; a
similar configuration is found in some western districts, where popular
and decaying dwellings of the 1950s stand alongside grander residential
housing. The northern part of the city (narrow stripes) is characterized by a white-collar population as well as by first-generation blue-
collar immigrants, fairly well integrated into the urban and social
context having benefited from previous industrial development. The

most disadvantaged areas are the southern districts (wide stripes), often hostels where recently built working-class housing inhabited by low-skilled young workers and resident immigrants started decaying shortly after construction.

AN IDENTIKIT OF POVERTY BASED ON SOCIAL ASSISTANCE RECIPIENTS

It can be asserted that in Milan social exclusion is not (or not yet) a matter of numerical size. Instead, it seems to involve a qualitative transformation of the pauperization process which, given the declining support offered by social institutions, tends to become more and more severe under the pressure of cumulative and interacting events.

The life cycle passages which seem to be most vulnerable to the risk of poverty are two: youth and the entry into adulthood between 16–18 and 25 years of age; and late adulthood at about 45–50 years of age. This does not imply an underestimation of the condition of elderly people, who form a growing part of the population and whom the welfare system, though relatively effective[8] in their case, does not succeed in protecting. On one side, the evidence[9] does not provide a thorough understanding of the still severe situation of the elderly, even though it is not as serious as was thought some decades ago. On the other side, the elderly often run the risk of becoming poor, but at the same time this risk is specifically related to their age; suffice it to mention the loss of physical autonomy which often adds to social isolation. Intervention in this area can be difficult to organize, and is confined to offering specialized assistance at a low cost in order to meet the needs also of other low-income groups (Facchini, 1993).

Table 13.2 Social assistance recipients (UAD, SAM-Caritas, RN) by age

	UAD	%	SAM	%	RN	%
<34	122	18.5	440	30.8	28	11.0
35–44	152	23.1	334	23.4	41	16.1
45–54	205	31.1	301	21.1	79	31.2
55–64	162	24.7	202	14.1	76	29.9
>65	17	2.6	151	10.6	30	11.8
Total	658	100	1428	100	254	100

Source: elaboration of data from UAD and SAM-Caritas

Table 13.3 Social assistance recipients (UAD, SAM, RN) by sex

	UAD	%	SAM	%	RN	%
Men	460	69.4	1175	77.4	223	87.8
Women	203	30.6	343	22.6	31	12.2
Total	663	100	1518	100	254	100

Source: elaboration of data from UAD and SAM-Caritas

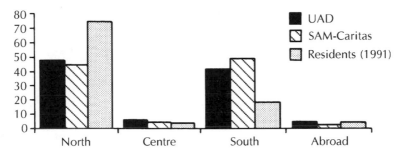

Figure 13.4 Social assistance recipients (UAD and SAM-Caritas) and total Milanese residents by area of birth (percentage) (*elaboration of data from UAD and SAM-Caritas*)

According to the data, the typical individual who runs a higher risk of becoming poor is male; and does not receive or no longer receives unemployment benefit or social security. Consequently, he does have not, or has lost, any identity as a working subject.

Geographical origin represents a key factor in the understanding of poverty in Milan (figure 13.4). People born in southern Italy are largely over-represented among those who applied for the assistance considered here (UAD and SAM). They share specific features, both among the older component – who came to Milan in the 1960s – and the younger component – who have recently fallen into extremely degraded conditions. As Ghezzi points out, 'emigration and geographical mobility often represent the first sign of crisis' (1995: 37). Immigrants to large cities start in a precarious state and do not always improve their conditions.

> . . . my father came to Milan. Then we lived apart for about a year, you know, he couldn't keep us with him, he went there to find a job . . . he left us with our grandparents . . . When he got the job, he sent for us.

> But it was bad, too little money. We came to Milan in 1953, we didn't
> have a house, anything, we lived in a . . . well, let's say hotel. A very low
> kind of hotel.

Besides difficult or precarious housing and economic conditions, the
individual or the family lives apart, isolated from the social and
emotional context which normally provides effective protection and
guarantees a minimum standard of consumption and resources. Given
the constant need for money, children start working very young
without any professional training.

> I started working as soon as I came here, when I was twelve. There
> wasn't much going here in Milan. Galvanizer, that's what I was . . .
> You know, if you want to make a living in Milan, you have to work.

On one hand, women adapt more quickly to poor jobs and are less
likely to lose their familial, parental and communitarian bonds; on the
other, as changing socio-economic, demographic and cultural conditions have changed, a growing proportion of women have found a
paid job, which exposes them to the risk of poverty in a still
discriminatory occupational and social context (Weitzman, 1985;
Garfinkel and McLanahan, 1986; Daly, 1992). Finally, the age of
individuals at risk of becoming poor tends to shift down towards the
younger cohorts.

The deprivation and exclusion condition is characterized by certain
features:

- *Loneliness*: more than half of social assistance recipients live on their own;
  family units formed by one or two persons account for 83 per cent.
- *Difficult housing*: by which is meant precarious housing conditions. During
  the last three years, the quota of people facing eviction increased from 21
  per cent to 62 per cent; one half of those applying for social service aid live
  in rented working-class housing, the number of house owners being only 6
  per cent.
- *Low education level*: only 13 per cent have a secondary school leaving
  certificate; more than 30 per cent dropped out from compulsory school.
- *Unemployment and precarious work conditions*: unskilled manual workers with a
  low educational level are increasingly likely to be out of work. The data
  suggest that unemployment is the standard and chronic condition for 80
  per cent of cases, while only in 43 per cent is it classified as the cause of
  poverty.
- *Illness*: more than the 80 per cent of cases suffer from degenerative diseases,
  mental illness, drug and alcohol abuse or other traumas. As we shall see
  later, health and psychiatric research shows that there are substantial
  differences between men and women, while illness is particularly rife
  among the homeless (Maranese, 1995).

- *Imprisonment*: about 40 per cent – almost exclusively men – have been sent to gaol; this rate rises to 60–80 per cent among people over 45. The figure may have been overestimated; however, imprisonment is a rather common experience among new male poor. In any case, it represents a relevant obstacle towards familiar and occupational reinsertion.

Table 13.4 Social assistance recipients (UAD and SAM-Caritas) by job condition and age (percentage)

	<34	*35–44*	*45–54*	*55–64*	*>64*
UAD					
worker	71.4	71.9	61.5	66.7	72.2
low tertiary[a]	10.9	7.3	12.7	5.7	9.0
medium tertiary[b]	8.5	15.6	16.4	14.9	18.2
artisan	6.1	5.2	3.6	12.6	–
SAM					
worker	52.8	47.7	43.9	30.4	14.3
low tertiary[a]	34.3	32.2	30.8	21.4	11.4
medium tertiary[b]	9.3	14.1	15.4	12.5	2.9
artisan	3.7	2.0	3.8	1.8	–
pensioner	–	4.0	6.2	33.9	71.4

[a]Cleaning staff, poorly qualified seasonal workers, mac jobbers, etc.
[b]White collars, porters, non-skilled personnel.
Source: elaboration of data from UAD and SAM-Caritas

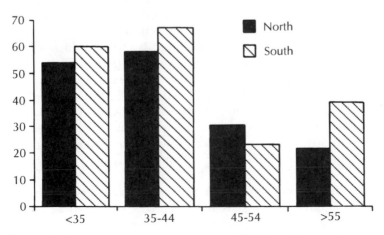

Figure 13.5 Social assistance recipients (UAD) with imprisonment experiences by age and area of birth (percentage) (*elaboration of data from UAD*)

THE CAUSES OF EXCLUSION:
SUFFICIENT BUT NOT ALWAYS NECESSARY

The process of pauperization comprises a host of negative events and conditions, which accumulate and intertwine (see Micheli herein). It is difficult to put in a chronological or causal sequence all those negative events which can determine a progressive detachment and isolation from vital worlds, job networks, social life and social services (Berzano, 1991). Moreover, a condition of need is the outcome not only of structural or incidental factors but also of knowledge, values and individual ability. While an integrated analysis that is both quantitative (social services data) and qualitative (individual biographies) makes it possible to delineate the boundaries and paths of the exclusion process, it is always hard to know the subjective significance of these dramatic events.

Life histories tell us that there is a 'negative synergy', that is, a process in which disadvantages accumulate and combine with pre-existing conditions in individuals' lives. The outcome of a condition of poverty is not always attributable to a cause-effect chain. This is true for two reasons: (a) different poverty conditions may be the result of the same triggering situation, most often in *borderline* situations and; (b) an identical final outcome may be due to many different causal chains, each of them sufficient – as Micheli points out very clearly – but not necessary. If social exclusion is to be explained as a cumulative process, then the crisis of the familial context and primary social networks, poor work conditions or unemployment and low pensions are necessary but not sufficient elements in a chain of events which ends in multiple deprivation. Consequently, we should not look for *the* causes of poverty but for the *inus-causes* (*insufficient but necessary part of a condition which is itself unnecessary but sufficient*) in each individual marginalization process (Laffi and Micheli, 1995). It is seldom a matter of a precipitating event which suddenly alters the equilibrium: 'The most problematic situations are those in which we observe a worsening individual or familial condition after a quickening of some destructuring event or the failure of one's own life strategies which accumulate over time' (Benassi, 1995: 52).

While complex phenomena like poverty do not allow us to pinpoint a single triggering cause, it is none the less still possible to outline the most frequent typological sequences corresponding to different categories of individuals. These sequences never have a decisive feature, but we can still try to distinguish between mechanisms which start in a 'normal' condition and those paths where 'the fall has taken place progressively, after some complicated events whose intertwining depends partly on some deterministic cause and partly on the individual's adaptive behaviour' (Negri, 1995: 10).

THE YOUNG: A GROUP AT A HIGH EXCLUSION RISK

About 45 per cent of clients of social services are aged between 18 and 44. Recently, operators report a higher demand coming from people aged 25–34, while in 1991 for the first time even the young between 18 and 24 applied for aid. As can be seen, the age at which the process of social marginalization begins is tending to decrease; the dropouts from the educational system and the young thrown out of low-income households run the highest risk. Although in Milan there is a wide range of job chances, many young people have hardly any professional qualifications, which makes it difficult to find a job.

During the 1980s the demand for qualified and specialized workers increased, causing the expulsion (−34 per cent) of workers with little or no educational training. Many low-qualification job opportunities in the private service sector – the so-called mac jobs (Sassen, 1991) – are precarious and deskilled and tend to favour the social marginalization process since they do not permit a progressive stabilization and strengthening of job careers as happened for previous working generations with the move from apprenticeship to skill qualification.[10] This group is not very visible (Saraceno, 1990) and has not yet been perceived from the usual poverty observation points; they are seldom classified as unemployed or as workers on too low an income, or as clients of social assistance or recipients of reinsertion measures. Undoubtedly, the family still plays a crucial role in the primary socialization and solidarity network for meeting young people's needs; on the other hand, it is in the past history of relations within the family that we find the core elements which structure the preconditions of poverty. The point is that the family is not always present and, even when it is, it may not be able to fulfil its role; primary social networks may be highly ambivalent, representing at the same time a positive resource and a source of tension which can even break up the family itself. It is often a question of inter-generational conflict, which is made unmanageable by the cultural gap and the difference in primary and reference contexts between parents and offspring.

They (parents) don't give a fuck about me. Why should I care about them!

> You couldn't talk to my father . . . I always had a bad relationship, an old-fashioned mind. He didn't understand we were born and lived in Germany. Nothing could be done. He wanted his children to obey and that was that. We were not allowed to go out . . . to put make-up on. He didn't want it because he was jealous.

The combination of more than one negative element in the family environment (father unemployed or on supplementary benefit,[11] low cultural background, large families sometimes with separated parents, violence, alcoholism, etc.) increases the possibility of family and individual crises, especially when the young subject has dropped out of school very early. Young people who find themselves in this condition are often characterized by a low educational level and a low occupational profile, associated with a difficult family situation: 'In a poor context, where positive models are lacking, one takes part in a system of values favouring a self-penalizing attitude and deviant behaviour which, once added to structural difficulties, lead to exclusion' (Benassi, 1995: 54). Drug abuse, alcoholism, the emergence or worsening of psychological problems, the fall into microcriminality are all elements that go together with this kind of youth syndrome.

> Soft drug abuse begins at 15–16 years of age and ends in hard drug abuse at 18: 'I went straight in . . . I couldn't get out.' The impression one gets from his story is that it had an almost natural ending, given the degraded environment he lived in. 'I went around with this boy with lots of problems, he took me to other boys with all the problems of poverty and stuff like that.'

The process that brings these individuals from childhood to social exclusion, if not to true social marginalization, seems somehow to be inevitable. It is not characterized by some special negative event; rather it involves a continuum of material deprivation, drug abuse and several bouts of imprisonment.

> Thrown out of the house at 12, ended up in a boarding-school, then lived on the street since 15, drug abuser, imprisoned for theft more than once . . .

> She starts taking drugs at 14, runs away from home several times, has a daughter (who lives with her grandparents), tries drug addiction treatment, now she's HIV-positive, and doesn't know what to do . . .

WOMEN AND MEN: EQUALITY IN POVERTY?

Is urban poverty gender specific? Could it be said that the causes of hardship and exclusion paths are different for men and women? The available evidence points to a positive answer, in the sense that men's and women's hardship show different qualitative and temporal features.

Although women are less numerous than men, the female rate among clients of the UAD has increased over time – from 39 per cent in 1990, to 42 per cent in 1991 and 52.6 per cent in 1992 – while it is stable among those of the SAM-Caritas. Since the latter service is devoted to the homeless, it seems that women's poverty is less severe or acute than men's; thus we can say that men suffer from social exclusion more often than women.[12] Men belong more often to categories at risk of poverty in their youth, while women are more likely to become poor as a result of events which take place in adulthood. Women's poverty becomes manifest when they are about 35, increases until 54 and then seems to diminish, probably because they succeed in getting the old age pension or becoming recipients of the domiciliar assistance service (CADA). On the other hand, men's poverty may be already critical at 25, then its rate increases, reaching a peak between 45 and 59. In sum, as other researches show (CIPE, 1985), poverty among women is less linked to disadvantaged conditions than to particular phases of the life cycle.

As I have already pointed out, the demographic transformations which affected Milan resulted in a progressive weakening of the traditional household and a growing incidence of other ways of cohabiting, and also a growing instability inside the family leading to separation, divorce or children running away from home. Instability itself does not represent a real threat of deprivation; however, it does become a threat when added to unemployment, illness, precarious housing, difficult social relations.

> My problem is money. My health problems prevent me from working. Then I depend on my children.

> since our separation, (my husband) has never given me a penny, though there's a tribunal injunction. Now that I only have supplementary benefit, I have to ask for that money . . .

Given such conditions, the separation and divorce rates highlight how high the risk of poverty is for broken families, especially for women and children. On the other side, the Luxembourg Income Study data for Italy analysed by Garfinkel and McLahanan (1986) shows that being married determines a lower *gender poverty gap*, while single women (separated, divorced or widowed) are more vulnerable, have weaker ties with their familial network and sometimes have physically or mentally handicapped dependent small children.

> Separated, two sons who live with their father. No connection with the family of origin. Many health problems, 45 per cent civil invalidity.

> Widow, four children, only one of them (disabled) has a regular job. No income since her husband died.

> Separated since she was 24 because she could not have children. She applied for civil invalidity. She worked as home help in the black and as an auxiliary nurse; because of her health she had to stop working.

Without the support of a family or friendship network, or without sufficient money, it is difficult to cope with labour market demands and children's needs, mostly in households where only one spouse is responsible on both fronts. Data from the Mother and Child Social Service show that single-parent households account for almost half (44.2 per cent) of all its recipients; these parents often have low educational training and low-qualification jobs (workers, housewives, domestic help, petty traders). Moreover, in 1993 many new recipients belonged to adolescent and pre-adolescent cohorts (6–10, 11–13 and 14–18). The situation they live in is particularly difficult, especially when both mother and child benefit from social assistance or minors are sent into residential care or made wards of court.

> Boarding-school represents an experience which has marked his life because of its rigidity and the rupture it brought about in the development of his personality. After leaving it, he is no longer able to be with other people, he does not make friends . . . He says: 'They've been my ruin. They've just ruined my life.'

FAMILY INSTABILITY AND UNEMPLOYMENT: TWO CRUCIAL FACTORS

The listing of negative events tells us very little about the temporal sequence in which they take place in individual life-courses. In the case of the marginalization of minors and young people it is relatively easy to reconstruct, as the process of social exclusion begins very early, often on the basis of an already disadvantaged situation. In the case of adults, the understanding of how a condition of need arises is more difficult since the individual life paths are more differentiated and heterogeneous.

The biographies I analysed point to sequences of events which interwine and combine in a no longer recognizable way. In general, as noted above, being married decreases the risk of falling into poverty for both men and women but is more effective for women:

- separation, divorce, abandonment by their spouse, difficult relations with the family of origin often represent the starting point in the loss of a life's balance and project;
- emotional instability leads to greater economic and family problems: loneliness, difficulty in caring for children, forced separation from children;
- then, psycho-physical hardship occurs or becomes chronic, which seems to derive from a traumatic childhood (spent in a children's home), more often from unhealthy living conditions, and which is reflected in children's unease, for instance, drug abuse.
- finally, entry into a true marginalization circuit takes place.

The last step appears to be strongly linked with certain physical pathologies, as if the process of marginalization includes the sapping of mind and body. Data from the Office for Adults in Need show that women are more often affected by mental illness[13] (20.7 per cent, more than twice the rate for men) and degenerative disease (39 per cent) and men by drug abuse (14.4 per cent) and injuries (8.5 per cent).

> Separated, she has not worked since 1984. She is 46 per cent invalid because of scoliosis, arthritis, obesity and diabetes.

> Divorced. Health problems with thyroid gland and eyes, hypertension, anxiety. Unemployed since 1986. Application for invalidity rejected.

> Separated. Children in a home. Husband does not pay alimony. Serious mental illness.

In the case of women, on one side, the breaking of family bonds often acts as the triggering factor for the entire marginalization process; on the other, the illness and psychological problems that result – isolation, difficulty in accomplishing the tasks required by work and being a mother, inability to cope with the problems of everyday life – interact with dramatic family situations (drug abuser offspring, forced separation from children, unemployment), creating a negative synergy which accelerates the process of marginalization and contributes to the worsening of the subject's mental and physical state.

> Separated, two children. The male is a drug abuser and HIV-positive, the female has had a nervous breakdown. Her monthly income is 1,100,000 lire, but she is not able to support both herself and the children.

> Separated, she lives with her drug abuser son who has a criminal record. Eighty per cent invalid, she cannot work at all.

> Separated. Her two sons have been taken from her by court order: the first is on a detoxification programme, the second lives with his grandparents. Her health situation is serious.

> Eleven years in a children's home. Married and separated, a child died at the age of one and a half. A few hours of domestic help. Serious psycho-physical situation (has applied for civil invalidity).

Their precarious psycho-physical condition often induces these women to make explicit their need for help, that is, to cross the threshold of the social assistance system, which involves individual and public recognition of hardship.

Life histories tell a story of deprivation and exclusion caused by the accumulation of the negative events already mentioned, which lower the individual's capacity to react and lead him/her to a condition of chronic hardship.

> Thirty-nine years of age, separated, three daughters. Recipients of the SAM assistance since separation from her husband. Psychological instability and temporary poverty.

> The woman has had a difficult relationship with her job (a lot of time off work) and her husband (she has run away from home many times; now her husband does not want her back). She suffers from physical illness, does not look after her daughters, who live with their father. She is accepted at the public hostel.

> Forty-six years of age, separated and psychologically unstable, past prostitution and difficult family conditions (crises due to separation). Her parents have been separated for many years; she never had a true family; at 16 she married a man chosen by her mother and separated soon after. Her past was marked by some episodes of violence, which negatively affected her mental balance and led her to take tranquillizers. Her family of origin does not care about her problems.

A completely different path towards social exclusion comprises a 'normal' life trajectory until the occurrence of a sudden and destructuring event. Such is the case of male adults who have had a regular job for many years and then lose it and its accompanying socio-economic status.

The analysis of data from recipients of social assistance in Milan highlights the fact that men have an educational level slightly higher than that of women; nevertheless they often enter the labour market as unskilled manual workers, deskilled service labourers (dishwasher, barman) or artisans in an already obsolete sector. In 90 per cent of the cases looked at here, they become unemployed.

Barman, fired in 1989; his mother, with whom he lived, died. Now he's probably an alcoholic, heavily in debt. He lives in a council house.

Hotel porter. The hotel closed in 1989. He started to drink. No work. He often fought with his wife, then they separated. After living in very low-grade hotels for a while, he became homeless.

In general, they have no experience of marginalization and depriva-tion, though their individual and familial condition is already weak and the social security system is only able to prop it up to a limited extent. Where social and labour guarantees are weak – more and more frequent in post-Fordist cities – individuals not old enough to get a pension but too old to try for a new job qualification find themselves already out of the labour market at about 40. They run a serious risk of entering a downward mobility path together with their families.

The lack of balance within the family was generated exclusively by the fact that both parents lost their job. In R's case, who had always worked, to be on supplementary benefit is a shock, none the less he started looking for another job: 'I just went out and looked for a job . . . I kept looking for three or four months. Then I lost heart . . . How can it be that at my age (46) I am already old?' He doesn't know how to fill his days, what to do. The level of consumption drops: 'The eldest (15-year-old son) realizes that when I am at home, there's no money . . . Then I try to make him use his head; I tell him, well, you can't do what your friends do. They can go out and have a pizza every night, you can only do it once a month.' (Kazepov, 1995b: 65)

To pass from a normal everyday life to a condition which means a change in the individual and household status has a negative effect on the psychological well-being of the family head; he loses his self-confidence and develops a pessimistic attitude towards work and his family. Moreover, especially for single-earner families, this situation means a cut in consumption and a progressive shift towards a lower standard of life.

The critical event which hit the family was the loss of C's (family head) job. In the early eighties, his wife lost her job due to industrial restructuring; she became a housewife as her husband had a good job. In November '93, C was on supplementary benefit for eight months; the first decision was to renounce unnecessary expenses, which means their daughters' spending. In September '94 he was made temporarily redundant for no more than two years. At this point, finding a job was increasingly urgent, C became more and more anxious: 'I've done something, I didn't twiddle my thumbs . . . Well, one day here, the other there . . . porter, that's what I did, moving furniture, emptying cellars, stuff life that. I can't stay around here doing nothing, who knows when I'll get my temporary redundancy money.' (Kazepov, 1995b: 61)

In sum, a typology of more frequent events in men's biographies leading to poverty includes:

- Exclusion from the labour market (unemployment or non-employment) being by far the main cause of downdrift and chronic marginalization.
- Though poverty and marginalization are less linked to critical family events, emotional and family life are negatively affected.

> A happy marriage for 15 years, then his wife leaves him. The firm he works for goes bankrupt. One of his sons becomes a drug addict; his daughter throws him out of the house. He ends up on the streets, owing 20 million in rent arrears.

- Loss of housing can be an event which is hard to deal with.
- Frequent drug abuse.

> Born in 1941 in northern Italy, separated, no children, problem of alcoholism. Worker, term of imprisonment. After separation from his wife, the cause of which he does not want to talk about, he lived together with his old mother (75), who lives on a low old age pension. Then the house his mother rented was sold and she went to live with an older brother. He became homeless.

- Periods of imprisonment appear frequently in men's biographies.

This last fact can be explained in more than one way. It should be noted that after such an experience reinsertion in social life is very difficult, partly because the social service in support of ex-prisoners fails to do its job. On the other hand, going to jail is a good starting point for serious marginalization: a light sentence can have a very serious impact and imprisonment may be a de-socializing rather a re-socializing experience.

> Born in 1949, from southern Italy, married, one daughter. He came to Milan in 1979. He's a cook. His biography is almost completely characterized by precarious jobs lasting no more than ten days because of arguments with his employers and because, as he claims, his previous imprisonment does not allow him to get a better job. In 1989 he had to send his wife and daughter back to their home town since he was unable to maintain them. He sleeps anywhere, a train, a station waiting room, a bench, a hostel.

> Mario (35) hoped that, after imprisonment (for theft) and separation from his wife, his life might take a turn for the better. His job as a

bricklayer, which he got thanks to a friend, seemed to lead him back to a normal life, though at that time he was working in the black. When he was about to be regularly hired the firm went bankrupt and he lost his job. Since he separated from his wife, he has lived together with his mother, who is a pensioner, without any difficulty. Problems arose with his sister even before he lost his job, after her husband died and she and her little baby came to live with them.

CONCLUSION

Although poverty and severe marginalization do not affect a sizeable part of the resident population of Milan, they none the less represent a serious challenge of growing importance. Even in a wealthy city like Milan, syndromes of chronic exclusion are emerging which, unlike general social inequality, directly threaten the cohesion of the citizenship system and create serious problems of social reinsertion. As in many other urban contexts (see Micheli as well as Buck, Morliccho and Häussermann and Kazepov in the present volume), poverty in Milan is a multidimensional process in which many negative events combine together. It is seldom a question of a single event which suddenly alters a pre-existing equilibrium; rather we find a temporal chain of events and conditions which determine, worsen or crystallize a condition of social marginalization. The path towards margin-alization can vary: drug abuse, prostitution, isolation from reciprocity networks, atypical family structures, poor individual biographies or long-term and repeated imprisonment. All these trajectories share a common feature: deprivation, experienced passively, feeds on itself in a self-reproductive process which weakens the individual's capacity to plan his/her future.

It is easy to understand that those who apply for social assistance have already followed their own personal path made up of hardship, accidents, troubles, which have exhausted their individual, family and community resources. Moreover, the social drift has undermined their psycho-physical balance, or the vicious circle has started from psychological and health problems which have worsened as the marginalization process becomes more severe. Social services are intended to cope with this kind of serious marginalization and deprivation; however, they lack the means to implement an effective reinsertion process and confine their actions to partial interventions that only relieve but do not solve the problem. Social services are like hospitals for the seriously ill that can offer nothing except aspirin. In some instances, intervention succeeds in helping the individual to regain his or her strength and escape from social marginalization; in the majority of cases, the deficit of integrated resources is evident. People who experience severe marginalization do not need only small-scale help in terms of money, a shelter for the night, a hot meal, a decent job, medical and psychological care, drug addiction treatment or regaining self-esteem; what they need more is an appropriate, repeated and long-lasting infusion of all these things in order to break the negative synergy which builds up their multidimensional condition of exclusion. Obviously, one cannot be sure that an integrated intervention is always really effective, though a combination of work, housing, health care, financial aid and constant monitoring would probably increase the effectiveness of interventions.[14]

The wide fragmentation and the low integration of social service actions is undoubtedly due to a cultural and institutional deficit at the centre. However, in a context like that of Milan, where severe marginalization is not yet very widespread and there are abundant resources, it should be possible to reverse this situation. The most evident difficulties are not lack of means or the difficult reorganization of and co-ordination between various services, a different use of already available resources and the support of synergies in organization and programming between the public and the private sector; an effort in terms of co-ordination could start a deep transformation. The main difficulty is represented by cultural attitude and political will. Once these obstacles have been overcome, it will become possible to discuss the different available synergies between public and private, as well as how to design those 'integral' trajectories which are needed to favour social reinsertion and prevent social exclusion.

In conclusion, let us return briefly to the question of the social and territorial concentration of the poor. As was said above, the distribution of social marginalization in Milan is characterized by a juxtaposition of well off and decaying areas over the whole territory. However, some factors contribute to the creation of slum areas: the acute decay of working-class housing districts where not only the elderly but also first- and second-generation immigrants from the south live; the constant tendency of public institutions to concentrate highly discriminated groups (gypsies, immigrants from developing countries) leads to a dangerous combination of expulsion from some areas and attraction to others where social assistance is more available. The analysis of life histories highlights what could be the consequence – mostly for young people – of growing up in degraded territorial contexts (Benassi, 1995). When the structural deficiencies of the socio-economic context (mostly poor job chances for those with a low educational level) are combined with those of the referential microcontext, the growing risk of entering an early and often irreversible exclusion path becomes fully apparent.

NOTES

1 The estimate also includes immigrants from non-EU countries, equal to 40 per cent of the total.

2 The estimate of 'poor' households made for an economic well-being index revealed that from 1989 to 1992 the percentage of households earning less than 12 million lire per year grew from 12.3 per cent to 13.8 per cent (Associazione MeglioMilano, 1989–1993).

3 Poor families with three or more children amount to 9.7 per cent in the north, 6 per cent in the centre and 22.6 per cent in the south.

4 The life histories are taken from two different researches: the first, by Kazepov, Mingione and Zajczyk (1995), considers data from clients of the UAD (Office for Adults in Need) of the municipality of Milan and SAM-Caritas; the second is on new poverty in Lombardy (Kazepov, 1995b).

5 Milan may be considered a 'global city' according to some factors highlighted by Sassen (1991): local hegemony in an advanced tertiary system; financial control over a large international area; node of a global information network; network of economic, financial and research-and-development decision making.

6 The most evident increase is found in credit and assurance activities and services to private firms (+83 per cent), public administration (+27 per cent) and trade (+17 per cent).

7 People over 65 living in such housing comprise 40.3 per cent, while the rate for the entire resident population is 18.3 per cent. About 61 per cent of households whose head is over 65 and 71 per cent of single elderly have an average income between 11 and 15 million lire per year.

8 Beside the old age pension, which is the only universalistic intervention of financial aid, there are other indirect measures, mostly in the health sector, and specific services (the Domiciliar Assistance for the Elderly).

9 My analysis is based on data from the following services supplied by the Municipality of Milan: (a) Mother and Child Social Service (SSMI), whose recipients are households in need with one or more minors; (b) Office for Adults in Need (UAD), whose recipients are single people or households in need without minors and aged between 18 and 55 for women, 18 and 65 for men; (c) Night Shelters (RN), for homeless people between 18 and 65; (d) Domiciliary Assistance for the Elderly (CADA).

10 The psychological climate which has recently spread among young people should be taken into account. As a recent qualitative analysis illustrates, young workers who joined Alfa Romeo on a training contract are discouraged about their professional future.

11 Workers on supplementary benefit receive 80 per cent of their regular salary.

12   This conclusion is supported by data from the public hostel, the place of the most chronic marginalization, where women account for 11 per cent of users.

13   According to Istat (1989), women more than men, and housewives and retired persons more than others, claim to suffer from mental illness. Some research results, mainly from abroad, show that depression as a psychic pathology affects women more than men. Its causes should be looked for, not only in the differences in metabolism, but in the conditions of women's role in our societies.

14   The experience of the *Revenue Minimum d'Insertion* in France moves in that direction; see Milano (1988), UNIOPSS (1992), Autès (1992) and Paugam (1993).

14

Exclusion from Work and the Impoverishment Processes in Naples

Enrica Morlicchio, University of Naples

INTRODUCTION

This chapter on poverty in Naples will attempt to highlight some of the specificities of the impoverishment processes and social exclusion which have occurred over the last few decades, linking them with the question of unemployment. The central assumption is that the typologies of the social groups in danger of pauperization in Naples are determined not so much by the social and cultural characteristics of the urban environment in which the involved subjects live, as by the more general structural processes which have taken place in the city: since the 1970s these processes have been marked by phenomena of de-industrialization.

The specific analysis of the Neapolitan case requires two further assumptions. The first is that the aggravation of the problem of poverty in Naples is a salient aspect of the Italian model of inequality founded, as we know, on the territorial division between North and South (Paci, 1993; see also Mingione and Zajczyk, 1992). The second is that the general process of transformation of the economy and production in a post-Fordist sense affects a city like Naples most particularly.

The tertiary nature and the destructured labour market of post-Fordist cities are also reflected in the formation of poverty strata (see, for example, Peter Marcuse in this volume or Mingione, 1991a or b).

And the impoverishment processes which are specific to cities during this historical phase are most certainly present in Naples, though in the Neapolitan context they intermingle with the underdevelopment of the economic structures and the legacy of traditional forms of poverty.

As Castel observed, the novelty of the present impoverishment processes is that they are associated with certain changes which have occurred along two principal axes: an axis of occupational integration/ non-integration and an axis of inclusion/non-inclusion in family and community networks (Castel, 1991: 147).[1]

These changes are due on the one hand to the destructuralization of the labour market (an increase in the unemployment of adult males and the reduction of prospects for the traditional 'victims of the labour market'[2]), on the other to a slackening of social ties produced by the decline of the family and community networks of solidarity and the associative forms specific to the working class. According to Castel the combination of these two processes produces an increase in social vulnerability which, in its turn, can become a process of 'loss of affiliation' (*désaffiliation*) (Castel, 1991: 152).

The first part of this chapter will deal with the themes of the destructuralization of both the labour market and the role of social networks, and go on to consider the phenomena of the territorial concentration of poverty in Naples. It will end with a description of the principal specificities of the Neapolitan situation and how this differs from that of other metropolitan contexts.

THE DETERIORATION OF THE LABOUR MARKET IN THE NEAPOLITAN AREA AND THE CHARACTERISTICS OF UNEMPLOYMENT

We will start with the question of the labour market and unemployment: the last two decades have witnessed the consolidation of extremely high unemployment rates both in Naples and in the entire Mezzogiorno. As we shall see in greater detail later, the unemployment rate in the Mezzogiorno is 19 per cent as against the average national rate of 8 per cent.

The link between poverty and unemployment is particularly evident here for it is not by mere chance that both phenomena are concentrated in the Mezzogiorno, which absorbs over 60 per cent of the Italian unemployed and two-thirds of the poor (while little more than one-third of the country's population lives there). Besides, according to the 1992 data provided by the governmental Commission on poverty and underprivilege (CIPE, 1994), the incidence of poor families among the total families living in the Mezzogiorno is three times higher than in the Centre-North (respectively 21 per cent and 7 per cent).

But we should bear in mind another element: that is, that Naples presents the highest concentration of unemployment and is one of the principal centres of organized crime in Italy. Neither of these phenomena is a novelty, but from the second half of the 1970s on they have become an essential trait of the social structure of the city.[3] Their coexistence is certainly not accidental; they have the same identical matrix. However, the deterioration processes of the economy must be taken into account in order to explain both phenomena.

This theme should be stressed, as well as the way in which structural, institutional and socio-cultural aspects have contributed to determine the present situation. In fact in recent years the socio-economic situation of the Mezzogiorno regions, and of Naples, has received considerable attention from an anthropological point of view and from the point of view of political processes (see Becchi, 1989; Gribaudi, 1993). The situation of economic deterioration has been linked with the role of values and the evolution of the political structures accompanying the modernization process. The mentality and culture of the Mezzogiorno, the role of institutions such as the family (the revival of 'amoral familism' is not accidental) and the absence of civic culture are more and more frequently invoked to explain the situation of economic deterioration of the Neapolitan context.

In other words, as with other social realities, poverty is interpreted with reference to the culture of the victims of poverty and the labour market. Undoubtedly factors of an institutional nature have played an important role in determining the processes of impoverishment, unemployment and the spread of phenomena of deviance which have also been influenced by variables of an anthropological and cultural nature. But, at least where Naples is concerned, the progressive deterioration of the labour market, due mainly to the reduction of occupational prospects in the core sector, has played a decisive role.

This contraction has particularly affected industrial occupations; according to data provided by national population censuses, industrial employment in the city of Naples decreased by 26 per cent between 1981 and 1991. This decrease has not been compensated by development in the services sector, nor can it be attributed to processes of relocation like those which occurred in all the major metropolitan areas in order to deal with problems of congestion, the high cost of land and labour, social conflict, etc. (the Milanese area can be considered a typical example of these processes, see Zajczyk in this volume). It is simply the result of a reorganization of the city's industrial structure induced by the crisis of maritime and port activities, the closing of the larger industrial settlements and the decline of the manufacturing urban structure of artisan or semi-artisan work (on the process of de-industrialization in the city of Naples see Giannola, 1984; Rebeggiani, 1990). In this setting tertiary activities too have deteriorated, offering poor quality work especially in the areas of retail commerce and personal services.

The decrease in manufacturing/industrial occupations has corresponded to an increase in unemployment: according to population census data the number of unemployed in Naples has increased from 155,000 in 1981 to 179,000 in 1991, an even higher figure than that of the registered unemployed provided by the Ministry of Labour for the same year (150,000 registered). Census data reflects, as everyone knows, the perception of self of the interviewed person (or, more precisely, the perception of her/his position on the labour market) at the moment of the census survey.

The Ministry of Labour figure is an administrative datum which expresses availability for work or the expectation of obtaining work through the unemployment bureau. This is the first time that the Istat figures on unemployment are higher than the number of people registered with the unemployment bureau. In the past this latter category was accused of 'fake' unemployment, that is, of not really looking for work and using registration for welfare advantages or in the hope of some kind of artificial, state protected, job. Another accusation of 'fake unemployment' is based on the conviction that the registered unemployed have in fact some kind of informal activity (for a critique of this interpretation see Liguori and Veneziano, 1982). What emerges today is, if anything, a general loss of confidence in the possibility of finding work through unemployment bureaus in proportion to the protraction of the period of unemployment. In Naples 77 per cent of the people registered with the unemployment bureau have been looking for work for over two years and of these a significant quota (22 per cent, which rises to 34 per cent if we consider only the male component) is represented by heads of families. This is useful evidence of the link between poverty and the labour market: the family of an unemployed person in Naples is very often a poor family (see, for example, Cerase, Morlicchio and Spanò, 1991).

The high incidence of young people among the Neapolitan unemployed also indicates how unemployment is not so much an effect of expulsion from the productive process as the effect of non-entry. In a context in which industrial-sector employment is not expanding (or at all events is growing less than the labour market supply) young people end up in a situation of marginalization. This was already the Neapolitan situation before the 1980s and it naturally deteriorated still further through de-industrialization processes.

The decrease of industrial employment has particularly affected the working-class nuclei formed during the 1960s and 1970s in the wake of the great flow of industrial investment from private and state-run companies which converged on the city itself or the Neapolitan metropolitan area. This is particularly evident if we consider the number of unemployed in the upper bracket: that is, people who were regularly employed in medium or large productive structures who now are registered in special lists (so-called mobility lists).[4] In Naples, 16,556 workers are registered in these lists. Of these, one quarter is under 33 years of age and a further half belongs to the cohorts of the next age group (33–49). We are thus speaking of workers who are mostly in a central phase of their life cycle, and this makes the prospect of unemployment even more serious. In Naples the percentage of women in 'mobility lists', that is, women who have lost their jobs, is 30 per cent (in the whole of Italy the same percentage is 60 per cent). This low incidence of women can be explained by their relatively limited presence in industrial worker occupations, where they represent little more than 10 per cent. However, if we calculate the quota of women registered in the mobility lists as a percentage of the total number of women employed in industry we see that it reaches 6.1 per cent while the male component is 2.4 per cent – even though it is larger in absolute terms. It is therefore clear that the processes of expulsion from the central productive system tend to further reduce the already low female rate of participation in industrial employment.[5]

At this point we should ask ourselves to what extent the deterioration processes have affected the informal sector of the economy too. Some authors have stressed that, 'poverty and lack of opportunities are neither a necessary condition nor a sufficient condition for informal activities to develop' (Cotugno, et al., 1990: 158). During the period of most intense industrial development and social modernization in Naples some aspects of the informal economy declined and it lost, to a great extent, the characteristics of an urban subsistence economy. The modification of consumption and access to a wider market eliminated some of the traditional activities specific to the so-called street corner economy, which was extremely closed and characterized by under-consumption. Only a few aspects of this economy (for example, the sale of smuggled cigarettes at street corners) – which stimulated such interest in scholars of the city of Naples in the past (see Allum, 1973) – have survived (after many ups and downs), especially in the central areas. The evolution of 'informal' manufacturing activities is more

interesting (though these are 'informal' only from a fiscal point of view
– in the sense of tax evasion – and because no social security is paid for
the workers, and building, health and contractual regulations are not
observed). The 'poor' traditional crafts for the local market were in
fact replaced little by little in the course of the 1960s and 1970s by a
sweatshop system in the manufacturing sector which became the
modern informal market sector (see mainly Pugliese, 1983). In more
recent years this has been accompanied by a new area of unskilled
tertiary activity (for example, cleaning work) which is not very
different from that observed in many metropolitan areas in Europe
and the United States. If anything, these activities differ from the
forms of peripheral work specific to the 'Third Italy'; in fact – apart
from some cases of jobbing, such as the production of bags and shoes
with the trade marks of well-known local firms – their production is
not directed towards medium-high or innovative sectors of the market
but to residual ones (the market of non-authorized imitations, of
second quality goods, etc.) (Mingione, 1990).

At all events there is a marginal and poor labour market on which
various segments of the population depend, and the traditional
components of these segments have now been joined by third world
immigrants. So far this group is not very numerous though it is
quite relevant from the point of view of the problems it poses of social
and labour integration. One of the questions we have to take into
consideration is that the presence of foreign immigrants in Naples
is not incompatible with the existence of a high and growing number
of unemployed, in fact the city of Naples itself has the highest
concentration of both unemployed and immigrants. The characteristics of the labour market of the area act as an attraction for
immigrants who perform poorly paid interstitial jobs with such an
absence of any guarantees that their working conditions are even
worse than those of the secondary level (Calvanese and Pugliese, 1991;
de Filippo and Morlicchio, 1992).

During the last ten years the reduced opportunities in official
employment have caused an increase in the competition among
workers even in the marginal-poor labour market. The unemployed
without school-leaving certificates,[6] who form 70 per cent of those
registered with the unemployment bureau, have thus to 'compete with
the other components for the offer of irregular and provisional jobs,
often at the price of sinking deeper and deeper into itineraries of de-
professionalization which end by accentuating the risk of pauperization'
(Mingione, 1990: 57). Women in particular are de-professionalized and
discouraged by the occupational structure and are therefore tendentially
forced into the exclusive role of housewife.[7] Whether this is a

constriction or, as some people maintain, a 'preference' is debatable (for a critique of this second point of view see Pugliese, 1993). However, one fact is certain: the condition of housewife is dominant in Naples among women of working age. The number of housewives (246,369) exceeds that of women present in the labour market (135,143). It must, however, be noted that in spite of persistent and high levels of exclusion (the unemployment rate among young women in Naples is 78 per cent, that is, three out of four young women between the ages of 14 and 29 in the labour market are unemployed) women do not move back into the non-active population as they used to do: in fact from 1981 to 1991 the number of women in search of employment increased from 52,454 to 66,001. A complex framework of labour market victims has thus developed: from women who have been discharged from precarious and not at all encouraging jobs and those employed in the sector of small informal manufacturing, to those employed in the expanding services of the city with its growing tertiary sector, to employment in jobs often on the edge of legality, to the young unemployed in the strict sense of the term. In the meantime, occupation in the core sector – stable occupation protected by a system of guarantees in the private sector of the economy – is very clearly decreasing.

Precisely this deterioration of the labour market after a phase of development and numerical and political consolidation of the core working class[8] helps us understand a particularly significant phenomenon in Naples: that is, the 'movement of the organized unemployed', which started in the mid-1970s with an initial nucleus of unemployed and precariously employed people who established their seat in the San Lorenzo quarter in the historical centre. The protagonists of the movement of the organized unemployed were not the proletariat who had recently moved to the city and had no industrial socialization or the underprivileged city dwellers but specific social subjects who saw themselves first of all as unemployed and whose goal was that of emerging through work from a condition of marginalization and precariousness.[9] And, as Judith Chubb stresses, this did not only mean state employment in the public sector since guaranteed industrial work also represented an aspiration, for 'in Southern Italy, the precariousness of economic survival in general is such that the primary aspiration of every worker is a guarantee of stable employment – and this means either the public sector (doormen, garbage men, bus drivers, etc.) or a regular factory job' (Chubb, 1982: 48).

Even though the mobilization of the 'organized unemployed' continued in later periods, its significance and quality were considerably inferior. As the de-industrialization process continued (between

1971 and 1981 Naples lost 12,000 jobs in the manufacturing industry, down from 70,000 to 58,000) the prospects of entering into the central occupational structure decreased significantly – also as a consequence of the solutions proposed by the municipality and the central state, based more on the distribution of subsidies and short-term jobs in the public sector than on the promotion of new jobs. And these prospects had raised hopes of change among unemployed and temporarily employed Neapolitans (see Becchi, 1989).

CAPACITY AND LIMITATIONS OF FAMILY SUPPORT NETWORKS

Bearing in mind this structural setting, we should evaluate considerations such as Castel's on the slackening of solidarity and family networks and ties as a cause of the intensification of poverty conditions. In fact the role of family support networks in Naples has often been stressed in the present Italian debate, especially in connection with the cultural and survival aspects of archaic phenomena (for a comment, see Gribaudi, 1993). These networks certainly still play a central role in the survival strategies of the weaker layers of the population.

Among other things it is interesting to note how the importance of these forms and their tenacious persistence is being stressed now, during this phase of the long crisis of modern manufacturing and industry, which themselves influenced the modification of the social structure, contributing to the development of forms of aggregation and solidarity typical of industrial societies (for example, trade unions) which provided a far more solid and formal – though not yet sufficiently extended – system of solidarity and guarantee. One can say that a complex process occurred in Naples involving the slackening of traditional ties and forms of solidarity, though also the persistence of other forms of solidarity.

For example, according to research carried out in the Pendino quarter in the historic city centre, the family network is a fundamental dispenser of both monetary and non-monetary help.[10] In fact about a quarter of the interviewed families living below the poverty line have recourse to this kind of help and an equally significant quota (19 per cent) help needy relatives (providing money or domestic help). On the other hand, only 6 per cent of the poor families are helped by the Church or by volunteer associations.[11]

Consequently even though poor families have frequent recourse to informal help, because of the scarcity of monetary and service resources, they can only do so within a rather limited network generally consisting of relatives, while there is little recourse to the assistance of volunteer or self-help groups whose capacity for organization is on the whole equal to the extent of public intervention. But this centrality of the family and the network of relatives is not what it was in the past as a consequence of the strength of traditional family values and models and of the backwardness of the productive structure, which was still characterized by the 'street corner economy'. What is happening today is a revitalization of these networks concomitant with the downgrading of the labour market which – as we have seen – started during the second half of the 1970s (on this point see Pugliese, 1992).

The family typologies most exposed to the risk of poverty confirm this. Generalizing the results of the research carried out in the historic city centre we can say that in Naples poverty involves both large households[12] (which are composed of several nuclear family units) – in which the father has temporary or low-income work, and the children (young adults with poor qualifications) only rarely are engaged in black work – and classic nuclear families (father, mother and one or two children) who depend entirely on the stable income of the head of the family. The former suffer from the absence of stable job incomes and the cumulative effect of the disadvantages due to a large family and forced cohabitation; the latter suffer from having to deal with the needs of the family in a particularly difficult phase of the cycle of family life. Besides, this second category cannot count on the integration of a complementary salary (also since, as we have seen, there are few job possibilities for women, especially if they have had little schooling) and on a system of welfare services which is insufficient both quantitatively and qualitatively in the Italian Mezzogiorno.[13]

This does not mean that some subjects have not become poor individually (former inmates of psychiatric hospitals, old people with chronic diseases, unmarried girls with children). A selection of biographies we collected in June and July 1994 in the only free hostel in Naples, in the Pendino quarter, shows a substantial presence of young unemployed without family connections or who have lost touch with their families. The latter present the combination of isolation from social networks and of marginality on the labour market which, according to Castel, tends to generate vicious circles of impoverishment and phenomena of the loss of affiliation.[14] At all events Mingione and Zajczyk's consideration that 'the principal syndrome of poverty is unburdened on the families and, consequently, amplified to a certain extent rather than attenuated by this fact' (Mingione and Zajczyk, 1993: 19) is perfectly valid in Naples too.

In some cases family poverty is set off by the existence of specific problems or individual needs (for example, the problems caused by a handicapped child) which low-income families are not able to deal with in a context characterized by the lack of welfare services and a market of private services in which the high cost does not correspond to a decent quality of service. In this case the course of poverty is linked not only to general structural processes but also, and above all, to the deficiencies of the local welfare system (and to the accompanying modest force of the family and neighbourhood networks). Other elements, besides, like widespread drug addiction among young people in various quarters (see next section), contribute to further exacerbate the course of family and individual poverty.

Finally we should remember an internal aspect of the question of poverty: that is, the fact that the family is the reference point for the analysis of social disadvantages and exclusion must not lead us to underestimate generational differences as well as significant gender differences in the allocation of family resources. For example, a study on unemployment carried out in the Scampia and Montecalvario quarters shows that, when looking for jobs, family relational resources are activated more frequently for men than for women (Cerase, Morlicchio and Spanò, 1991).

DOES A 'GHETTO POVERTY' EXIST IN NAPLES? TERRITORIAL DIVISION OF POVERTY IN THE CITY

After identifying the subjects at the highest risk of being below the poverty level we need to identify the urban space in which they tend to live. The following question should be asked: to what extent do the phenomena of social and job exclusion we have described above tend to be territorially concentrated in Naples, thus giving rise to pockets of chronic and localized poverty in specific areas or quarters? In other terms, ought we to verify whether Naples has a degree of concentration of poverty corresponding to the process Tosi (1994: 162) highlighted when he said that 'the cumulative nature of hardships may correspond to the evidence of territories in which excluded populations are concentrated, or with whom the excluded populations are identified.'

Undoubtedly processes which move in this direction exist, but available documentation and the literature on the city do not indicate an accumulation of disadvantages in one or more quarters likely to determine the creation of a ghetto. On the other hand if we agree with Wilson, for whom 'extreme poverty neighborhoods' exist only where at least 40 per cent of the population is poor, we have to exclude the existence in Naples of quarters which can be thus defined.[15] In fact varying factors of hardship, exclusion and poverty interact in different quarters and are not always territorially cumulative and concentrated. According to Itsuki Nakabayashi (quoted in Sassen, 1993) four indicators are needed for the identification of areas characterized by an accumulation of disadvantages: (a) physical and housing decline, (b) local economic decline, (c) the decline and impoverishment of social relationships in the neighbourhood, and (d) the presence of underprivileged minorities.[16]

Though we do not have sufficient empirical documentation on which to be able to construct indicators of this kind for the city of Naples, on the basis of the shared knowledge of the urban social reality one can say that no single neighbourhood rather than another sums up these disadvantages. In the first place the indicators do not always tally or have the same meaning they have in other social contexts. Thus – as we will see further on – the presence, for example, of underprivileged minorities in cities does not run parallel with the other indicators. Of these the most significant is possibly the first (housing) which effectively shows a concentration in the historic city centre[17] where, among other things, a quota of the population lives in *bassi*, one-room ground-floor lodgings (in most cases not legally habitable) or in decrepit historic buildings.

A study carried out at the beginning of the 1980s (IRES Campania, 1987) tried to evaluate the extent of this deterioration on the basis of criteria concerning housing characteristics (the presence of lodgings with bathrooms, the average coefficient of the 1980 earthquake damage, the presence of one-room lodgings) and the stable settlement intensity (the index of the crowding of lodgings, the density of inhabitants, the index of cohabitation). According to this study 6 per cent of the historic city centre is in an 'abnormal' state of deterioration: these areas are concentrated in Montecalvario, in the high areas of the Quartieri Spagnoli, in some blocks in San Lorenzo (Duchesca and Forcella), in Stella (Sanità), in the Avvocata (Cavone) and Pendino (Piazza Mercato). Eighty-six per cent suffers from substantial and widespread deterioration (defined as 'very high' in 14 per cent of the cases, 'high' in 35 per cent of the cases and 'medium' in 37 per cent of the cases) and only the remaining 8 per cent from 'slight' deterioration or the absence of deterioration. And yet these quarters with a high degree of physical deterioration contain many 'islands' of buildings

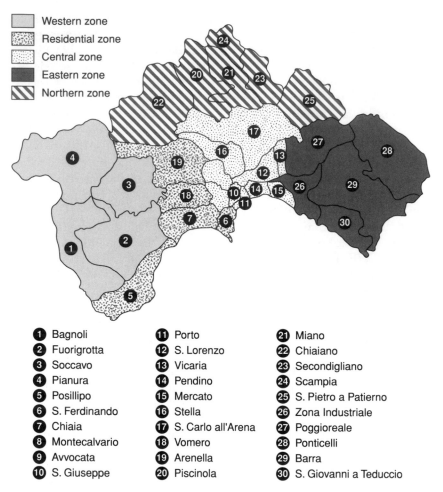

Western zone
Residential zone
Central zone
Eastern zone
Northern zone

❶ Bagnoli	⓫ Porto	㉑ Miano
❷ Fuorigrotta	⓬ S. Lorenzo	㉒ Chiaiano
❸ Soccavo	⓭ Vicaria	㉓ Secondigliano
❹ Pianura	⓮ Pendino	㉔ Scampia
❺ Posillipo	⓯ Mercato	㉕ S. Pietro a Patierno
❻ S. Ferdinando	⓰ Stella	㉖ Zona Industriale
❼ Chiaia	⓱ S. Carlo all'Arena	㉗ Poggioreale
❽ Montecalvario	⓲ Vomero	㉘ Ponticelli
❾ Avvocata	⓳ Arenella	㉙ Barra
❿ S. Giuseppe	⓴ Piscinola	㉚ S. Giovanni a Teduccio

Map 14.1 The neighbourhood of Naples

or entire blocks of prevalently bourgeois or upper-bourgeois dwellings. This does not involve (or does not only involve) processes of gentrification since we are often in the presence of the persistent residence of people belonging to upper social classes in old family houses or palaces.

On the other hand, urban deterioration is not only limited to the central quarters: the old centres encapsulated in the heart of the eastern industrial zone (Ponticelli, S. Giovanni and Barra) and some residential neighbourhoods in the western suburbs where unauthorized building has predominated (an emblematic case is that of Pianura) equally present conditions of absence of services and processes of social isolation. The diffusion of poverty and social underprivilege in neighbourhoods not included in the inner city, and in fact the concentration of some of the more serious forms of exclusion like labour market exclusion in the peripheral quarters also, suggests the possibility of using the concept of hyperghetto, as Wacquant uses it, also for areas like the Neapolitan metropolitan area, even though the social and institutional context is different.[18]

Where indicators of an economic nature are concerned, the decline of the local economy has had different manifestations in the central, semi-central and peripheral quarters of the city. In the former it is connected with the disappearance of manufacturing and artisan activities or to their relocation to extra-urban and peripheral neighbourhoods (like Secondigliano). The 1980 earthquake acted as an accelerator for these changes, and the relocation of traditional manufacturing activities took place not so much because of direct damage to the physical structures – which were already crumbling – as because of indirect effects and, in particular, the acceleration of the expulsion process of the population from the historic centre. In the peripheral quarters of the north-west and eastern industrial areas this decline was expressed, instead, in terms of the downsizing of the urban manufacturing sector – dependent mainly on centralized decision making – and on the transformation of the old factories into unproductive storage depots. But in the periphery itself we should distinguish between residential dormitory quarters (which never have had an industrial productive fabric) and the quarters which have been hit by de-industrialization processes like, for example, Barra S. Giovanni and more recently Bagnoli, the seat of the great steelworks and the heart of the Neapolitan working class in this century.

As for the third indicator (social decline), the areas which have suffered most from phenomena of social decline are again the central quarters: in the wake of outmigration – whether spontaneous or induced by reconstruction policies – these neighbourhoods have seen profound modifications in their social make-up. Throughout the 1980s job opportunities have both diminished and become impoverished for the fringe groups of the population, and young people in particular have become more exposed to the risk of deviance. While in some more favoured and less degraded areas of the historic city centre the flow of public resources activated by the earthquake has attracted the interest of big construction companies and individual members of the middle-upper classes, most of the *rioni* (districts) have undergone an impoverishment process of their human and productive resources. At the same time the nature of these *rioni* and the availability of low-cost crumbling dwellings has allowed immigrants to settle in them. This process has involved the Quartieri Spagnoli and the *rione* Sanità in particular.[19]

Though the processes of social decline are particularly evident in the central quarters the situation is no better in the low-cost housing residential areas (Ponticelli, Piscinola-Marianella) where new neighbourhoods for the population which was moved out of the centre after the earthquake have grown up.[20] In fact post-earthquake reconstruction policies followed procedures which increased the sense of social isolation connected with living in a given neighbourhood rather than carefully renovating the entire area. As Savastano pointed out, 'a 13-year-old boy attending a neighbourhood middle school today, in 1993, is a child born in the year of the earthquake who most probably lost his home in the first months of his life and lived for five, six, seven years in a container camp, or in a hotel, or in an occupied school, before being 'transferred', through decisions which his family feels that it neither took nor shared, to the new neighbourhood' (Savastano, 1994: 79). Consequently, for many families, the allocation of a lodging in the neighbourhoods in which reconstruction was concentrated implied acquiring the status of 'welfare subject' as well as being isolated from their family and neighbourhood network. Besides, some of the lodgings of the special reconstruction programme were taken over by squatters. This provoked on the one hand conflictual situations with the legitimate assignees and on the other it favoured the spread of the stigmatization of the new arrivals.

Where the more peripheral neighbourhoods are concerned, one must speak of the absence of a social and institutional fabric rather than of social decline. While the inner quarters have many institutional infrastructures and service activities (from schools to health facilities, from shops to public offices), many of the peripheral neighbourhoods are absolutely lacking in these which not only lowers the quality of life but represents a deteriorating situation of poverty (see Waquant in this volume for a comparison with other urban realities).

We now come to the last indicator (concerning the concentration of underprivileged minorities). As we have said, the presence of immigrants is not very substantial numerically in Naples, in view of the relatively recent nature of the phenomenon and the possible conditions of social integration. Consequently specific ethnic groups do not predominate in given neighbourhoods as they do in the American inner cities. The presence of immigrants is spread out and on the whole follows the pattern of the opportunities for work. Women immigrants (especially Cingalese, Capeverdians, Eritreans and Filipinos) who work as 'day and night' servants live in the homes of their employers in the residential hillside and central areas (Vomero, Posillipo, Chiaia). The men, on the other hand, work mainly as pedlars and sleep in pensions and lodgings near the main railway station where rents are very high considering the conditions of the lodgings. This is why a high number of compatriots (three or four per room) share them. On the other hand, the families of immigrants, as mentioned earlier, are concentrated in the central quarters. In recent years, however, their presence has been recorded in the peripheral, illegal building areas and particularly in Pianura. Consequently a neighbourhood is not dequalified by the presence of immigrants but rather the social deterioration of a neighbourhood attracts this type of population. In these neighbourhoods a situation of 'equilibrium in marginality' develops, which offers very few occasions for conflict with the local population and in fact favours the diffusion of solidaristic behaviour.

But even if there are no real ghettos in Naples, the immediate outskirts present cases of this kind of situation. The 'ghetto of Villa Literno' – a shanty town which has developed in a suburban Neapolitan area – is a significant example. It presents many of the characteristics of a ghetto: the domination of an ethnic group (Burkina Faso), social and institutional isolation (most of the immigrants do not have regular residence permits), territorial stigmatization (isolated episodes of prostitution and drug peddling have been abundantly emphasized by the press and by local institutions) and finally marginalization in the labour market (the ghetto dwellers work as unskilled labourers in the building trade and, mainly, as agricultural pickers, receiving far less pay than with contractual salaries and far less than local workers).

CONCLUSION

The degenerative processes of the Neapolitan labour market and the weakening of social ties consequent to the decline of social movements, as well as the decrease of the protective capacity of the family, have increased the risk Naples is running of entering into chronic itineraries of pauperization.

Even if it is difficult at present to quantify the phenomenon, the number of underprivileged poor subjects who are fundamentally external to the material and cultural networks of the working classes is increasing. However, these subjects cannot really be compared to the 'ghetto poverty' described in studies of the inner cities, both because of the absence of a 'closure' of ethnic and racial discrimination and because they are less socially isolated and spatially concentrated. The only element in common with the black ghetto situation of the American inner cities is the very high concentration of youth unemployment. The exclusion of young people from the labour market is characteristic of most of the central and suburban poor quarters and it brings to mind the situation of the black ghettos. But other contextual characteristics are radically different. Thus, for example, the importance of the family and the way in which family roles are seen is certainly different. For, in spite of a certain slackening, in almost every Neapolitan neighbourhood the family has held its ground and cases of the socialization of young people in one-parent families run by the mother are certainly not the rule. From this point of view there is, if anything, an analogy with another situation of urban poverty in the USA, that is, that of the Hispanics.

One certainly cannot say that urban poverty is localized in ghetto situations in Naples. The term 'hyperghetto' – according to Wacquant's definition – is suitable in its sense of a 'reconfigured, decentred and spatially differentiated' ghetto. But, as we have seen, the spatial differentiation also corresponds to a social differentiation: the elements of exclusion operate with greater or lesser force in the different quarters which form the hyperghetto area or, more simply, in the traditionally poorer quarters. The basic common element of the thrust towards impoverishment in all these quarters is, however, the disadvantageous labour market situation together with the decrease in occupational possibilities due to the weakening of the productive structures. In this sense the downward thrust towards impoverishment processes does not operate within territorially restricted localities but over a very wide area which transcends the city. The cause of the high concentration of poverty in areas like Naples stems in the first place from the territorial imbalance between North and South. Poverty does not only strike particular subjects or social and ethnic groups (the homeless, young blacks, etc.) on an individual level but also, on a general level, it strikes the populations resident in economically and socially underprivileged areas. Besides, the most targeted subjects are not the same as those of other contexts. Poverty does not mainly target single mothers but large families, according to a prevalent model in traditional contexts. What must be stressed is that this configuration of poverty represents a 'new' element; not because post-materialist or relational aspects prevail (as the Italian debate sometimes insists) but because it is deeply rooted in the material processes which have concerned not only uprooted subjects or the traditional victims of the labour market during the past ten years but also people belonging to what was the strong segment of the working class, in which the popular strata had placed their hopes of change and modernization of the city.

NOTES

1 For a commentary on Castel's interpretative model, see Bergamaschi (1993: 117–19) and Tosi (1994: 159–61).
2 This is how Offe defined the subjects and social groups most exposed to labour market risks: young people, women, mature workers, the disabled and underprivileged minorities (1985: 43).
3 Unlike the Palermo mafia the camorra played a marginal role in the urban transformation of Naples in the 1960s.
4 Registration in 'mobility lists' provides for the possibility of collecting a kind of unemployment indemnity for a period which varies from one to two years.
5 This data comes from a volume edited by the Agenzia per l'Impiego della Campania (1993).
6 In Naples the phenomenon of school truancy starts in early childhood: according to data provided by the Neapolitan Provincial Education Office, in the year 1989–90 the rate of school truancy (children who had never been to school or who stopped going without giving any justification out of the total school-age population) was 3 per cent in the elementary school and 10 per cent in the middle school. However, these are average figures which do not reflect the real situation in educational centres in the more underprivileged neighbourhoods where the truancy rates involve a quarter of the student population.
7 In view of the general disadvantageous conditions of the labour market, women without educational qualifications have to compete with the male labour force for low-prestige and low-qualification jobs too. In Naples the presence of women in unskilled tertiary jobs (school caretakers, cleaners) is considerably lower than the national average.
8 See the following observation by Giannola: 'Naples is one of the major Italian industrial poles and, of these, one of those undergoing the most profound crisis' (1984: 36).
9 Therefore the movement of the organized unemployed must not be confused with marginal urban mass movements or mobilizations, the 'poor people movements', which have been analysed in the international literature (see, for example, Piven and Cloward, 1979).
10 This research, consisting in the administration of a structured questionnaire to a sample of 576 families resident in the Pendino quarter, was carried out in 1990–91 by a group of researchers directed by G. Ragone, which included E. Amaturo, E. Morlicchio, A. Spanò.
11 This reflects solely the Pendino quarter. In another quarter in the historic centre – Montecalvario – in 1987 the Associazione Quartieri Spagnoli founded, for example, a small company called '081' to help people engaged in the black economy to produce leather goods. The Association

has also developed a pilot project financed by the EEC, the 'Work Park', which provides training and sets up firms for young people working in the shadow economy. Other activities of the Association include 'Anna's house', a *basso* which has become a centre for welcoming and listening to particularly underprivileged subjects (young social outcasts, the children of women detained in the Pozzuoli female prison, recent immigrants), the 'Via Nova' youth centre and the 'Butterfly-City' project for the creation of a documentation centre on the socio-economic conditions of the area.

12   Large families (five or more people living together) still form a quarter of Neapolitan families.

13   It is a known fact that in the Mezzogiorno in particular the Italian welfare system has specialized in granting monetary transfers in the form of subsidies and pensions to a very-low-income section of the population to the detriment of the development and modernization of the public services (IRES Campania, 1987).

14   As for the effect of these processes on job-hunting, this is what Vito (21 years old) said: 'Even if we want to look for work, we have no address to leave.' According to another person interviewed: 'If I say that I live in the Dormitory people think that there is something wrong' (Flavio, 23 years old). The fact that poverty is condensed within families rather than in situations of individual hardship therefore does not exclude the possibility of an increase in the number of subjects who are not protected by family networks. In fact between 1981 and 1991 the number of unemployed males in Naples who had previously worked almost doubled, passing from 16,044 to 29,033. This increase in the unemployment of adult male heads of families – together with the reduction of the area and quality of provision of income guarantees – makes extended living at home more and more difficult for young family members looking for jobs, so much so that in some cases it represents a factor of family breakup.

15   For Wilson this type of quarter coincides *de facto* with the black ghetto (1993: 13).

16   The indicators were constructed on the basis of 32 variables in relation to the 23 neighbourhoods of Tokyo; in this context they were used mainly in a qualitative sense.

17   The historic city centre includes the quarters of San Ferdinando, Montecalvario, Avvocata, Stella, San Giuseppe, Porto, Pendino, San Lorenzo, Mercato.

18   Wacquant used the term 'hyperghetto' to define a 'reconfigured, decentred and spatially differentiated ghetto' (1993: 367).

19   The largest immigrant communities present in these quarters are Cingalese, Tamil, Capeverdian and Eritrean, since they are consolidated communities within which there is the highest presence of family units.

20   The special reconstruction programme provided for the building of 20,000 lodgings partly in the city of Naples and partly in the provincial municipalities.

15

Urban Poverty in Germany: A Comparative Analysis of the Profile of the Poor in Stuttgart and Berlin

Hartmut Häussermann, Humboldt University of Berlin, and Yuri Kazepov, University of Milan

INTRODUCTION

The main purpose of this chapter is to analyse the situation the unified German welfare institutions must cope with – in particular the new risk of poverty resulting from different ongoing transformation processes: on one hand the long-lasting economic restructuring process and on the other the political reunification process between East and West Germany. The two cities we chose could be taken as very particular points of observation. The affluent context of Stuttgart, which has to face a structural economic crisis, and a city like Berlin, involved in a complex process of social, political and economic reunification and transformation.

What we want to look at is how these two processes of transformation change the profile of the poor, pointing out the groups at risk of poverty in the two contexts. The two cities are not typical examples of the way these two transformation processes affect German society in general, but what we are interested in is the impact of the two different processes on the profile of the poor as they are defined by social assistance. In this sense considering two particular contrasting cases like Stuttgart and Berlin could be of some interest, because the processes of transformation are affecting also what were, up till the end of the 1980s, relatively stable socio-economic contexts – Stuttgart because of its long-lasting positive economic performance, and Berlin (West) because of its subsidized economy up to 1990.

Although German reunification extended the positive economic trend till the beginning of the 1990s, mainly through growing internal demand from the new eastern *Länder*, this did not prevent the structural crisis from affecting in more recent years also affluent contexts like Stuttgart. This positive short-term effect on the West German economies was more than counterbalanced by the long-term adjustment crisis in the new *Länder*. The process of social change that the transition to the market economy has initiated raised the level of unemployment between 1990 and 1994, and this had a great impact, particularly on the East German cities. That East Germany will become a German Mezzogiorno, characterized by a high concentration of poverty, long-term unemployment and difficulties in entering the labour market (as shown by Morlicchio herein for Naples) is unlikely, although the present performance of these regions shows indicators not very different from the least industrialized economies within Europe. The high level of state transfers, however, is having some positive effects in the medium run, although the institutional change is having deeper consequences than were expected, or admitted, by politicians.

In the following paragraphs of this chapter we will show the institutional context within which the transformation processes are embedded and the difficulties the institutional asset has to deal with. In particular we will show the different profiles of poverty emerging from these changes in the two cities and the need of new instruments to face adequately these processes.

THE INSTITUTIONAL FRAME OF SOCIAL CITIZENSHIP IN GERMANY: EAST AND WEST BEFORE AND AFTER 1990

The System of Social Assistance

Before 1990, East and West Germany had formally similar systems of social assistance. This may sound curious, but in both countries there was in fact a Hilfe zum Lebensunterhalt (HLU), a financial help devoted to grant minimum life conditions to persons in a situation of need. Although the two systems developed autonomously after the

Second World War, they were rooted in the same historical background characterized, as far as social policies are concerned, by Bismarck's reforms at the end of the nineteenth century.[1] This imprinting defined some common lines in the design of social policies in the two contexts, although the two political regimes shaped their role in their respective social contexts. Formerly both subsidies were means-tested, determined more (West) or less (East) by the families' sheltering capacities and had a specific and strong relation with the work-centred policies. Their amount had to be below the minimum wage so as to avoid the paradoxical situation of higher subsidies which discourage work.[2] Given these similarities, the two assistance systems played different roles both in terms of the amount paid and because of the radically different role of the firms providing employment. As far as the amount paid is concerned, although it was determined by a similar procedure,[3] its adequacy was very different. In West Germany it could reach 50–60 per cent of the average income, while in East Germany it reached only 25–30 per cent. This was not so much a problem in East Germany, because the 'right to work', rooted in the constitution since 1968 (Frerich and Frey, 1993a: 173), in practice implied full employment. Consequently, most social problems became invisible, because alcoholics, ex-prisoners and so on were on the payroll of big firms, even if they didn't come to their workplace regularly. This kept the number of persons in receipt of social assistance very low: in 1989 they numbered only 5,500 in the whole of East Germany (Priller, 1994 3), that is, 0.03 per cent of the population. In the same year in West Germany, 5.8 per cent of the population were in receipt of social assistance (Statistisches Bundesamt, 1991).

After reunification and starting from 1 January 1991, the West German system of social assistance has been extended to the new East German *Länder*. There are, in any case, still some important differences. The most important is the fact that while in the western *Länder* a person in a condition of need has a right to income support, that is, this right could be claimed before a court, in the East German *Länder* this is not possible: the right can be claimed only if the local contextual (and financial) conditions allow it. This restriction has not been limited in its duration, so that the perspectives are, from the point of view of entitlements, not particularly good for the Germans in the new *Länder*.

Further differences are related to the gaps existing between the amounts paid in basic subsidy and for supplementary benefit in the West and in the East. Although the first gap has been reduced from 11 per cent to 4 per cent in four years,[4] the second one is still existing as supplementary benefits are not yet paid in the eastern *Länder*. The situation was worsened by being embedded in the overall retrenching policies of 1994, which restricted the indexation of subsidies to the cost of living, freezing the subsidy to a fixed increase of 2 per cent in 1993–4 and to 3 per cent in 1994–6, while the real cost of living increase was 2–3 per cent higher. Also *ad hoc* economic aid (for example, for clothing) and other integrative supplementary benefits were restricted by making the conditions of access more severe or increasing the age limits. These limitations have been compensated only partially by a massive investment in active labour policies.

The Labour Market in the Two Contexts

As mentioned above, the role played by firms in the two Germanys was very different. In East Germany the firms were the privileged system of social integration. This meant that there was no unemployment, and that an income was guaranteed to all through participation in the labour market. This was true in general, and in particular for women, who had in East Germany a very high activity rate.[5] This was encouraged by a wide range of labour policies which allowed mothers and single parents to combine childcare and work. There was an entitlement to maternity leave (up to one-and-a-half years' paid leave at 65–90 per cent of the net wage), financial support (relatively generous child allowances ranging from 95–215 DM, per month and child) and infrastructural services (kindergarten and other state childcare services open 9–12 hours a day, covering up to 94 per cent of all children).[6] In East Germany the *right to work* was paralleled by an *obligation to work*. Economic incentives also contributed to the high activity rate of women, because for a family an average level of consumption was only possible when both parents went to work.

In West Germany, while there is also a relatively wide range of social policies, covering risky situations (unemployment, conditions of economic need) and a basic distrust in market forces, we have a greater degree of commodification and stigmatization of the conditions of need. The firms follow micro-economic planning without having social policy goals as in the East. It is not by chance that unemployment, as we will see later on, is in West Germany one of the main causes of the condition of need and of dependence on social assistance, while in East Germany there was practically no unemployment. The fact was that in East Germany a firm, in order to lay off a worker, had to find him/her a new job, as his/her right to a job was fundamental. This may have led to lower productivity, less competitiveness and subsidized employment, but the situation was surely also less stigmatizing. In West Germany, although there are restrictions too, if a person has not the required capabilities to re-enter the labour market there is an institutional path downwards and the West German stigma of being unemployed is related to it. Besides its cultural aspects, which we will mention later on, the stigma derives, as in most welfare states where entitlements are connected to the position in the labour market, from the fact that unemployment benefits are limited in time and related to the payment of contributions.[7] This implies that if a person is unemployed for a long time he/she will drift down first to unemployment subsidy[8] and then to social assistance. Both measures are means-tested and undergo the subsidiarity principle. This implies that near relations have to support these persons if they are in a condition of need.

After reunification and the introduction of the western market regulatory mechanisms in the eastern *Länder*, the system of social citizenship based on the firm changed radically. Unemployment increased rapidly (see table 15.1), with a shocking effect on the

Table 15.1 Unemployment rates in Germany (new and old *Länder*) 1990–1994 by sex (year average)

		1990	1991	1992	1993	1994
Eastern *Länder*	Males	6.4[a]	8.5	11.4	11.0	10.9
	Females	8.2[a]	12.3	21.2	21.0	21.5
	Total	7.3[a]	10.1[b]	15.4[b]	15.1[b]	15.2[b]
			10.3	16.1	15.8	16.0
Western *Länder*	Males	6.3	5.8	6.2	8.0	9.2
	Females	8.4	7.0	7.2	8.4	9.2
	Total	6.4[b]	5.7[b]	5.9[b]	7.3[b]	8.2[b]
		7.2	6.3	6.6	8.2	9.2
Germany	Males	–	–[c]	7.1	8.6	9.5
	Females	–	–[c]	10.2	11.3	12.0
	Total	–	–[c]	7.7[b]	8.9[b]	9.6[b]
			8.5	9.8	10.6

Source: Bundesanstalt für Arbeit (1995a, 1995b: 36)
[a]Data for the new *Länder* is available only starting from the second half of 1990.
[b]Unemployment rate calculated as a percentage of the labour force. For all other cases the unemployment rate is calculated as a percentage of all persons in 'dependent' employment, that is, subject to social security contributions.
[c]Unemployment rates for 1991 have not been calculated because of the heterogeneous data base.

Table 15.2   Labour market policy effects on the labour force in the new *Länder* (in thousands and percentages) 1990–1995 (year average)

	1990[a]	1991	1992	1993	1994	1995[b]
(1) Total employment	8035	7182	6359	6208	6299	–
(2) Total persons in labour market measures[c]	1391	1958	1802	1455	1201	1039
(3) 2 as % of potential labour force (1+2)	15	22.5	20.5	16.5	14	12
(4) Shortfall of regular employment[d]	2033	2898	2914	2593	2267	2079
(5) 4 as a % of potential labour force (1+4)	22	34	31	27.5	25.5	24

Source: own calculations on: European Commission (1995: 2)
[a]Second half of the year.
[b]April.
[c]Labour market measures include: (a) job creation measures (ABM); (b) wage-cost subsidies east (§249h AFG), starting from 1993, (c) full-time equivalent of loss of working hours in case of short-time working, (d) full-time further training measures, (e) early retirement.
[d]Shortfall of regular employment includes total unemployed persons and total persons in labour market measures.

population, whose level of employment dropped by more than 40 per cent between 1989 and 1994.[9]

The consequences of this situation have been limited only by strong state investment in active labour market policies (see table 15.2).[10] Budgetary constraints and the short- and medium-term nature of these measures, however, have resulted in a retrenchment of their funding from 1992 onwards, without a corresponding development in job opportunities. This has brought about once again an increase in unemployment, leading to new measures intended to cover an 'extended' period of transition. For instance, paragraph 249h of the Employment Promotion Act introduced the wage cost subsidy for East Germany starting on 1 January 1993 and valid until 31 December 1997. This measure, using funds which would otherwise have been spent on passive measures in the form of unemployment benefit or unemployment subsidy, supports investment in the provision of productive regular employment for those who draw benefits. Particular projects aimed at improving the environment (in 1994, 45.4 per cent of all projects), social services or child and youth welfare (in 1994, 19 per cent) are supported. One of the major points of debate is that the amount paid must not exceed 90 per cent of the local wage for comparable work and that these measures are creating a secondary labour market which bears the risk of wage dumping.[11]

PATTERNS OF INEQUALITY AND POVERTY IN GERMANY

The previous paragraphs concentrated on the institutional mechanisms and, therefore, lack two important aspects:

1 the extent of poverty in Germany (East and West);
2 the spatial patterns of inequality and poverty in Germany.

(1)   The debate on the measurement of poverty in terms of income deprivation is complex (Krause, 1993, 1994; Leibfried et al., 1995, Øyen, 1992, Mingione herein). In any case their use depends upon the purpose of the research design. To measure the diffusion of poverty on a federal level, researchers normally use data from the socio-economic panel which has existed in West Germany since 1984 (first wave) and was extended to the eastern *Länder* in 1990. According to this data, in West Germany nearly 12 per cent of the population in the mid-1980s had an income below the 50 per cent threshold. The tendency was for a slightly decreasing poverty rate until 1992 (10 per cent). Most affected groups were immigrants, who, along with single mothers, were over-represented among the poor.

In East Germany before reunification there was officially no poverty, but the work-centredness of social policies and the concentration of the entitlements to benefits towards those in employment put non-working groups in a particularly disadvantaged position: pensioners, disabled, that is, groups not, or no longer, active, with below average incomes and marked disadvantages in some areas of provision (Priller, 1994). According to the estimates of Günter Manz (1992: 88), in 1988 about 10 per cent of the East German population lived in a condition of poverty, with a particular concentration among the elderly: 45 per cent of all retired people lived in a condition of poverty. As we will see, the social policies based on the general availability of basic (subsidized) goods did succeed in avoiding social exclusion only at a low level of provision (Leibfried et al., 1995).

After reunification income-related poverty slightly increased in the western *Länder*, while, after an immediate and rapid increase, it decreased in the eastern ones, particularly when we use the West German threshold (see table 15.3). When we use the East German threshold, that is, the average household income in the eastern *Länder*, poverty increases. Misleading at a first glance, this is explained by the fact that East German incomes are lower than West German ones, but are growing faster, constantly reducing the gap (Leibfried et al., 1995: 259; Hanesch et al., 1994: 138–9).

In order to measure poverty on a local level researchers usually use social assistance data. This entails some problems, which change according to the purpose for which the data are used. If we use them to count the poor, we will

Table 15.3   People living below the 50 per cent income threshold in Germany (East and West), 1990–1994 (percentage of the population)

	1990	1991	1992	1993	1994
Germany	14.0	12.2	11.5	12.1	11.6
Western *Länder*[a]	10.5	10.0	10.0	11.1	11.1
Eastern *Länder*[a]	26.7	20.5	17.8	16.0	13.8
Eastern *Länder*[b]	3.5	4.3	6.0	6.3	7.9

Source: Krause (1993: 31), table 23; (1994: 18 and following), tables 10, 11. Socio-economic Panel, Leibfried et al. (1995)
[a]50% threshold of the West German income.
[b]50% threshold of the East German income.

get only the persons entitled to the subsidy and not the poor *tout court*. Moreover an increase of the threshold will, paradoxically, increase more than proportionally the number of the poor and, vice versa, a low threshold will lower the entitled more than proportionally.[12] As our purpose is to analyse how the institutional set-up copes with the ongoing transformation processes, the use of social assistance data is to be considered adequate and one of the very few sources at the municipal level. Table 15.4 shows the different tendencies in social assistance dependency (HLU) at the moment of reunification and after two years both in old and new *Länder*. The East–West convergence of the dependency rates is very clear and confirms the institutional prestructuring of the downward path of social exclusion.

(2)   The different socio-economic and institutional contexts in the two parts of Germany resulted in different territorial outcomes. In eastern Germany the social homogeneity corresponded to a relative territorial homogeneity in terms of per-capita income and per-capita product before reunification. In western Germany, on the contrary, there was (and still is) a south–north drift, both in terms of income distribution and unemployment patterns. Regions and cities in the south, with their more competitive firms and more innovative industrial systems, have lower unemployment rates and higher incomes.[13] Nevertheless, different researchers (for example, Krämer-Badoni and Ruhstrat, 1986) show that higher incomes in southern cities are counterbalanced by many factors which lead to higher living costs in these cities. In Stuttgart and Munich, for example, a person has to pay higher rents than in Bremen or Dortmund. Although this drift does not necessarily affect the standard of living in northern and southern Germany, revealing an unexpected success of the redistribution mechanisms, it surely contributes to differentiate the distribution of the risks of impoverishment and the quota of people who depend on social assistance. Krug and Rehm (1986; Krug, 1987) partially confirm this view, but show that the influence of the economic performance is embedded in a wider cultural dimension which shapes attitudes both towards work and social assistance. The importance of non-economic factors is underlined also

Table 15.4 Persons depending upon social assistance (HLU) as a percentage of the resident population, western and eastern *Länder*, 1990–1992

	1990	*1992*	*Δ1990–1992*
Western *Länder*	6.6[a]	6.8[a]	+0.2[a]
Schleswig-Holstein	6.4	6.6	+0.2
Hamburg[b]	11.1	10.7	−0.4
Niedersachsen	6.4	7.0	+0.6
Bremen[b]	9.8	9.2	−0.6
Nordrhein-Westphalen	7.2	7.1	−0.1
Hessen	5.7	6.3	+0.6
Rheinland-Pfalz	4.7	5.1	+0.4
Baden-Württemberg	4.1	4.8	+0.7
Bayern	4.0	4.2	+0.2
Saarland	6.8	7.4	+0.6
Berlin (west)	10.6	8.2[c]	
Eastern *Länder*	0.9[a]	4.4[a]	3.5[a]
Berlin (east)	1.3		
Brandenburg	0.9	5.6	+4.7
Mecklenburg-Vorpommern	1.1	4.6	+3.5
Sachsen	0.5	3.2	+2.7
Sachsen-Anhalt	1.0	4.8	3.8
Thüringen	0.6	3.8	3.2

Source: own calculations on Statistisches Bundesamt (1992a, 1992b) tables 1.4., 1.2. and 8.2. (1994) table 17.2
[a]Without Berlin.
[b]City-states.
[c]Berlin west and east.

by the fact that the regional distribution of unemployment is explained in Germany by economic factors in only 60–65 per cent of cases (Klemmer, 1988: 17). Also the correlation between unemployment and social assistance dependency, although existing, explains only 58 per cent of long-term unemployment (Hotz, 1987: 598). This is also confirmed by more recent research (Grüske, Lohmeyer and Miegel, 1990; Miegel, Grünewald and Grüske, 1991) which points out the importance of the cultural dimension in understanding economic behaviour and the stigma affecting the condition of being unemployed in southern regions. In the cities the influence is not so strong as in the countryside, but the south–north drift is confirmed also at this level. In northern regions and cities the unemployed feel socially more accepted and no blame is attached to being unemployed.

The two cities we present in this section can be taken as examples of the ongoing processes of transformation impacting Germany. Stuttgart is an example of the affluent south which is facing an unexpected structural crisis and Berlin is an example of the ambivalence of German reunification.

Stuttgart

Stuttgart is in the middle of one of the richest regions of the world, highly industrialized and with a very differentiated productive structure based on high-tech goods.[14] This situation is reflected in the fact that among the big West German cities Stuttgart has one of the lowest concentrations of poverty in terms of *Sozialhilfe* recipients in the population. In 1992 there were 35,712 persons dependent on social assistance and getting Hilfe zum Lebensunterhalt (HLU), with 6 per cent of the resident population receiving social assistance at an annual cost of 222 million DM in 1993. However, as we have seen before, economic success is not the only explanation of why poverty rates are low. To take a broader view of these low rates, we have to consider the regional context in which Stuttgart is embedded: Baden-Württemberg, a *Land* where three features play an important role:

1   The hidden poverty of the elderly. This aspect is related to their sense of shame and lack of information and characterizes more the regional level than the urban context, but it is still important in order to understand the overall cultural climate.[15] The institutional mechanisms also play an important role, because the shame of the elderly is connected to, and activated by, the subsidiarity principle upon which the German system of social security is built. According to this principle the state intervenes only when 'lower' social institutions, in this case the sheltering capacities of the family, are no longer effective in preventing conditions of need. The elderly usually do not want to be a burden upon their children, and for this reason they do not apply for social assistance as doing so would imply a check being made of their financial capacities.

2   The hidden poverty of part of the immigrants. This aspect, typical for regions and cities with a high quota of foreigners in the resident population,[16] is related to a differentiated citizenship status on one hand, and to the different access to social network resources on the other. Marissen has shown (1989) that immigrants from different countries, both from EU and non-EU *Gastarbeiternationen*[17] (guest-worker nations), often do not apply for social assistance because they are afraid of being expelled. Moreover he has shown that the different access to primary social networks influences the foreigners' social assistance dependency rate more than the German rate. In Stuttgart, for instance, Greek and Spanish people, living mostly in families with children, show much lower rates than Turks or Italians, who often live alone.

3   The cultural embeddedness of an individualistic and work-centred

Weltanschauung. This third aspect is more difficult to deal with, although several researchers are trying to investigate its historically rooted influence and dimension. The diffusion in Württemberg, and especially in the Stuttgart area, of pietism, a faction of Protestantism in the seventeenth century, is seen, for example, as particularly important (Scharfe, 1977; Trautwein, 1984; Boelke, 1989; Borst, 1992; Wehling, 1991). Pietism considered efficiency and economic success as signs of divine grace, and work was no longer a punishment as in the Old Testament, but a way to participate in the creation. This view was strongly connected to the belief in individual responsibility, according to which the single person had to justify his/her own destiny before God without hiding him/herself behind collective bodies (Trautwein, 1984). Pietism underlined the importance of education and individual action as the basis for trust, faith and the work ethos, which was characterized by the motto: 'Everybody, given his/her will, can multiply their own properties through diligence, industry, loyalty and initiative.' In this view poverty was not chance but a matter of guilt, and the poor were considered mostly undeserving for their lack of initiative and will. This basic attitude towards work and poverty was embedded in a context of pervading social control deriving from the socialization of the practices of the *Kirchenkonvente* (1644–1891) over many centuries. Instituted at the beginning as an instrument of moral rigour they soon became an instrument of pervasive social control of every aspect of daily life.[18]

These three aspects, which are strongly interconnected, contribute to lower the poverty rates through cultural obstacles to social assistance dependency, on one hand, and fostering entrepreneurship and individual problem-solving strategies on the other. If their influence is particularly evident for Baden-Württemberg, it is also undeniable that the modernization process did not radically change the traditional characteristics of the local cultures.[19] On the contrary it exalted them partially in the new forms of production which required *dicto puncto*, flexibility, individual initiative and entrepreneurship. It is also for these very reasons that the economic crisis of the 1970s and the 1980s affected Stuttgart and Baden-Württemberg proportionally less compared to other urban and regional contexts in Germany.[20] Nevertheless, the changes in the economic structure and in the labour market were part of the cause of social assistance dependence also in Stuttgart. In order to understand how these trends impacted the profile of the socially assisted, we have to consider in particular the increase of unemployment and of migration flows during the last 15 years. The available data on the principal causes of social assistance dependency reflect clearly these two processes.

Figure 15.1 shows how unemployment has become the main cause of the condition of need and social assistance dependency, being also

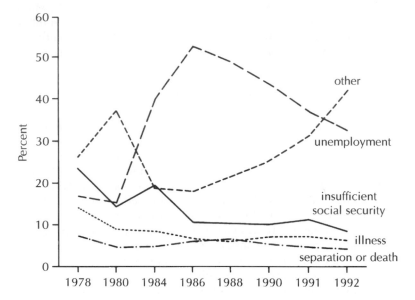

Figure 15.1   Households dependent on social assistance (HLU) in Stuttgart, according to the main cause of the condition of need (*calculations on data from Statistisches Landesamt Baden-Würtemberg, Statistische Berichte KI j78–92*)

the cause of the marked increase in the number of social assistance recipients from 1978 up to the end of the 1980s.[21] This trend is more (in the north) or less (in the south) common to all German cities and characterized the German debate on the 'new poverty'.[22] Only in the second half of the 1980s did its incidence decrease *vis-à-vis* an increase of 'other' causes. At first this could seem misleading and confusing, as in absolute terms unemployment continued to increase till 1990 as a cause of dependency, although the unemployment rate decreased constantly from 1983 (5.6 per cent) to 1991 (3.7 per cent). To understand the data we have to consider two important aspects. A first aspect is connected to the fact that long-term unemployment increased till 1991. The consequence was that many people, whose right to unemployment benefits ended after two years, drifted down to social assistance. These are mainly 40–45-year-old males, unskilled with very poor chances of re-entering the labour market. A second aspect is the fact that the term 'other' includes, especially from the mid 1980s, asylum seekers and other foreigners; it is their increase[23] in the last decade that lowered the incidence of unemployment which still remained the main cause of the condition of need till the early 1990s.

These two processes, that is, the unemployment and the immigration increase, determined both a change in the socio-demographic profiles of the welfare recipients on one hand and a revitalized debate on social policy issues on the other (Hauser and Hübinger, 1993; Leibfried et al., 1995 are the most recent significant examples). From a socio-demographic point of view the main effects have been the lowering of recipients' age and a more balanced gender composition. In fact, while in the 1970s elderly females living alone were the largest group, at the beginning of the 1990s we have a majority of males, mainly singles concentrated in the cohort 25–49. In Stuttgart in 1973 females comprised 62 per cent of the *Sozialhilfe* (HLU) recipients; over 50 per cent of them over 50 years old. However, in 1991 over 51 per cent of the recipients were male, with 43 per cent in the age range 25–49.[24] To these weak groups we have to add single mothers with children. This group, typically at risk in all welfare systems based on occupational entitlements, is in absolute terms less numerous than that of single persons. This is true for the urban context of Stuttgart, whereas for the regional context it is other way around.[25] In both cases the importance of the family in facing the conditions of need is underlined by the fact that persons within a household are under-represented among benefit recipients.

To sum up, the groups with a higher incidence among the benefit recipients are (in decreasing order of importance):

1 single unemployed males, German, middle-aged, sometimes homeless;
2 young male recent asylum seekers;
3 single old women with a weak reciprocity network or with none;
4 single mothers with children;
5 young couples with children where both adults are unemployed.[26]

Although each group has a different relation to the citizenship system and needs different solutions and projects of social reinsertion, there is no significant spatial concentration of cumulative conditions of need. Map 15.1 shows the distribution of persons receiving social assistance (HLU) weighted on the resident population. The levels are very low even where they reach their highest values: downtown, in the valley, and in the northern and eastern industrialized periphery along the River Necker. All other areas, mostly on the slopes of the surrounding hills are affluent or mixed areas: the few exceptions to this picture are small social housing quarters. These quarters (2–7 in the map) have a higher concentration of unemployed (in 1987 about 5.5–15 per cent) and single-mothers (in 1987 about 20–28 per cent of the households with children below 18 years of age), but are not particularly significant in terms of poverty concentration if compared

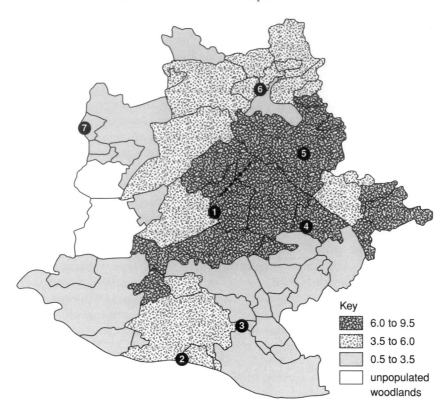

Key

6.0 to 9.5

3.5 to 6.0

0.5 to 3.5

unpopulated
woodlands

Map 15.1 Stuttgart: social-assistance-dependent (HLU) persons as a
percentage of the resident population, 1992 *(calculations on unpublished
data from Amtsstatistik 1992, Einwohnerzahlen und Sozialhilfeempfaenger, and
estimates on fieldwork carried out by the author and data from census (1987)
and Marissen and Mueller, 1990)*

to other case studies in the United States or the United Kingdom (see
Logan, Alba and McNulty, Marcuse and Morris herein).

This does not deny the existence of quarters with more problems
than others, but as in Berlin or in Milan (see Zajczyk herein), the
problems do not reach a significant level of social alarm.

Stuttgart is a city where we can find the typical side effects of
economic success: high living costs and a particularly overheated
housing market with high rents (the highest in Germany after
Munich). To this situation must be added the lowest rate of social
housing in Germany (after Karlsruhe): only 14 per cent of the whole
housing stock (Amt für Wohnungswesen, 1992). These aspects

contribute to the marginalization of, in addition to the above mentioned groups, new households, that is, young couples and recent immigrants with low incomes.

The high costs of the location (rents, infrastructure, labour costs) could be afforded by firms because of their positive performance. The overall change in the structure of international markets and the generalized shortening of the life cycle of products are challenging this situation. The necessity to rationalize and restructure constantly, mainly at a technological and organizational level, has considerable effects on the structure of employment both in terms of quantity and quality, and the high exchange rate of the German mark poses serious problems to the export orientation of the area. Also the deep structural crisis that has affected sectors like machinery, electronics, chemicals and particularly the automobile industry, which form the industrial core of Stuttgart, threatens the ability to maintain the traditionally high occupational levels. In 1993–4 the Stuttgart region had a shortfall in the number of incoming orders of nearly 40 per cent. The greatest danger in this situation is the possible relocation of firms outside of the area and a potential over-dependence upon the automobile industry. The consequences for the employment structure and on the labour market are evident: a less differentiated occupational structure, from the point of view of the qualifications required, is more vulnerable and dependent upon the fluctuations of the market. First signs of recession are recognizable – unemployment has increased more than proportionally compared to other German cities and regions. The effects of long-term unemployment, however, will be apparent in 1996 when the end of the institutionally prestructured downward path will have been reached: from unemployment benefit, through unemployment subsidy to social assistance. These emerging difficulties together with the high cost of living are a dangerous mix within a context where the life conditions of the poor are framed with a high degree of stigmatization. The poor may be fewer than elsewhere in Germany, but their condition is probably worse.

Poverty in East and West Berlin after Reunification

To analyse the changing poverty patterns in Berlin we have to face two important aspects which were not present in the context of Stuttgart:

1 Before reunification West Berlin had a special status in the history of German urban development. Both economic development and financing of public expenditure were subject to specific regulations. Industry was subsidized more than proportionally so that there was a higher quota of

unskilled workers compared to other German cities. Public expenditure
was independent from the trends of the local economic system, as more
than 50 per cent of the municipal budget was allocated by the federal
government.
2   Berlin was a divided city, both from the social and from the economic
point of view. Besides the influence of the different socio-economic
systems, the different welfare systems, lasting for over 40 years, had a deep
and pervasive influence which continues to affect the social morphology of
poverty in the two parts of the city.

These two aspects are framing and determining the trends of
growing poverty after reunification. In order to show this tendency, we
will refer to: (1) the increasing unemployment; (2) the housing supply;
(3) the trends amongst social assistance recipients.

(1)   Presently, there is no noticeable difference between East and West
Berlin's unemployment rate. During the month of October 1993, 12.4 per cent
of the labour force in West Berlin and 13.1 per cent in East Berlin were
unemployed. Regarding the enormous loss of jobs in East Berlin in 1990, the
relatively low unemployment rate can be explained by the high participation
in employment measures. In East Berlin about 34,400 persons were
'retrained' and 52,200 persons were given early retirement. More people were
registered as participating in employment measure programmes (about
86,000) than those registered as unemployed (about 80,000). Hence,
unemployment in East Berlin would be twice as high if no *ad hoc* labour
market policies were being offered.

In comparison, in West Berlin 122,000 persons were unemployed and only
11,000 persons participated in labour market programmes. Since German
reunification unemployment in West Berlin has grown faster than in East
Berlin and has caused an increase of competition on the labour market. Fewer
jobs than applicants and about 15,000 people who are willing to commute from
East to West Berlin reflect this situation. In West Berlin the unemployment rate
has increased among foreign workers, who have been replaced by skilled East
German workers. Between 1989 and 1993 the unemployment rate for foreign
workers almost doubled, whereas it only increased by a third among the German
population. We will later reflect on the question of whether foreign workers will
become a part of the new urban underclass.

(2)   Both halves of the city show clear social differences in respect to housing.
The system of state-run housing in the GDR did not use income as a deciding
factor in the distribution of housing, and apartments were allocated by the
local administration on the basis of need: one person, one room, even children
were considered as one person. Since income was not as differentiated as in
West Germany, segregation by income did not exist. However, the socialist
housing system did acknowledge status by selectively distributing attractive,
large apartments as a way of favouring certain citizens, such as doctors,
artists, political officials and managers. Other social groups that were not
particularly important to the system or who had been disloyal to the state

were supposed to be punished by receiving less desirable apartments, which were located in run-down pre-Second World War buildings, the interiors reminiscent of the nineteenth century.[27] Low-income households who continued to live in such apartments after reunification are now at risk of being greatly disadvantaged in two ways. First, with the introduction of the free market and private property, they will have no chance of improving their living/housing conditions. Secondly, if buildings are renovated, households are then faced with higher rents and gentrification. The worsening of their housing condition, however, is related to the fact that low-income households are either unaware of the housing laws or do not contact the department of social assistance. It is this difficulty in dealing with the new welfare mechanisms which explains to some extent the increase of homelessness, a phenomenon which was previously unknown in East Germany.

In 1994, 1,700 people were registered as homeless in East Berlin, but the real number is probably twice as high. East Germans have not yet fully understood the effects of private property ownership. In the socialist system no negative consequences followed if a person did not pay his/her rent; the housing authorities would contact his/her employer who, in turn, would subtract the outstanding *minimum* rent from the tenant's wage. An eviction without an alternative solution was impossible. Today, if tenants are unable to pay the still state-regulated prices (till the end of 1995), they can apply for a housing allowance or social assistance. Hence, in theory, no tenant would have to leave his/her apartment, and in the case of an eviction the Social Assistance Office would have to provide alternative housing. So far this system seems to work because at present the government still has access to the former state-run housing supply.[28] However, due to privatization and a continuous decrease of the housing supply this will change in the near future. Since East Germans are not aware of the negative consequences not paying their rent and not answering payment reminders, the housing administration finally takes the last step and asks the court for an eviction order. In January 1993, about 57,600 East Berlin households did not pay their rents; this figure corresponds to about 8 per cent of all tenant households. From January 1993 up to March 1994, 2,317 evictions had taken place.

Since 1989 homelessness has drastically increased in West Berlin also. It increased by 5 per cent between 1989 and 1994, that is from 6,000 to 12,000 persons. The main cause for this rapid increase is unemployment: after the loss of job and the consequent decrease in income, many households are helpless, often too embarrassed to go to the social assistance office and, finally, are unable to pay their rent on a regular basis. They fall into a spiral of increasing debts, and lose all control over their daily lives. The result of this downward path is that they end up among the group of the poor.

(3) At the end of 1991, social assistance recipients comprised 7.8 per cent in West Berlin and 3.9 per cent in East Berlin. Unemployment was the main cause for 37.7 per cent of West Berlin social assistance recipients and 31.1 per cent of East Berlin social assistance recipients. In West Berlin 12.7 per cent of them were senior citizens; in East Berlin, only 3 per cent. The elderly in the

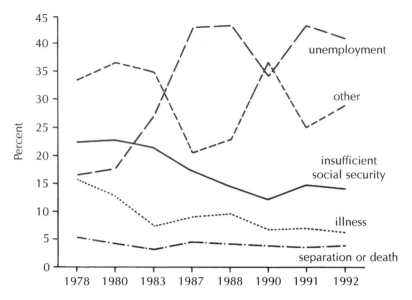

Figure 15.2   Households dependent on social assistance in Berlin, according to the main cause of the condition of need (*calculations on data from Berliner Statistik, Statistiscche Berichte KI j/78–92*)

East count themselves as the *winners* of German reunification; poverty among them is not at present very noticeable.

In the near future there is a large chance of growing poverty since many of the unemployed have been out of work for a long period of time. For this reason, as we have seen before, if they are unable to find a new job, they will receive unemployment subsidy instead of unemployment benefit. This will be supplemented by social assistance if its amount is lower than the social assistance threshold. At the same time the number of persons participating in employment measures programmes will decrease. However, a massive increase of jobs is not to be expected in the near future. Hence, unemployment and particularly long-term unemployment will continue to grow. In the long run unemployment affects retirement benefits, because the benefits are determined by the duration of employment and by the amount of income. Irregular employment leads to low benefit entitlement, and thus poverty among the elderly is expected to increase again in the long run.

Is there an urban underclass in Berlin?   Even though the number of poor has been increasing it is questionable whether an urban underclass is developing. The urban underclass is by definition dependent on spatial structural conditions. Generally, with the increase of households that are affected by poverty, the concentration of the poor in the cities has also increased. Due to cumulating social problems, a few areas, particularly located in large cities, are faced with urban blight. The *Deutsche Städtetag*[29] has identified these areas as 'socially troubled areas' (*soziale Brennpunkte*): 'Socially troubled areas are housing quarters in which certain negative factors influence the life chances of tenants, especially those of children, and occur on a regular basis' (Deutscher Städtetag, 1979: 12). The term 'socially troubled areas' not only refers to the concentration of socially disadvantaged groups, but also to the disadvantages that are caused by the housing quarters themselves. This does correspond with the category of the urban underclass. The general question of the extent to which housing quarters impact the life chances of an individual need not necessarily be seen in negative terms. A spatial concentration of homogeneous social groups forms a *milieu* (see Herlyn, Lakemann and Lettko, 1991). *Milieu* terminology does not define how far the influence of a housing quarter in respect to the social position of inhabitants has positive or negative effects. Herlyn's study in Hannover shows that the concentration of socially disadvantaged groups as an independent factor does not explain much about life chances. *Milieus* can have numerous qualities, and also provide specific resources, such as information, informal economy, social ties, etc. We refer to an urban underclass when marginal groups, that is, groups of persons who are faced with a multiple lack of resources, are segregated in specific areas and when this causes an additional disadvantage. Additional disadvantages develop if certain residential areas are stigmatized and this, in effect, negatively affects the inhabitants' opportunities on the labour market, for example, if people are no longer able to reach their places of work due to poor infrastructure (see: Wilson, 1987, 1991 and Marcuse, Wacquant herein). Another disadvantage is that segregation hinders opportunities for 'informal' improvement, for example by taking on odd jobs. Also, segregation can mean severance of information channels through which otherwise an individual could improve his/her housing situation by using personal ties. Finally, in all cases spatial segregation intensifies social marginalization.

Although Berlin shows a higher concentration of people dependent upon social assistance than Stuttgart, in comparison to other German cities, we can find only a slight tendency towards segregation. However, clear signs of segregation can be seen among foreign households; neither the unemployed, nor households with a minimum income or in receipt of welfare benefits, are as spatially concentrated as the foreigners are. We will therefore focus on the spatial concentration of foreigners because it is this group that is mostly disadvantaged in respect to housing and the labour market. Foreigners are usually portrayed as

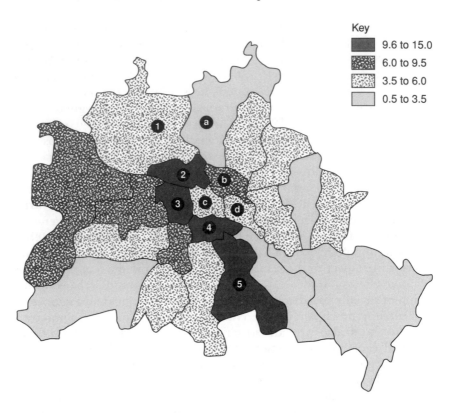

Key
- 9.6 to 15.0
- 6.0 to 9.5
- 3.5 to 6.0
- 0.5 to 3.5

Map 15.2   Berlin: social-assistance-dependent (HLU) persons as a percentage of
the resident population, 1992 (*Sozialhilfe in Berlin 1992, Berliner Statistik,
Statistishe Berichte KI 1-j92*)

unqualified workers, even if they are in possession of a degree because
their degrees are not accepted in Germany. Up to 1990, hardly any
foreigners lived in East Berlin. Because of the absence of freedom of
movement only contract workers from Vietnam and Africa lived in
East Berlin. These contract workers had little contact with the local
population since they were housed in separate dormitories.

During the early 1990s, West Berlin's districts showed the same
spatial concentration of foreigners as had already been established in
the 1980s (for example, Kreuzberg (4 on the map), which is one of the
areas with the highest concentration of social assistance recipients after
Tiergarten (3)). During this period, processes of spatial segregation
became apparent. During the 1970s foreigners were pushed into inner
city areas which had been declared 'urban renewal' zones, peripheral to
West Berlin's central areas (1–5) during the time of the Wall. Now these

districts (2–4) have become the central areas of the unified city and are expected to become gentrified in the long run. In these areas the buildings had been neglected due to scheduled upgrading and renewal. During the following years though, urban planning policy changed from urban renewal to 'careful' upgrading. The city's policy focused now on upgrading rather than removing entire buildings and city blocks. 'Careful' upgrading refers to raising housing and social standards without displacing the inhabitants. Some foreign households have benefited from this improvement.

Since the late 1980s and the early 1990s the housing situation has taken on the following characteristics: foreigners live in West Berlin, particularly in pre-Second World War buildings. In 1993, 16 per cent of the population of West Berlin were foreigners, and in inner city areas, up to 30 per cent of residents were foreign, mostly living in pre-Second World War buildings near the Wall. This concentration was mostly made up of Turkish households.

Foreign households have less living space at their disposal than German households. On average, foreign households (tenants) in West Berlin have 22 square metres per person, whereas German households have 38 square metres (Tuchscherer, 1993). Foreign households live in more poorly equipped apartments than Germans do; 17.1 per cent are not equipped with a shower (Germans: 3.9 per cent) or with a bath and 4 per cent have no toilet in their apartment (Germans: 0.9 per cent). Furthermore, 53.3 per cent of foreign households (Germans: 30 per cent) are situated in pre-Second World War buildings and are less represented (30 per cent of the Turkish households) among social housing than German households (42 per cent).

Poor living conditions and overcrowding are a burden for foreign households. These conditions are not a result of free choice, as is often argued. On the contrary, foreign households are willing to pay higher rents for better housing. Their housing situation is rather a result of discrimination on the housing market. The example of Turkish families demonstrates this. Turks are dependent on ethnic ties when trying to find an apartment; this is usually done through friends and family members. Also, professional Turkish businesses, such as translating, travel and insurance agencies are a part of this network. Foreigners, especially Turks, have hardly any access to safe, decent housing. Even co-operative housing is hard to access, but none the less, many Turkish households still put their names down. Although the city government has demanded that the public co-operative housing authorities should raise the foreign quota to the general average level, Turkish households are still being discriminated against

(Kapphan, 1994). The share of the foreign population living in social housing is clearly below the percentage of foreigners in the population as a whole.

Although foreigners are discriminated against and segregated, one cannot automatically assume that segregation is strictly a disadvantage. Rather, the example of Turkish families shows that spatial proximity can also provide a resource, such as easy access to social ties and also to Turkish stores and restaurants. Many Turks view the ethnic concentration in their housing quarters generally as an advantage, that is, they are in favour of not having to live among only Germans (Kapphan, 1994).

The recent changes in urban development may cause a growing problem regarding the housing situation for foreigners, and hence this group could possibly become the core of an urban underclass. Especially, the economic situation has changed due to de-industrialization and growing competition in the labour market with East Berlin's cheap labour force. This is shown by the high unemployment rate among foreigners, and as the decline in manufacturing and low-paying jobs is expected to continue, the situation will worsen. Also, the restructuring of Berlin as Germany's new capital is going to increase the demand for labour in the larger service sector, but foreigners are hardly qualified for these jobs and an improvement in their situation cannot be expected.

At the same time, residential areas that are located near the Wall, which used to form the fringe of the city, have now become inner city neighbourhoods. They have been turned into areas of gentrification, from which foreigners and marginal groups are being pushed out. Due to the deregulation of the housing market, affordable housing and public-administered housing will diminish, and then affordable housing might only be found in the new housing estates located on the fringes of East and West Berlin.

During a time in which the share of the foreign population is growing, the opportunities in the housing market and in the labour market are diminishing. Three trends are decisive in predicting the socio-spatial structuration of the future: (a) less regulation, more market-led distribution of housing provision; (b) loss of unskilled jobs in the manufacturing sector, growth of insecure, short-term, badly paid jobs in the service sector, (c) growth of population only among immigrants. These trends point toward a less accessible labour market, decreasing housing availability for low-income households and spatial concentration in certain urban areas increasingly contributing to the shaping of an urban underclass.

In conclusion, the following developments could lead to the formation of an urban underclass:

1 The continuing high unemployment rate leads to the exclusion of certain groups that in the long run would not have access to the (primary) labour market; this especially concerns problem groups, such as people without qualifications, people over 45 years of age, those in poor health and the long-term unemployed.

2 Urban policies are oriented towards international competition and neglect measures to prevent the formation of socially troubled areas.

3 Immigration of asylum seekers and refugees is going to increase. Due to specific regulations regarding their legal status, social and spatial integration is going to be difficult, if not impossible.

4 The situation for low-income groups in the housing market is going to deteriorate and a growing concentration of foreigners, particular refugees and asylum seekers, will be found in certain areas (1 to 4).

CONCLUSION

The structure of poverty in Germany has many profiles, depending on regional differences in economic performance, on fundamental chances of the welfare system in East Germany, and on labour market policies. However, the profiles of poverty for the two cities we have presented here are basically similar. Only the degree of poverty is different, although in both cities poverty (in terms of receipt of social assistance) is increasing.

One striking difference, as shown partially also by the maps, is the potential spatial concentration/segregation of poverty: in Stuttgart relatively small pockets of poverty are developing, whereas in Berlin there are indications of an emerging pattern of concentration due to the relative size of unemployment and the crisis of the public budget. Up to now it is still not clear to what extent this is caused by the special situation of transformation, but all signs of economic and demographic change point towards growing social polarization in Berlin, whereas in Stuttgart it is less apparent.

NOTES

1 Bismarck's social reform bills based the entitlement to benefit on the claimant's position in the labour market, that is, on past contributions and earnings. The adoption of particular schemes against sickness (1883), industrial accidents (1884) and invalidity or old age (1889) implied, therefore, a strong work-relatedness of social policies. The schemes, made compulsory by law, were financed by the insured, the employer and the state; see Alber (1986). For the history of social assistance in East and West Germany after the Second World War, see Frerich and Frey, respectively 1993a and 1993b.

2   The debate on this point developed particularly in western Germany where it has been used politically in a very misleading way; in fact what has to be asked is whether the minimum wage is sufficient or not, instead of arguing that the subsidy is too high.

3   To determine the amount of the subsidy in West Germany the social worker has to sum: (a) a basic amount which should enable the person to cover all 'fixed' basic needs; (b) all supplementary benefits – 20–30 per cent of (a) – paid for particular needs of single parents, the elderly, etc.; (c) all 'variable' costs, like rent and heating. The sum of a+b+c constitutes the threshold according to which the subsidy is still determined. With an income equal to zero, the whole amount is paid. In East Germany the procedure was similar, although there were more restrictions. Practically, the subsidy was envisaged to support those who were not able to work, that is, the elderly with insufficient pension, women with children below three years of age, etc.

4   In 1994 the basic subsidy corresponded to 519 DM in the western *Länder* and 505 DM in the eastern *Länder*.

5   In 1992 in the eastern *Länder* the activity rate (that is, the labour force as a percentage of the population aged between 15 and 65) was 81.6 per cent against 70.5 per cent in western *Länder*. This difference was largely due to women's activity rate, which was 74.8 per cent against 59.5 per cent. Men's activity rate, on the other hand, was higher in the western *Länder* (82.2 per cent against 80.2 per cent). In any case, the trend in the eastern *Länder* is of a decreasing activity rate, due to higher educational participation, to the increase in early retirement and to women quitting the labour market.

6   For details see Gutachten des wissenschaftlichen Beirats für Familienfragen (1992); for an overview see Hanesch et al. (1994: 90–6).

7   In order to claim unemployment benefit, a person has to have at least 180 days of contribution. In this case, if he/she is under 42, he/she is entitled to claim benefit for up to 312 days. The maximum duration of the claim depends on both the previous periods of employment and the unemployed person's age. The maximum duration is 832 days for persons over 54 years of age. The benefit is payable at 60 per cent of the wage (67 per cent in case of a worker with at least one child).

8   Unemployment subsidy, unlike unemployment benefit, is mostly granted for an unlimited period, until the claimant reaches the age of 66, assuming the condition of need persists. The amount corresponds to 57 per cent of the wage for workers with at least one child (53 per cent for others). The strong relation with social assistance derives from the fact that usually the amount is below the social assistance threshold, so that the person has to integrate the first amount with the difference up to the threshold.

9   In eastern Germany in the first half of 1989, 93 per cent of the population of working age were employed (9.9 million persons); in the first half of 1994, only 57 per cent were employed (6.1 million), some of them (about 5 per cent) commuting to the western *Länder*.

10 In 1993 the Federal Employment Service (BA, Bundesanstalt für Arbeit) invested in general job creation measures (ABM, *Arbeitsbeschaffungsmaßnahmen*) in the new *Länder* nearly 75 per cent of the 12 billion DM budget foreseen for ABM for all Germany. Considering all measures the new *Länder* absorbed more than half of the BA's total budget (62 billion DM).

11 The number of supported workers according to paragraph 249h increased to over 100,000 by August 1994, 20 months after its inception. For the debate on this point see Bergmann et al. (1993); for a synthesis, Hanesch et al. (1994). For data see Bach, Jung-Hammon and Otto, (1994). The measure is similar to the *lavori di pubblica utilità* in Italy. The great difference with the German measures is that in Germany contributions to the social security system (for pensions, unemployment benefits, health) are paid, while in Italy they are not (except for pensions to some extent). In Italy the scheme lasts for 12 months and has involved 70,000 unemployed up to September 1995.

12 For the debate see Hanesch, 1990; Döring, Hanesch and Huster, 1990; Øyen, 1992; Sen, 1981 and 1992; Leibfried et al., 1995; see also Mingione herein.

13 For a description of the south–north drift debate see Friedrichs, Häussermann and Siebel (1986); for Baden-Württemberg see Kunz (1986).

14 In 1991 in Stuttgart (in 1993; 575,756 inhabitants) the gross national per capita product was nearly 70,000 DM (the second in Germany after Frankfurt-on-Main) and more than 34 per cent of the work-force was occupied in the manufacturing sector in the city and 46 per cent in the metropolitan area.

15 Hartmann (1981) found out that hidden poverty could reach the ratio of 1:1 and is widespread particularly among the elderly and in southern regions. This implies that the potential number of persons entitled to social assistance is double. In more recent research the ratio seems to have changed to 1:0.75 or 1:0.5 (Krause, 1993).

16 Baden-Württemberg is the *Land* with the highest rate of resident foreigners (in 1993 over 10 per cent); Stuttgart is, after Frankfurt-on-Main (in 1993, 28.3 per cent), the city with the highest rate of resident foreigners (in 1993, 23.7 per cent).

17 Usually it is not citizenship which determines the right to social assistance, but the conditions of need. A foreigner has to have a residence permit, but this is not so important for the social worker as for the bureaucrats working on the administrative aspects of the subsidy. Asylum seekers and refugees have a special status, but still receive social assistance; since 1993 the matter is newly regulated through separate, and slightly lower, subsidies.

18 Each month the population of the town, or of the quarter, met in the church and, under guidance of the priest, gave publicity to the infringements of individuals, blaming them in front of the congregation.

For a description of the role of the *Kirchenkonvente* see Schnabel-Schüle (1990) and Wehling (1991).

19   According to Krug and Rehm (1986) the dispersion of social assistance dependency rates around the respective regional mean has its highest values in Baden-Württemberg. This means that the gap between city and countryside is higher than anywhere else in Germany. However, given the low values of both territorial contexts (HLU in Baden-Würtemberg at 3.7 per cent and in Stuttgart at 6 per cent in 1992) its significance is not so high. It is probably more important to note the different weight which the cultural (more directly on the regional level) and the economic (more directly on the urban level) dimensions have in influencing these rates.

20   The economic history of south West Germany has been thoroughly studied as an example of a successful transition to post-Fordist flexible production systems. Within most of the analyses the cultural dimension has been pointed out, together with the poverty of natural resources and some institutions with specific regulatory functions, as an important argument in explaining the success, although it is, of course, not the only one. Other given conditions and contingencies contributed to the development of a differentiated industrial structure focused not only on the mass production of standardized goods, no longer able to compete with low-wage countries (mainly NICs), but also on the production of high quality, often custom-oriented items, characterized by price rigidity. Local policies fostering research and development activities are strongly related to this. The whole region is investing nearly 4 per cent of the GNP in R&D, that is, more than the USA and Japan do, and even more than the German average (2.8 per cent in 1990). See Megerle (1982), Maier (1987), Sabel et al. (1987), Boelcke (1989), Wehling (1991), Kunz (1992).

21   Between 1973 and 1991 the recipients of *Sozialhilfe* increased by 416.7 per cent, while there was a decrease in the resident population of nearly 10 per cent (own calculations on: Statistische Berichte, 1973–1991; Statistische Blätter, Jahresübersicht 1992).

22   Unlike the debate in the USA, where the debate on 'new poverty' was more related to the question of ghettoization and the underclass (see Wilson (1987, 1991), Marcuse, Mingione, Silver and Wacquant herein) or Italy, where the debate was related on one hand to post-material needs (see Calvaruso, 1993; Guidicini and Pieretti, 1993) and on the other hand to the institutional prestructuring of cumulative processes of impoverishment (Kazepov, Mingione and Zajczyk, 1995; Kazepov, 1995a and 1995b), the German debate on 'new poverty' was concentrated, as the French one, on the increase of unemployment (Lompe, 1987). For a discussion of the topic see Silver herein.

23   The incidence of foreigners on receiving social assistance increased from the second half of the 1980s, reaching 32.6 per cent of the total number of social assistance dependent in 1991 at the regional level. Of this 32.6 per cent, 60.4 per cent were asylum seekers. These rates are far higher than

the proportion of foreigners in the population, which is about 10 per cent in Baden-Württemberg. In Stuttgart the percentage of foreigners depending on social assistance is nearly 40 per cent compared to 23.7 per cent of the resident population. Source: own calculation on data from the Statistisches Landesamt Baden-Württemberg, Linder (1992) and Statistische Berichte (1993).

24 Source: own calculations on data from Statistische Berichte KI 1 j/73–91/1 (1993).

25 In 1988 in Stuttgart 47.3 per cent of the benefits recipients were individuals, single males (67.9 per cent) and single females (32.1 per cent), against 23.1 per cent who were single parents with children (95 per cent of them females). In Baden-Württemberg, however, in the same year 26.6 per cent were individuals (57 per cent males and 43 per cent females) against single parents with children who comprised 30.1 per cent. Sources: for Stuttgart (Stiefel, 1990) and for Baden-Württemberg (Statistische Berichte, 1989).

26 These groups emerge partially from Statistische Berichte published data and from other sources: (a) two *ad hoc* researches on unpublished data (Marissen, 1989; Stiefel, 1990); (b) 12 qualitative interviews with social workers carried out in Stuttgart by the author; (c) 12 qualitative interviews with experts in Stuttgart and Baden-Württemberg; (d) interviews with persons in a condition of need carried out by Astrid Springer (mimeo).

27 In the year of reunification in East Berlin, 11.2 per cent of all apartments were without a bathroom and 5.2 per cent of apartments were without a WC.

28 In 1993 about 700,000 apartments in East Berlin were administered or owned by the state. This figure corresponds to about 65 per cent of the housing supply.

29 The *Deutsche Städtetag* is the German association of large cities which deals with urban and regional development issues.

16

Conclusion

Enzo Mingione, University of Padova

URBAN POVERTIES: CONVERGENCE OR SPECIFICITY

In the first chapter I raised several problems that are worth discussing again in this concluding chapter. These problems involve a questioning of the conventional comparative approach because they embrace phenomena that are very diverse or because the related research methods are different.

Urban poverty in the US, highly concentrated among ethnic minorities, has been seen to be so specific as to lie completely outside the theoretical debate on poverty in industrial societies (see, for example, Danziger, Sandefur and Weinberg, 1994). The same has been more or less true of the high rates of unemployment in many European countries. They are regarded more as the result of particular institutional set-ups than as one of the possible consequences of the historical transformation that is affecting all advanced industrial societies in diverse ways. Within such a context, a comparative approach gives a distorted picture. The capacity of the US to create a large number of jobs in a strongly deregulated labour market context is greatly admired by many European politicians and academics, who consider it a model to be emulated. At the same time – as if the phenomena were in no way connected – the 'Americanization' of European cities and the importation of the underclass are dreaded. On both sides of the Atlantic, state welfare intervention is demonized for being wasteful and stifling economic growth, while at the same time it is extolled as the only means available to prevent urban poverty becoming chronic. The essays contained in this volume have been brought together to help correct this distorted vision. Beyond this, they aim to go more deeply into the interplay of differences and convergences that characterize a common transition in which all the different systems of social integration are being radically transformed as a result of the weakening of the protective capacity provided by diverse combinations of social institutions, from the labour market to the stability and homogeneity of families and communities and the effectiveness of different welfare programmes.

The book had to face various difficulties. An important one arises from the well-established division of intellectual labour between on one side the measurement and identification of the poor, always discussed as a matter of social policy, and on the other the conceptualization and causal analysis of social structure, which are examined rather in terms of general problems of social stratification, inequalities, organization and consensus in societies. Two-way movement between the different activities is necessary in order to achieve a comparative vision that cuts across conventional divisions but it remains highly problematic.

A further difficulty comes from the fact that in order to understand the question of urban poverty properly it is insufficient to compare across countries the standards of life of different groups of the population: what is needed is to look at dynamic processes and their perception within changing social integration systems. From the very beginnings of industrial societies and the social sciences this link has been crucial, even if as part of ideologically different visions and in conditions that changed with time and cultural context. Poverty is no longer the typical condition of the vast masses in contrast to that of the few rich and powerful, but rather a qualitative threshold that excludes people from the competitive individualistic and consumerist behaviour typical of industrial societies. This is what Adam Smith was pointing out when he referred to the need to possess certain goods without which one would be ashamed to show one's face in society and not have access to the normal opportunities open to others. This is also what Alexis de Tocqueville had in mind when he predicted that in the most advanced industrial societies a number of subjects would be in serious difficulty due to their having no access to sources of subsistence and community solidarity, and thus be destined to depend on state intervention. By pinpointing the link between poverty and systems of social integration we can more easily reconstruct the chain of logic by which the meaning of impoverishment processes is situated within the construction of citizenship systems. Problems then emerge on two fronts.

First, there are diversified visions of the question of social integration. It is on this very terrain that the rift has opened up between the 'critical' literature, to which the authors included herein belong, though in differing tones, and the conservative conceptions of the social order. The first approach holds that poverty is a deficit of integration existing independently of the will and behaviour of the poor and thus a structural fissure in the citizenship pact, which should be repaired through intervention to restore to the poor opportunities for social insertion equal to those enjoyed by the other subjects. For the authors adopting the second approach the condition of poverty is in most cases voluntary. Consequently, it is not a question of helping the poor to reacquire the opportunities and forms of behaviour typical of the majority but of keeping under control the public nuisance resulting from the 'deviance' of the undeserving poor.[1] What we have are two divergent visions of the social order and in each the concept of poverty and also the qualitative threshold that delimits it from non-poverty is different. In the first case, emphasis is placed on structural conditions or event chains that condition life chances largely independently of individual will and moral attributes. In the second, the fracture is perceived mainly in the domain of moral attributes and behaviour. It is for this very reason that the poor have to be divided into the deserving, subjects who are particularly unfortunate but still preserve a moral status shared by the majority of the population and may therefore be helped, and the undeserving, those who from the start or during impoverishment lose their moral link with the majority and, consequently, should not be helped but merely kept under control. Already very fragile in itself, this second demarcation line between the deserving and undeserving poor is thrown into crisis by the theory of the 'culture of poverty'. If it is true that in order to face up to particularly difficult life conditions, when poverty obviously is not just a transitory misfortune, all the poor have to adopt strategies and behaviours that are very unlike those of the majority, then it must also be the case that all the 'truly poor' are characterized by a moral, cultural and behavioural divergence from the rest of the population. The deserving poor do not exist since they either die off due to privation or quickly escape from poverty.

The second difficulty concerns the qualitative nature that is attributed in all the diverse narratives on poverty, beyond the ideological and terminological disputes, to the threshold that divides those who are integrated into society from those who are excluded. I have already addressed this problem extensively in the first chapter. Here I will confine myself to underlining its intractable methodological difficulty. All the various criteria adopted by those interested in poverty, including the authors in this book (some are working on poverty lines; some, like Nick Buck, select an indicator of exclusion from official stable employment; others, like Francesca Zajczyk, dwell on the conditions of the users of services to help those facing particular economic hardship; and, lastly, both Tosi and Marcuse give special prominence to the category of the homeless), are legitimate and compatible with one another under two conditions. The first is the awareness that no indicator, however sophisticated, can identify the poor exhaustively in the way that they are marked in reality by the qualitative fracture underlying the various theoretical constructions of the concept of poverty. The second is that the logical reconstruction of the significance of the indicators with respect to the theoretical narrative on poverty must be clear. It is precisely on this terrain of compatibility that the contributions included herein provide comparable visions since the differences take on meanings that can be traced back to a common matrix. Apropos, as declared in the first chapter, we will have to come back to the question of how to combine the two different paths followed by the authors in this volume: that oriented towards the individual drift perspective of Micheli and Zajczyk and that oriented more towards the analysis of social areas of chronic poverty undertaken by the others.

POVERTY AS INDIVIDUAL DRIFT OR BELONGING TO CHRONIC GROUPS

In the first chapter I insisted on the methodological complementarity between the two above-mentioned paths in analysing urban poverty. The first is more suited to tracing the features of individual or familial itineraries where there are no extensive chronic areas and highlights the conditions and stages of impoverishment trajectories. The second, in contrast, stresses the particular conditions for the chronic reproduction of poverty in socially and geographically concentrated segments. It is also the case that both paths emphasize two different interconnections between poverty and the city in the current historical transition from one system of social integration to another. Independently of whether large areas of chronic poverty have already formed in it or not, the urban environment sets in motion malign circuits of impoverishment that are unmanageable in terms of social reinsertion.

The drift trajectories illustrated by Micheli and Zajczyk, but also those by Tosi and Marcuse for the homeless, represent this type of phenomenon. They may not be numerous or greatly on the increase but, as Marcuse stresses in relation to the difference between homelessness and advanced homelessness, they are phenomena for which no way out can be seen; the only prospect in sight is that the separation from the rest of society will become chronic. In this perspective, above all, the perverse effects are highlighted of the cumulative concatenation of negative events and disadvantages that end by giving rise to complex syndromes in the face of which interventions aimed at reinsertion are doomed to failure. This happens especially because, at best, they are intended as solutions to only one of the multiple facets of social hardship (hospitalization or a temporary job, a supplementary income or family counselling).[2]

In tandem with the triggering of malign circuits of impoverishment, under the conditions of the current transition in the social and employment system the already formed areas of chronic poverty are being consolidated along diverse lines of social and cultural discrimination. In this case too, numbers may be large and on the increase or not. The essential question is another: that of the widening of the gap separating a segment of the population from the rest of society, the formation of a marked borderline between the included and the excluded. As mentioned by Robert Castel in a very recent book (1995), the radical change within the social–employment regime from relative stability to increasing precariousness of working careers shifts the poverty question from the area of inequality and mobility to that of permanent divisions and discriminations. A part of the population has no hope of finding reasonable jobs and hence of being socially integrated under conditions normal for the rest of the community. In this sense the debate on the underclass in the US and the UK and the one on social exclusion in continental Europe,[3] even though their political and cultural premises differ, as is well highlighted by Silver, both reflect and are consistent with the perception of this widening fracture in society.

Both the path centred on impoverishment trajectories and the one centred on chronic pockets of urban poverty point in the same direction in two respects. In both cases, the factors that bring about a widening of the gap between inclusion and exclusion are the same and connected with the transformations affecting the employment and family systems and that for the public protection of subjects in difficulty. Saskia Sassen's observations on the social implications of the new services employment regime[4] show how the changes in question contribute to making individuals more vulnerable to impoverishment drift as well as to consolidating the exclusion of already chronically poor groups. The consequences in terms of poverty risk are the same both when difficulties result from the diffusion of unstable underpaid jobs and when they derive from an increase in long-term unemployment, with its direct (deskilling and chronic marginalization from work opportunities) and indirect (the erosion of the family's or the welfare state's economic support capacity) effects. The selectivity of the labour market generates malign circuits that are increasingly difficult to reverse. Moreover, they are often concentrated among disadvantaged social groups where location in a ghetto plays an important role. This is especially the case for minorities or immigrants but also, as Enrica Morlicchio shows in her chapter on Naples, for those simply exposed to an unfavourable social life context in terms of access to welfare services and job opportunities.

Then, the two different interpretative paths both point out that it is the very social context in industrial cities that functions as a privileged generator of poverty. It is not only a matter of the old discourse on the more rarefied and fragile sociality of the cities, as in the analyses of the development of the industrial labour market from Engels to Polanyi and, along different lines, in the contribution of the Chicago School, but also of a different set of considerations. The contemporary city comes later than both the solid but isolated sociality of nuclear families and the stable working careers of male family breadwinners. In this sense, a large number of subjects are ensnared in life destinies that are blind alleys. They may be ghettoized members of minorities or disadvantaged communities or it may be a case of individual drift in which the stages of the cumulative malign circuit are the loss of a job, a family crisis, mental or physical illness, drug dependency and the inability to find or keep a dwelling.

As Marcuse has explained well in his contribution, the post-Fordist city – an incisive though improper expression – produces poverty also relatively independently of the economic cycle and the community's level of available wealth. What lies behind this process are in fact phenomena that have little to do with the course of the economy, ranging from the dynamics of feasible jobs for subjects in difficulty that avoid their falling from one form of poverty into another (from poor because jobless to poor because of poor job) and from the capacity of local authorities to support these subjects with effective programmes to the question of family stability. Among the cases considered in this book, only that of Naples does not follow this pattern and reveals a close connection between the depressed local economy and the consolidation of poverty. But even here questions arise as to why there are such high peaks of social privation in what remains of the largest and most dynamic centre in the southern Italian economy. Besides, no special attention has been paid in this volume to those regions and cities that have been the main victims of the process of de-industrialization and industrial restructuring, from Liverpool to Detroit and Bremen. This was partly a conscious choice so as not to shift attention away from the general problem of urban poverty and onto the particular one of the devastating effects of economic restructuring. The various chapters in this volume clearly show that social conditions in Milan and Stuttgart are very different from those in Naples and Berlin and that a convincing explanation for this lies in their respective economic situations. What is important to stress is that in all urban contexts, including rich cities like Milan and Stuttgart, are found a significant number of impoverishment paths that lead to almost invariably irreversible social exclusion. As we have seen in this book, the fact that these paths are more or less numerous and on the increase, particularly concentrated in some neighbour-hoods and involve certain ethnic and social groups depends on various factors and conditions, which cannot, however, be related in a mechanical fashion to the level of wealth or economic development. This makes comparative discussion more complicated. The fact that the city and the main transformation tendencies constitute a matrix of common factors is not a sufficient basis on which to construct a solid comparative framework if we are unable to formulate a narrative on poverty that encompasses all the diverse phenomena indicated in this volume and that is adequately structured to explain the differences. Along these lines, it is possible to renew the debate on the underclass starting from a question posed by Norman Fainstein in his chapter.

To What Extent do the Underclass and the Other Poor Represent Different Problems?

Leaving aside the disputes over terminology that have led to the term 'underclass', overloaded with behaviourist connotations, being aban-doned in favour of 'ghetto poor', Fainstein criticizes the dramatization of the question of territorially concentrated poverty or ghetto poor. If one starts from the consideration that also in the US and also with regard to the condition of African-Americans most of the urban poor do not live in ghettos, there is no reason for the whole debate to focus on the ghetto poor. With the problem posed in these terms, Fainstein is undoubtedly right, also because documentation on poverty in general is too often used to talk exclusively about the underclass. However, the problem may be posed in a different way, which I believe is the approach adopted by the authors in this volume and is not in contradiction with the reconceptualization of the question undertaken by Wilson in the 1980s.

The premises for this different approach to the problem have in fact already been postulated on several occasions throughout this volume and they form the cornerstone of the comparability of the various contributions and the unity of the narrative on urban poverty, beyond the profound cultural and material differences that characterize the phenomenon. It has been underlined that what lies behind present-day urban poverty are the structural transformations of the social institutions that guarantee insertion, from the family systems to the composition and distribution of work chances and the efficacy of public welfare, though in different mixes in the different social situations. Furthermore, we have seen that the outcome of these transformations is always the generation of poverty in the form of social exclusion, that is, a heightened and difficult-to-reverse divergence from normal conditions of social insertion. Given these two assumptions, the ghetto poor are simply variants of the same phenomenon whether they are (as in the case of African-Americans) or are not (as in the case of the poor concentrated in the inner city or peripheral quarters of Naples) a disadvantaged minority. Clearly, there are differences that are worth discussing at greater length, as has to a large extent been done in this book, but they do not necessarily invalidate the narrative's unity.

The question remains whether – and if so to what point – territorial concentration and, possibly, the condition of being a homogeneously disadvantaged minority alter impoverishment syndromes to such an extent that they become qualitatively different forms of poverty from those typically affecting most of the other urban poor. In this sense, both Sen's and Wilson's arguments that territorial concentration is a factor making for a higher risk of poverty is not at stake. This signifies only that some social groups, starting out with extremely limited and distorted bundles of resources, slide into poverty even without that cumulative concatenation of negative events illustrated herein by Micheli. In fact the reverse is often the case. In order to exit from the poverty risk area, the inhabitants of poor neighbourhoods are in increasing need of a cumulative concatenation of positive events. The pre-Wilson behaviourist narrative on the underclass resolved the question in a clear-cut fashion, but one which we find unacceptable also because almost invariably falsified by the data. The underclass was different from the other poor because it behaved differently; it crossed the moral divide between deservedness and undeservedness.[5] If it is unacceptable to run this dividing line through the poor or between the ghetto poor and the non-ghetto poor or between diverse ethnic groups, then it is impossible to break the unity of the discourse on urban poverty.

What, then, is the importance of the attention paid to the ghetto poor and of Wilson's contribution, which still lies behind many of the chapters in this book? It seems to me that we should and can confine ourselves to the question of the privileged modes of production of the social exclusion risk, that this question is of great importance and lies entirely within the debate on poverty in general. If today the cities are in general factories of social exclusion, ghettoization – even more, according to Wilson, than belonging to a disadvantaged minority – constitutes an intensive production unit. The population is completely exposed to the high probability of malign circuits, starts from an already extremely low resource equilibrium threshold and must of necessity adopt behaviours that are very likely to speed up the malign circuits, independently of aspirations, vocations and moral inclination (Gans, 1994). Wilson's contribution was of great importance in explaining the specific historical and social modes by which the ghetto has become a hyperghetto (the term used herein by Wacquant and Marcuse in this precise sense), namely, an intensive generator of social exclusion. This transformation of the ghetto does not produce different, more deviant, immoral or dangerous poor than the other poor, but it begets them by way of a 'different', accelerated and multiplicative, social process; hence both the interest in analysis and the political concern. As Marcuse explains well, the segregation of a substantial minority of poor in ghettos tends to alter and speed up the process of social exclusion. And even more so if the ghettoization is institutionally enforced and to the detriment of disadvantaged and discriminated ethnic minorities, as happens with blacks and Puerto Ricans in the US and, in different ways, with the immigrants from Central America and the immigrants to European cities from underdeveloped countries. From this there also derives the necessity to understand why and how an ethnic minority community is transformed into a hyperghetto or economic enclave, as Logan et al. and Marcuse attempt to do in their chapters. These considerations also serve to explain the interest and political alarm surrounding the question in Europe, given that the capacity to contain the hyperghettoization of the poor, even though as we have seen it in no way resolves the problem of poverty, at least allows a diminution of the intensity with which European cities are creating chronic and irreversible forms of social exclusion.

EXCLUSION AND POST-FORDIST REGIMES OF SOCIAL INTEGRATION

Starting from the observations in the previous section, the argument can be developed on the basis of a dual comparative grid covering the intensity of production of the social exclusion risk and the ways in which social exclusion is generated in different social contexts. The initial condition becomes gradually more unfavourable as we run down the typologies from top to bottom in figure 16.1. The left-hand column shows the hypothesized levels of high social exclusion risk, calculated as an average and using relatively lower values than the poverty lines. The real levels change in line with the extensive presence or not of groups of ghettoized poor, above all because in these cases the creation of a high exclusion risk does not depend on the selection of paths characterized by a concatenation of negative events but involves the life conditions and the limited chances available to many or all of the ghettoized community's members, as the right-hand column attempts to show. The intensity of risk is greatest and the modes of exclusion are largely independent of subjects' life-courses in

	Production of social exclusion in general	Percentage of social exclusion independent of downdrifts caused by negative events
In society in general	5%	1-2%
In big cities	10%	up to 5%
Within cities:		
Disadvantaged ethnic groups and social classes	25%	up to 15%
Segregated and ghettoized groups without social stigma	more than 35%	up to 60%
Stigmatized groups in closed ghettos institutionally penalized	more than 50%	all

Figure 16.1 Production of areas of social exclusion in general and also independently of individual downdrift caused by negative events within different social contexts

the case of closed ghettos with a high ethnic-social stigma attached, like those analysed by Wilson and Wacquant and others in this volume. It is, however, also high in the cases of ghettoization without stigma and under relatively more open conditions, as can be seen in Morlicchio's chapter on Naples.

The contributions in this book appear to me to all largely go in the direction of confirming the hypotheses listed below, which make up an interpretational paradigm able to explain the meaning assumed by both the convergences and the divergences in the processes of social exclusion and also to absorb the differences in methodological approach.

1   The transformation tendencies in the regimes of social integration, the diverse combinations of increasing familial and employment instability and the declining efficacy of welfare protection are bringing about, above all in the cities, serious forms of marginalization leading to chronic exclusion from the life conditions of most of the population.

2   All the authors in this book insist on the fact that exclusion should be viewed and studied as a process rather than a fixed condition. The processes of exclusion are different particularly when we take into consideration the case of disadvantaged groups versus that of individuals or households subject to drift into pauperization.

3   Even if the modalities of marginalization are different, the outcome of the exclusion process is the same. Consequently, it is not possible to distinguish between different categories of excluded persons on the basis of wide conceptual divisions or by starting from behavioural syndromes (the deserving divided from the undeserving) or from the exclusion process modalities (processes produced by a concatenation of negative events against those produced by particularly unfavourable socio-territorial environments).

4   Unfavourable environments, above all the closed ghettos characterized by ethnic-social stigma, generate a strong risk of exclusion even independently of the cumulative concatenation of negative life events. This occurs exactly as explained in Wilson's narrative on the ghetto poor, which in this interpretation may be applied to different social realities, obviously changing the conditions. The significance of this narrative derives precisely from the fact that the contextual variables are very important in explaining the intensity and modes of generating exclusion, and not from the fact that the ghetto poor are more or less dangerous or undeserving than the other poor.

5   Ghettoization, and even more so the hyperghettoization recorded in some American cities, tends to intensify and speed up the process producing social exclusion even though the ghetto poor are still everywhere a minority of the poor.

One important question has remained open throughout this book. To what extent does hyperghettoization constitute a specific cultural and institutional modality of the US case, or is it rather one of the tendencies in the transformation process of the social integration system which European countries are more willing and able to resist, starting with their different welfare systems and cultures? I would opt for the second interpretation, but the existing documentation does not as yet provide any decisive evidence. On the basis of the contributions contained herein and the debate on the underclass that has begun also in Europe, we know both that here too areas of segregated poverty involving immigrants, minorities and local inhabitants are gradually being consolidated where, as in the US, social exclusion processes are becoming more intense and that the institutional apparatus has been used at least to promote a certain degree of social mobility in the ghetto (see apropos the section in Loïc Wacquant's chapter on La Corneuve). In order to clarify the matter, longitudinal and ethnographic analyses would be required on the life conditions in the poor districts of Naples, Paris, Berlin or London, like those undertaken in the ghettos of American cities in past decades.

Moreover, another question arises from the comparison between the US and European societies. In preventing the consolidation of urban ghettos as intensive producers of social exclusion, are institutional strategies against ghettoization more effective or those that preserve a more regulated labour market even at the cost of a higher unemployment rate? In this case also there is no clear answer. But it could be easily maintained that both kinds of strategy clearly underlie the difference between the higher levels of urban poverty in the US and the lower ones in Europe, where the welfarist socio-cultural climate still, for the time being, favours resistance against the negative impact of the transition to a different social integration system.

In conclusion, I think it is worthwhile to make some observations on the significance of social exclusion in respect of the system of integration that is being formed. In *The Great Transformation* Karl Polanyi, taking above all the English experience as a benchmark, laid great stress on the enormous amount of suffering and poverty that had been caused by industrialization. Critical philanthropists, men and women of culture and academics in the last century were horrified by and felt helpless in the face of the devastating social effects of the advent of the still totally unregulated labour market. The historical events and social conflict that led to this situation being overcome were neither predicted nor predictable. Thus, it may be assumed that all transitions from one system of social integration to another generate strong currents of marginalization, privation and suffering, but also that the mobilizations and battles against social injustice represent an essential experience in overcoming the most devastating effects of 'great transformations'. Having said this, however, many questions still remain open. I will confine myself to a few remarks on avenues that deserve to be investigated more thoroughly.

None of the diverse visions of integration are at all incompatible with even marked social inequalities. In two articles far apart in time (1972 and 1994), Herbert Gans points to the latent functions of poverty and the undeserving poor. The integration systems of individualized societies are in reality founded on inequalities and the presence of even strongly marginalized groups, reflected both in tensions and disfunctions and in latent functions. But unlike what occurred in premodern societies, where social divisions were legitimized by a religious-transcendental order, it is now maintained that chronic persistent fissures are hard to tolerate. This is perhaps the central problem of the urban poverties as they are emerging during the current transition between different systems of social integration. It is for this reason that greater attention is being paid to the areas of chronic poverty, namely, the ghetto poor, even though they form a minority of the poor. Here, indeed, the stigma of exclusion exists from birth.

Another line of discussion regards the question as to which resources can be mobilized within the new integration systems to combat social exclusion. On this front, too, many questions have arisen that await more exhaustive answers. The combined message from the contributions by Saskia Sassen and Lydia Morris is that a division of labour, where a large share of working activities are precarious and underpaid and systematically performed by women, immigrants and disadvantaged minorities, will be inevitably engendered in an area of chronic social disadvantage (see also Castel, 1995). On this front the room for manœuvre appears to be very limited. Neither a generalized reduction in working hours nor a wider recourse to minimum income contracts for socially useful jobs, even though they might have positive effects, impinge upon the malign circuit of the division of labour.

On a different front, there is the question of how far family and kinship resources can be remobilized even beyond the erosion of the stable nuclear family firmly inserted in the social context. The long-term cohabitation of young people with their families or the return to their parental home by divorcees, with or without children, are undoubtedly cultural practices typical of some societies rather than others. There are, however, signs that these are spreading and they need to be discussed also in terms of responses to social exclusion tendencies. Furthermore, one wonders how far and in what way the mobilization of voluntary solidarity can compensate for the difficulties in public welfare intervention.

It is with regard to public intervention that it seems interesting to me to raise a last question. There are three tendencies in social exclusion that are giving cause for concern. A very intense debate is centred around the first two relating to the growing financial problems and the limited effectiveness of intervention. Very little is said, on the other hand, about the third tendency. This is the malign circuit that has been found in all advanced industrial societies, though more markedly in the US and the other liberal variants, linking the increase in the poor and their separateness from the rest of society with the growing opposition on the part of taxpayers to intervention aimed at helping them (Lafer, 1994). It is evident that if this malign circuit is not broken, what we can expect in the future is not 'wars on poverty' but rather the continuation of the 'war against the poor' (Gans, 1995).

NOTES

1   This division in approach is very clear with regard to welfare dependence. The first criticizes it as a myth invented to take public protection away from the poor, whereas the second maintains that a large part of the poor exploit community support as a way to shirk their moral duty to work and contribute to the well-being of the whole community.

2   A recent investigation of the users of public and private welfare services in Milan (Kazepov, Mingione and Zajczyk, 1995) reveals this aspect in a clear light and shows that a useful intervention is often nullified by the impossibility of intervening in the other aspects of present-day social exclusion syndromes. In chapter 4, Tosi stresses the difficulties met with by political innovations, paying particular attention to the questions posed by the *Revenue Minimum d'Insertion* contracts in France.

3   It is not by chance that the Commission of the European Union has in the early 1990s gradually replaced the term 'poverty' with 'social exclusion'. While doing so, its attention has been concentrated almost exclusively on two groups: immigrants or ethnic minorities and the long-term unemployed.

4   It is worth mentioning here that Sassen works along the same lines as Castel (1995). They both point to the impact of the structural transformation of the employment regime but with the variant, in the case of Sassen, of highlighting the radical leading role of large cities within this process and, consequently, the fact that the social fracture (the production of new forms of poverty) is more visible and opens up faster in global cities.

5   On closer inspection, in Auletta's version (1983) there is no special emphasis on either ghetto or race. What we have, instead, is a renewed version of the concept of 'undeserving poor'. Even in the more sophisticated development of this line subsequently proposed by Murray (1984, 1990) territorial and ethnic segregation play a decidedly unimportant role.

Bibliography

Abou Sada, G., Anderson, J., Estivil, J., Henriques, J. M. and Swiergiel, C. (1994) *Integration through Economic Means Within the Framework of Poverty 3*. European Commission, DG V/E/12, Brussels.

Abrahams, R. D. (1970) *Positively Black*. Prentice Hall, Englewood Cliffs.

Abu-Lughod, J. (1993) *From Urban Village to 'East Village': the battle for New York's Lower East Side*. Blackwell, Oxford.

Agenzia per l'Impiego della Campania (1993), *La mobilità in Campania*, quaderno n. 5.

Aïchoune, F. (1991) *Nés en banlieue*. Editions Ramsay, Paris.

Alba, R. (1990) *Ethnic Identity: the transformation of white America*. Yale University Press, New Haven.

—— and Logan, J. R. (1991) Variations on two themes: racial and ethnic patterns in the attainment of suburban residence. *Demography*, 28 (August), 431–53.

—— and Logan, J. R. (1992) Analyzing locational attainments: constructing individual-level regression models using aggregate data. *Sociological Methods and Research*, 20, 367–97.

—— and Logan, J. R. (1993) Minority proximity to whites in suburbs: an individual-level analysis of segregation. *American Journal of Sociology*, 98, 1388–427.

Alber, J. (1986) Germany. In P. Flora (ed.), *Growth to Limits. The Western European Welfare States since World War II*, de Grayter, Berlin, vol. 2, 4–149.

Alisch, M. and Dangschat, J. S. (1993) *Die solidarische Stadt. Ursachen von Armut und Strategien für einen sozialen Ausgleich*. VWP (Verlag für wissenschaftliche Publikationen), Darmstadt.

Allen, S. and Macey, M. (1990) Race and ethnicity in the European context. *British Journal of Sociology*, 41, 375–93.

Allum, P. A. (1973) *Politics and Society in Post-war Naples*. Cambridge University Press, Cambridge.

Amart, L. (1987) 'La fréquentation du parc de La Courneuve'. Laboratoire d'économétrie de l'Ecole Polytechnique, Paris, mimeo.

Amt für Wohnungswesen der Stadt Stuttgart (1992) *Stuttgarter Wohnungsbericht 1987/1991*. Stuttgart.

Amtliche Nachrichten der Bundesanstalt für Arbeit (1994) *Arbeitsmarkt 1993*, Jg. 42. Nürnberg.

Anderson, B. (1991) *Imagined Communities: reflections on the origin and spread of nationalism*. Verso, London.

Anderson, E. (1991) *Streetwise*. The University of Chicago Press, Chicago.

Anderson, P. (1991) *English Questions*. Verso, London.

André, C. (1994) La France des pauvres. *Alternatives Economiques*, 114 (February), 23–32.

Aponte, R. (1990) Definition of the underclass: a critical analysis. In H. Gans (ed.), *Sociology in America*, Sage, Newbury Park, CA, 117–137.

Appelbaum, E. and Albin, P. (1990) Shifts in employment, occupational structure, and educational attainment. In T. Noyelle (ed.), *Skills, Wages, and Productivity in the Service Sector*, Westview Press, Boulder, 31–66.

Ashford, D. (1986) *The Emergence of the Welfare States*. Basil Blackwell, London.

Associazione MeglioMilano (1989–1993) L'osservatorio sulla qualità della vita a Milano (various papers).

Atkinson, A. B. and Micklewright, J. (1983) On the reliability of income data in the Family Expenditure Survey 1970–1977. *Journal of the Royal Statistical Society*, vol. 146, 33–61.

—— (1989) Turning the screw: benefits for the unemployed, 1979–1988. In A. B. Atkinson (ed.), *Poverty and Social Security*, Harvester Wheatsheaf, Hertfordshire.

Auletta, K. (1983) *The Underclass*. Vintage Books, New York.

Autés, M. (1992) Les paradoxes de l'insertion. In R. Castel and J.-F. Laé (eds) (1992) 93–120.

Avery, D. (1987) *Civilisations de La Courneuve. Images brisées d'une cité*. L'Harmattan, Paris.

Avramov, D. (1994) 'Homelessness: a condition or a social process? An overview for the 12 member states of the European Union'. Paper presented at the XIII World Congress of Sociology, Bielefeld, 18–23 July.

Bach, H.-U., Jung-Hammon, T. and Otto, M. (1994) *Aktuelle Daten vom Arbeitsmarkt*. Neue Bundesländer, Stand Oktober 1994, IAB Werkstattbericht, Nr. 1.10/15.10.1994.

Bachmann, C. and Basier, L. (1989) *Mise en images d'une banlieue ordinaire*. Syros, Paris.

Bailey, T. and Waldinger, R. (1991) Primary, secondary, and enclave labour markets: a training systems approach. *American Sociological Review*, 56, 432–45.

Balazs, G. and Abdelmalek Sayad (1991) La violence de l'institution. Entretien avec le principal d'un collège de Vaulx-en-Velin. *Actes de la recherche en sciences sociales*, 90 (December), 53–63.

Baldwin, J. A. (1971) *The Mental Hospital in the Psychiatric Service: a case-register study*. Oxford University Press, Oxford.

Baldwin-Edwards, M. (1991) Migration after 1992. *Policy and Politics*, 19, 199–211.

Balibar, E. (1991a) Race, nation and class. In M. Silverman, (ed.), *Race, Discourse and Power in France*, Avebury, Aldershot, UK, 71–83.

—— (1991b) Es gibt keinen Staat in Europa: racism and politics in Europe today. *New Left Review*, 186 (March–April), 5–19.

—— (1992) Inégalités, fractionnement social, exclusion: nouvelles formes de l'antagonisme de classe? In J. Affichard and J.-B. de Foucald (eds), *Justice sociale et inegalités*, Editions Esprit, Paris, 149–161.

Bane, M. J. (1988) Politics and policies of the feminization of poverty. In M. Weir, A. S. Orloff and T. Skocpol (eds), *The Politics of Social Policy in the United States*, Princeton University Press, Princeton, 381–396.

—— and Ellwood, D. T. (1986) Slipping into and out of poverty: the dynamics of spells. *Journal of Human Resources*, 21, 1–23.

Banfield, E. C. (1970) *The Unheavenly City: the nature and future of our urban crisis*. Little, Brown, Boston.

Barker, M. (1981) *The New Racism*. Junction Books, London.

Barrou, J. (1992) *La place du pauvre. Histoire et géographie sociale de l'habitat HLM*. L'Harmattan, Paris.

—— (1993) Les paradoxes de l'intégration: de L'infortune des mots à la vertue des concepts. *Ethnologie Française*, 23 (2) (April-June), 169–76.

Bastide, J. (1982) Les enfants immigrés et l'enseignement français: enquête dans les établissement du 1er et 2nd degré. *Travaux et Documents*, 97, INED/PUF.

Baudrillard, J. (1970) *La societé des consommation, ses mythes, ses structures*. Syros, Paris.

Becchi, A. (1989) Napoli contro Napoli. Città come economia e città come potere. *Meridiana*, n 5.

Beckmann, P. and Bender, S. (1993) Arbeitslosigkeit in ostdeutschen Familien. Der Einfluss des Familienkontextes auf das individuelle Arbeitslosigkeitsrisiko. *Mitteilungen aus der Arbeitsmarktund Berufsforschung*, 2 (93), 222–235.

Bednarzik, R. (1990) A special focus on employment growth in business services and retail trade. In T. Noyelle (ed.), *Skills, Wages, and Productivity in the Service Sector*, Westview Press, Boulder, 67–80.

Bellah, R. et al. (1985) *Habits of the Heart*. Harper and Row, New York.

Bellamy, E. (1888) *Looking Backward, 2000–1887*. Houghton Mifflin, Boston (repr. 1987, Harvard University Press, Cambridge, MA).

Benassi, D. (1995) 'I percorsi di formazione del bisogno' and 'Le strategie di fronteggiamento del bisogno'. In IARD, *I neopoveri in Lombardia. Sistemi di welfare e traiettorie di esclusione sociale*, research report.

Bergamaschi, M. (1993) Rottura dei legami sociali nei sistemi urbani complessi: un'ipotesi di lettura. In P. Guidicini and G. Pieretti (eds), *La residualità come valore. Povertà urbane e dignità umana*, Angeli, Milan.

Bergmann, C. et al. (1993) *Initiative für einen öffentlich geförderten Beschäftigungssektor (zweiter Arbeitsmarkt)*. Edited by Senatsverwaltung für Arbeit und Frauen, Berlin.

Berstein, S. and Rudell, O. (1992) *Le modèle republicain*. Presses Universitaires de Paris, Paris.

Berzano, L. (1991) Introduzione. In M. Pellegrino and V. Verzieri (eds,) *Senza tetto né legge. L'emarginazione grave, le nuove povertà, i 'senza fissa dimora'*, Edizioni Gruppo Abele, Torino.

Best, J. (ed.) (1995) *Images of Issues: typifying contemporary social problems*. Aldine de Gruyter, Hawthorne, NY.

Betelli, M. (1994) *Gli Avviamenti al Lavoro a Milano nel '92–'93*, Agenzia per l'Impiego della Lombardia.

Beveridge, A. (1992) maps. *New York Times* (15 July).

Beveridge, W. (1942) *Report on the Social Insurance and Allied Services*. Cmnd 6404, London.

Bianchi, S., Farley, R. and Spain, D. (1982) Racial inequalities in housing: an examination of recent trends. *Demography*, 19, 37–51.

Blackmar, E. (1989) *Manhattan for Rent, 1785–1850*. Cornell University Press, Ithaca, New York.

Blasi, G. (1994) And we are not seen: ideological and political barriers to understanding homelessness. *American Behavioral Scientist*, 37 (4), 553–85.

Blauner, R. (1972) *Racial Oppression in America*. Harper and Row, New York.

Body-Gendrot, S. (1993) Migration and the racialization of the postmodern city in France. In M. Cross and M. Keith (eds), *Racism, the City and the State*, Routledge, London, 77–92.

Boelke, W. (1989) *Sozialgeschichte Baden-Württembergs 1800–1989. Politik, Gesellschaft, Wirtschaft*. Kohlhammer, Stuttgart.

Bok, D. (1993) *The Cost of Talent: how executives and professionals are paid and how it affects America*. The Free Press, New York.

Bonetti, M., Conan, M. and Allen, B. (1991) *Développement social urbain, stratégies et méthodes*. L'Harmattan, Paris.

Booth, C. (1889) *Life and Labour of the People in London*. William and Norgate, London.

—— (1902) *Life and Labour of the People of London*. Macmillan, London.

Borst, O. (ed.) (1992) *Aufruhr und Entsagung. Vormarz 1815–1845 in Baden und Württemberg*. Theiss Verlag, Stuttgart.

Bourdieu, P. (1991a) L'ordre des choses. Entretien avec des jeunes gens du Nord de la France. *Actes de la recherche en sciences sociales*, 90 (December), 7–19.

—— (1991b) Mission impossible. Entretien avec Pascal Rémond, chef de projet dans le Nord de la France. *Actes de la recherche en sciences sociales*, 90 (December), 84–94.

—— et al. (1993) *La misère du monde*. Editions du Seuil, Paris.

Bourgois, P. (1989) In search of Horatio Alger: culture and ideology in the crack economy. *Contemporary Drug Problems* (Winter), 619–49.

—— (1992) Une nuit dans une 'shooting gallery': enquête sur le commerce du crack à East Harlem. *Actes de la recherche en sciences sociales*, 94 (September), 59–78.

Braghin, P. (ed.) (1978) *Inchiesta sulla miseria in Italia*. Einaudi, Torino.

Breton, E. (1983) *Rencontres à la Courneuve*. Messidor/Temps Actuel, Paris.

Briggs, A. (1961) *Social Thought and Social Action: a study of the work of Seebohm Rowntree*. Longman, London.

Brown, G. W. and Harris, T. (1978) *Social Origins of Depression*. Tavistock, London.

Brown, J. (1989) *Why don't they go to Work?* HMSO, London.

Brown, P. and Scase, R. (1991) *Poor Work: disadvantaged and the division of labour*. Open University Press, Milton Keynes.

Brubaker, R. (1992) *Citizenship and Nationhood in France and Germany*. Harvard University Press, Cambridge.

Brubaker, W. R. (1990) Immigration, citizenship, and the nation-state in France and Germany: a comparative historical analysis. *International Sociology*, 5–4 (December), 379–407.

Brückner, H. (1995) 'Times of poverty': lessons from the Bremen longitudinal social assistance sample. *Research in Community Sociology*, 5, 203–24.

Buck, N. (1991) Social polarization in the inner city: an analysis of the impact of labour market and household change. In M. Cross and G. Payne (eds), *Social Inequality and the Enterprise Culture*, Falmer, London, 79–101.

—— (1992) Labour market inactivity and polarisation: a household perspective on the idea of an underclass. In D. J. Smith (ed.), *Understanding the Underclass*, Policy Studies Institute, London, 9–31.

—— and Gordon, I. R. (1987) The beneficiaries of employment growth: an analysis of the experience of disadvantaged groups in expanding labour markets. In V. Hausner (ed.), *Critical Issues in Urban Economic Development*, vol. 2, Oxford University Press, Oxford, 77–115.

—— Gershuny, J., Rose, D. and Scott, J. (1994) *Changing Households: the British Household Panel Survey 1990–1992*, ESRC Research Centre on Micro Social Change, University of Essex, Colchester.

Buhr, P., Leibfried, S., Ludwig, M. and Voges, W. (1989) Passages through welfare. The Bremen approach to the analysis of claimants' careers in 'Publicly Administered Poverty'. Working paper, University of Bremen.

Bundesantalt für Arbeit (1995a) *Geschäftsbericht 1994*. Nürnberg.

—— (1995b) *Arbeitsmarkt 1994*. Sondernummer der Amtlichen Nachrichten der Bundesanstalt Für Arbeit (ANBA), Jg. 43.

Bundesanstalt für Landeskunde und Raumordnung (BfLR) (1993) *Obdachlosigkeit in den neuen Bundesländern*. Materialien zur Raumentwicklung, Heft 55.

Burgess, R. (1939) Introduction. In R. E. L. Faris and H. W. Dunham (eds) (1939).

Burnett, J. (1994) *Idle Hands: the experience of unemployment, 1790–1990.* Routledge, London.

Burt, M. (1991) *Over the Edge: the growth of homelessness in the 1980s.* Urban Institute Press and Russell Sage Foundation.

Burtless, G. (1994) Public spending on the poor: historical trends and economic limits. In S. H. Danziger, G. Sandefur and D. H. Weinberg (eds) (1994).

Business Week (1994) Inequality. How the gap between rich and poor hurts the economy. 15 August.

Calhoun, C. J. (1980) Community: toward a variable conceptualization for comparative research. *Social History*, 5 (1), 105–29.

Calogirou, C. (1989) *Sauver son honneur: rapports sociaux en milieu défavorisé.* L'Harmattan, Paris.

Calvanese, F. and Pugliese, E. (eds) (1991) *La presenza straniera in Italia: il caso della Campania.* Angeli, Milan.

Calvaruso, C. (1993) Povertà materiali e immateriali, in Europa. *Tutela*, 8 (2–3), 26–9.

Campiglio, I. (1988) Il costo economico del cambiamento in una metropoli in transformazione. In IReR-Progetto Milano, *Equilibrio economico ed equilibrio sociale in una metropoli che cambia*, Franco Angeli, Milan.

Carabelli, G. and Micheli, G. A. (1986) *Sofferenza psichica in scenari urbani. Strategie individuali nei percorsi istituzionali della malattia mentale.* Unicopli, Milan.

Cardia, C. (1987) *Ils ont construit New York: histoire de la métropole au XIX siècle.* Georg Editeur, Geneva.

—— (forthcoming) Population change in New York City. In P. Marcuse (ed.), *The Permanent Housing Crisis* (forthcoming).

Carens, J. H. (1988) Immigration and the welfare state. In A. Gutman (ed.), *Democracy and the Welfare State*, Princeton University Press, Princeton, NJ, 207–30.

Carnoy, M. (1994) *Faded Dreams.* Cambridge University Press, New York.

Caro, R. A. (1974) *The Power Broker. Robert Moses and the fall of New York.* Alfred A. Knopf, New York.

Carre, F. J. (1992) Temporary employment in the eighties. In V. L. DuRivage (ed.), *New Policies for Part-time and Contigent Workers*, M. E. Sharpe, Armonk, NY.

Castaing, M. (1994) L'éxclusion sans réponse. *Le Monde Dossiers et Documents*, 227 (December).

—— (1995a) Des milliers de personnes ont manifesté en France contre l'exclusion. *Le Monde* (11 April), 12.

—— (1995b) Le zones d'ombre d'une evaluation statistique. *Le Monde* (9–10 April), 12.

Castel, R. (1991) De l'indigence à l'exclusion: la désafiliation. In J. Donzelot (ed.), *Face à l'exclusion. Le modèle français*, Editions Esprit, Paris, 137–68.

—— (1995) *Les métamorphoses de la question sociale. Une chronique du salariat.* Fayard, Paris.

—— and Laé, J. -F. (eds) (1992) *Le revenu minimum d'insertion. Une dette sociale*. L'Harmattan, Paris.

—— and Laé, J. -F. (1992) La diagonale du pauvre. In R. Castel and J.-F. Laé (eds) (1992), 9–30.

Castellan, M., Marpsat, M. and Goldberger, M. F. (1992) Les quartiers prioritaires de la politique de la ville. *Insés Première*, 234 (December).

Castells, M. and Aoyama, Y. (1994) Paths towards the informational society: employment structure in G-7 countries, 1920–1990. *International Labor Review*, 133 (1), 5–33.

Castles, F. and Mitchell, D. (1991) Three worlds of welfare capitalism or four? LIS Working Paper n. 63, CEP/INSTEAD, Luxembourg.

Castles, S. (1984) *Here for Good*. Pluto Press, London.

—— and Kosack, G. (1985) *Immigrant Workers and Class Structure in Western Europe*. Oxford University Press, Oxford.

Centre for Contemporary Cultural Studies (1982) *The Empire Strikes Back: race and racism in 70s Britain*. Hutchinson, London.

Cerase, F. P., Morlicchio, E. and Spanò, A. (1991) *Disoccupati e disoccupate a Napoli*, CUEN, Napoli.

Chevalier, L. (1984) *Classes labourieuses, classes dangereuses*. Hachette Pluriel, Paris.

Chicago Tribune (1991) 849 homicides places 1990 in a sad record book. 2 January, 1 and 14.

—— (staff of the) (1992) *The Worst Schools in America*. Contemporary Press, Chicago.

Chubb, J. (1982) *Patronage, Power and Poverty in Southern Italy: a tale of two cities*. Cambridge University Press, Cambridge.

Clark, K. (1965) *Dark Ghetto: dilemmas of social power*. Harper and Row, New York.

Cohen, C. and Dawson, M. (1993) Neighborhood poverty and African American politics. *American Political Science Review*, 87 (2) (June), 286–302.

Cohen, R. (1987) *The New Helots*. Gower, Aldershot.

Cohen, S. and Zysman, J. (1987) *Manufacturing Matters: the myth of the post-industrial economy*. Basic Books, New York.

Commissariat Géneral du Plan (CGP) (1992) L'exclusion, rupture du lien social. *Problèmes économiques*, 2 (282) (1 Juillet), 1–4.

—— (1993) *L'insertion des adolescents en difficulté*. La Documentation Française, Paris.

Commission of the European Communities (1992) *Toward a Europe of Solidarity: intensifying the fight against social exclusion, fostering integration*. Brussels, 12 December.

Commissione d'Indagine sulla Povertà e l'Emarginazione (CIFT) (1985) *La povertà in Italia*. Istituto Poligrafico dello Stato, Roma.

—— (1992) *Secondo rapporto sulla povertà in Italia*. Franco Angeli, Milan.

—— (1994) *III rapporto sulla povertà in Italia*. Angeli, Milan.

—— (1995) *La povertà in Italia, 1993–1994*. Presidenza del Consiglio dei Ministri, Roma.

Contardi, R., Kazepov, Y. and Laffi, S. (1995) Crisi individuali e contesto sociale negli ospiti dei Ricoveri Notturni di Milano. In Y. Kazepov, E. Mingione and F. Zajczyk (eds), *Povertà estrema: istituzioni e percorsi a Milano*, Franco Angeli, Milan.

Cook, T. and Curtin, T. (1987) The mainstream and the underclass: why are the differences so salient and the similarities so unobtrusive? In J. Masters and W. Smith (eds), *Social Comparison, Social Justice and Relative Deprivation*, Lawrence Erlbaum, Hillsdale, NJ, 217–64.

Cools, R. and Dodd, P. (eds) (1986) *Englishness: politics and culture 1880–1920*. Croom Helm, London.

Cotugno, P., Pugliese, E. and Rebeggiani, E. (1990) Mercato del lavoro e occupazione nel secondo dopoguerra. In *Storia d'Italia. Le Regioni dall'Unità a oggi*, Einaudi, Torino.

Council of Europe (1993) *Homelessness*. Bruxelles.

Crowley, J. (1992) Minorités ethnique et ghettos aux Etats-Unis: modèle ou anti-modèle pour la France? *Esprit*, 182 (Juin), 78–94.

Dahrendorf, R. (1985) *Law and Order*. Westview, Boulder.

—— (1988) *The Modern Social Conflict: an essay on the politics of liberty*. Weidenfeld and Nicolson, London.

—— (1989) The underclass and the future of Britain. St George's House Tenth Annual Lecture, Windsor.

Dalton, R. (1988) *Citizen Politics in Western Democracies: public opinion and political parties in the United States, Great Britain, West Germany, and France*. Chatham House, Chatham, NJ.

—— Flanagan, S. and Allen Beck, P. (eds) (1984) *Electoral Change in Advanced Industrial Democracies: realignment or dealignment?* Princeton University Press, Princeton.

Daly, M. (1992) Europe's poor women? Gender in research on poverty. *European Sociological Review*, 8 (1) (May), 1–12.

Danziger, S. and Gottschalk, P. (eds) (1993) *Uneven Tides*. Russel Sage Foundation, New York.

—— with Sandefur, G. and Weinberg, D. (eds) (1994) *Confronting Poverty. Prescriptions for Change*. Russel Sage Foundation and Harvard University Press, New York and Cambridge, MA.

Day, L. H. (1978) *Demographic Concerns of the 1980s and the Applicability of Economic and Sociological Frames of Reference to their Analysis*. Proceedings IUSSP Conferences, III, Helsinki.

Deakin, S. and Wilkinson, F. (1991) Labour law, social security and economic inequality. *Cambridge Journal of Economics*, 15, 125–48.

Dean, H. and Taylor-Gooby, P. (1993) *Dependency Culture: the explosion of a myth*. Harvester Wheatsheaf, New York and London.

de Filippo, E. and Morlicchio, E. (1992) L'immigrazione straniera in Campania. *Inchiesta*, 22 (95) (January–March), 40–9.

Delahaye, V. (1994) *Politiques de lutte contre le chômage et l'exclusion et mutation de l'action sociale*. Ecole National d'Administration, Paris.

DeMott, B. (1990) *The Imperial Middle: why Americans can't think straight about class*. Yale University Press, New Haven.

Denton, N. and Massey, D. (1988) Residential segregation of blacks, Hispanics, and Asians by socioeconomic status and generation. *Social Science Quarterly*, 69, 797–817.

Désir, H. (1992) Villes ou ghetto. L'édito de Harlem. *Melting potes. Le mensuel de SOS Racisme* (May), 3.

Deutscher Städtetag (1979) *Heinweise zur Arbeit in sozialen Brennpunkten. Beiträge zur Sozialpulitik*. Reihe D, Heft 10, Deutscher Städtetag, Köln.

Devine, J. A. and Wright, J. D. (1993) *The Greatest of Evils. Urban Poverty and the American Underclass*. Aldine de Gruyter, New York.

Donati, P. (1991) Equità generazionale: un nuovo confronto sulla qualità familiare. In P. Donati (ed.), *Secondo rapporto sulla famiglia in Italia*, Edizioni Paoline, Torino.

Donnison, D. (1991) *Urban Poverty: the economy and public policy*. Combat Poverty Agency, Dublin.

Donzelot, J. (ed.) (1991) *Face à l'exclusion. Le modèle français*. Editions Esprit, Paris.

—— (1991) Le social du troisième type. In J. Donzelot (ed.) (1991), 15–40.

—— and Roman, J. (1991) Le déplacement de la question sociale. In J. Donzelot (ed.), *Face à l'exclusion. Le modèle français*, Editions Esprit, Paris, 5–11.

Döring, D., Hanesch, W. and Huster, E.-U. (eds) (1990) *Armut im Wohlstand*. Suhrkamp, Frankfurt-on-Main.

Drake, St C. and Cayton, H. R. [1945] (1962) *Black Metropolis: a study of negro life in a northern city*. 2 vols, rev. and enlarged edition, Harper and Row, New York.

Drennan, M. P. (1992) Gateway cities: the metropolitan sources of US producer service exports. *Urban Studies*, 29 (2), 217–35.

Dubet, F. (1987) *La galère: jeunes en survie*. Fayard, Paris.

—— and Lapeyronnie, D. (1992) *Les quartiers d'exil*. Seuil, Paris.

Dubrow, N. F. and Garbarino, J. (1989) Living in the war zone: mothers and young children in a public housing development. *Child Welfare*, 68 (1) (January).

Dulong, R. and Paperman, P. (1992) *La reputation des cités HLM: enquête sur le langage de l'insecurité*. L'Harmattan, Paris.

Duncan, A. (1987) 'The values, aspirations, and opportunities of the urban underclass'. Unpublished BA thesis, Harvard University, Cambridge, Mass.

Duncan, G. J. (ed.) (1984) *Years of Poverty, Years of Plenty*. Institute of Social Research, University of Michigan, Ann Arbor.

—— Gustafsson, B., Hauser, R., Schmaus, G., Jenkins, S., Messinger, H., Muffels, R., Nolan, B., Ray, J.-C. and Voges, W. (1995) Poverty and social-assistance dynamics in the United States, Canada and Europe. In K. McFate, R. Lawson and W. J. Wilson (eds) (1995), 67–108.

Duncan, J. (1986) *Years of Poverty, Years of Plenty*. Institute for Survey Research, University of Michigan, Ann Arbor.

EC Commission (1992) *Towards a Europe of Solidarity: intensifying the fight against social exclusion, fostering integration*. Brussels, 12 December.

The Economist (1995) *The far-right factor*. 4 March, 53.

Edin, K. (1991) Surviving the welfare system: how AFDC recipients make ends meet in Chicago. *Social Problems*, 38 (4) (November), 462–74.

Ellwood, D. (1988) *Poor Support: poverty in the American family*. Basic Books, New York.

Elshtain, J. B. (1993) Issues and themes: spiral of delegitimation or new social convenant? In M. Nelson (ed.), *The elections of 1992*, Congressional Quarterly, Washington, 109–24.

Engbersen, G. (1989) Culture of long-term unemployment in the New West. *The Netherlands Journal of Social Science*, 25 (2) (October), 75–96.

—— Schuyt, K., Timmer, J. and Van Waarden, F. (1993) *Cultures of Uemployment: long-term unemployment in Dutch inner cities*. Westview Press, Boulder.

Engelbrech, G. (1994) Erwerbsverhalten im Umbruch? Erwerbswünsche ostdeutscher Frauen und Möglichkeiten von Arbeitsmarktpolitik. In Arbeitskreissozialwissenschaftliche Arbeitsmarktforschung (ed.), *Erwerbsverhalten und Arbeitsmarktsituation von Frauen im nationalen Vergleich*, Arbeitspapier 1994-I.

Ercole, E. and Martinotti, G. (1988) Le aree metropolitane: la regione metropolitana lombarda. *Amministrare*, XVIII, (1) (April), 141–95.

Esping-Andersen, G. (1990) *The Three Worlds of Welfare Capitalism*. Polity Press, Cambridge.

—— (1993) *Changing Classes. Stratification and mobility in post-industrial societies*. Sage, London.

Etienne, B. (1987) *L'islamisme radical*. Hachette, Paris.

European Commission (1995) East Germany. Labour market developments in the new German Länder. *Employment Observatory*, no. 15 (June).

European Commission (DG V) (1993) *Ostdeutschland, Arbeitsmarktentwicklungen und Arbeitsmarktpolitik in den neuen Bundesländern*. Beschäftigungsobservatorium Nr. 9.

Eurostat (1988) *Long Term Unemployment*. Luxembourg. Brussels.

Euvremer, L. and Euvremer, Y. (1985) La honte. *Archivari* (July), 6–9.

Facchini, C. (1993) Anziani e assistenza domiciliare: caratteristiche degli utenti, modalità del servizio. *Inchiesta*, n. 100–1.

Fainstein, N. (1993) Race, class and segregation: discourses about African Americans. *International Journal of Urban and regional Development*, 17, 384–403.

—— (forthcoming) Did the black ghetto have a golden age? *Journal of Urban History*.

Fainstein, S. S. and Fainstein, N. (1990) Technology, the new international division of labor, and location: continuities and disjunctures. In R. Beauregard (ed.), *Economic Restructuring and Political response*. Sage, Beverly Hills.

—— Gordon, I. and Harloe, M. (eds) (1992) *Divided Cities: New York and London in the Contemporary World*. Blackwell, Oxford.

Faris, R. E. L. and Dunham, H. W. (eds) (1939) *Mental Disorders in Urban Areas*. Chicago University Press, Chicago.

Farley, R. and Allen, W. (1987) *The Color Line and the Quality of Life in America*. Oxford University Press, New York.

Farrugia, F. (1993) *La crise du lien social: essai de sociologie critique*. L'Harmattan, Paris.

Feagin, J. R. (1991) The continuing significance of race: anti-black discrimination in public places. *American Sociological Review*, 56 (1) (February), 101–16.

Feffer, A. (1993) *The Chicago Pragmatists and American Progressivism*. Cornell University Press, Ithaca.

Ferrera, M. (1993) *Modelli di solidarietà. Politica e riforme sociali nelle democrazie*. Il Mulino, Bologna.

Field, F. (1989) *Losing Out: the emergence of Britain's underclass*. Basil Blackwell, London.

Foley, D. (1990) *Learning Capitalist Culture: deep in the heart of Texas*. University of Pennsylvania Press, Philadephia.

Foucauld, J. B. de (1992a) Une citoyenneté pour les chômeurs. *Droit Social*, 7 (6) (Juillet-Août), 653–60.

—— (1992b) Vouloir faire, savoir faire. In J. Affichard and J. B. de Foucauld (eds), *Justice sociale et inégalités*, Editions Esprit, Paris, 257–68.

Foucault M. (1977) *Discipline and Punish: the birth of the prison*. Pantheon, New York.

Fourcault, A. (ed.) (1992) *Banlieue rouge, 1920–1960: années Thorez, années Gabin*. Autrement, Paris.

Fragonard, B. (1993) *Cohésion sociale et prévention de l'exclusion*. Commissariat Général du Plan, Paris, February.

Frattini, L. (1994) *Milano 1994. Percorsi nel presente metropolitano*. Feltrinelli, Milan.

Freeman, R. (ed.) (1994) *Working under Different Rules*. Russel Sage Foundation, New York.

—— and Katz, L. (1994) Rising wage inequality: the United states v. other advanced countries. In R. Freeman (ed.) (1994), 29–62.

Frerich, J. and Frey, M. (1993a) *Handbuch der Geschichte der Sozialpolitik in Deutschland, vol. 2, Sozialpolitik in der Deutschen Demokratischen Republik*. Oldenbourg Verlag, München.

—— —— (1993b) *Handbuch der Geschichte der Sozialpolitik in Deutschland, vol. 3, Sozialpolitik in der Bundesrepublik Deutschland bis zur Herstellung der Deutschen Einheit*. Oldenbourg Verlag, München.

Friedrichs, J., Häussermann, H. and Siebel, W. (eds) (1986) *Süd-Nord-Gefälle in der Bundesrepublik?* Westdeutscher Verlag, Opladen.

Frost, M. and Spence, N. (1993) Global city characteristics and central London's employment. *Urban Studies*, 30 (3), 547–58.

Gaffikin, F. and Morrissey, M. (1992) *The New Unemployed*. London, Zed Books.

Gaffney, J. (1991) French political culture and republicanism. In J. Gaffney and E. Kolinsky (eds), *Political Culture in France and Germany*. Routledge, London.

Gallie, D. (1988) Employment, unemployment and social stratification. In D. Gallie (ed.), *Employment in Britain*. Blackwell, Oxford, 465–92.

—— (1993) Are the unemployed an underclass? Some evidence from the Social Change and Economic Life Initiative. Estudio Working Paper 1993/4 (June).

—— (1994) Are the unemployed an underclass? Some evidence from the Social Change and Economic Life Initiative. *Sociology*, 28, 737–58.

Gallie, W. B. (1956) Essentially contested concepts. *Aristotelian Society Proceedings*, 56, 167–98.

Gans, H. J. (1972) The positive functions of poverty. *American Journal of Sociology*, 78 (2), 275–89.

—— (1990a) Deconstructing the underclass. *APA Journal*, 52, 271–7.

—— (1990b) Planning for worksharing: the promise and problems of egalitarian work time reduction. In K. Erikson and S. P. Vallas (eds), *The Nature of Work: sociological perspectives*, Yale University Press, New Haven.

—— (1990c) *Sociology in America*. Sage, Newbury Park.

—— (1991) *People, Plans, and Policies: essays on poverty, racism, and other national urban problems*. Columbia University Press, New York.

—— (1993) From 'underclass' to 'undercaste': some observations about the future of the postindustrial economy and its major victims. *International Journal of Urban and Regional Research*, 17 (3), 327–35.

—— (1994) Positive functions of the undeserving poor: uses of the underclass in America. *Politics and Society*, 22 (3), 269–83.

—— (1995) *War against the Poor: the underclass and antipoverty policy*. Basic Books, New York.

Garfinkel, I. and McLanahan, S. S. (1986) *Single Mothers and their Children*. The Urban Institute Press, Washington.

Genestier, P. (1991) Pour une intégration communautaire. *Esprit*, 169 (February), 48–59.

Gershuny, J. and Miles, I. (1983) *The New Service Economy: the transformation of employment in industrial societies*. Praeger, New York.

Ghezzi, S. (1995) Le reti sociali primarie: la famiglia e gli eventi critici. In IARD, *I neopoveri in Lombardia. Sistemi di welfare e traiettorie di esclusione sociale*, research report.

Giannola, A. (1984) L'industria napoletana in crisi. In A. Becchi (ed.), *Napoli 'miliardaria'. Economia e lavoro dopo il terremoto*, Angeli, Milan.

Giddens, A. (1973) *The Class Structure of the Advanced Societies*. Harper & Row, New York.

Gilroy, P. (1987) *There ain't no Black in the Union Jack*. Hutchinson, London.

Glasgow, D. (1980) *The Black Underclass: poverty, unemployment and the entrapment of black ghetto youth*. Jossey-Bass, San Francisco.

Glass, R. (ed.) (1964) *London: aspects of change*. MacGibbon & Kee, London.

Glazer, N. and Moynihan, D. P. (1963) *Beyond the Melting Pot*. The MIT Press, Boston.

Glendon, M. A. (1991) *Right Talk*. Free Press, New York.

Goffman, E. [1958] (1963) *The Presentation of Self in Everyday Life*. Penguin Books, Harmondsworth.

Goldberg, D. T. (1993) 'Polluting the body politic': racist discourse and urban location. In M. Cross and M. Keith (eds), *Racism, the City and the State*, Routledge, London, 45–60.

Golding, P. (ed.) (1986) *Excluding the Poor*. Free Press, New York.

Goldsmith, W. and Blakeley, E. (1992) *Separate Societies: poverty and inequality in U.S. cities*. Temple University Press, Philadelphia.

Golini, A. (ed.) (1994) *Tendenze demografiche per la popolazione*. Il Mulino, Bologna.

Gordon, I. (1989) The role of international migration in the changing European labour market. In I. Gordon and A. P. Thirwall, *European Factor Mobility*, Macmillan, London, 13–29.

Gottdiener, M. and Feagin, J. R. (1988) The paradigm shift in urban sociology. *Urban Affairs Quarterly*, 24 (2) (December), 163–87.

Green, D. G. (1992) Liberty, poverty and the underclass: a classical-liberal approach to public policy. In D. Smith (ed.), *Understanding the Underclass*, Policy Studies Institute, London, 68–87.

Green, G., Coder, J. and Ryscavage, P. (1991) International comparison of earnings inequality for men in the 1980s. LIS Working Paper n. 58, Luxembourg, CEP/INSTEAD.

Greenstone, J. D. (1993) *The Lincoln Persuasion: remaking American liberalism*. Princeton University Press, Princeton.

Gribaudi, G. (1993) Familismo e famiglia a Napoli e nel Mezzogiorno. *Meridiana*, 17, 13–42.

Grüske, K.-D., Lohmeyer, J. and Miegel, M. (1990) *Der Einflußausserökonomischer Faktoren und Beschäftigung. Eine Fallstudie für die Arbeitsamtsbezirke Leer und Balingen*. Bertelsmann Stiftung, Gütersloh.

Guidicini, P. and Pieretti, G. (eds) (1993) *La residualità come valore*. Franco Angeli, Milan.

Guillaumin, C. (1991) 'Race' and discourse. In M. Silverman (ed.), *Race, Discourse and Power in France*. Avebury, Aldershot, UK, 5–13.

Gutachten des wissenschaftlichen Beirats für Familienfrügen (1992) *Leitsätze und Empfehlungen zur Familienpolitik im vereinigten Deutschland*, Schriftenreihe des Bundesministeriums fuer Familie und Senioren, Band 1, Kohlhammer, Stuttgart.

Gwaltney, J. L. (1980) *Drylongso: a self-portrait of black America*. Vintage, New York.

Halimi, S. (1994) I cantieri della demolizione sociale. In *Le Monde Diplomatique*, it., *Il Manifesto*, 4 (1) (luglio).

Hall, S. (1979) The great moving right show. *Marxism Today*, 23 (January), 14–20.

—— (1988) *The Hard Road to Renewal: Thatcherism and the crisis of the left*. Verso, London.

Hammar, T. (1990) *Democracy and the Nation State*. Avebury, Aldershot.

Hamnett, C. and Randolph, B. (1986) Tenurial transformation and the flat break-up market in London: the British Condo experience. In N. Smith and P. Williams (eds), *Gentrification and the City*, Allen and Unwin, Boston, 121–52.

Hanesch, W. (1990) Armut und Armutsberichterstattung in Kommunen. In H.-U. Otto and M.-E. Kartsten (eds), *Sozialberichterstattung. Lebensräume gestalten als neue strategie Kommunaler Sozialpolitik*, Juventa, Munich, 58–76.

—— et al. (1994) *Armut in Deutschland. Der Armutsbericht des DGB und des Paritätischen Wohlfahrtsverbandes*. Rowohlt, Hamburg.

Hannerz, U. (1969) *Soulside: inquiries into ghetto culture and community*. Columbia University Press, New York.

Harris, D. (1987) *Justifying State Welfare: the New Right vs. the Old Left*. Basil Blackwell, Oxford.

Hartmann, H. (1981) *Sozialhilfebedurftigkeit und Dunkelziffer der Armut*. Kohlhammer, Stuttgart.

Hartz, L. (1955) *The Liberal Tradition in America*. Harcourt, Brace, and World, New York.

Harvey, B. (1994) 'Europe's homeless people and the role of housing'. Paper presented at the European Network for Housing Research Workshop on Housing, May 16–18, Copenhagen.

Hatzfield, H. (1989) *Du paupérisme à la sécurité sociale 1850–1940*. Presses Universitaires de France, Nancy.

Hauser, R. and Hübinger, W. (1993) *Arme unter uns, Teil 1: Ergebnisse und Konseqünzen der Caritas-Armutsuntersuchung*. Lambertus Verlag, Freiburg i.B.

Häussermann, H. and Siebel, W. (1987) *Neue urbanität*. Suhrkamp, Frankfurt am Main.

Haut Conseil à l'Intégration (1991) *Pour un modèle français d'intégration*. La Documentation Française, Paris.

Heath, A. (1992) The attitudes of the underclass. In D. J. Smith (ed.), *Understanding the Underclass*, Policy Studies Institute, London.

Held, D. (1989) Citizenship and autonomy. In D. Held and J. B. Thompson (eds), *Social Theory of Modern Societies*, Cambridge University Press, Cambridge, 162–84.

Henretta, J. (1984) Parental status and child's homeownership. *American Sociological Review*, 49 (February), 131–40.

Herlyn, U., Lakemann, U. and Lettko, B. (1991) *Armut und Milieu. Benachteiligte Bewohner in grosstädtischen Quartieren*. Birkhäuser Verlag, Basel.

Herpin, N. (1993) L'urban underclass chez les sociologues americains: exclusion sociale et pauvreté. *Revue Française de Sociologie*, 34, 421–39.

Hill, M. et al. (1985) *Motivation and Economic Mobility*. Institute for Survey Research, University of Michigan, Ann Arbor.

Hill, R. (1978) *The Illusion of Black Progress*. National Urban League, Washington, DC.

Himmelfarb, G. (1984) *The Idea of Poverty: England in the early industrial age*. Alfred A. Knopf, New York.

Hobsbawm, E. and Ranger, T. (eds) (1983) *The Invention of Tradition*. Cambridge University Press, Cambridge.

Hofemann, K. (1992) Sozialhilfe in den neuen Bundesländer. Arbeitslosenunterstüzung sichert nicht mehr das Existenzminimum. *Zeitschrift für Sozialhilfe und Sozialgesetzbuch*, 12, 625–9.

Hoffman, S. (1963) Paradoxes of the French political community. In S. Hoffman, C. Kindleberger, L. Wylie, J. Pitts, J.-B. Duroselle and F. Goguel (eds), *In Search of France*, Harvard University Press, Cambridge, 1–117.

Hollifield, J. F. (1991) Immigration and modernization. In J. F. Hollifield and G. Ross (eds), *In Searching for the New France*. Routledge, New York, 113–50.

—— (1994) 'Immigration and Republicanism in France: the hidden consensus'. Paper presented at the International Conference of Europeanists, Council for European Studies, Harvard University.

Hoogenboom, T. (1992) Integration into society and free movement of non-EC nationals. *European Journal of International Law*, 3, 36–52.

Hopper, H. and Baumohl, J. (1994) Held in abeyance: rethinking homelessness and advocacy. *American Behavioral Scientist*, 37 (4), 522–52.

Hopper, K. (1983) *1933–1983 Never Again: a report on homelessness in New York*. Association Task Force on the Homeless, New York.

Hotz, D. (1987) Arbeitslosigkeit, Sozialhilfeausgaben und Kommunales Investitionsverhalten. *Informationen zur Raumentwicklung*, no. 9–10, 593–610.

Hunter, J. D. (1991) *Culture Wars: the struggle to define America*. Basic, New York.

Hyman, H. (1942) The psychology of status. *Archives of Psychology*, 38, 269.

IMI (1992) *La exclusiòn social y la vivienda*. Ingreso Madrileno de Integraciòn, Madrid.

Immergut, E. (1993) 'Dilemmas of the welfare state in the current conjuncture'. Paper presented to the Study Group on Citizenship and Social Policy, Center for European Studies, Harvard University.

Industrie- und Handelskammer Stuttgart (1990) *Die Wirtschaftsregion Stuttgart. Strukturen und Entwicklungen*. IHK-Stuttgart.

—— (1991) *Stuttgart im Standort-Wettbewerb. Acht Städte und Regionen im Vergleich*. IHK-Stuttgart.

Inglehart, R. (1990) *Culture Shift in Advanced Industrial Society*. Princeton University Press, Princeton.

—— and Hochstein, A. (1972) Alignment and dealignment of the electorate in France and the United States. *Comparative Political Studies*, 5 (October), 343–72.

Institut für Medienforschung und Urbanistik GmbH (1988) *Gefährdung der Arbeitnehmer durch Umstrukturierungsprozesse in der Metallindustrie im Wirtschaftsraum Stuttgart*. IMU, München.

Institute for Social Research (1987) *Measurement of selected income flows in informal market 1981 and 1985–1986*. University of Michigan, Ann Arbor.

IReR (1991) *Istituzione della Città Metropolitana Milanese*. Milan.

IRES Campania (1987) *Welfare State e Mezzogiorno. Dall'assistenza allo Stato sociale*. Liguori, Napoli.

ISTAT (1989) *Collana di informazione*, n. 17.

—— (1993) *Statistiche e indicatori sociali*, supplemento all'Annuario Statistico Italiano.

Jackson, A. A. (1973) *Semi-detached London: suburban development, life and transport*. Allen and Unwin, London.

Jackson, K. T. (1984) Technology and the city: transportation and social form in New York. *Annals of the New York Academy of Sciences*, 424, 283–8.

Jacquier, C. (1991) *Voyage dans dix quartiers européens en crise*. L'Harmattan, Paris.

Janowitz, M. (1980) Observations on the sociology of citizenship: obligations and rights. *Social Forces*, 59 (1) (September), 1–24.

Jargowski, P. (1994) Ghetto poverty among blacks in the 1980s. *Journal of Policy Analysis and Management*, 13 (2), 288–310.

—— and Bane, M. J. (1990) Ghetto poverty: basic questions. In L. Lynn and M. McGeary (eds), *Inner-city Poverty in the United States*, National Academy Press, Washington, 16–67.

Jazouli, A. (1992) *Les années banlieue*. Seuil, Paris.

Jencks, C. (1985) How poor are the poor? *New York Review of Books*, 32 (8), 41–9.

—— (1991) Is the American underclass growing? In C. Jencks and P. E. Peterson (eds) (1991), 28–102.

—— (1992) *Rethinking Social Policy*. Harvard University Press, Cambridge, MA.

—— (1994) *The Homeless*. Harvard University Press, Cambridge, MA.

—— and Peterson, P. E. (eds) (1991) *The Urban Underclass*. The Brookings Institution, Washington, DC.

Jensen, J. (1991) The French left: a tale of three beginnings. In J. Hollifield and G. Ross (eds), *Searching for the New France*, Routledge, New York, 85–112.

Joffrin, L. (1991) Des lendemains qui flambent? *Le Nouvel Observateur* (20–26 June), 58–9.

Johnson, J. (1925) Making of Harlem. *Survey* (1) (March).

Jones, G. (1980) *Social Darwinism and English Thought*. Harvester Press, Brighton.

Jones, J. (1985) *Labor of Love, Labor of Sorrow: black women, work and the family from slavery to the present*. Vintage, New York.

Kahn, T. (1964) *The Economies of Equality*. National Urban League, Washington, DC.

Kamermann, S. B. (1995) Gender role and family structure changes in the advanced industrialized West: implications for social policy. In R. Lawson, K. McFate, and W. J. Wilson (eds) (1995), 231–56.

Kantor, H. and Brenzel, B. (1993) Urban education and the 'truly disadvantaged': the historical roots of the contemporary crisis. In M. Katz, (ed.) (1993), 366–404.

Kapphan, A. (1994) *Die Wohnsegregation nichtdeutscher Bevölkerung in West-Berlin*. Diplomarbeit, Humboldt Universität Berlin, Fachbereich Geowissenschaften.

Kasarda, J. (1992) The severely distressed in economically transforming cities. In A. Harrell, and G. Peterson (eds), *Drugs, Crime, and Social Isolation*, Urban Institute, Washington.

Katz, M. (1986) *In the Shadow of the Poorhouse: a social history of welfare in the United States*. Basic Books, New York.

—— (1989) *The Undeserving Poor: from the war on poverty to the war on welfare*. Pantheon, New York.

—— (1993) *The 'Underclass' Debate: views from history*. Princeton University Press, Princeton.

Katznelson, I. (1984) *City Trenches: urban politics and the patterning of class in the United States*. Pantheon, New York.

—— (1992) *Marxism and the City*. Oxford University Press, Oxford.

Kazepov, Y. (1995a) Ai confini della cittadinanza: il ruolo delle istituzioni nei percorsi di esclusione a Stuttgart e Milano. *Polis*, 9 (1/95), 45–66.

—— (1995b) I nuovi poveri in Lombardia. Sistemi di Welfare e traiettorie di esclusione sociale. Rapporto IARD, Quaderni Regionali di Ricerca, n. 1.

—— and Mingione, E. (1994) *La cittadinanza spezzata. Il dibattito teorico e metodologico su esclusione sociale e povertà*. Armando Siciliano Editore, Messina.

—— Mingione, E. and Zajczyk, F. (eds) (1995) *Povertà estrema: istituzioni e percorsi a Milano*. Franco Angeli, Milano.

Keil, R. (1994) Going up the country: internationalization and urbanization on Frankfurt's northern fringe. *Environment and Planning D; Society and Space*, 12.

Keith, M. and Cross, M. (1993) Racism and the postmodern city. In M. Keith and M. Cross (eds), *Racism, the City and the State*, Routledge, London, 1–30.

Keithley, T. (1989) United Kingdom, In J. Dixon and R. P. Scheurell (eds), *Social Welfare in Developed Market Countries*, Routledge, London.

Képel, G. (1987) *Les banlieues de l'Islam. Naissance d'une religion en France*. Seuil, Paris.

Kesteloot, C. (1994) 'Three levels of socio-spatial polurization in Brussels'. Paper presented at the ISA International Congress, Bielefeld, Germany.

Killian, L. M. (1990) Race relations and the nineties: where are the dreams of the sixties? *Social Forces*, 69 (1) (September), 1–13.

King, D. (1987) *The New Right: politics, markets and citizenship*. Macmillan, London.

—— (1992) The establishment of work-welfare programs in the United States and Britain. In S. Steinmo, K. Thelen and F. Longstreth (eds), *Structuring Politics: historical institutionalism in comparative analysis*, Cambridge University Press, Cambridge, 217–50.

Kirchheimer, D. W. (1989–1990) Sheltering the homeless in New York City: expansion of an era of government contraction. *Political Science Quarterly*, 104 (4).

Klanfer, J. (1965) *L'exclusion sociale*. Bureau de Recherches Sociales, Paris.

Klausen, J. (1995) Social rights advocacy and state-building: T. H. Marshall in the hands of social reformers. *World Politics* (January).

Klein, J. (1995) Firm an affirmative action. *Newsweek* (31 July), 31.

Klemmer, P. (1988) *Arbeitsmarktentwicklung in ländlichen Regionen – Auswirkungen der Wirtschaftsförderung.* Vortragsmanuskript anläßlich des 'Dorf-Forums Berlin 1988' der Deutschen Akademie der Forschung und Planung im ländlichen Raum am 27. Januar 1988, Berlin.

Kluegel, J. R. and Smith, E. R. (1986) *Beliefs about Inequality: Americans' views of what is and what ought to be.* Aldine de Gruyter, New York.

Knowles, C. (1992) *Race, Discourse and Labourism.* Routledge, London.

Kohl, J. (1992) Armut im internationalen Vergleich. Methodische Probleme und empirische Ergebnisse. In S. Leibfried and W. Voges (eds), Armut im modernen Wohlfahrtsstaat. *Sonderheft der Kölner Zeitschrift für Soziologie und Sozialpsychologie*, 32/92, 272–99.

Kornblum, W. (1984) Lumping the poor: what is the 'underclass'? *Dissent*, 31 (Summer), 295–302.

Kotlowitz, A. (1991) *There are No Children Here.* Doubleday, New York.

Kozol, J. (1988) *Rachel and her Children: homeless families in America.* Crown Publishers, New York.

—— (1991) *Savage Inequalities: children in America's schools.* Crown Books, New York.

Krämer-Badoni, T. and Ruhstrat, E.-U. (1986) Soziale Folgen des Süd-Nord-Gefälles. Ein Vergleich zwischen Bremen und Stuttgart. In J. Friedrichs, H. Häussermann and W. Siebel (eds), *Süd-Nord-Gefälle in der Bundesrepublik? Sozialwissenschaftliche Analysen*, Westdeutscher Verlag, Opladen, 262–78.

Krause, P. (1992) *Einkommensarmut in der Bundesrepublik Deutschland.* In 'Aus Politik und Zeitgeschichte', Beilage zur Wochenzeitung 'Das Parlament', Heft B 49/92, 3–17.

—— (1993) *Einkommensarmut im vereinigten Deutschland.* Ruhr-Universität Bochum, Fakultät für Sozialwissenschaft, Diskussion papier no. 93–09.

—— (1994) Zur zeitlichen Dimension von Einkommensarmut. In W. Hanesch (ed.), *Armut in Deutschland*, Rowohlt, Hamburg, 189–214.

Krivo, L. (1986) Home ownership differences between Hispanics and Anglos in the United States. *Social Problems*, 33 (April), 319–34.

Krug, W. (1987) Nord-Süd- und Stadt-Land-Gefälle in der Sozialhilfedichte der Bundesrepublik Deutschland. *Informationen zur Raumentwicklung*, Hf. 9/10, 527–35.

—— and Rehm, N. (1986) *Disparitäten der Sozialhilfedichte. Eine Statistische analyse.* Schriftenreihe des Bundesministers für Jugend, Fraün und Gesundheit, Bd. 190, Kohlhammer, Stuttgart.

Kuhn, R. (1985) Lösung der Wohnungsfrage als soziales Problem in ihrem Einfluß auf Lebensweise und Stadtgestaltung. Akademie für Gesellschaftwissenschaften beim Z.K. der S.E.D., Berlin, April.

Kuhn, T. (1970) *The Structure of Scientific Revolutions*, 2nd edn. University of Chicago Press, Chicago.

Kumar, K. (1994) ' "Britishness" and "Englishness": what prospect for a European identity in Britain today?' Paper presented at the International Conference of Europeanists, Chicago, March.

Kunz, D. (1986) Anfänge und Ursachen der Nord-Süd-Drift. *Informationen zur Raumentwicklung*, Hf. 11/12, 829–37.

—— (1992) *Die wirtschaftliche Position der Region Stuttgart und ihre Gefährdung*. ISW-Papiere, 1992/2, Institut für Südwestdeutsche Wirtschaftsforschung, Stuttgart.

Kunzmann, K. R. and Wegener, M. (1991) *The Pattern of Urbanisation in Western Europe 1960–1990*. Report for the Directorate General XVI of the Commission of the European Communities as part of the study 'Urbanisation and the function of cities in the European Community', Institut for Raumplanung, Dortmund (Germany), March 15.

Laé, J. -F. and Murard, N. (1985) *L'argent des pauvres. La vie quotidienne en cité de transit*. Seuil, Paris.

—— (1988) Protection et violence. *Cahiers Internationaux de Sociologie*, 84 (January-June), 19–40.

Lafer, G. (1994) The politics of job training. Urban poverty and the false promise of JTPA. *Politics and Society*, 22 (September).

Laffi, S. (1992) Il povero, homo non oeconomicus. *Inchiesta*, 97–98, pp 89–93.

Lapeyronnie, D. (1987) Les jeunes Maghrébins nés en France: assimilation, mobilisation et action. *Revue française de sociologie*, 28(2), 287–318.

—— (1992) L'exclusion et le mépris. *Les Temps Modèrnes* (December), 2–17.

—— (1993) *L'individu et les minorités: la France et la Grande Bretagne face à leurs immigrés*. Presses Universitaire de Paris, Paris.

—— and Frybes, M. (1990) *L'intégrazion des minorités immigrées: étude comparative France-Grande Bretagne*. ADRI, Issy-les-Moulineaux.

Lawson, B. E. (ed.) (1992) *The Underclass Question*. Temple University Press, Philadelphia.

Leavitt, J. and Goldstein, C. (1990) The doors are closed, the lights are out. *Architecture California* (August).

Leborgne, D. and Lipietz, A. (1994) Nach dem fordismus. In P. Nolle et al. (eds), *Stadt-Welt*, Campus Verlag, Frankfurt, 94–111.

Le Debat (1994) Le Nouveau Paris. Special Issue, Summer.

Legget, J. (1968) *Class, Race and Labor*. Oxford University Press, New York.

Leibfried, S. (1992) Towards a European welfare state? On integrating poverty regimes into the European Community In Z. Ferge and J. Eivind Kolberg, (eds), *Social Policy in a Changing Europe*, Westview Press, Boulder, Colorado, 245–79.

—— Leisering, L., Buhr, P., Ludwig, M., Mädje, E., Olk, T., Voges, W. and Zwick, M. (1995) *Zeit der Armut. Lebensläufe im Sozialstaat*. Suhrkamp Verlag, Frankfurt-on-Main.

Lenoir, R. (1974) *Les exclus: un français sur dix*, 2nd edn. Seuil, Paris.

Lesthaeghe, R. (1991) The second demographic transition in Western countries: An interpretation. IPD working paper, n. 2, Vrjie Universiteit, Bruxelles.

Levine, L. (1977) *Black Culture and Black Consciousness*. Oxford University Press, Oxford.

Levitan, S. A. and Shapiro, I. (1993) *Working but Poor: America's contradiction*. The Johns Hopkins University Press, Baltimore.

Levy, F. and Murnane, R. (1992) US earnings levels and earnings inequality: a review of recent trends and proposed explanations. *Journal of Economic Literature*, 30 (September), 1333–81.

Lewis, P. (1995) As French elections approach, investors ponder 'what if'. *New York Times* (20 March), D4.

Light, I. (1984) Immigrant and ethnic enterprise in North America. *Ethnic and Racial Studies*, 7, 195–210.

—— and Bonacich, E. (1991) *Immigrant Entrepreneurs: Koreans in Los Angeles, 1965–1982*. University of California Press, Los Angeles.

Liguori, M. and Veneziano, S. (1982) *Disoccupati a Napoli*. ESI, Napoli.

Linder, P. (1992) Asylanten in der Sozialhilfe. *Baden-Württemberg in Wort und Zahl*, 11, 576–81.

Lindner, H., Graf, H.-W., Klee, G. and Kleinmann, R. (1992) *Schaffung von Arbeitsplätzen für Sozialhilfeempfänger durch Beschäftigungsgesellschaften*. Gutachten im Auftrag des Bundesministers für Arbeit und Sozialordnung, Institut für Angewandte Wirtschaftsforschung, Tübingen, Forschungsbericht 221, Bundesministerium für Arbeit und Sozialordnung, Bonn.

Linhart, V. (1992) Des Minguettes à Vaulx-en-Vélin: les réponses des pouvoirs publics aux violences urbaines. *Revue Française de Sciences Politique*, 3 (June), 91–111.

Link, B. G. et al. (1994) *Life-time and Five-year Prevalence of Homelessness in the United States*. Columbia University and the New York State Psychiatric Institute.

Lipietz, A. (1992) *Towards a New Economic Order. Postfordism, Ecology and Democracy*. Polity Press, Cambridge.

Lister, R. (1990) *The Exclusive Society*. Child Poverty Action Group, London.

Lockwood, D. (1987) Schichtung in der Staatsbuergergesellschaft. In B. Giesen and H. Haferkamp (eds), *Soziologie der sozialen Ungleichheit*, Westdeutscher Verlag, Opladen, 31–48.

Logan, J. R. and Alba, R. D. (1993) Locational returns to human capital: minority access to suburban community resources. *Demography*, 30, 243–68.

—— and Molotch, H. L. (1987) *Urban Fortunes: the political economy of place*. University of California Press, Berkeley.

—— Alba, R. D. and McNulty, T. (1994a) Ethnic economies in metropolitan regions: Miami and beyond. *Social Forces*, 72, 691–724.

—— Alba, R. D. and McNulty, T. (1994b) 'The racially divided city: housing and labor markets in Los Angeles'. Department of Sociology, State University of New York at Albany, typescript.

Lompe, K. (ed.) (1987) *Die Realität der neuen Armut. Analysen der Beziehungen zwischen Arbeitslosigkeit und Armut in einer Problemregion*. Transfer Verlag, Regensburg.

McFate, K. (1991) 'Poverty, inequality and the crisis of social policy. Summary of findings'. Paper, UCLA, Los Angeles.

—— (1995) Introduction: Western states in the new world order. In K. McFate, R. Lawson and W. J. Wilson (eds) (1995), 1–28.

—— Lawson, R. and Wilson, W. J. (eds) (1995) *Poverty, Inequality and the Future of Social Policy. Western States in the New World Order.* Russel Sage Foundation, New York.

—— Smeeding, T. and Rainwater, L. (1995) Markets and states: poverty trends and transfer system effectiveness in the 1980s. In K. McFate, R. Lawson and W. J. Wilson (eds) (1995), 29–66.

McGoldrick, M. and Carter, E. A. (1991) Il ciclo di vita della familia. In F. Walsh (ed.) (1991).

Mackie, J. L. (1974) *The Cement of Universe. Study of Causation.* Clarendon Press, Oxford.

McLanahan, S. and Garfinkel, I. (1986) *Single Mothers and their Children: a new American dilemma.* Urban Institute, Washington.

—— (1993) Single mothers, the underclass and social policy. In W. J. Wilson (ed.) (1993), 109–21.

McLeod, J. (1988) *Ain't no Makin' it.* Westview Press, Boulder.

Maclouf, P. (1992) L'insertion, un nouveau concept opératoire des politiques sociales. In R. Castel and J.-F. Laé (eds) (1992), 121–44.

Macnicol, J. (1986) In pursuit of the underclass, *Journal of Social Policy*, 16 (3), 293–318.

Madsen, R. (1991) Contentless consensus: the political discourse of a segmented society. In A. Wolfe (ed.), *America at Century's End*, University of California Press, Berkeley, 321–9.

Magri, S. and Topalov, C. (eds.) (1989) *Villes ouvrières, 1900–1950.* L'Harmattan, Paris.

Mahler, S. (1996) *American Dreaming: immigrant life on the margins.* Princeton University Press, Princeton.

Maier, E. H. (1987) *Das Modell Baden-Württemberg. Über institutionelle Vorraussetzungen differenzierter Qualitätsproduktion. Eine Skizze.* WZB Discussion paper IIM/LMP 87–10a, Berlin.

Malthus, T. R. (1806) *An Essay on the Principle of Population, V II.* Reprinted in 1989 by P. James (ed.). Cambridge University Press, Cambridge.

Manz, G. (1992) *Armut in der 'DDR' Bevölkerung. Lebensstandard undKonsumtionsniveau vor und nach der Wende.* Maro Verlag, Augsburg.

Maranese, T. (1995) 'La psichiatria di strada'. Paper presented at the Convegno della Caritas Ambrosiana about 'I senza fissa dimora a Milano, in Italia, in Europa: realtà e strategie di intervento', Milano, 10–11 February 1994.

March, J. and Olsen, J (1984) The new institutionalism: organizational factors in political life. *American Political Science Review*, 78 (3), 734–49.

Marcus, S. (1974) *Engels, Manchester and the Working Class.* Random House, New York.

Marcuse, P. (1979) The deceptive consensus on redlining. *Journal of the American Planning Association*, 45 (4) (October).

—— (1981) The targeted crisis: on the ideology of the urban fiscal crisis and its uses. *International Journal of Urban and Regional Research*, 5 (3), 330–55.

—— (1985) Gentrification, abandonment, and displacement: connections, causes, and policy responses in New York City. *Journal of Urban Contemporary Law*, 28, 195–240.

—— (1987) The grid as city plan: New York City and laissez-faire planning in the nineteenth century. *Planning Perspectives*, 2, 287–310.

—— (1988a) Divide and siphon: New York City builds on division. *City Limits*, 13 (3) (March), 8–11, 29.

—— (1988b) Neutralizing homelessness. *Socialist Review*, 88 (1), 68–97.

—— (1989a) Dual city: a muddy metaphor for a quartered city. *International Journal of Urban and Regional Research*, 13 (4) (December), 697–708.

—— (1989b) The pitfalls of specialism: special groups and the general problem of housing. In S. Rosenberry and C. Hartman (eds), *Housing Issues of the 90s*, Praeger, Westport, 67–82.

—— (1991) Housing markets and the labor markets in the quartered city. In C. Hamnett and J. Allen (eds), *Housing and Labor Markets: building the connections*, Unwin Hyman, London, 118–35.

—— (1992a) *The Goal of the Wall-less City: New York, Los Angeles, and Berlin.* UCLA Graduate School of Architecture and Urban Planning, Los Angeles.

—— (1992b) 'The unwalled city'. Perloff Lecture, UCLA, April.

—— (1993) What's new about divided cities. *International Journal of Urban and Regional Research*, 17 (3), 355–65.

—— (1994a) Empowering New York. *City Limits* (March).

—— (1994b) Walls as a metaphor and reality. In S. Dunn (ed.), *Managing Divided Cities*, Ryburn Publishing, Keele, Staffordshire.

—— (1995a) *Global Transitions and Urban Spatial Structures. Implications for Economic Apartheid in South Africa.* Department of Sociology, University of Witwatersrand, Working Paper no. 4.

—— (1995b) *Is Australia Different? Globalization and the New Urban Poverty.* Australian Housing for Urban Research Institute, Melbourne, Working Paper.

—— and Vergara, C. (1992) Gimme shelter (homelessness in New York City), *Artforum* (Spring).

—— Medoff, P. and Pereira, A. (1982) Triage as urban policy. *Social Policy*, 12 (3) (Winter), 3ff.

Marissen, N. (1989) Sozial Schwache in Bedrängnis. Über die Sozialhilfeabhängigkeit Stuttgarter Haushalte. *Beiträge aus Statistik und Stadtforschung*, Sonderheft 2/1988, 37–63.

—— and Müllcr, W. (1990) Räumliche Strukturen der Armut. *Beiträge aus Statistik und Stadtforschung*, Sonderheft 12/1989.

Marklund, S. (1990) Structures of modern poverty. *Acta Sociologica*, 33 (1), 125–40.

Markusen, A. and Giwasda, V. (1994) Multipolarity and the layering of functions in the world cities: New York City's struggle to stay on top. *International Journal of Urban and Regional Research*, 18 (2), 167–93.

Marshall, T. H. (1950) *Citizenship and Social Class and Other Essays*. Cambridge University Press, Cambridge.

Martinotti, G. (1993) *Metropoli*. Il Mulino, Bologna.

Marx, K. [1867] (1961) *Capital. Critical Analysis of Capitalist Production*. Foreign Languages Publishing House, Moscow.

—— and Engels, F. (1850) *The Communist Manifesto*. Reprinted in K. Marx and F. Engels (1953) *Selected Works*, Lawrence and Wishart, London.

Massa, R. et al. (1992) *La dispersione scolastica degli istituti professionali*. Franco Angeli, Milano.

Massey, D. (1985) Ethnic residential segregation: a theoretical synthesis and empirical review. *Sociology and Social Research*, 69, 315–50.

—— (1990) American apartheid: segregation and the making of the underclass. *American Journal of Sociology*, 96, 329–57.

—— and Denton, N. (1987) Trends in the residential segregation of blacks, Hispanics, and Asians: 1970–1980. *American Sociological Review*, 52, 802–25.

—— and Denton, N. (1988) Suburbanization and segregation in US metropolitan areas. *American Journal of Sociology*, 94 (November), 592–626.

—— and Denton, N. (1989) Hypersegregation in US metropolitan areas: black and Hispanic segregation along five dimensions. *Demography*, 26 (3) (August), 373–92.

—— and Denton, N. (1993) *American Apartheid: segregation and the making of the underclass*. Harvard University Press, Cambridge.

—— and Kanaiaupuni, S. M. (1993) Public housing and the concentration of poverty. *Social Science Quarterly*, 74 (1) (March).

—— Gross, A. and Shibuya, K. (1994) Migration, segregation, and the geographic concentration of poverty. *American Sociological Review*, 59, 425–45.

Mauger, G. and Fossé-Poliak, C. (1983) Les loubards. *Actes de la Recherche en Sciences Sociales*, 50, 49–57.

Mayhew, H. (1861) *London Labour and London Poor*. London.

Mead, L. M. (1986) *Beyond Entitlement: the social obligations of citizenship*. Free Press, New York.

—— (1992) *The New Politics of Poverty*. Basic Books, New York.

Megerle, K. (1982) *Württemberg im Industrialisierungsprozess Deutschlands. Ein Beitrag zur Regionalen Differenzierung der Industrialisierung*. Klett-Cotta, Stuttgart.

Meinlschmidt, G., Imme, U. and Kramer, R. (1990) *Eine statistisch-methodische Analyse mit Hilfe der Faktorenanalyse*. Senatsverwaltung für Gesundheit und Soziales, Berlin.

Mendras, H. and Cooke, A. (1991) *Social Change in Modern France: towards a cultural anthropology of the Fifth Republic*. Cambridge University Press and Editions de la Maison des Sciences de l'Homme, Cambridge.

Merton, R. K. [1949] (1957) *Social Theory and Social Structure*. The Free Press, New York.

Michael, T. T. and Tuma, N. B. (1985) Entry into marriage and parenthood by young men and women: the influence of family background. *Demography*, 22 (4), 515–44.

Micheli, G. A. (1991) *Generazioni. Il comportamento procreativo nell'ottica di una demografia comprendente*. Franco Angeli, Milan.

—— (1992) La riproduzione sociale tramite la famiglia. In L. Mauri et al. (eds), *Vita di famiglia. Social Survey in Veneto*, Franco Angeli, Milan.

—— (1993) Scenari demografici. In M. Livolsi (ed.), *L'Italia che cambia*, La Nuova Italia, Firenze.

—— and Laffi, S. (eds) (1995) *Derive. Stati e percorsi di povertà non estreme in una survey nel Veneto*. Franco Angeli, Milan.

Miegel, M., Grünewald, R. and Grüske, K.-D. (1991) *Wirtschafts- und arbeitskulturelle Unterschiede in Deutschland. Zur Wirkung ausserökonomischer Faktoze auf die Beschäftigung*. Bertellsmann Stiftung, Gütersloh.

Migration News Sheet (1991) The Churches Commission for migrants in Europe, edited by A. Cruz in Brussels, February.

Milano, S. (1988) *La Pauvreté Absolue*. Hachette, Paris.

Miles, R. (1992) 'Explaining racism in contemporary Europe: problems and perspectives'. Paper presented at the Annual Meeting of the American Sociological Association, Pittsburgh, August.

—— (1993) *Racism after 'Race Relations'*. Routledge, London.

Mills, N. (1995) Affirmative action on the ropes. *Dissent* (Spring), 189–90.

Mincy, R. (1988) 'Is there a white underclass?' Paper presented at the 63th International Conference of the Western Economic Association, Los Angeles.

—— (1994) The underclass: concept, controversy, and evidence. In S. Danziger et al. (eds) (1994) 109–46.

Mingione, E. (1986) Ristrutturazione del welfare e politiche sociali nel Mezzogiorno. *Politica ed Economia*, 6, 65–9.

—— (1990) Ritratto del giovane povero tra Inserimento e Salario Garantito. *Politica ed Economia*, n. 10.

—— (1991a) *Fragmented Societies. A Sociology of Economic Life Beyond the Market Paradigm*. Basil Blackwell, Oxford.

—— (1991b) 'The new urban poor and the crisis of the citizenship/welfare systems in Italy'. Paper presented at the Working Conference on 'Pauvreté, immigration et marginalités urbaines dans les sociétés avancées', Paris, Maison Suger, May.

—— (1995) New aspects of marginality in Europe. In C. Hadjimichalis and D. Sadler (eds), *Europe at the Margins. New Mosaics of Inequality*, Wiley and Sons, Chichester, 15–32.

—— and Pugliese, E. (forthcoming) Modelli occupazionali e disoccupazione giovanile di massa nel Mezzogiorno. *Sociologia del Lavoro*.

—— and Zajczyk, F. (1992) Le nuove povertà urbane in italia: modelli di percorso a rischio nell'area metropolitana milanese. *Inchiesta*, 97–98, pp. 63–79.

—— and Zajczyk, F. (1993) Le nuove povertà: nodi problematici. *Marginalità e Società*, 22, 11–21.

Mitchell, D. (1991) *Income Transfers in Ten Welfare States*. Avebury, Aldershot.

Model, S. (1992) The ethnic economy: Cubans and Chinese reconsidered. *Sociological Quarterly*, vol. 33, 63–82.

Mollenkopf, J. H. and Castells, M. (eds) (1991) *Dual City: restructuring New York*. Russel Sage Foundation, New York.

Le Monde Diplomatique (1991) La ville partout et partout en crise. Manier de voir, 13, Octobre.

Mongin, O. (1992) Le contrat social menacé? *Esprit*, 182 (June), 5–11.

Monroe, S. and Goldman, P. (1988) *Brothers: black and poor – a true story of courage and survival*. William Morrow, New York.

Moore, J. and Pinderhughes, R. (eds) (1993) *In the Barrios. Latinos and the Underclass Debate*. Russel Sage Foundation, New York.

Moore, R. (1977) Migrants and the class structure of western Europe. In R. Scase (ed.), *Industrial Society; class, cleavage and control*, Allen and Unwin, London.

Moore, W., Livermore, C. and Galland, G. Jr. (1973) Woodlawn: the zone of deconstruction. *Public Interest*, 30, 41–59.

Morlicchio, E. and Spanò, A. (1992) La povertà a Napoli. *Inchiesta*, 22 (97–98) (July–December), 80–8.

Morris, L. D. (1990) *The Workings of the Household: a US–UK comparison*. Cambridge, Polity Press.

—— (1992) The social segregation of the long term unemployed. *Sociological Review*, 38, 344–69.

—— (1993) Is there a British underclass? *International Journal of Urban and Regional Research*, 17 (3), 404–12.

—— (1994) *Dangerous Classes: the underclass and social citizenship*. Routledge, London.

—— and Irwin, S. (1992) Employment histories and the concept of the underclass. *Sociology*, 26, 401–20.

Morris, M. (1989) From culture of poverty to the underclass. *The American Sociologist*, 20 (2), 123–33.

Mothé, D. (1991) Le progrès de l'exclusion. *Esprit*, 169 (February), 73–92.

Mulhall, S. and Swift, A. (1992) *Liberalism and Communitarism*. Blackwell, Cambridge.

Müller, W. (1989) Sozialhilfe. Landesweite Entwicklung in der Sozialhilfe unter besonderer Berücksichtigung der Stadt Stuttgart. *Beiträge aus Statistik und Stadtforschung*, Sonderheft 2/1988, 4–36.

Murie, A. (1991) Tenure conversion and social change: new elements in British cities. In J. Van Weesep and S. Musterd (eds), *Urban Housing for the Better-off: gentrification in Europe*. Stedelijke Netwerken, Utrecht.

Murphy, R. (1988) *Social Closure: the theory of monopolization and exclusion*. Clarendon Press, Oxford.

Murray, C. (1984) *Losing Grounds*. Basic Books, New York.

—— (1989) Underclass. *The Sunday Times Magazine* (26 November), London.

—— (1990) *The Emerging British Underclass*. Institute of Economic Affairs

Health and Welfare Unit, London (with commentaries by F. Field, J. C. Brown, A. Walker and N. Deakin).

Mutual Information System on Employment Policies (1995) *Federal Republic of Germany. Institutions, Procedures and Measures 1994.* Employment Observatory, Policies series, Commission of the European Communities, DG V, Bruxelles.

Myrdal, G. (1944) *American Dilemma: the Negro problem and the modern democracy.* Harper and Brothers, New York.

—— (1963) *Challenge to Affluence.* Pantheon, New York.

Nanton, P. (1991) National frameworks and the implementation of local policies. *Policy and Politics,* 19, 191–7.

Nasse, P. (1992) *Exclus et exclusion: connaître les populations, comprendre les processus.* Commissariat Général du Plan, Paris, Janvier.

Negri, N. (ed.) (1990) *Povertà in Europa e trasformazione dello Stato sociale.* Franco Angeli, Milan.

—— (1991) Storie di povertà e di incapacità. In P. Guidicini (ed.), *Gli studi sulla povertà in Italia,* Franco Angeli, Milan, 49–68.

—— (1993) Le conseguenze dei disagi imprevisti: note sulla costruzione sociale degli eventi della biografia. *Rassegna Italiana di Sociologia,* 4, 487–514.

Newman, K. (1992) Culture and structure in 'The truly disadvantaged'. *City and Society,* 6 (1) (June), 3–25.

New York City Human Resources Administration (1984) *New York City Plan for Homeless Adults.*

New York City Mayor's Office of Operations (1987) *Mayor's Management Report.*

New York Times (1995a) Gap in wealth in US called widest in West. 17 April, 1.

—— (1995b) America's opportunity gap. 4 June, sec. 4, p. 4.

Nicole-Drancourt, C. (1991) *Le labyrinthe de l'insertion.* La Documentation Française, Paris.

Nicolet, C. (1982) *L'idée républicaine en France: essai d'histoire critique.* Gallimard, Paris.

Noel, J.-F. (1991) L'insertion en ettente d'une politique. In J. Donzelot (ed.) (1991) 191–202.

Noir, M. (1992) Factories of exclusion. *New York Times* (6 June), 23.

Noiriel, G. (1988) *Le creuset français: histoire de l'immigration XIXe–XXe siècles.* Seuil, Paris.

Novak, T. (1988) *Poverty and the State: an historical sociology.* The Open University Press, Milton Keynes.

Noyelle, T. and Dutka, A. B. (1988) *International Trade in Business Services: accounting, advertising, law and management consulting.* Ballinger Press, Cambridge, MA.

Nuy, M. (1993) *The Legal and Social Reality. The Second National Report for The Netherlands.* Feantsa, Bruxelles.

OECD (1991) *Employment Outlook.* OECD, Paris.

—— (1993) *Employment Outlook.* OECD, Paris.

Offe, C. (1984) *Contradictions of the Welfare State*. Hutchinson, London.
—— (1985) *Disorganized Capitalism*. MIT Press, Cambridge, MA.
O'Higgins, M., Schmaus, G. and Stephenson, G. (1990) Income distribution and redistribution: a microdata analysis for seven countries. In Smeeding, T., O'Higgins, M. and Rainwater, L. (eds), *Poverty, Inequality, and Income Distribution in Comparative Perspective: the Luxembourg Income Study*, Urban Institute Press, Washington, 20–56.
—— (1993) *Social Policy and Welfare State in Sweden*. Arkiv, Lund.
Ong, P. et al. (1989) *The Widening Divide: income inequality and poverty in Los Angeles*. The Research Group on the Los Angeles Economy, Los Angeles.
—— and Lawrence, J. R. (1992) *Pluralism and Residential Patterns in Los Angeles*. Graduate School of Architecture and Urban Planning, Los Angeles.
Orfield, G. (1985) Ghettoization and its alternatives. In P. Peterson (ed.), *The New Urban Reality*, The Brookings Institution, Washington, 161–93.
—— (1986) Minorities and suburbanization. In R. Bratt et al. (eds), *Critical Perspectives on Housing*, Temple University Press, Philadelphia, 221–9.
Ormerod, P. and Salama, E. (1990) The rise of the British underclass. *The Independent* (19 June).
Orshansky, M. (1965) Counting the poor: another look at the poverty profile. *Social Security Bulletin*, 28.
Osofsky, G. (1968) *Harlem: the making of a negro ghetto: New York, 1890–1930*. Harper and Row, New York.
Øyen, E. (1992) Some basic issues in comparative poverty research. *International Social Science Journal*, 44 (4), 615–26.
Paci, M. (1989) *Pubblico e privato nei moderni sistemi di welfare*. Liguori, Napoli.
—— (1990) *La sfida della cittadinanza sociale*. Edizioni Lavoro, Roma.
—— (1992) *Il mutamento della struttura sociale in Italia*. Il Mulino, Bologna.
—— (ed.) (1993) *Le dimensioni della diseguaglianza*. Il Mulino, Bologna.
Padilla, F. M. (1992) *The Gang as an American Enterprise*. Rutgers University Press, New Brunswick.
Pahl, R. (1989) *Money and Marriage*. Macmillan, London.
Pahl, R. E. (1984) *Division of Labor*. Blackwell, New York.
—— (1988) Some remarks on informal work, social polarisation and the social structure. *International Journal of Urban and Regional Research*, 13 (4), 709–20.
Parcel, T. (1982) Wealth accumulation of black and white men: the case of housing equity. *Social Problems* 30 (December), 199–211.
Park, R. E. (1925) The city: suggestion for the urban environment. In R. E. Park, E. W. Burges and R. D. McKenzie (eds), *The City*, University of Chicago Press, Chicago.
Parker, R. (1994) Reviews of Derek Bok. *The Nation* (3 January), 28.
Parkin, F. (1974) Strategies of social closure in class formation. In F. Parkin (ed.), *The Social Analysis of Class Structure*, Tavistock, London, 1–18.
Patemen, C. (1989) *The Disorder of Women*. Polity Press, Cambridge.
Patterson, J. (1981) *America's Struggle Against Poverty 1900–1980*. Harvard University Press, Cambridge.

Patterson, O. (1972) Toward a future that has no past: reflections on the fate of blacks in the Americas. *The Public Interest*, 27 (Spring), 25–62.

Paugam, S. (1991) *La disqualification sociale. Essai sur la nouvelle pauvreté*. Presses Universitaires de France, Paris.

—— (1993) *La société française et ses pauvres*. Presses Universitaires de France, Paris.

Peterson, G. and Vroman, W. (eds) (1992) *Urban Labor Markets and Job Opportunity*. The Urban Institute, Washington, DC.

Peterson, W. C. (1994) *Silent Depression: the fate of the American Dream*. W. W. Norton, New York.

Pétonnet, C. (1979) *On est tous dans le brouillard*. Galilée, Paris.

—— (1982) *Espace habités. Ethnologie des banlieues*. Galilée, Paris.

Pettigrew, T. F. (1971) *Racially Separate or Together*. McGraw-Hill, New York.

Pialoux, M. (1979) Jeunesse sans avenir et travail intérimaire. *Actes de la Recherche en Sciences Sociales*, 26–27 (April), 19–47.

Pinçon, M. (1982) *Cohabiter: groupes sociaux et modes de vie dans une cité HLM*. Plan Construction, Coll. 'Recherche', Paris.

Pinçon-Charlot, M., Preteceille, E. and Rendu, P. (1986) *Ségregation urbaine. Classes sociales et équipement collectifs en région parisienne*. Editions Anthropos, Paris.

Piven, F. and Cloward, R. A. (1979) *Poor People's Movements. Why they Succeed, How they Fail*. Vintage Books, New York.

Plant, R. (1978) Community: concept, conception, and ideology. *Politics and Society*, 8 (1), 79–107.

Polanyi, K. (1944) *The Great Transformation*. Rinehart & Winston Inc., New York.

Port Authority of New York and New Jersey, Office of Economic and Policy Analysis (1994) Demographic trends in the NY–NJ metro region: income distribution and poverty.

Portes, A. (ed.) (1995) *The Economic Sociology of Immigration*. The Russel Sage Foundation, New York.

—— and Bach, R. L. (1985) *The Latin Journey: Cuban and Mexican immigrants in the United States*. University of California Press, Berkeley.

—— and Stepick, A. (1993) *City on the Edge: the transformation of Miami*. University of California Press, Berkeley.

Potter, L. B. (1991) Socioeconomic determinants of white and black males' life expectancy differentials. *Demography*, 28 (2), 303–22.

Priller, E. (1994) Unemployment-induced poverty. Social change and the risk of impoverishment in the new federal states. *Employment Observatory: East Germany*, nr. 12, VIII, 3–6.

Procacci, G. (1993) *Gouverner la misère*. Seuil, Paris.

Pugliese, E. (1983) Aspetti dell'cconomia informale a Napoli. *Inchiesta*, 13 (59–60) (January–June), 89–97.

—— (1992) Famiglia, occupazione e mercato del lavoro. In F. P. Cerase (ed.), *Dopo il familismo, cosa? Tesi a confronto sulla questione meridionale negli anni '90*, Angeli, Milan.

—— (1993) *Sociologia della disoccupazione*. Il Mulino, Bologna.

Quirk, P. and Dalager, J. (1993) The election: a 'New Democrat' and a new kind of presidential campaign. In M. Nelson (ed.), *The elections of 1992*, Congressional Quarterly, Washington, 57–88.

Raskin, J. B. (1995) Supreme Court's double standard. *The Nation* (6 February), 167ff.

Rebeggiani, E. (1990) *Disoccupazione industriale e Cassa Integrazione*. Liguori, Napoli.

Reed A. (1991) The underclass as a myth and symbol: the poverty of discourse about poverty. *Racial America*, 24, 21–40.

Reeves, F. (1983) *British Racial Discourse*. Cambridge University Press, Cambridge.

Rex, J. (1986) *Race and Ethnicity*. Open University Press, Milton Keynes.

—— (1988) *The Ghetto and the Underclass*. Avebury, Aldershot.

—— and Tomlinson, S. (1979) *Colonial Immigrants in a British City*. Routledge and Kegan Paul, London.

Reyneri, E. (1994) Italy: A long wait in the shelter of the family and of safeguards from the state. In O. Benoît-Guilbot and D. Gallie (eds), *Long-term Unemployment*, Pinter Publishers, London, 97–110.

Ricketts, E. and Sawhill, I. (1988) Defining and measuring the underclass. *Journal of Policy Analysis and Management*, 7 (2), 316–25.

Rieder, J. (1985) *Canarsie: the Jews and Italians of Brooklyn against liberalism*. Harvard University Press, Cambridge.

Roche, M. (1992) *Rethinking Citizenship*. Polity Press, Cambridge.

Romero, C. J. (1991) La naissance des hyperghettos. *Libération* (22 June), 27–30.

Room, G. (1990) *'New Poverty' in the European Community*. St Martin's, London.

Room, G. et al. (1992) *Observatory on National Policies to Combat Social Exclusion. Second Annual Report*, Directorate General V, Commission of the European Communities, Bruxelles.

Rosanvallon, P. (1992) *Le sacré du citoyen: histoire du suffrage universel en France*. Gallimard, Paris.

Rowntree, S. B. (1901) *Poverty, a Study of Town Life*. Macmillan, London.

—— (1941) *Poverty and Progress, a Second Social Survey of York*. Longmans, London.

—— and Lavers, G. R. (1951) *Poverty and the Welfare State. A Third Social Survey of York Dealing only with Economic Questions*. Longmans, London.

Roy, O. (1991) Ethnicité, bandes et communautarisme. *Esprit*, 169 (February), 37–47.

Ruano-Borbalan, J.-C. (1993) L'imaginaire de l'exclusion. *Science Humaines*, 28 (Mai), 29–30.

Ruggles, P. (1990) *Drawing the Line: alternative poverty measures and their implications for public policy*. Urban Institute Press, Washington.

Runciman, W. G. (1990) How many classes are there in contemporary British society? *Sociology*, 24, 377–96.

Saardon, J. P. (1986) Evolution de la nuptialité et de la divortialité en Europe depuis la fin des années soixante, in *AIDELF*, Les familles d'aujourd'hui, Paris, pp. 15–29.

Sabel, F. C., Herrigel, B. G., Deeg, R. and Kazis, R. (1987) *Regional Prosperities compared: Massachusetts and Wurttemberg in the 1980's.* WZB Discussion papers III M/LMP87 10b.

Safford, J. (1987) *Pragmatism and the Progressive Movement in the United States.* University Press of America, Lanham, MD.

Sahlins, M. D. (1972) La sociologia dello scambio primitivo. In E. Grendi (ed.), *L'antropologia economica*, Einaudi, Torino.

Samuel, R. (ed.) (1989) *Patriotism: the making and unmaking of British identity.* 3 vols, Routledge, London.

Sánchez-Jankowski, M. (1991) *Islands in the Street: gangs in urban American society.* University of California, Berkeley.

Sanders, J. and Nee, V. (1987) Limits of ethnic solidarity in the enclave economy. *American Sociological Review*, 52, 745–67.

Saraceno, C. (1990) Nuove povertà o nuovi rischi di povertá? In N. Negri (ed.) (1990).

Sassen, S. (1989) New trends in the sociospatial organization of the New York City economy. In R. A. Beauregard (ed.), *Economic Restructuring and Political Response*, Sage, Newbury Park, 69–114.

—— (1990) Economic restructuring and the American city. *Annual Review of Sociology*, 16, 465–90.

—— (1991) *The Global City. New York, London and Tokyo.* Princeton University Press, Princeton.

—— (1993) 'Urban marginality in transnational perspective: comparing New York and Tokyo'. Paper presented at conference, Milan, December 1993.

—— (1994a) *Cities in a World Economy.* Pine Forge/Sage Press, Thousand Oaks, CA.

—— (1994b) The informal economy: between new developments and old regulations. *The Yale Law Journal* (Summer), 2289–304.

—— (1995) Immigration and local labor markets. In A. Portes (ed.) (1995), 87–127.

—— and Orloff, B. (forthcoming) *Trends in Purchases of Services in Multiple Industries over the last Twenty Years.* Department of Urban Planning, Columbia University.

Savastano, F. (1994) Cronache di un'esperienza. *Dove sta Zazà*, 3–4, 74–9.

Sawhill, I. (1989) The underclass: an overview. *Public Interest* (Summer), 3.

Sayad, A. (1975) Les foyers des sans-famille. *Actes de la Recherche en Sciences Sociales*, 32–33 (June), 89–104.

Sayer, A. and Walker, R. (1991) *The New Social Economy: reworking the division of labour.* Blackwell, Oxford.

Scharfe, M. (1977) Protestantismus and Industrialisierung. In I. Hampp and P. Assion (eds), *Forschungen und Berichte zur Volkskunde in Baden-Württemberg 1974–1977*, Landesdenkmalamt Baden-Württemberg, Stuttgart, 149–62.

Schmitter-Heisler, B. (1991) A comparative perspective on the underclass:

questions of urban poverty, race, and citizenship. *Theory and Society*, 20 (4) (August), 455–84.

Schnabel-Schüle, H. (1990) Calvinistische Kirchenzucht in Württemberg? Zur Theorie und Praxis der Württembergischen Kirchenkonvente. *Zeitschrift für Württembergische Landesgeschichte*, vol. 49, 169–223.

Schnapper, D. (1991) *La France de l'intégration: sociologie de la nation en 1990*. Gallimard, Paris.

Schuz, A. (1970) *On Phenomenology and Social Relations*. University of Chicago Press, Chicago.

Sen, A. (1981) *Poverty and Famine. An Essay on Entitlement and Deprivation*. Clarendon Press, Oxford.

—— (1985) A sociological approach to the measurement of poverty: a reply to prof Peter Townsend. *Oxford Economic Papers*, 37, 669–76.

—— (1992) *Risorse, valori, sviluppo*. Bollati Boringhieri, Torino.

—— (1993) *Il tenore di vita*. Marsilio, Venezia.

Sennet, R. (1992) 'The origins of the modern ghetto'. Paper delivered at Arden Urban Forum on Place and Right, mimeo.

Shklar, J. (1991) *American Citizenship: the quest for inclusion*. Harvard University Press, Cambridge, MA.

Shorter, E. (1975) *The Making of the Modern Family*. Fontana Books, London.

Silver, Allan (1990) The curious importance of small groups in American sociology. In H. J. Gans (ed.), *Sociology in America*, Sage, Newbury Park, CA, 61–72.

Silver, H. (1991) State, market and community. *Netherlands Journal of Housing and the Built Environment*, 6 (3), 185–203.

—— (1993) National conceptions of the new urban poverty: social structural change in Britain, France and the United States. *International Journal of Urban and Regional Research*, 17 (3), 336–54.

—— (1994) Social exclusion and social solidarity: three paradigms. *International Labour Review*, 133 (5–6), 531–78.

Silverman, M. (1992) *Deconstructing the Nation: immigration, racism and citizenship in modern France*. Routledge, London.

Simon, P. (1992) Banlieues: de la concentration au ghetto. *Esprit*, 182 (June), 53–64.

Sinfield, A. (1980) Poverty and inequality in France. In V. George and R. Lawson (eds), *Poverty and Inequality in Common Market Countries*, Routledge and Kegan Paul, London.

Sivanandan, A. (1990) *Communities of Resistance: writings on black struggles for socialism*. Verso, London.

Skogan, W. G. (1986) Fear of crime and neighborhood change. In A. Reiss and M. Tonry (eds), *Communities and Crime*, University of Chicago Press, Chicago, 203–30.

—— (1988) Community organization and crime. In M. Tonrey and N. Morris (eds), *Crime and Justice: an annual review*, University of Chicago Press, Chicago, 39–78.

Smeeding, T., O'Higgins, Y. and Rainwater, L. (eds) (1990) *Poverty, Inequality and Income Distribution in Comparative Perspective*. Harvester Wheatsheaf, Hemel Hempstead.

Smeeding, T., Rainwater, L., Rein, M., Hauser, R. and Schaber, G. (1990) Income poverty in seven countries. In T. Smeeding, M. O'Higgins and L. Rainwater (eds) (1990) 57–76.

Smith, R. [1776] (1812) *An Inquiry into the Natural Causes of the Wealth of Nations*. Ward Lock, London.

Smith, D. J. (1992) Defining the underclass. In D. J. Smith (ed.), *Understanding the Underclass*, Policy Studies Institute, London.

Smith, N. (1992) New city, new frontier: the lower East Side as wild wild west. In M. Sorkin (ed.), *Variations on a Theme Park: the new American city and the end of public space*, Farrar Straus and Giroux, New York, 61–93.

—— and Williams, P. (eds) (1986) *Gentrification and the City*. Allen and Unwin, London.

Smith, S. (1989) *The Politics of 'Race' and Residence*. Polity, London.

Social Justice (1993) Global crisis, local struggles. Special Issue, 20 (3–4) (Fall-Winter).

Solomos, J. (1993) *Race and Racism in Britain*, 2nd edn. Macmillan, London.

Spengler, E. H. (1930) *Land Values in New York in Relation to Transit Facilities*. Columbia University Press, New York.

Spicker, P. (1993) *Poverty and Social Security: concepts and principles*. Routledge, London.

Squires, G. D., Bennett, L., McCourt, K. and Nyden, P. (1987) *Chicago: race, class, and the response to urban decline*. Temple University Press, Philadelphia.

Stadtplanungsamt Stuttgart (1991) *Der Wirtschaftstandorf Stuttgart*. Stuttgart.

Stafford, W. and Ladner, J. (1990) Political dimension of the underclass concept. In H. Gans (ed.), *Sociology in America*, Sage, Newbury Park, 138–55.

Stanback, F. et al. (1981) *Services: the new economy*. Allenheld, Osmun, New Jersey.

Standing, G. (1995) Labor insecurity through market regulation: legacy of the 1980s, challenge for the 1990s. In K. McFate, R. Lawson and W. J. Wilson (eds) (1995), 153–96.

Staples, R. (1987) Black male genocide: a final solution to the race problem. *Black Scholar*, 18 (3) (May–June).

Statistische Berichte – Baden-Württemberg (1974–) Ausgaben und Einnahmen der Sozialhilfe in Baden-Württemberg, K I 1 – j/74–91, Teil 1, öffentliche Sozialleistungen, Statistisches Landesamt Baden-Württemberg, Stuttgart.

—— (1974–) Empfänger von Sozialhilfe in Baden-Württemberg, K I 1 – j/ 74–91, Teil 2, öffenthche Sozialleistungen, Statistisches Landesamt Baden-Württemberg, Stuttgart.

Statistische Berichte – Berlin (1974–) Ausgaben und Einnahmen der Sozialhilfe in Berlin, K I 1 – j/74–91, Teil 1, öffentliche Sozialleistungen, Statistisches Landesamt Berlin.

—— (1974–) Empfänger von Sozialhilfe in Berlin, K I 1 – j/74–91, Teil 2, öffentliche Sozialleistungen, Statistisches Landesamt Berlin.

Statistische Blätter (1992) *Jahresübersicht 1992*. Statistisches Amt, Stuttgart.

Statistisches Amt, Stuttgart (1992) Strukturdatenatlas, Stuttgart. *Beiträge aus Statistik und Stadtforschung*, Sonderheft 1/1991, Stuttgart.

Statistisches Bundesamt (1991) *Sozialhilfe*. Fachserie 13, Reihe 2, Metzler-Poeschel, Stuttgart.

—— (1992a) *Sozialleistungen 1990*. Fachserie 13, Reihe 2, Sozialhilfe, Metzler Pöschel Stuttgart.

—— (1992b) *Sozialleistungen 1990*. Fachserie 13, Reihe 2.S.1, Sozialhilfe in den neün Bundesländern, Metzler Pöschel, Stuttgart.

—— (1993) *Bevölkerung und Erwerbstätigkeit*. Reihe 3: Haushalte und Familien 1991, Metzler Pöschel, Stuttgart.

—— (1994) *Sozialleistungen 1992*. Fachserie 13, Reihe 2, Sozialhilfe, Metzer Poeschel, Stuttgart.

Statistisches Landesamt Berlin, Statistisches Jahrbuch, several years.

Stedman-Jones, G. (1971) *Outcast London*. Oxford University Press, London.

Stehli, J.-S. (1991) Etats-Unis: Etat de guerre. *Le Point*, 978 (17 Juin), 48–9.

Stern, M. (1993) Poverty and family composition since 1940. In M. Katz (ed.), *In the 'Underclass' Debate: views from history*, Princeton University Press, Princeton, 220–53.

Stiefel, M.-L. (Federführung) (1990) *Soziale Ungleichheit und Armut. Sozialhilfe Bericht für die Stadt Stuttgart*. Beiträge zur Stadtentwicklung, 30, Stuttgart, Sozial- und Schulreferat.

Stoléru, L. (1977) *Vaincre la pauvreté dans les pays riches*. Flammarion, Paris.

Stone, D. (1994) Helter shelter. *The New Republic* (June 27), 29–34.

Stouffer, S. A. (1949) *The American Soldier. I: adjustment during army life*. Princeton University Press, Princeton.

Stovall, T. (1990) *The Rise of the Paris Red Belt*. University of California Press, Paris.

Suchindran, C. M., Koo, H. and Griffith, J. (1985) The effects of post-marital childbearing on divorce and remarriage. *Population Studies*, 39 (3), 471–86.

Sullivan, M. L. (1989) *'Getting Paid'. Youth Crime and Work in the Inner City*. Cornell University Press, Ithaca, NY.

—— (1993) Absent fathers in the inner city. In W. J. Wilson (ed.) (1993), 65–75.

Suttles, G. (1968) *The Social Order of the Slum*. University of Chicago Press, Chicago.

Taylor, C. (1995) Un entretien. *Le Monde* (14–15 Mai), 12.

Terkel, S. (1992) *Race: how blacks and whites think and feel about the American obsession*. Doubleday, New York.

Testa, M., Astone, N. M., Krogh, M. and Neckerman, M. (1993) Employment and marriage among inner-city fathers. In W. J. Wilson (ed.) (1993), 96–108.

Thernborn, G. (1986) *Why some People are more Unemployed than Others?* Verso, New York.

Tienda, M. (1989) Puerto Ricans and the underclass debate. *Annals of the American Academy of Political and Social Science*, 501, 105–19.

Time Magazine (1977) The American underclass. 110 (28 August), 14–27.

Titmuss, R. (1965) Goals of today's welfare state. In P. Anderson and R. Blackburn (eds), *Towards Socialism*, Cornell University Press, Ithaca.

Tobier, E. (1984) *The Changing Face of Poverty: trends in New York city's population in poverty*. Report prepared for the Community Service Society, New York.

Tocqueville, A. (1835) Mémoires sur le paupérisme. *Mémoire de la Société Académique de Cherbourg*, 294–344.

Topalov, C. (1994) *Naissance du chômeur 1880–1910*. Albin Michel, Paris.

Tosi, A. (1994) *Abitanti. Le nuove strategie dell'azione abitativa*. Il Mulino, Bologna.

—— and Cremaschi, M. (1989) 'Poverty, social marginality and housing in Italy'. Paper presented at the XXIX International Congress, International Institute of Sociology, Rome, June.

—— and Ranci, C. (1993) *Italy*. Report for the European Observatory on Homelessness, Feantsa, Bruxelles.

Touraine, A. (1990) American sociology viewed from abroad. In H. J. Gans (ed.), *Sociology in America*, Sage, Newbury Park, 239–52.

—— (1991) Face à l'exclusion. *Esprit*, 169 (February), 7–13.

—— (1992a) Inégalités de la société industrielle, exclusion du marché. In J. Afficard and J.-B. de Foucauld (eds), *Justice sociale et inégalités*, Editions Esprit, Paris, 163–76.

—— (1992b) Di fronte all'esclusione. *Iter*, 2–3, 13–20.

Townsend, P. (1952) Poverty: ten years after Beveridge. *Planning*, 19, 21–40.

—— (ed.) (1970) *The Concept of Poverty*. Heinemann, London.

—— (1979) *Poverty in the United Kingdom. A Survery of Households' Resources and Standard of Living*. Penguin, London.

—— (1985) A sociological approach to the measurement of poverty: a rejoinder to Prof. Amartya Sen. *Oxford Economic Papers*, 37, 659–68.

—— (1990) Deprivazione del centro urbano e polarizzazione sociale a Londra. In N. Negri (ed.) (1990) 73–104.

—— Corrigan, P. and Kowarzick, U. (1987) *Poverty and Labour in London*. Low Pay Unit, London.

Trautwein, J. (1984) Pietismus, ein erfolgreicher Sonderfall. *Der Bürger im Staat.*, Jg. 34, 2, pp. 124–33.

Tuchscherer, C. (1993) Die Wohnsituation ausländischer Haushalte in Berlin West am 25. Mai 1987. *Berliner Statistik*, no. 10/93.

Tucker, W. (1990) *The Excluded Americans: homelessness and housing policy*. Regnery Gateway and the Cato Institute, Washington.

Turner, J. (1995) The fairest cure we have. *New York Times* (16 April), 11.

UNIOPSS (1992) *Des outils pour l'insertion. Guide pratique*. Syros, Paris.

US Bureau of the Census (1990) *Decennial Statistical Studies Division*. REX Memorandum Series P-14.

US Department of Commerce (1980) *The Current Population Survey, May 1980*. US Bureau of the Census, Washington, DC.

—— (1983) *Census of Population and Housing, 1980: public-use microdata sample (A)*. US Bureau of the Census, Washington, DC.

—— (1993) *We the American Asians, and we the American Blacks*. US Bureau of the Census, Washington, DC.

Van de Kaa, D. (1980) Recent trends in fertility in Western Europe. In R. W. Hiorns (ed.), *Demographic Patterns in Developed Societies*, Taylor and Francis, London.

—— (1987) Europe's second demographic transition. *Population Bulletin*, 41 (1), Population Reference Bureau, Washington.

Van Kempen, R. (1994) 'Spatial segregation, spatial concentration, and social exclusion: theory and practice in Dutch cities'. Paper presented at European Network for Housing Research Workshop, Copenhagen, 3.

Van Parijs, P. (ed.) (1992) *Arguing for Basic Income: ethical foundations for a radical reform*. Verso, London.

Verdès-Leroux, J. (1978) Les 'exclus'. *Actes de la Réchérche en Sciences Sociales*, 19 (January), 61–6.

Vergara, C. (1989) 'Housing the poor in New York City: intensifying racial and economic segregation', typescript.

—— (1991) Lessons learned, lessons forgotten: rebuilding New York City's poor communities. *The Livable City*, n. 15/1 (March), 3ff.

Vernoy, A. (1993) *The Enclave as a Strategy of Urban Revitalization*. School of Architecture and Planning, University of Texas at Austin, Fall, Working paper 039.

Vieillard-Baron, H. (1987) Chanteloup-les-Vignes: le risque du ghetto. *Esprit*, 132 (November), 9–23.

—— (1994) *Le ghetto impossible*. Aube Editions, Paris.

Wacquant, L. (1992a) Pour en finir avec le mythe des 'cité-ghettos': les différence entre la France et les Etats-Unis. *Annales de la recherche urbaine*, 52, 20–30.

—— (1992b) Banlieues françaises et ghetto noir américain: De l'amalgame à la comparaison. *French Politics and Society*, 10 (4) (Fall), 81–103.

—— (1992c) Décivilisation et démonisation: la mutation du ghetto noir américain. In C. Fauré and T. Bishop (eds), *L'Amérique des français*, Editions François Bourin, Paris, 231–76.

—— (1992d) 'The zone': le métier de 'hustler' dans le ghetto noir américain. *Actes de la Réchérche en Sciences Sociales*, 92 (June), 38–58.

—— (1993) Urban outcasts: stigma and division in the black American ghetto and the French urban periphery. *International Journal of Urban and Regional Research*, 17 (3), 366–83.

—— (1994a) 'Advanced marginality in the city: notes on its nature and policy implications'. Report prepared for the Experts' Meeting on Distressed Urban Areas, OECD, Paris, March.

—— (1994b) The new urban color line: the state and fate of the ghetto in postfordist America. In C. J. Calhoun (ed.), *Social Theory and the Politics of Identity*, Basil Blackwell, Oxford and Cambridge, 231–76.

—— (1995a) Pour comprendre la 'crise' des banlieues. *French Politics and Society*, 13 (4) Fall, 68–81.

—— (1995b) The comparative structure and experience of urban exclusion: 'race', class, and space in Paris and Chicago. In R. Lawson, W. J. Wilson and K. McFate (eds), *Poverty, Inequality, and the Future of Social Policy: western states in the new world order*, Russell Sage Foundation, New York, 543–70.

—— and Body-Grendrot, S. (1991) Ghetto: un mot de trop. *Le Monde* (17 July), 2.

—— and Wilson, W. J. (1989) The cost of racial and class exclusion in the inner city. In W. J. Wilson (ed.) (1993), 25–42.

Wagner, D. (1993) *Checkerboard Square. Culture and Resistance in a Homeless Community*. Westview Press, Boulder.

Waldinger, R. (1986–1987) Changing ladders and musical chairs: ethnicity and opportunity in post-industrial New York. *Politics and Society*, 15, 369–402.

—— (1993) The ethnic enclave debate revisited. *International Journal of Urban and Regional Research*, 17(3), 444–52.

Walker, A. (1990) Blaming the victims. In C. Murray (1990), 49–58.

Walker, J. B. (1970) *Fifty Years of Rapid Transit: 1864–1917*. Arno Press, New York (original edition 1918).

Wallock, L. (1987) Tales of two cities: gentrification and displacement in contemporary New York. In M. Campbell and M. Rollins (eds), *Begetting Images*, Peter Lang, New York.

Walsh, F. (1991) Concettualizzazioni del funzionamento della famiglia normale. In F. Walsh (ed.), *Stili di funzionamento familiare*, Franco Angeli, Milan, 45–98.

Walton, J. (1993) Urban sociology: the contribution and limits of political economy. *Annual Review of Sociology*, 19, 301–20.

Walzer, M. (1990) What does it mean to be an 'American'? *Social Research*, 57(3) (Fall), 591–614.

Weaver, R. C. (1948) *The Negro Ghetto*. Harcourt, Brace and Company, New York.

Wehling, H.-G. (ed.) (1991) *Baden-Württemberg. Eine politische Landeskunde*. Teil II, Landeszentrale für Politische Bildung, Stuttgart.

Weiler, J. (1987) Wirtschaft und Arbeitsmarkt in Stuttgart. Situation und Perspektiven bis 2000. *Beiträge zur Stadtentwicklung*, 24, Stuttgart, Stadtplanungsamt.

Weinberg, A. and Ruano-Borbalan, J.-C. (1993) Comprendre l'exclusion. *Sciences Humaines*, 28 (Mai), 12–15.

Weir, M. (1993) From equal opportunity to 'the new social contract': race and the politics of the American 'underclass'. In M. Cross and M. Keith (eds), *Racism, the City and the State*, Routledge, London, 93–107.

Weitzman, L. (1985) *The Divorce Revolution. The Unexpected Social and Economic Consequences for Women and Children in America*. The Free Press, New York.

White, M. (1994) Unemployment and employment relations in Britain. In O. Benoît-Guilbot and D. Gallie (eds), *Long-term Unemployment*, Pinter Publishers, London, 34–53.

—— Biddlecon, A. and Guo, S. (1991) 'Immigration, naturalization, and residential assimilation among Asian Americans in 1980'. Paper presented at the annual meeting of the American Sociological Association.

Wiebe, R. (1985) *The Opening of American Society*. Knopf, New York.

Wieviorka, M. (1991) Face à l'exclusion. *Liberation* (3 June), 4.

—— et al. (1994) *Le Racism en Europe*. La Découverte, Paris.

Wihtol de Wenden, C. (1993) Prélude: l'image des banlieues hante ces années '90. *Panoramiques*, numéro speciale, pp. 6–8.

Wilkinson, D. (1992) 'Living with the underclass'. Unpublished BA Honors Thesis, Harvard University, Cambridge, MA.

Willets, D. (1992) Theories and explanations of the underclass. In D. J. Smith (ed.), *Understanding the Underclass*, Policy Studies Institute, London.

Williams, J. (1995) White man's burden. *Washington Post*, weekly edition (10–16 April), 24.

Williams, R. (1976) *Keywords: a vocabulary of culture and society*. Oxford University Press, New York.

Williams, T. (1992) *The Crackhouse: notes from the end of the line*. Addison-Wesley, Reading.

Williamson, J. B. (1974) Beliefs about the motivation of the poor and attitudes toward poverty policy. *Social Problems*, 21 (5) (June), 634–47.

Willis, P. (1982) *Learning to Labor: how working-class kids get working-class jobs*. Columbia University, New York.

Wilson, K. and Martin, W. A. (1982) Ethnic enclaves: a comparison of the Cuban and black economies in Miami. *American Journal of Sociology*, 88, 135–60.

Wilson, K. and Portes, A. (1980) Immigrants enclave: an analysis of the labor market experiences of Cubans in Miami. *American Journal of Sociology*, 86, 295–319.

Wilson, W. J. (1978) *The Declining Significance of Race: blacks and changing American institutions*. University of Chicago, Chicago.

—— (1987) *The Truly Disadvantaged: the inner city, the underclass, and public policy*. University of Chicago Press, Chicago.

—— (1989) The ghetto underclass: social science perspectives, edited volume, in *Annals*, vol. 501 (January).

—— (1991) Studying inner-city social dislocations: the challenge of public agenda research (1990 presidential address). *American Sociological Review*, 56, 1–14.

—— (1993) The underclass: issues, perspectives, and public policy. In W. J. Wilson (ed.) (1993) 1–24.

—— (ed.) (1993) *The Ghetto Underclass*, Sage, London.

—— (1994) 'Crisis and challenge: race, class, and the new American poverty'. Paper presented to the Russell Sage Foundation seminar, New York, 21 February.

Wirth, L. (1964) *On Cities and Social Life*. Edited and with an introduction by Albert J. Reiss, University of Chicago Press, Chicago.

Wittgenstein, L. (1958) *Philosophical Investigations*, 3rd edn. Macmillan, New York.

Wodon, Q. (1992) *Logement. Le droit des exclus*. Les Editions Ouvrières, Paris.

Wolfe, A. (1989) *Whose Keeper? Social Science and Moral Obligation*. University of California Press, Berkeley.

Wolff, E. (1995) *Top Heavy: a study of increasing inequality of wealth in America*. Twentieth Century Fund, New York.

Wunsch, G. (1988) *Causal Theory and Causal Modeling. Beyond Description in the Social Sciences*. Leuven UP, Leuven.

Xiberras, M. (1992) *Théories de l'exclusion sociale*. Meridiens Kliensieck, Paris.

Young, I. M. (1990) The ideal of community and the politics of difference. In L. J. Nicholson (ed.), *Feminism/postmodernism*. Routledge, London.

Yuval-Davis, N. (1990) 'Women, the state and ethnic processes'. Paper presented at the Racism and Migration in Europe Conference, Hamburg.

Zajczyk, F. (1991) Ricerche sulla povertà: un itinerario metodologico. In P. Guidicini (ed.), *Gli studi sulla povertà in Italia*, Franco Angeli, Milan, 129–52.

—— (1992) Quartieri storici dell'IACPM: un profilo socio-demografico. AAVV, *Recupero di quartieri storici di Milano*, IACPM, Milan.

—— (1994) Gli studi sulla povertà in Europa: approcci metodologici e problemi di comparabilità. Y. Kazepov and E. Mingione (eds) (1994) 38–70.

—— (1995) *Le fonti per le statistiche sociali*. Franco Angeli, Milan.

Zhou, M. and Logan, J. R. (1989) Returns on human capital in ethnic enclaves: New York City's Chinatown. *American Sociological Review*, 54, 809–20.

Index